THE HISTORY OF ARMENIA

FROM THE ORIGINS TO THE PRESENT

Simon Payaslian

palgrave
macmillan

THE HISTORY OF ARMENIA
Copyright © Simon Payaslian, 2007.
Softcover reprint of the hardcover 1st edition 2007 978-0-230-60064-5

First published in 2007 by
PALGRAVE MACMILLAN™
175 Fifth Avenue, New York, N.Y. 10010 and
Houndmills, Basingstoke, Hampshire, England RG21 6XS
Companies and representatives throughout the world.

PALGRAVE MACMILLAN is the global academic imprint of the Palgrave Macmillan division of St. Martin's Press, LLC and of Palgrave Macmillan Ltd. Macmillan® is a registered trademark in the United States, United Kingdom and other countries. Palgrave is a registered trademark in the European Union and other countries.

ISBN 978-1-4039-7467-9   ISBN 978-0-230-60858-0 (eBook)
DOI 10.1007/978-0-230-60858-0
Library of Congress Cataloging-in-Publication Data

Payaslian, Simon.
    History of Armenia / Simon Payaslian.
        p. cm.—(Palgrave essential history series)
    Includes bibliographical references and index.

    1. Armenia—History. 2. Armenians—History. 3. Armenia—Civilization.
    I. Title.

DS175.393 2007
956.6'2—dc22   2007015374

A catalogue record for this book is available from the British Library.

Design by Newgen Imaging Systems (P) Ltd., Chennai, India.

First edition: December 2007

10 9 8 7 6 5 4 3 2 1

PALGRAVE ESSENTIAL HISTORIES

General editor: Jeremy Black

This series of compact, readable, and informative national histories is designed to appeal to anyone wishing to gain a broad understanding of a country's history.

Published

A History of the Pacific Islands *Steven Roger Fischer*
A History of Israel *Ahron Bregman*
A History of the British Isles *Jeremy Black*
A History of the United States (2nd ed) *Philip Jenkins*
A History of Ireland *Mike Cronin*
A History of Spain *Simon Barton*
A History of Denmark *Knud J.V. Jespersen*
A History of Poland *Anita J. Prazmowska*
A History of Germany *Peter Wende*
A History of the Low Countries *Paul Arblaster*
The History of Armenia *Simon Payaslian*
A History of Slovakia (2nd ed) *Stanislav J. Kirschbaum*
A History of Russia *Roger Bartlett*
A History of India *Peter Robb*
A History of China (2nd ed) *J.A.G. Roberts*
The History of Mexico *Burton Kirkwood*
The History of Chile *John L. Rector*
The History of Argentina *Daniel K. Lewis*
The History of Brazil *Robert M. Levine*
The History of Havana *Dick Cluster & Rafael Hernández*
The History of Cuba *Clifford L. Staten*
The History of Venezuela *H. Micheal Tarver & Julia C. Frederick*
The History of Central America *Thomas L. Pearcy*
The History of Latin America *Marshall C. Eakin*

For my wife, Arpi

Contents

Preface

This volume presents a survey of the history of Armenia from antiquity to the present, with a focus on four major themes: East-West geopolitical competitions, Armenian culture (e.g., language and religion), political leadership (e.g., *nakharars* or the nobility, intellectuals and party leaders), and the struggle for national survival. It places Armenian history within the broader context of secularization, modernization, and globalization. It would be mere truism to state that the geography of Armenia directly affected the local cultures and economies. The mountain chains and valleys across the historic Armenian land created distinct regions, each with its own local customs and interests. The Armenian Plateau, rich in natural resources, in times of peace became a center for international commerce, but precisely because of its resources and strategic location, it also served as a battleground for military competition between major powers, such as the Persian, Roman, Byzantine, Arab, Ottoman, and Soviet empires. The history of the Armenian people, therefore, whether in ancient or modern times, as in the age of King Artashes I in the 180s–170s B.C. and as demonstrated in the twentieth century and since the collapse of the former Soviet Union in 1991, remains a constant struggle for security and survival.

This volume also challenges some of the conventional views on key aspects of Armenian history that are often presented through the traditional lenses of received wisdoms. For example, the historiography on the Armenian conversion to Christianity in the fourth century and the adoption of the Armenian alphabet in the fifth century is deeply rooted in theologically based analyses often blurring the line between history and mythology. Relying on more secular narratives (most of which are in the Armenian language), this book examines the political economy of the Christianization and transformation of Armenian culture. Further, one of the central themes in Armenian historical thought, as shaped by geographical determinism, has been the disadvantaged position historic Armenia had, and the current Republic of Armenia continues, to endure as a result of the lack of access to the sea. Of particular interest in this regard is the case of the Armenian kingdom in Cilicia (Armenian: Kilikia, Giligia), which in fact had access to the sea for nearly two hundred years. Yet despite Cilicia's various achievements, the advantages accrued from access to the sea proved nugatory, as the Cilician system failed to rectify effectively its shortcomings in international relations and internal governance.

This volume consists of four parts. Parts I and II (chapters 1 to 4) examine the emergence of the Armenian dynasties and the formation of the Armenian state as an independent entity, the role of the major powers in the development of the Armenian kingdoms, the conversion to Christianity and the adoption of the Armenian alphabet, and the strengths and weaknesses of the Armenian monarchies until the collapse of the last Armenian kingdom in Cilicia in 1375. Close attention is paid to some of the most successful leaders in the Armenian kingdoms, including Artashes I, Tigran the Great, Trdat the Great, and Hetum I. Part III (chapters 5 and 6) reviews the major issues involving the emergence of modern Armenian culture and political life in Western (Ottoman) Armenia and Eastern (Persian and later Russian) Armenia from the late seventeenth to the twentieth century. It focuses on the emergence of Armenian national movements, the conditions that gave rise to Turkish nationalism and the Young Turk dictatorship, the genocide, and the creation of the first Republic of Armenia. Part IV (chapters 7 to 9) evaluates the successes and failures of Soviet Armenia and reviews the reemergence of the Republic of Armenia in 1991 after the collapse of the Soviet Union and the current international and domestic issues confronting the republic.

I shall be greatly satisfied if this volume makes the history of Armenia accessible to a wide readership and generates debates on the various issues it examines. The genocide during World War I abruptly cut short the numerous intellectual currents that sought to address some of the fundamental issues at the time, such as religion and secularization, cultural revival and nationalism, civil and political rights and good governance. Since then, the evolving historiography in the former Soviet Armenia and across the diaspora has made a considerable contribution to our understanding of some of the old and new themes in Armenian history. I hope this survey will contribute to that historiography. Above all, I hope this book will be seen as a product of my intellectual curiosity in issues and ideas rather than as an expression of loyalty to ideas and political agendas.

Throughout this volume, I employ a simplified transliteration based on Eastern Armenian phonetics instead of the more scientific system with diacritical marks, except in citations to sources that utilize such technical transliteration. Turkish words and names are spelled according to the style used before the alphabet reforms in the late 1920s (e.g., *j* instead of *c*). Words in languages other than English are italicized only at first mention. Also, while it is common to include maps and photographs in books of this nature, the availability and far superior quality of such material on the

Internet to those found in print would make their inclusion here superfluous. I have therefore included at the end of the bibliography a sample of Internet links where the reader will find various useful materials.

I would like to thank the anonymous reviewers for Palgrave Macmillan for their suggestions and corrections that greatly improved the quality of the manuscript. Special thanks to Alessandra Bastagli, Yasmin Mathew, Brigitte Shull, and the editorial team at Palgrave Macmillan for their patience and for bringing this book to fruition. It gives me a great pleasure to take this opportunity to thank Professor John A.C. Greppin (Cleveland State University) for his comments and corrections on parts of the manuscript. I would like to express my gratitude to Professor Richard G. Hovannisian (UCLA) for his usual attention to details and for his invaluable criticism and corrections. Of course, I alone am responsible for any errors in facts and interpretations. I would also like to take this opportunity to express my intellectual debts to the pioneering historians of the previous generations: Leo (Arakel Babakhanian, 1860–1935), Nikoghayos Adonts (1871–1942), and Hakob Manandyan (1873–1952), and to professors Hovannisian and Nina Garsoian, who have all, as indicated throughout this volume, greatly influenced my understanding of Armenian history.

Thanks to my mother, Kohar Payaslian, my brother, Zareh Payaslian, and the Payaslian and Hedeshian families for their moral support and their understanding for my prolonged absences from and inattention to family affairs as I worked on this project. I want to express my deepest gratitude to my wife, Arpi. Without her love, patience, and constant support, I could not have completed this book.

Part I

Origins and Formation

This page intentionally left blank

1

Dynasties and the Geopolitics of Empire: The Ervanduni and the Artashesian Dynasties

The inhabitants of Armenia were in the throes of rebellion against their recent conqueror, King Darius I the Great of Persia, one of the greatest empire builders in history. Having briefly tasted local autonomy after the collapse of the Median empire, the rebels were in no mood to submit to yet another power. King Darius, a man of little tolerance for insubordination, had ascended to the Persian throne in 521 B.C. amid widespread political turmoil as rebellions shook the empire, and he was determined to resolve the crises. No sooner had he quelled the rebellions in the provinces of Elam and Babylon than fighting broke out in Media and Armenia, followed by uprisings in Sagartia, Hyrcania, and Margiana. By the ninth year of his reign, Darius I (521–485 B.C.) had suppressed eight major rebellions, including the revolt led by an ambitious imposter in Persia itself.[1] Having completed his military campaigns and consolidated power, Darius of the great Achaemenian empire ordered a set of commemorative inscriptions to be cut on the Rock of Behistun, located by the small village of Behistun (or Bahistun; Bisitun) on the caravan road between today's cities of Baghdad and Tehran. About 500 feet above the plain, the second column of the cuneiform inscriptions reads:

> XXVI. [Thus] saith Darius the king: An Armenian named Dâdarshish, my servant, I sent into Armenia, and I said unto him: "Go, smite that host which

is in revolt, and does not acknowledge me." Then Dâdarshish went forth. When he was come into Armenia, the rebels assembled and advanced against Dâdarshish to give him battle. At a place in Armenia named [Zuzza] they fought the battle. Auramazda brought me help; by the grace of Auramazda did my army utterly overthrow that rebel host. On the eighth day of the month Thuravâhara the battle was fought by them.[2]

Here was recorded "Armina," one of the earliest references to Armenia, the name used by foreigners for nearly three millennia.

Armenians refer to Armenia as Hayastan and to themselves as Hay. They are believed to have emerged in historic Armenia after centuries of cultural fusion among various native and migrating peoples, perhaps extending as far back as to the Hurrians, Hittites, and Phrygians, as suggested by Greek (Ionian) historian Herodotus (ca. 490–431 B.C), Strabo (ca. 63 B.C.–A.D. 21), and modern linguistic and cultural studies. During about the third and second millennia B.C, the Hurrians inhabited the area from the northeastern coast of the Mediterranean Sea to the Taurus Mountain range in Cilicia, across the Armenian highland to the Erzinjan region in the northeast, to present-day Kirkuk in Iraq in the southeast, and to modern Hama, Syria, in the south. The Hittites emerged as a dominant power in Asia Minor beginning in the nineteenth century B.C. and ruled the entire region from the Aegean Sea to the Mediterranean and to the Black Sea until their empire collapsed in the twelfth century B.C. The Thraco-Phrygians probably replaced the Hittites as a power in Asia Minor in about 1200 B.C. and expanded eastward to the Armenian highland by the eighth century B.C. As the historian Igor Diakanoff has noted, "The appearance in Asia Minor and the Armenian Highland of the Thraco-Phrygian ethnos means that all the basic components from which the Armenian people were ultimately formed were now present."[3] The proto-Armenian people inhabited the regions surrounding Lake Van: Nairi in the north and northeast; Arme-Shupria in the west and southwest; and Hayasa-Azzi farther west.[4] Their religio-cultural traditions developed over centuries in four major phases. The first represented the oldest proto-Armenian people as Hayassa-Azi in the region of Erznga (Erzinjan) on the plain of Erzerum. The second emerged in the region of Arme-Shupria, which included the vales of Kharpert and the Western Euphrates. The third developed on the shores of Lake Van, particularly the city of Van during the Urartian kingdom.[5] The fourth phase witnessed the spread of Armenian culture across the Araratian plain to the shores of Lake Sevan.[6]

The Armenian Plateau rises from an average of 3,000 feet to 7,000 feet above sea level and covers about 235,000 square miles. This vast territory of mountains and valleys, rivers and ravines, and fertile lands is historic Armenia, the homeland of Armenian civilization for three millennia. The Pontus Mountains extend from the north to the Lesser

Caucasus and farther east to the Karabagh range to the north and northeast. The Anti-Taurus mountain ranges and the Euphrates River are located in the west, the Arax River and Lake Urmia to the east and southeast, and the Tigris River, the Taurus Mountains, and Mesopotamia to the south. In the current Republic of Armenia, the Areguni, Sevan, Vardenis, and Gegham mountains surround Lake Sevan. The most famous Armenian mountain, however, is Mount Ararat, a climb of more than 16,800 feet, where, according to the Bible, Noah's ark is said to have landed. Historic Armenia consists of numerous rivers, including the Arax, the Western and Eastern Euphrates, the Tigris, the Hrazdan, and the Arpa. Armenians built their ancient capital cities (e.g., Armavir and Artashat) on the banks of the Arax River. The largest lakes are Van, Sevan, and Urmia.[7] Most of historic Armenian lands currently constitute eastern Turkey. The geography of Armenia directly affected Armenian culture and economy. The mountain chains across the Armenian Plateau created distinct regions, each with its own local culture, dialect, traditions, and interests. Rich in natural resources, historic Armenia became a major center for international commerce in times of peace but also a battleground for military and cultural competition between major empires seeking hegemonic spheres of influence.[8]

THE URARTIANS

The kingdom of Urartu emerged in the region of Arme-Shupria in about 870 B.C. under King Aramu I. During its formative years, Kings Sarduri I, Ishpuini, and Menua, who ruled from the capital city of Van (Tushpa; Tosp), united the western regions of Nairi, Arme-Shupria, and Hayasa, and expanded their armies from modern Erzerum to Mount Ararat, from Lake Urmia to Lake Sevan farther east.[9] The Urartians had their own indigenous culture and language, which were mixed with Hurrian, Hittite, Aramaic, and Assyrian influences.[10] The combination of these cultures and languages set the foundations for the Armenian culture and language, although the latter is of Indo-European origins.[11] Urartian religion venerated male and female gods, which were led by the male god Khaldi, the god of gods, whose wife, Arubani, served as the supreme female goddess. Appearing in military uniform, Khaldi often blessed the Urartian troops before they marched off to war. Other gods and goddesses included Teisheba (god of war) and his wife, Khuba; Shivini (the sun god) and his wife, Tushpua; Sardi, star goddess; Epaninaue, land goddess; Dsvininaue, sea or water goddess; and Babaninaue, mountain goddess. The local people worshiped the above gods, but also nature (e.g., tree worship [the concept of "holy tree"]) and the sun, the followers of which became known as the "arevordik."[12]

The most developed regions in the Urartian kingdom were the Lake Van basin and the area between Lakes Van and Urmia, followed by the region of Lake Sevan. During the reign of King Argishti I (r. ca. 786–764), when Urartian power is said to have reached its zenith, the Urartian military conquered the vast region across the Araratian plain to the eastern shores of Lake Sevan. Having strengthened his position in the region, he founded the geostrategically significant fortress town of Erebuni (present-day Erevan) in 782 B.C., where he deployed nearly 6,600 Urartian troops and non-Urartian military slaves.[13] The imperial economy centered on four principal sectors: the royal (state) economy, temple economies, individual or private land ownership, and the communes. The productive capacity of each sector rested on the political economy of slavery. The royal economy, based on large tracts of land that included hundreds and thousands of people, developed near rivers and lakes and on arable lands, and its agriculture included vineyards and large-scale farming. The Urartian king owned these lands, which were named after him—for example, Argishdikhenli (Armavir) on the Arax River and the Argishduna fortress south of Lake Van. The king and the members of the royal family granted lands and slaves as gifts and patronage to their supporters and relatives.[14] Armavir later emerged as the first capital of the Armenian people.

The temple economies played a very important role in the national economy. Each god in the Urartian pantheon had its own temples whose economies were based on agricultural production (as, for instance, the vineyards at the famed temple of Musasir located southeast of Lake Van), animal husbandry, and trade in domestic and regional markets. The economies of private landholders were run by the members of the nobility, including the leading members of the administrative and military bureaucracies. The economic and financial relations between the royal family and the military were particularly important as a strong monarchy required a prosperous economy, while the military establishment not only defended the borders but also brought in slaves whose labors contributed to the local economies. Equally important were the communes, which consisted of rural and urban economies and were owned mostly by *azat* (free) people who were neither part of the nobility nor slaves. Each commune had its own internal leadership structure and served as the primary base for taxation for royal revenues. The communes' cooperation with the royal court and the state bureaucracies were rewarded by a grant of additional land or slaves.

Wars and forced migrations constituted the primary means to capture slaves. In some wars, they totaled in the thousands. Argishti I, for example, is said to have brought 320,000 slaves to Urartu after his successful military campaign against the Hatti and Dsopk in the 780s. A large number were taken to the northeast to build the fortress city of Erebuni.[15] There was an inherent cycle in such ventures: the more successful a war, the greater the number of slaves; the greater the number of slaves, the greater the economic development (construction of cities, fortresses, irrigation canals, roads); the greater the economic development, the greater the need for slaves; and the greater the need for slaves, the greater the propensity to engage in wars. Loss in war led to loss of slaves and destruction. The most loyal among the slaves were employed in the royal economy, while others served in the temple economies. Most of them, however, worked for state bureaucracies on the construction and maintenance of cities, canals, roads, and fortresses. Some slaves escaped both Urartian and Assyrian rule and inhabited the areas between the two, in the region of Arme-Shupria west of Lake Van, and in the east of Urartu—that is, the Karabagh region—where (especially in the mountainous areas) they developed a tradition of guerrilla warfare.

The Urartian state hierarchy consisted of the central government and local principalities. At the apex of the political system stood the king, a hereditary office with absolutist powers. He led the royal court, which encompassed various ministries and a small circle of close advisers. The ministries included hundreds of high-level officials, thousands of administrators and secretaries, and hundreds of servants (including wine makers, architects, rug makers, and others). The administrative ministries were usually headed by the members of the royal family and included the military bureaucracies for internal security and war. Regional governors maintained law and order, transferred local agricultural production to the royal court and related financial institutions, and were responsible for the collection of taxes. These administrative institutions were available for the king to centralize or decentralize power as necessary, but weaknesses in the hierarchy could potentially undermine the king's leadership. Some kings were more successful than others as leaders, but wars proved to be the ultimate test of the loyalty of local officials and nobilities.[16]

Urartian kings Aramu (r. 870–845 B.C.), Sarduri I (r. 845–825), Menua (r. 810–785), and Argishti I (r. 785–760) were unusually powerful monarchs, but others, such as Sarduri II (r. 760–735) and Rusa I (r. 735–714), failed to maintain stability. Internal disunity and military failures against the Assyrians during the reign of Rusa II (r. 685–645) led to the decline of the Urartian kingdom, which finally collapsed in about 590 B.C. The demise of the Urartian empire should have enabled the Assyrian army to conquer a large part of the Urartian territories, but the Assyrian empire itself began to experience domestic turmoil, which by 600 B.C. proved insurmountable.[17]

The geopolitical vacuum created by the disintegration of both empires enabled the Medes to expand their power over most of former Urartian territories and Mesopotamian regions and to emerge as the dominant empire in the Middle East. The vast administrative structure of the Median empire became highly decentralized, allowing satraps, or local governors, wide latitude in the management of their territories.[18] Members of the local Ervanduni dynasty of Armenian origin served as satraps in the region of Lake Van and participated in the economic, cultural, and military affairs of the Median empire. Particularly significant was the Ervandunis' ability to mobilize considerable manpower for the military campaigns against the decrepit Assyrian monarchy to the south, in the process strengthening their own political and military base in the area. Relations with the Median empire deteriorated, however, when, confronted with financial difficulties, the imperial administration sought to tighten its control on the expanding domain. The Ervandunis, in turn, having contributed to that expansion, now demanded privileges of autonomous rule.[19]

In the meantime, the period between the eighth and sixth centuries B.C. witnessed the emergence of the Armenian nation on the banks of the Euphrates and Tigris rivers and in the regions of Mush (or Taron) and Van, the center of Urartian power where Armenians now established themselves as the predominant group. The disintegration first of the Urartian and Assyrian empires and subsequently of the Median empire, which collapsed in 550 B.C., provided the opportunity for the local Armenians, led by the Ervanduni dynasty, to conduct their affairs with a considerable degree of autonomy from the neighboring powers. An Armenian state thus took shape along the lines of Urartian institutions and heavily influenced by Urartian religious and cultural traditions and customs that themselves represented the amalgamation of various cultural and linguistic strata.[20]

THE EMERGENCE OF THE ERVANDUNI DYNASTY

In about 585 B.C. the Ervanduni dynasty emerged as the powerful overlords in historic Armenia. The Ervanduni (or Orontid) dynasty, a name derived from the Iranian origin of *arvand* (mighty), ruled Armenia during the period from the disintegration of the Urartian kingdom and the rise of the Armenian Artashesian monarchy by 190 B.C.[21] Although the origins of the Ervanduni family is not clear, historians suggest dynastic familial linkages to the ruling Achaemenian dynasty in Persia. The Greek historian Xenophon (ca. 431–355 B.C.) recorded in 401 B.C. as he passed through Armenia that a certain Ervand, the son-in-law of the Persian king Artaxerxes I, ruled as satrap in the eastern parts of Armenia.[22] Ervanduni leaders included Ervand I (r. 401–344 B.C.), Ervand II (r. 344–331), and Mithranes (r. 331–317). They were the immediate descendants of the

Achaemenians through Princess Rhodogune, the daughter of King Artaxerxes II and the wife of an Ervanduni satrap.[23] During the reign of the Achaemenian King Artaxerxes III, Kodomanus, who later ascended to the Persian throne under the regnal name of Darius III (r. 336–330 B.C.), the last Achaemenian king, had served as a satrap in Armenia. The Ervandunis certainly stressed their Achaemenian lineage to strengthen their political legitimacy.[24]

The Ervanduni dynasty ruled as satraps in the region of Van, once the capital of the Urartian kingdom, and named the city Ervandavan.[25] Subsequently its domain expanded to the southernmost territories of historic Armenia between lakes Van and Urmia, northward across the Armenian highland to Erebuni and Lake Sevan, and to the banks of the Upper and Lower Euphrates in the west. In the mid-sixth century B.C., a number of vassals, including the Ervandunis, led by King Cyrus II (r. 546–529 B.C.) of Persia, overthrew the Medes, whose empire at the time was rent by internal divisions and rebellions. Cyrus II strengthened the Achaemenian dynasty and with his eldest son, Cambyses, launched major military campaigns to India, the Mediterranean, and the Aegean.[26] Upon conquering Armenia in about 546 B.C., Cyrus maintained amicable relations with the Ervandunis and (like the Medes) supported their prominent position in society and government; in return he increased taxes and demanded Armenian troops for his campaigns. Confident of his relations with the Ervandunis, Cyrus granted them the freedom to establish their own political power and to practice their local customs.

The Armenians, however, having remained under Median control for more than a century, sought independence from outside powers, and in 521 B.C., when Darius I the Great assassinated Gaumata the Magian, who had succeeded Cyrus, they rebelled against Persian and pro-Persian authorities. To suppress the rebellions in Armenia, Darius I dispatched one of his loyal Armenian generals, Dadarshish, to impose stability. The general registered several victories but failed to end the crisis. Dissatisfied with the results, Darius I dispatched a Persian general, Vaumisa, who in fever-pitch battles destroyed the anti-Darius movements.[27] Thus Darius I, with the blessings of the great Persian god Ahuramazda, as he claimed, had successfully subdued the rebellious Armenians. Darius designated a number of Armenian families among the nobility to serve as satraps over the Armenian provinces, with Van serving as the principal administrative center. (Erebuni served as a center as well.)[28] Darius I eventually consolidated power over a vast empire, as indicated by the majestic portrayal of raw power and authority carved in the royal inscriptions of 518 B.C. at Behistun.

The Persian empire ruled the Armenian highlands, an area rich in tribal and linguistic diversity and populated by the descendants of Assyrians,

Hurrians, Urartians, and Scythians among others. The Achaemenians established a decentralized imperial administrative system encompassing more than twenty satrapies, whereby the Achaemenian King of Kings reigned supreme at his capital city of Susa. Under Darius I, the first Persian king to coin money, the Armenian financial system was based on the Achaemenian system, and Armenia was required to pay annual tribute and to serve in and supply horses for the Persian army.[29]

The integration of the Armenian Plateau into a single political and cultural unit within the Persian empire in general proved beneficial to the Armenian people. As long as the subjects remained peaceful and fulfilled their obligations, the empire's loosely organized political structure and tolerance for cultural diversity enabled the Armenians to maintain their traditions while the imperial regime provided security against external and internal threats. Armenians benefited from East-West international trade relations and the economic and infrastructural development (e.g., the extension of the Royal Road covering a distance of 1,500 miles and passing through Armenia) sponsored by King Darius I.[30] The generally close relations between Armenians and Persians enhanced the formers' sense of loyalty toward the empire. Armenians served in the imperial army against Greece in 480 B.C. and provided a contingent of 10,000 soldiers for the Persian campaign in Cilicia in 368 B.C. Armenian soldiers served loyally in the Achaemenian army under the reign of Darius III, as during the Battle of Issus in 333 B.C. and the Battle of Gaugamela (Arbela) in 331 B.C. against Alexander the Great.[31] As is often the case with imperial rule, however, the Achaemenian army failed to maintain absolute control, and on several occasions the Armenians, resentful of the high taxes, rebelled against the empire.[32]

Persian political and economic dominance in Armenia also resulted in heavy Persian cultural influence ranging from industry to language and religion. Achaemenian influences were apparent in Armenian ceramics, metallurgy, architecture, jewelry, and the like. The impact of Persian culture was demonstrated by pre-Christian Armenian language and Zoroastrian religio-mythological traditions. Persian words have survived in the Armenian language to this day, including, for example, Persian *mazda*-Armenian *imastutiun* (wisdom), *arda-ardarutiun* (justice), *azata-azat* (free), and *shakert-ashakert* (student). Moreover, Armenians were forced to replace some of the Urartian temples with Persian temples for fire-worship and the Zoroastrian pantheon, including, for example, Aramazd, the creator of heaven and earth; Mihr, the god of light; Astghik, the goddess of love; Vahagn, the god of war; and Anahit, the goddess of fertility and wisdom.[33] Like Persians, Armenians practiced polygamy and imposed severe limitations on women's role in society and on their individual freedom beyond the familial environs.

Outside influences were not limited to Persians. Some of the earliest local Armenian mythologies that perhaps originated in relations with Babylon included Hayk and his archenemy, Bel. Hayk, a descendant of Noah and a god worshiped by Armenians as the progenitor of the Armenian people, refused to submit to the repressive dictates of Bel, the god and ruler of Babylon and, upon defeating Bel, he is said to have led his followers to the land of Ararat, where he established the Armenian homeland. According to traditional Armenian narrative Hayk and his descendants ruled Armenia for generations, and King Paruir, also a descendant of Hayk, founded the first Armenian kingdom. The Armenian people thus call themselves Hay and their homeland Hayastan (the place of Hay).[34]

The collapse of the Achaemenian empire in the aftermath of Alexander the Great's invasions in 331 B.C. allowed the Ervandunis to claim sovereignty and to establish the first independent Armenian state.[35] By then "Armenia" consisted of three separate regions: Greater Armenia (Armenia Major); Lesser Armenia (Armenia Minor), situated northwest of the Euphrates; and Dsopk (Sophene). Greater Armenia comprised most of historic Armenia. Neither Greater Armenia nor Lesser Armenia was apparently listed among the divided lands in the post-Macedonian period, suggesting that Alexander the Great did not conquer Greater Armenia, although he probably appointed a handful of weak governors in Lesser Armenia. The latter administered the region for purposes of taxation, but Armenians under the Ervanduni leadership soon rebelled against them. Alexander's death in 323 B.C. led to power struggles among his top generals, who agreed, under the partitions of Babylon in 323 B.C. and of Triparadeisus in 320 B.C., to divide his vast empire into four areas. General Seleucus acquired the lands between the Euphrates and India. Upon assuming the throne in his capital Seleucia in 305 B.C., he rapidly expanded his domain from Central Asia to Asia Minor and to the Mediterranean Sea. He ruled until his death in 281 B.C. Meanwhile, the Ervandunis, taking advantage of the political turbulence, consolidated power in Greater Armenia (and at times Dsopk); the more Hellenistic Lesser Armenia at various times came under Seleucid, Pontic, or Cappadocian rule.[36] Armenia was not yet completely drawn into the East-West geopolitical struggles, but Alexander's campaigns against the Persian empire and the subsequent spread of Hellenistic culture throughout the Mediterranean basin heavily influenced Armenian culture and political economy.

ERVANDUNI ARMENIA AS AN INDEPENDENT STATE

The paucity of reliable information concerning the structure of the Ervanduni state remains a major obstacle for a comprehensive treatment of the subject. Nor is there a consensus with respect to the chronological sequence of successive rulers during this period.[37] The historical reconstruction presented here therefore is fragmentary, although the available material show direct lineage to the Urartian and Persian cultural heritage and social, economic, and political structures. The Ervandunis consolidated their domain and unified the different cultures into a highly centralized state in the region previously under Urartian rule.[38] The state structure consisted of a palace court, the imperial military command and personnel, chamberlains, councils, secret police, accountants, representatives of conquered lands, wine makers, craftsmen, huntsmen, musicians, and cooks. The higher echelons of the socio-economic structure consisted of the royal family and its palace economy, the nobility, and temple economy, as in the ancient city of Bagaran.[39] The Greek inscriptions at Armavir indicate that the upper classes used Greek as one of their languages.[40] The economy was based on agriculture, metalworks, animal husbandry, and various crafts, all of which contributed to the development of highly sophisticated functional complexes, which in turn contributed to Armenia's trade relations with the neighboring economies.

Under Ervand the Last (r. ca. 210–200 B.C.), the structure of government had begun to resemble Greek institutions, and Greek was used as the language of the royal court. Ervand had surrounded himself by the Hellenized nobility and sponsored the establishment of a Greek school in Armavir, the capital of the Ervanduni kingdom.[41] The Ervanduni kingdom registered significant economic successes, as demonstrated by the reconstruction and construction of several cities. It rebuilt the declining Urartian cities of Argishtikhinili (Nor Armavir), Erebuni (Erevan), and Tushpa (Van, perhaps Ervandavan),[42] the latter two having served as Achaemenian administrative centers with geostrategic significance for the empire. The Ervandunis built a number of major cities of their own, including Ervandashat, Ervandakert, and Vardgesavan.[43] Ervandashat, a city of approximately 50,000 families on the banks of the Akhurian and Arax rivers, replaced Armavir as the capital city for the Ervanduni state, and Vardgesavan set the foundation for what later became Vagharshabat. Armavir, where the temples of Apollo and Artemis/Anahit were located, continued to serve as the religious center of Ervanduni Armenia but, along with Ervandashat, also became an important center for international commerce.[44]

As the Ervanduni kingdom consolidated its domain over different tribes, rapid economic development, particularly in the newly emerging urban centers, created vast economic inequalities that pitted one local leader against another and gave rise to centrifugal forces. Local socioeconomic differences and tensions weakened Ervand the Last by 200 B.C.[45] In fact, the transfer of the capital from Armavir to Ervandashat reflected the deepening sense of insecurity prevalent in his court, as the internal divisions widened between the various pro- and anti-Ervanduni noble houses. The monarch refused to transfer some of the leading religious temples to the new capital, fearing that pilgrimages by a large number of people to the holy sites would occasion rebellion against him. The Seleucids, led by Antiochus III the Great (r. 223–187 B.C.), successfully exploited this internal structural loosening and the resultant political instability and supported Artashes (Artaxias) and Zareh (Zariadris), two of the leading anti-Ervanduni figures in Armenia, to rebel against the Ervandunis. The Artashesian-Ervanduni war commenced as the troops under the command of Artashes advanced across the northern shores of Lake Sevan and met Ervand the Last's army at Ervandavan on the northern banks of the Akhurian River, some distance from the capital. Ervand's army suffered heavy losses, and the king fled back to Ervandashat, pursued by Smbat, one of Artashes' loyal generals. The soldiers stormed the capital, and one stabbed Ervand to death. Then Artashes marched on to Bagaran, the last remaining stronghold of the Ervanduni government, and captured and killed Ervand's brother, Ervaz. Artashes, now in control, granted Bagaran to Smbat as a reward for his loyalty.[46] Thus the Ervanduni kingdom came to a tragic end in 200 B.C.

Antiochus III placed Artashes (now Artashes I) and Zareh as his new vassals in Greater Armenia and Dsopk, respectively, while his nephew, Mithradates, ruled as satrap over Lesser Armenia.[47] The Seleucid military command, having accomplished one of its geopolitical objectives in neutralizing Armenia, now turned to the grand strategies of conquering the whole of Asia Minor, Macedonia, and Egypt. Yet such territorial aspirations proved unrealistic at a time when the empire was in the process of disintegration, as a number of Seleucid satraps (e.g., in Cappadocia and Pontus) secured their independence from the empire. This situation was further complicated by the shifting tides favoring the successor to the Achaemenian empire in the east, the Parthian dynasty. In Armenia, the initial support from Antiochus enabled Artashes to assume the leadership; the death of the Seleucid emperor in 187 B.C. and the decline of his empire strengthened the hand of the Armenian king.

By then a new power had appeared from the west and radically altered the region's geopolitical power configuration. The Roman empire had conquered most of the territories on the Mediterranean Sea and prepared to advance across the Balkans and throughout Asia Minor. Beginning in 192–191 B.C., the Roman military launched its eastern offensive. In 192 B.C., the Roman navy defeated the Seleucid admiral Polyxenidas and disabled his entire naval fleet, while the Roman army advanced eastward to Asia Minor. In 190 B.C., after destroying the troops of Antiochus III at the Battle of Magnesia, the Romans entered the region for the first time. The Peace of

Apamea in 188 B.C., which concluded the war, forced the Seleucids to withdraw from Europe and Asia Minor. Under the agreement, the Roman Senate also granted Artashes and Zareh sovereignty over Greater and Lesser Armenia, respectively. The military defeat at Magnesia and the internal instability caused by the death of Antiochus III eliminated the Seleucid threat and permitted Artashes, Zareh, and Mithradates to maneuver for autonomy. The Roman victory and recognition of Artashes as the sovereign king of Greater Armenia raised expectations among Armenian leaders that they could rely on Rome to strengthen their position vis-à-vis the rising Parthian power.[48]

THE ARTASHESIAN KINGDOM

Artashes I (r. ca. 189–160 B.C.) hoped to cultivate amicable relations with Rome and Antioch. Yet the geopolitical competition between the Roman empire from the west and the Persian empire from the east, on one hand, and internal factionalism as witnessed under Ervand the Last, on the other, had greatly impressed on the king the necessity of military strengthen. This *machtpolitik* reality of strengthening Armenia and the Armenian monarchy shaped his policies. As the Ervandunis had inherited the Urartian and Achaemenian sociopolitical structures, so did the Artashesians inherit and maintain those structures and traditions. The monarchy was essentially absolutist in orientation. The office of the king was hereditary, a tradition continued since the Ervanduni dynasty, which in turn was shaped during the Achaemenian period and Persian tutelage. In matters of domestic policy, the king served as the source of legal and political legitimacy. All laws and policies were instituted in the name of the king, who held ultimate authority in the implementation and review of laws for repeal and amendments.[49] The king was the commander in chief of the armed forces. In foreign affairs, he and the royal court (*arkunik*), which consisted of a close circle of advisers, including the king's relatives and loyal members of the nobility, were the principal policymakers, especially in issues involving declaration of wars, signing of treaties, and alliances. As the country expanded and the economy became more prosperous, the role of the royal court increased and further contributed to the centralization of power.[50]

Below the king were the royal functionaries, appointed by the royal court. They supervised the administrative bureaucracies, fiscal policy, transportation, commerce and customs, agriculture, and public works. These high offices were monopolized by or closely associated with individual *nakharar tuns* (noble houses) and eventually emerged as the nakharar hereditary offices. The monarch granted ministerial offices as patronage to members of noble houses representing important sectors of economy, as determined by their loyalty to him, landownership, and location of land (access to rivers, irrigation networks, mountains). Whether the nakharar structure developed under the Artashesians or the next dynasty, the Arshakunis, has been the subject of much debate, but suffice it to note here that some of the nobles and the offices they held were clearly in place during the Artashesian period. The father of Armenian historiography, Movses Khorenatsi, for example, referred to the office of the coronant (*tagakap* or *tagadir*), which was perhaps established even before the Artashesians.[51] Although the nakharar houses exercised enormous power in their loyalty or opposition to the monarchy, the nakharar structure formed the foundation of the Armenian political system, providing the prerequisite institutional strength for stability. The Armenian elite, however, was not monolithic and was rarely unified. The geography of Greater Armenia rendered members of the aristocracy highly divided along lines of local interests, converging and colliding with the priorities of the monarchy depending on political circumstances. Leadership required enormous balancing skills on the part of the Armenian monarch.

Urban social and economic structures represented above all else the interests of the prominent nakharar houses, whose commercial and agricultural interests constituted an essential component of the economy. They consisted of economically and politically powerful groups with their own individual and collective (commune-style) sectors, the "free" or half-free (*kisakakhial*) individuals, and slaves with minimum rights.[52] The king maintained close economic relations among the cities and granted certain rights and privileges to city administrators. It was inevitable that cities, as they became more populous and prosperous, would seek greater local autonomy from the central government.

The construction of new cities—at least ten were built during the Artashesian period—had both positive and negative consequences for the monarchy. As Artashes I sponsored the construction of new cities, the interests of the predominantly agricultural sectors in remote and isolated rural areas sharply diverged from the growing power of the urban centers. The nakharar houses were often divided due to familial ties (*khnamiutiun*) and regional and commercial interests. Cities became centers of foreign merchants and dissemination of Greek cultural values; they extended Hellenistic cultural influences to Greater Armenia, with enormous domestic and geopolitical implications for the nation. As cities became centers of Hellenistic culture, factional divisions appeared between pro-West (pro-Rome) and pro-East (pro-Persia) nakharars and between urban and rural interests.[53] The capital city of Artashat (Artaxata) built by Artashes I symbolized his sovereign status as the king of Armenia and became one of the principal political, administrative, economic, and cultural centers in

Greater Armenia. Its geographical location made it easily accessible to international trade, linking commercial routes with neighboring empires.[54]

Landownership, of course, represented the most important source of wealth and hence of economic and political power. It was divided into two separate categories: royal lands and landowning elites. The king used the royal lands for the accumulation of wealth and revenues for the royal treasury and for the distribution of patronage to military generals, religious leaders, and heads of administrative offices.[55] Loyal servants of the monarchy received personal and hereditary lands as rewards, which led to the solidification of the nakharar system under powerful noble houses. The landowning elites included the relatives of the king, the temples, the noble families, principal administrators in state agencies, and private landowners. As patriarchal values and customs dominated prefeudal and feudal Armenian society, the head of the nakharar house and his sons governed the affairs of their estates with minimum input by women, who possessed no rights in public life. Except in rare cases among the noble families, women lacked the legal right to inheritance and the means to secure financial independence. To be sure, they were not totally powerless, but their influence remained confined to matters of domestic responsibilities and family affairs.[56]

An important economic sector, inherited from the Ervandunis, was the temple complex, religious and economic. Armenian kings and elites had promoted ancestor worship, and this practice had led to proliferation of temples with vast properties and wealth. The temples were dedicated to ancestors and pantheons, including, for example, Anahit, Vahagn, Aramazt, and Naneh, all worshiped by the polytheistic Artashesian elite. The religious leaders, the *kurms*, especially their chief *krmapet*, usually were members of the king's dynasty. Although ancestor worship had been central to the Armenian religion, Artashes I was the first to introduce worship of the king's dynasty, although he did not institute deification of the monarch. Like the urban sectors, the temple economies retained a certain degree of autonomy from the central government and possessed rights and privileges in matters of market relations and ownership and management of property. In fact, some temple complexes were similar to urban centers. Often referred to as *tacharayin kaghakner* (temple cities), they had their own self-sufficient economic base and commercial networks.[57]

Among the lower classes, the peasants possessed certain rights on the land they worked, although they did not benefit significantly from the revenues accrued from their physical labor. The peasants were "free" but paid heavy taxes. The slaves were not "free"; their owners included members of the royal court, households, and temples. The state also employed slaves for the construction and maintenance of roads and canals, irrigation systems, cities, and buildings. Slavery thus constituted an essential component of the Artashesian economy.[58]

Artashes I introduced various reforms and relied on territorial expansion to improve domestic social and economic conditions, which in turn substantially increased the role of the state. The reforms were in response to the centrifugal tendencies of the emerging urban elites and temple economies that could potentially threaten his rule. He codified landholding to better manage relations between the landowning and the administrative-military elites. Administrative reforms aimed at improving the royal treasury and accounting, the efficient use of water transportation for trade and economic development, and the centralization of decision-making authority. For military purposes, Artashes I divided the country into four military regions (*strategos*),[59] each with its own administrative subdivisions and governed by governors appointed by the king. These four zones integrated into the nakharar structure the semi-autonomous lords, the *bdeshkhs*, who received vast lands in return for their loyal service and commission as guardians of the monarchy's borders. Although at this time the position of border guards had not yet become a hereditary office, nevertheless, along with the ministerial posts, it set the foundations for the nakharar system. Territorial expansion created opportunities for the accumulation of wealth and strengthened the symbiotic ties between the landholding families and the military and administrative agents of the state. However, territorial expansion and centralization of authority also created tensions, as powerful landowners competed for a greater share of the expanding domain.[60]

In the area of foreign policy, Artashes I launched successive military campaigns into the lands of the Medes, the Caucasian Albanians, and the Georgians (Iberians). He failed, however, to annex Lesser Armenia and Dsopk, then under the control of Pontus and Zareh, respectively. He initially pursued an equidistant policy, balancing relations with the two major powers: Rome from the west and Parthia in the east. But when competition between the two intensified, virtually threatening the survival of Armenia proper, Artashes I sided with Rome.[61] In hopes of enlisting Zareh's cooperation in military matters, he also signed a security treaty with him in about 180 B.C., although the latter's troops, concerned with their own security, refused to participate in the military campaigns led by Artashes I. Their bilateral cooperation remained limited to immediate interests, particularly as the government of Dsopk preferred to maintain its independence, despite Artashes's efforts to the contrary.[62]

Meanwhile, the polarization of Asia Minor between pro-Roman and pro-Seleucid camps posed a complicated problem. Mithradates III and Parnak I of Pontus pursued close relations with the Seleucids, whose empire had already collapsed, to check Roman geopolitical ambitions, while Cappadocia in turn relied on Rome to defend itself against both Pontus and the Seleucids. Artashes I sought alliances with Pontus in part to maintain access to its port cities on the Black Sea, which were essential for the Armenian economy, and to exert sufficient influence in the region so as to control Lesser Armenia as a buffer zone for his kingdom. The governor of Lesser Armenia, Mithradates, an ally of Parnak in Pontus, was not so inclined, however. As relations among neighbors deteriorated and the constellation of alliances led to wars between 183 and 179 B.C., Greater Armenia and Dsopk drew closer against Pontus and Rome.

The declining Seleucid empire encouraged Artashes I to preempt a potential threat, and in 168 B.C. he launched a series of invasions across the southern border into Mesopotamia, instigating a war with the Seleucid Antiochus IV Epiphanes.[63] The latter first attacked Dsopk and continued his campaign farther into Greater Armenia. The military offensive posed a serious threat to Artashes I, but he defended the capital and maintained his sovereignty.[64] However, Antiochus's primary target at this time was Parthia. He made a final attempt at invading Parthia and Armenia in 165 B.C., but again he failed.[65] Internal political crises weakened his position in the region at a time when the Arshakuni Parthians were in the process of consolidating power at Ctesiphon, their capital city in Mesopotamia,[66] and Rome was not yet prepared for heavy engagement in the Near East. The dissolution of the Seleucid empire created a geopolitical vacuum, providing an opportunity for the Parthians, led by Mithradates I the Great (r. ca. 171–138 B.C.) and Mithradates II (r. 123–87 B.C.), to expand their domain over most of Mesopotamia and emerge as a dominant regional power,[67] which ineluctably drew the Roman empire into the region.

Artashes I died in about 160 B.C., leaving behind six sons: Artavazd, Vruyr, Mazhan, Zareh, Tiran, and Tigran. His death coincided with the Parthian imperial drive to conquer the neighboring lands. The Persian army defeated Artashes's successors, Artavazd I (r. 160–115 B.C.) and Tigran I (r. 115–95 B.C.),[68] and forced Greater Armenia to pay tribute to Parthia in return for peace. In the meantime, however, political stability at home had enabled the Roman empire to redirect its attention to the Near East. The subsequent widening of Roman involvement in regional politics and greater control over Cappadocia, Commagene, and Syria, on one hand, and Parthian territorial ambitions, on the other hand, pitted the two empires against each other over Seleucid territories and Armenia. Neither Artavazd I nor Tigran I had the luxury of remaining neutral.[69] In 96 B.C., Roman and Parthian representatives signed an agreement to partition these disputed lands, a partition that the Armenians viewed as a humiliating defeat at the hands of foreign powers and that Tigran's son, Tigran II, sought to rectify. Upon his accession to power, Tigran II revived Artashes I's expansionist policies and conquered the lands where his grandfather had failed. The Artashesian dynasty reached its zenith during the reign of Tigran II the Great (r. 95–55 B.C.).

TIGRAN THE GREAT AND PAX ARMENNICA

Tigran the Great had been held captive by the Parthians since the Armeno-Parthian clashes, but he secured his release with a promise to surrender southeastern lands. Mithradates II of Parthia, who had married Tigran II's daughter Avtoman and sought to strengthen his position in Greater Armenia, supported his father-in-law's return to his homeland and enthroned him as successor to Tigran I. Family ties, albeit briefly, encouraged amicable relations.[70] Immediately after the agreement of 96 B.C., internal problems in both Rome and Parthia created a political vacuum, allowing Tigran the Great an opportunity to reassert his own power and independence from the foreign conquerors. Undoubtedly, a key motivating factor in his expansionist thrust was to avenge past Armenian military defeats and humiliations.[71] But the effective mobilization of his extensive military capabilities certainly required other essential ingredients as well.

Both domestic and external factors contributed to his imperial expansion. Decades of population growth had augmented the manpower available for the Armenian military. Further, the expansion in landownership begun under Artashes I had continued under his successors and contributed to vibrant commercial relations and rapid economic development, which in turn enabled the nobility to mobilize vast resources for external expansion at a time when Armenia was not yet fully drawn into East-West imperial scrambles for hegemony.[72] External factors included the demise of the Seleucid empire and the failure of the Parthians, under Mithradates II, to strengthen their position in the region. Unlike Artashes I, Tigran the Great could not maintain good relations with Rome, in part because of his expansionist policies but also because Rome, determined to become increasingly involved in the region, would not tolerate the emergence of yet another military and economic competitor. European scholars have viewed western policies of Tigran as a mere extension of the geopolitical aims of his powerful father-in-law, King Mithradates VI the Eupator of Pontus. Tigran the Great, however, devised his own calculations and objectives for the strengthening of his economy and imperial expansion.[73]

Once secure in power, Tigran the Great launched a number of ambitious military campaigns. He directed his first operation toward Dsopk, which he conquered in 94 B.C., thus consolidating his power over much of the former Ervanduni territories.[74] Tigran hoped to remove Dsopk (which he considered a second-rate kingdom) as a significant factor in regional politics, but his policy of outright annexation gravely complicated matters with Rome. The seizure of Dsopk threatened Roman interests in neighboring Cappadocia, although at this point the Roman army refrained from action. In 92 B.C. Tigran invited Mithradates VI to enter into a mutual security alliance regarding the kingdom of Cappadocia.

The agreement provided that Mithradates VI would gain control over the conquered lands in the region, while Tigran would receive the slaves and all movable goods. They sealed the alliance with the Armenian king marrying Cleopatra, one of the daughters of Mithradates VI. Encouraged by the alliance and in cooperation with Tigran, Mithradates invaded Cappadocia, drawing the Roman army directly into the conflict. Although the initial phase of Tigran's territorial ambitions had not moved the Roman empire, his alliance with Mithradates and the latter's annexation of Cappadocia provoked Roman intervention. General Lucius Cornelius Sulla was dispatched to defend Cappadocia, and while he and Mithradates were at war over Asia Minor, Tigran the Great in 90 B.C. recaptured the territories that he had earlier surrendered to Parthia in exchange for his freedom. Subsequently, he conquered the kingdom of Osroene and its capital city of Edessa (Orhai), Commagene, Cilicia, Syria, and Phoenicia, creating an Armenian empire stretching from the Caspian Sea to the Mediterranean.[75] Exploiting the opportunity provided by Parthian internal weaknesses, he assumed the Persian title of *shahanshah* (king of kings).[76]

Like Artashes I, Tigran the Great also built a new capital city, Tigranakert (Tigranocerta),[77] as the political, economic, and cultural center of his kingdom to symbolize the advent of a new Armenian imperial era under his leadership. The new capital, situated near the Achaemenian Royal Road, soon acquired strategic and commercial advantages as a growing center for international trade, while military victories and economic prosperity generated unprecedented wealth for the Armenian empire.[78] Tigran's empire encompassed a vast territory, rich in resources and slaves, dynamic economic centers (Antioch, Latakia, Damascus), and experienced civil and military administrators (Mtsbin became the imperial administrative center for the southern command)—all of which enabled the Armenian nobility to accumulate enormous wealth. The nakharar system was further solidified during the reign of Tigran the Great, as the empire expanded and provided opportunities for consolidation of power and wealth.[79]

This prosperity could be maintained so long as territorial expansion continued and the conquered peoples remained loyal to the Armenian monarchy and contributed to its treasury. Tigran II required the local leaders throughout the empire to provide soldiers for his army and taxed them heavily. He resettled large number of Jews and Syrians from the Middle East in the major commercial centers (e.g., Ervandashat, Armavir, Vardgesavan, and Van). By one estimate, over half a million foreigners were resettled in Armenia, and the commercial and industrial developments across his empire were managed by Armenians as well as by Jews, Assyrians, and Greeks. The use of such words as *shuka* (market), *khanut* (store), and *hashiv* (account) indicate Assyrian influence on Armenia's economic development.[80] Nevertheless, throughout the major cities and the vast expanse of his empire, non-Armenian inhabitants remained his vassals, albeit in a loosely structured system. So long as his subjects pledged loyalty and paid their taxes, they were granted some degree of local autonomy.[81] There were no guarantees, however, that the king's subjects would remain loyal as political and economic conditions deteriorated. By about 70 B.C., the empire had become unsustainable for a number of reasons.

Tigran the Great and his supporters did not view the empire as an exclusively "Armenian" empire but rather as an international enterprise, whose beneficiaries could include all participants in its promotion and protection. This approach to empire-building contributed to the most serious structural deficiency: Its highly decentralized imperial administration. It not only relied too heavily on local nobilities in the conquered lands, but also on subjects whose loyalty to the Armenian crown were suspect. Both groups could claim to be loyal only so long as the benefits of loyalty outweighed the burdens of foreign imperial rule. Had Tigran the Great achieved the degree of centralization of power witnessed under Artashes I, he could have organized an empire that perhaps could have proved sustainable long after his reign. A related structural deficiency in the imperial scheme was the absence (perhaps due to the short duration of the empire) of a strong institutional arrangement to facilitate circulation of capital and benefits of commerce between the core and peripheral economies. The relationship was strictly unidirectional: Wealth acquired in the conquered territories served to enrich the royal treasury. Such shortcomings could be overlooked only so long as the two major empires, Rome and Parthia, did not challenge Tigran II.

THE FALL

Beginning in 79 B.C., changes in Roman military leadership stimulated a more aggressive policy toward the Near East. General Lucius Licinus Lucullus (110–56 B.C.), having succeeded Sulla, invaded Pontus and appeared ready to attack Armenia. Despite warnings of Roman intentions, Tigran the Great ignored the threat. The Armenian *shahanshah* had become too arrogant and refused to negotiate with Lucullus to avert a crisis. Rather than declare war on Armenia at this time, Roman officials secretly recruited alliances with the nobility at Antioch. Having secured the northern flank by 70 B.C., the Roman army led by Lucullus marched through Dsopk (Sophene) in the spring of 69 B.C. It crossed the Taurus on October 6 and attacked Tigranakert.[82] During the battle, the local non-Armenian population sided with the Roman army, leaving the Armenians to fend for themselves. In his book *The Art of War*, Niccolò Machiavelli (1469–1527), one of the most influential Italian political theorists, attributes Tigran II's military failure to his excessive reliance on his cavalry. Machiavelli comments:

> Tigranes, king of Armenia, brought an army of 150,000 cavalrymen into the field, many of whom were armed like our men-at-arms and called *cataphracti* [soldiers clad in iron mail], against the Roman general Lucullus, whose army consisted of only 6,000 cavalrymen and 25,000 infantrymen. When Tigranes saw the enemy army, he said, "These are enough for an ambassador's train." Nevertheless, when they engaged, the king was routed; and the historian imputes the defeat entirely to the little service done by the *cataphracti*, whose faces were covered in such a manner that they could hardly see—much less annoy—the enemy and whose limbs were so overloaded with heavy armor, that when any of them fell from their horses, they could hardly get up again or use their arms.[83]

To make matters worse, Tigran's two sons, Zareh and Tigran, rebelled against him, and the younger Tigran fled to his father-in-law, the Parthian king Phraates III, who later provided him with an army contingent to invade Armenia.[84] Having lost confidence in their king's military capabilities, the Armenian nobility also rebelled, leaving the civilian and military leadership deeply demoralized. The Romans captured and destroyed the city of Tigranakert, forcing Tigran to withdraw from Syria and Mesopotamia; however, Lucullus failed to advance farther northeast to the region of Ararat and Artashat, thus enabling Tigran to recover some of his losses. Several factors conspired against Lucullus during his winter campaign to capture Artashat. A large number of his soldiers had been killed and wounded, while heavy snow and logistical problems (e.g., food shortages) impeded movement across the mountainous terrain. His troops, away from home and family for too long, refused to move forward and rebelled on several occasions. Rome could not tolerate such a loss and subsequently recalled Lucullus. Encouraged by the favorable turn in fortune, Tigran the Great and Mithradates retaliated by reconquering Pontus, northern Syria, and Commagene.[85]

Rome refused to relinquish its eastern policy. The appointment of General Pompey (Gnaeus Pompeius), at the time in Cilicia, as successor to Lucullus indicated Rome's determination to continue its conquest of Armenia. Intrigue and ambition caused Tigran's son, Zareh, who had already refused to defend his father, to ally with Pompey; internal rebellions had now considerably weakened Tigran's hold on power. In order not to lose its influence in the rapidly changing events in Armenia, Parthia capitalized on Tigran's sudden weakness and attacked from the east. Although the Armenian emperor defended Artashat against Parthian attacks, the arrival of Pompey made the two-front defense against the major empires virtually impossible. In 66 B.C., he finally agreed to sign the

Peace of Artashat, relegating the Armenian *shahanshah* to the position of a symbolic ruler now on friendlier terms with, but serving as a buffer for, Rome against Parthia.[86] Under the treaty, Tigran the Great was forced to pay war taxes and to withdraw from Syria, Phoenicia, Mesopotamia, Cilicia, Commagene, and Dsopk. His domain remained limited to Greater Armenia proper until his death in 55 B.C. at the age of eighty-five.[87] The Treaty of Artashat signified the decline of the Artashesian empire, not unlike the Treaty of Apamea in 188 B.C., which had signaled the decline of the Seleucids.

Beginning in 54 B.C., Rome intensified its policy toward Armenia, the Middle East, and Parthia. Although Parthian leaders at first sought to strengthen relations with Armenia against Rome and expected cultural ties to draw Armenia closer to them, Phraates III and Pompey arrived at an understanding: In return for Parthian support in Armenia, Pompey would restore the provinces of Corduene and Adiabene, lands annexed by Tigran, to Parthia.[88] Although the new Armenian king, Artavazd II (r. 55–35 B.C.), Tigran the Great's son and successor, preferred to maintain close ties with Rome, that relationship became untenable as Roman and Armenian interests diverged.

In the spring of 54 B.C. the Roman general Marcus Licinius Crassus, notorious for his immense fortunes amassed through both legal and illegal means and now envisioning himself as the conqueror of the East, arrived in Syria with plans to destroy Parthia. It is not clear whether the Roman Consul had approved his Parthian campaign, but he began his military operations across the Euphrates and advanced toward enemy territories, registering victories in successive battles.[89] Unwilling to clash with the Roman general head on, early in 53 B.C. the Parthian king Orodes II (r. ca. 57–38 B.C.) dispatched his envoys to meet with Crassus. They found the Roman general in a confident mood, energized with the prospect of gaining land and loot.

In the meantime, the Parthians had invaded Armenia to remove Artavazd's army as a potential threat. Artavazd rushed to propose that Crassus and his army march across the flat lands of Armenia to launch its attack on Parthia. The Armenian king offered 16,000 cavalry and 30,000 infantrymen as his seal of cooperation in the Roman campaign. Roman military presence in Armenia and Armenian engagement in the offensive, Artavazd reasoned, would provide sufficient defense against further aggression and a potential Parthian counteroffensive. Artavazd must have been aware of the gravity of his gamble in associating himself too closely with Roman military objectives, for Parthian defeat of Crassus would render Armenia vulnerable to greater attacks. Be that as it may, Crassus showed no interest in Artavazd's plans and ordered his army to march eastward across the Mesopotamian plains into Parthia.[90]

Disagreements between Artavazd II and Crassus caused frictions between the two and compelled Artavazd to gravitate toward Parthia. This strategic shift in foreign policy came at a time when King Orodes had ordered his army into Armenia to prevent, through negotiation or war, an Artavazd-Crassus alliance. After brief skirmishes, the negotiations between Orodes and Artavazd culminated in the marriage of Artavazd's sister to the Parthian heir apparent, Bakur (Pacorus). Artavazd continued to hope to remain Rome's ally as well; Crassus, of course, saw Artavazd's sudden alignment with Orodes as a treasonous act against Rome but, more personally, against him. The Roman general, however, did not have an opportunity to punish Artavazd. At Artashat, during the festivities celebrating the wedding between Bakur and Artavazd's sister, as the Armenian and Parthian monarchs and guests were drunk in jollification and merrymaking, a Parthian satrap entered the palace hall and proudly displayed Crassus's head. At the Battle of Carrhae in 53 B.C., an event of enormous significance for Parthia and, as one historian has commented, "without doubt the most celebrated episode in Parthian history,"[91] the Parthian military had captured and decapitated Crassus.[92] Plutarch wrote:

> Now when the head of Crassus was brought to the king's door, the tables had been removed, and a tragic actor, Jason by name, of Tralles, was singing that part of the "Bacchae" of Euripides where Agave is about to appear. While he was receiving his applause, Sillaces stood at the door of the banqueting-hall, and after a low obeisance, cast the head of Crassus into the centre of the company. The Parthians lifted it up with clapping of hands and shouts of joy. . . . Then Jason handed his costume of Pentheus to one of the chorus, seized the head of Crassus, and assuming the role of the frenzied Agave, sang these verses through as if inspired:
>
> "We bring from the mountain
> A tendril fresh-cut to the palace,
> A wonderful prey."

Changes in Roman military leadership did not bode well for Armenia, however. Hoping for stability in the region, Artavazd II opted for an equidistant policy toward both Rome and Parthia, but in Rome Julius Caesar decided to renew the military drive against Parthia. While plans were under way to that effect, a civil war broke out in Rome between Caesar and Pompey in 49–48 B.C. and forced Caesar to postpone his eastern campaign. In 47 B.C., having defeated Pompey, Caesar went to Syria and Asia Minor, where his military successes gave occasion to his famous words *"Veni, Vidi, Vici"* in an address before the Senate.[94] Plans were set for Caesar to return to the Middle East and to resume his military operations against Parthia, but a conspiracy in the Roman Senate led to his assassination on March 15, 44 B.C. Undaunted by the loss, the pro-Caesar faction nevertheless relentlessly fought and recaptured power.

Having secured peace at home, the Roman leadership resumed plans for the eastern campaign. General Marc Antony, one of the most prominent pro-Caesar leaders, led the eastern war in Asia Minor and against Parthia. In early 36 B.C., the Roman general demanded full cooperation from Artavazd II in the campaign. The Armenian king vacillated but entered a secret alliance with him and promised to supply 6,000 cavalry and 7,000 infantrymen to accompany the Roman military force of "sixty thousand Roman legionaries, with ten thousand Iberian and Celtic cavalry, and thirty thousand Asiatic allies," a force far greater than commanded by Crassus two decades earlier.[95] Marc Antony, then too engrossed in his love affair with Queen Cleopatra of Egypt, lost much valuable time and did not commence the offensive until summer. Confronting massive resistance on the Euphrates, he entered Armenia, where Artavazd II, faced with no choice, welcomed him. Artavazd advised Antony to avoid further direct confrontation with the Parthian king Phraates IV on the Euphrates and instead to march via Media Atropatene (Azerbaijan). Unfortunately for the Roman general, the advice proved near fatal, as the Parthian army pursued his troops in open field in Atropatene and killed about 10,000 Roman soldiers. The carnage continued until Antony finally escaped from Tabriz. Artavazd II, who now opposed Armenian engagement in the conflict, refused to support him.[96]

Marc Antony returned to the bosom of Cleopatra to recover, and while in Alexandria he received in 34 B.C. an offer by a delegation from the king of Media, a vassal of Phraates IV, to cooperate in battle against Armenia and Parthia. Antony seized the opportunity to punish Artavazd; the blame for the failure of the Roman army to conquer Parthia, the general believed, rested squarely on the shoulders of Artavazd. In 33 B.C. he attacked Artashat and took Artavazd as hostage to Egypt. Cleopatra ordered the beheading of Aravazd as a demonstration of her love for Marc Antony. Artashes II, Artavazd's son, escaped to Parthia.[97]

Despite the reverses suffered during the Roman campaigns, Parthia attempted, albeit briefly, to reestablish its hegemony, and in 30 B.C. supported Artashes II's return to recapture Armenia. In the process, Artashes II ordered the eradication of all Roman influences as a means to restore Armenia's autonomy and particularly to avenge Roman invasions there. By this time, based on their experiences with the virulence of Roman hostility toward Armenia, some Armenian leaders preferred to maintain closer alliances with Parthia, a relationship strengthened especially because of the nobility's familial ties.[98] While initially the Romans had presented themselves as "liberators" of the Armenian kingdom against the East, the pro-Parthian nakharars argued, their military engagement had proved far more destructive than any encountered by the local population. The Macedonian invasions in the Near East had given rise to prosperous cities and rapid economic development, while Parthian rule had proved more lenient toward the subject peoples. The Roman invasions, however, had brought massive physical and cultural destruction.[99] Yet, despite Armenian preference for closer ties with Parthia at this time, the Parthian engagement in Armenian affairs ended abruptly. The Parthian military under Phraates IV withdrew from Armenian lands, allowing Rome to exercise exclusive control over the situation in Armenia.[100]

In 20 B.C. news arrived that the emperor Augustus (r. 27 B.C.–A.D.14) had dispatched his adopted son, Tiberius, and Tigran, the son of Artashes II, to Armenia. The pro-Roman aristocrats seized this opportunity to plead their case to Augustus: Tigran should replace his father, who had shown clear preference for Parthia. The Romans agreed, and a pro-Roman conspiracy orchestrated the assassination of Artashes II and placed Tigran III on the Armenian throne. After Artashes II's death in 20 B.C., the ensuing domestic conflicts, especially between pro-Rome and pro-Parthia factions, so weakened the Artashesian dynasty that neither the pro-Roman Tigran III nor his son pro-Parthian Tigran IV could muster sufficient power to maintain even a semblance of unity.[101]

Tigran III (r. 20–6 B.C.) had spent ten years in Rome, where he received his education and political training. Rome supported his accession to the Armenian throne and expected full compliance with its policies in the East. Roman poets composed lyrics praising the imperial military successes in Armenia, while the government minted gold and silver coins celebrating Roman rule over Armenia—*Armenia capta* and *Armenia recapta.* The emperor Augustus reportedly commented that Rome could have annexed Armenia after the assassination of Artashes II but the emperor, following precedent, instead preferred to grant the monarchy to its rightful Armenian heir, Tigran. While Tigran III at first supported Roman policy in the region, he gradually shifted his orientation in favor of Parthia, a policy further pursued by his son, Tigran IV (r. 6–1 B.C.).

Tigran IV sought Parthian military support to strengthen his position against pro-Roman families and Rome, but the Parthian monarchy itself was experiencing a turbulent period. In return for his withdrawal from Armenia, Phraates IV had received from Augustus a Roman slave woman, Musa, as a present. Soon thereafter Musa bore a son, Phraataces (diminutive for Phraates), for the king and became Parthia's queen. In 2 B.C. Musa poisoned her aged husband and placed her son on the Parthian throne. Augustus subsequently ordered his military to conquer Parthia.[102] Neither Parthia nor Armenia could withstand the vicissitudes of Roman intrigue and machinations, and by A.D. 10 the Artashesian dynasty had declined beyond repair. Rome ruled Armenia for the rest of the first century A.D.

2

Culture, Language, and Wars of Religion: Kings, Marzpans, Ostikans

The imperial expansion under Tigran the Great demonstrated that the effective management of domestic competing interests in the context of East-West clashes required at minimum a strong military leadership. Although the Arshakuni (Arsacid) dynasty in Greater Armenia instituted fundamental changes that transformed the national culture and the structure of political economy at home, it nevertheless failed to counter the pressures exerted by the international geopolitical situation. In fact, the emergence of the Arshakuni kingdom in Armenia was itself the outcome of the East-West rivalry.

THE DANCE OF EMPIRES

Arshakuni influence in Armenia gained saliency in the early decades of the first century A.D. when widespread antagonism to the pro-Roman sympathies held by the Parthian Arshakuni king Vonones I led to his expulsion from Persia. He had hardly organized his kingdom in Armenia when three years later the Romans exiled him to Syria.[1] The conflict between Rome and Parthia escalated during the reign of the Roman emperor Nero (r. A.D. 54–68) and the Parthian king Vologeses I (Armenian: Vagharsh, r. 51–75), the eldest son of Vonones II by a Greek mistress of the harem. Virulently opposed to all things western, Vologeses I insisted on eradicating foreign cultural influences, a position that found strong support among the Parthian elite. Refusing to grant Rome exclusive jurisdiction over Armenia, he attacked Artashat and Tigranakert (Tigranocerta) and, with the blessings of the pro-Parthian *nakharar* or noble houses, installed his younger brother Trdat I (Tiridates, r. 62/66–75) on the Armenian throne.[2]

Rome refused to accept a potentially threatening Armenian-Parthian alignment and redoubled efforts to reassert its influence in Armenia. Upon accession to power, the emperor Nero, for domestic and geopolitical reasons, in A.D. 55 dispatched the revered general Domitius Corbulo to the east to secure Syria and Dsopk (Sophene) as client states, erecting a cordon sanitare against Greater Armenia. Vologeses I, determined to deny Nero a free hand in the region, declared Armenia a vassal state and launched his own offensive, to which Corbulo responded in 58 by a full-scale invasion of Armenia, which, one observer has noted, "had the misfortune to be the 'cockpit of the Near East.' "[3] The Roman army marched east from Erzerum, while Roman ships arriving at the docks of Trebizond and other ports on the southern coast of the Black Sea extended logistical support. Corbulo sacked Artashat and directed his southern contingent to the southern shores of Lake Van and onward to the city of Tigranakert. Vologeses retaliated in kind. Before the invasions and counter invasions had ceased in 58/59, Corbulo had captured Tigranakert and Artashat and the entire region between the two cities and farther north to Erzerum, forcing Trdat to seek refuge in Persia. Rome installed a governor in Tigranakert and actually sought to annex all of Armenia, but in 62 Vologeses defeated General Caesennius Paetus and forced him to withdraw from Armenia.[4] Internal political difficulties in Rome and Parthia led to the cessation of hostilities, and in 64 they agreed to the Rhandeia Compromise, which established Roman-Parthian co-suzerainty over Armenia, whereby Parthian Arshakunis would nominate the candidates to the Armenian throne and Rome would confer legitimacy through coronation. The Armenian nakharars, too exhausted by the chaotic situation and perhaps unable to decide whether to side with Rome or Parthia, accepted this mutually satisfactory resolution.

Trdat, with his wife, children, and nephews (sons of Vologeses and Bakur), traveled overland to Rome for his coronation by Nero, who financed the journey of his entire entourage of about 3,000 Armenians and Parthians.[5] Trdat arrived at Naples in 66, probably later than Nero had expected. The emperor received him with honors and gladiatorial contests for entertainment. Thence they traveled to Rome for the coronation, which was held at the Forum. There Nero, seated on the rostra, opened the ceremonies. Trdat knelt before Nero and "acknowledged vassality in terms that contained the formula proclaiming the supernatural attributes of the Iranian sovereign."[6]

Master . . . I have come to thee, my god, to worship thee as I do Mithras. The destiny thou spinnest for me shall be mine, for thou art my *Fortune and my Fate.*

The Roman emperor accepted the honor with great content; he crowned Trdat as king of Armenia, and they resumed celebrations at the theater in Pompey. The theater "had been entirely covered with gold for the occasion and shaded from the sun by purple curtains stretched overhead, so that people gave to the day itself the epithet of 'golden.'"[7] Vologeses I's brother Trdat I returned triumphantly to Armenia and assumed the throne, as "the sun" and "supreme ruler of Greater Armenia," attested the inscriptions found at Garni. Trdat thus established the Arshakuni dynasty in Armenia. With Nero's blessings, he launched major reconstruction projects throughout Armenia, rebuilt the cities, including the capital city of Artashat, destroyed by Corbulo, expanded commercial relations, and urged the Arshakuni residents in Armenia to assimilate into the local culture. Trdat also built a temple dedicated to the god Tir north of Artashat.[8]

The recurring imperial competition would not permit luxuries of peace and stability. The decline of the Parthian empire encouraged Rome to pursue an aggressive policy to control Armenia. The emperor Vespasian (r. 70–79) in 72 incorporated Lesser Armenia into the Roman province of Cappadocia, and shortly after Trdat's death in 88, Greater Armenia fell victim to Roman expansionist strategies against Parthia.[9] In 114, in clear violation of the Rhandeia Compromise, the emperor Trajan (r. 98–117) refused to install a Parthian to the Armenian throne and, under the Roman governor L. Catilius Severus, briefly annexed Armenia to the Roman empire.[10] After Trajan's death in August 117, Rome failed to maintain the vast territories under its domain. Fearing growing Parthian presence in Armenia under Vagharsh I (r. 117–138/144), founder of the new cities of Vagharshapat, Vagharshavan, and Vagharshakert, the Roman army intensified its campaign to force Parthia's withdrawal from Armenia.[11]

ECONOMIC AND CULTURAL CLASHES

The social structure in Arshakuni Armenia retained the deep imprints of Persian political customs and administrative practices.[12] The key Armenian institutions in the second century A.D. consisted of, in hierarchical order, the monarchy, the nakharars or nobles, *azats* (or knights), *ramiks* (the masses, city dwellers, laborers), *shinakans* (peasants), and *struks* (slaves). The Armenian king ruled as an "Oriental despot,"[13] and among the nobility, loyalty to the king and military service in his army yielded as reward all the accouterments of high offices, land, and slaves.[14] The Arshakuni kings, like their Artashesian predecessors, carried such titles as king, great king, and king of kings, each reflecting his own personal proclivities, wealth, and power as recognized at home and abroad. Following the Persian tradition, the king claimed "supernatural glory" (*park*) and was believed to possess "fortune and glory" (*bakht u park*) that legitimized his rule. In fact, the king represented *the* source of policy and political legitimacy. He revived and strengthened old rules and regulations, and issued new edicts that superseded them; he also had the authority to mint new coins and to build new cities. The principal functions and powers of the Armenian king included the declaration and conduct of war, signing treaties, representation of the Armenian state, and management of inter- and intradynastic relations. The latter often blurred the line between domestic and foreign policy issues because of the close *khnamiutiun* (familial) relations across the Armenian and Persian dynasties.[15]

The administrative bureaucracies, headed by the Royal Ministries, comprised of such offices as *sparapetutiun* (commander in chief of the armed forces), *hazarapetutiun* (seneschal), *tagadir-aspetutiun* (coronant), *maghkhazutiun* (chief of the royal escort), *mardpetutiun* (administrator of the royal treasury and fortresses), and *mets datavorutiun* (supreme court). The *hayr mardpet* as the head of the royal treasury was also responsible for the supervision of the royal harems and the citadels. *Mets datavorutiun* of the ministry of justice included the office of the high priest (*krmapet*) and, after Armenia's Christianization, the Catholicos Hayots (Supreme Patriarch of Armenians). Other offices included the *senekapet*, who administered the secretarial offices (run by secretaries, *dpirs*) and served as the king's secretary, while the royal archivist (*arkuni divan*) supervised the archives.[16]

Next in the social class structure were the nakharars,[17] the nobility. The most loyal and powerful members of the elite *nakharar tuns* (noble houses) enjoyed vast powers, and in return for their services they were granted land (or estate, *gavar*) in addition to honors and privileges of the court. Originally, the term nakharar referred to governorship or prefects, but over the centuries governorship became ownership of gavars, while nakharardom became hereditary. By the third and fourth centuries, this system eventually contributed to the development of feudalism in Armenia.[18] Arshakuni Armenia consisted of large and small nakharardoms[19] in hierarchical arrangement, each nakharar inheriting his rank and insignia (*bardz u pativ*; literarily, "cushion and honor") according to his status according to the *Gahnamak* (Rank List) and *Zoranamak* (Military List). The major nakharar houses held such positions as the *bdeshkh* (quasi-autonomous nobles guarding the borders), coronant, and *sparapet*, each with its own privileges and responsibilities and could maintain up to ten thousand cavalry troops. The nakharars were expected to provide their *tsarayutiun* (services), including military services in times of war, to the king, who in turn would consult with them on matters of importance.[20] The nakharars could cooperate with the king in promoting his policies and protecting his monarchy against internal and external enemies; they could withhold their cooperation and compel the king to seek protection from outside sources; or they could conspire to oust him from power.

As one of the highest and most powerful offices, the seneschal, for example, administered the country's finances and collected taxes from cities and villages. It coordinated the country's infrastructural development policies and provided laborers (usually based on some form of forced labor) for the construction of cities, fortresses, bridges, and irrigation and transportation networks. The coronant, in addition to his role during coronations, functioned as the head of royal ceremonies and determined each minister's relative status (*bardz u pativ*) within the palace according to the *Gahnamak* and *Zoranamak*.[21] Some "royal" ministerial offices were hereditary to individual houses. For example, the Mamikonian house headed the sparapetutiun, the Bagratuni house held the office of the coronant, and the Gnunis held the offices of the seneschal and administrator of the royal treasury and fortresses.[22]

This dominant aristocratic class consisted of autonomous *tun*s (houses), each led by the *tanuter* (head of the house), with its own *hayrenik* (inherited land) and *pargevagank* (granted estates). An Arshakuni king, for example, was the tanuter of the Arshakuni house. When a noble relinquished his land, it was transferred to a male heir in his house or the house of the nearest female heir's husband.[23] This system enabled the nakharars to prevent fragmentation of their lands and to maintain a certain (at times, a high) degree of autonomy from the center. Below the nakharars were the *sepuhs* (minor princes), followed by the small landowning class *azats* (corresponding to European knights), and the lower classes, the *anazats* (not free), which included *ramiks* and *shinakans*. The slaves were not considered a class as such and were therefore called *ankarg* (not classified). Most of the urban population were *ramiks* (laborers) employed by merchants and artisans, while urban slaves worked in households. Some economic sectors became virtual household industries engaged in production and sale of military hardware, clothing, furniture, jewelry, ceramic plates, and the like exhibiting various degrees of sophistication for the wealthy and mass consumers. The administrative districts and territorial divisions in Arshakuni Armenia reflected the hierarchical arrangement and social order. These included the royal domain and lands (or *gavark arkunakank*) owned by the king; the *gavars* (private estates) and land grants owned by the nobles (e.g., *bdeshkh gavars*); *gavars* owned by the Arshakuni minor princes; temple lands and complexes dedicated to the worship of deceased members of the dynasty; and village communes.[24]

The pre-Christian Arshakuni kings continued the traditions of self-deification and ancestor worship. As part of their patronage, they designated certain princely landholdings as sacred places for pilgrimage, which developed into temple complexes with their own estates, farm animals, and slaves. For example, after King Trdat I proclaimed himself god Helios "the sun," he declared a number of royal territories as pilgrimage sites in honor of his deceased relatives: Artavanian, located south of Van city, for his uncle the Parthian king Artavan III; Bakurakert (Bakur village), a suburb of Marand city, for his brother Bakur; and Vagharshakert (Alashkert), in memory of his brother King Vagharsh (Vologeses).[25] Their agricultural production contributed to the local economies, the royal treasury, and international commerce.

ARMENIA BETWEEN THE SASANIAN AND ROMAN EMPIRES

By the time Vagharsh II had ascended the Parthian throne in 191 (regnal name, Vologeses IV), tensions between the two major empires had escalated, pressuring the Arshakuni leadership in Armenia to decide whether to favor or abandon Parthia. Initially Khosrov I (r. ca. 191–216/217), Vagharsh's less capable son and successor in Armenia, sought to maintain neutrality in East-West conflicts but, as the Roman threat intensified during the latter's campaign to capture the Parthian capital Ctesiphon in 197/198, he eventually sided with Rome.[26] In 216, the Roman military command invited Khosrov I to a conference, imprisoned him and his family, and installed a Roman governor, Theocretes, in Armenia. The Armenian nakharars, and Armenians in general, rebelled against Rome for the treacherous act and incessant meddling in Armenian affairs and overthrew the Roman governor.[27] By the early 220s the Parthian empire itself became the battleground for internal clashes. Opposition to the Parthian Arshakunis in Ctesiphon came most notably from the rising leader of the Sasanian dynasty, Ardashir I, the son of Sasan who ruled Persis (modern Fars province). After a prolonged struggle for power, the Parthian kingdom collapsed, leaving the Armenian branch of Arshakunis to govern at Artashat.[28] The Armenian Arshakunis gained greater freedom to govern their internal affairs independently of their Persian relations, particularly in matters of succession to the throne. The Arshakunis thus emerged as an independent kingdom in the second half of the third century and ruled Armenia from 180 to 428 (with a brief interruption between 252 and 278/9). The Sasanians controlled Persia thereafter until 651.

Trdat II (r. ca. 216/217–252), the first Arshakuni king raised in Armenia, expected to manage his domestic and foreign affairs free of external interventions. The Parthian empire had collapsed, and Rome appeared to favor his government. The Sasanians, however, pursued a far more hostile policy toward Rome than their predecessors. Faced with this threat and in the absence of Arshakuni support from Persia, Trdat II requested protection from Rome, but to no avail.[29] The Sasanians, determined to create their own empire, constantly engaged in wars with their neighbors. Intensely opposed to the West and Greco-Roman cultural and political influences in the region, King Shapur I (r. 240–271) sought to impose Persian Zoroastrianism at home and abroad, launched massive military campaigns to expand his imperial domain, and eventually defeated the Roman army in the Middle East, scoring a major military victory particularly at the Battle of Massice (or Anbar) in 244. He subsequently captured the great cities of Antioch and Caesarea before his death in 271. One of his sons, Hurmazd I (Hormizd), succeeded him as the Sasanian king at Ctesiphon, while another son, Narseh, having deposed Trdat II, much to Rome's chagrin, ruled as the king of Armenia until 293.[30]

The Roman emperor Aurelian (r. 270–275) challenged Sasanian power. Their struggle was resolved in 278, when the emperor Probus (r. 276–282) and Narseh agreed to partition Armenia. Rome successfully installed the pro-Roman Khosrov II to rule the western or Roman provinces of Armenia, but the Sasanians orchestrated his assassination in 287 and removed the pro-Roman nakharars from power. Their meddling in Armenian affairs notwithstanding, the Sasanian government failed to exercise direct rule in Armenia at this time, particularly after 293, when Narseh left Armenia to assume the Persian throne.[31] Internal crises in Ctesiphon briefly permitted the Roman military to strengthen its hold on geostrategic regions in Armenia and the Middle East. No sooner had Rome installed Trdat III on the Armenian throne than Narseh, having consolidated power against his opposition at home, launched a sustained offensive in 296–297 against Armenia and Rome and removed Trdat III from power. Trdat IV, one of Khosrov II's sons, who had sought refuge with the Roman army, in cooperation with a Roman army contingent led by Galerius, routed Narseh's troops from Armenia. The Emperor Diocletian's army imposed the Peace of Nisibis (Mtsbin) on Narseh in 297 and placed Trdat IV on the Armenian throne in 298/9. Under the terms of this treaty, the Sasanians recognized the autonomy of Armenia under Roman suzerainty. The treaty also placed the former Persian satrapies under Roman directorate as *civitates feoderatae liberae et immunes* (free territories) and required their loyalty in matters of imperial foreign policy. The treaty also pushed the border of the Roman East across northern Mesopotamia and to the southern shores of Lake Van to secure for Roman merchants the trade routes in the region.[32] The Sasanians hated the humiliating treaty, but neither Narseh nor his successor, Hormizd II (r. 302–309), could rectify the situation. Shapur II, who ascended to the throne in 309 at a very young age, did not inspire much confidence. During the course of the next twenty years, Shapur concentrated his energies at home and normalized relations with Rome rather than risk defeat in military adventures. The rise of Roman emperor Constantine to power radically altered the relations between the two empires.

THE ADOPTION OF CHRISTIANITY AND
THE ARMENIAN ALPHABET

The accession of Trdat IV the Great to the Armenian throne in 298 or 299 followed tortuous events as Rome and Sasanian Persia competed for power.[33] Upon recognition of the Armenian king, Narseh returned the Armenian cities under his jurisdiction, including Tigranakert, and Trdat established his capital at Vagharshapat. The ensuing brief period of political stability enabled Trdat to consolidate Greater Armenia as a single political entity. In matters of domestic policies, he sought greater administrative centralization to strengthen the monarchy and reorganized the territorial jurisdictions of local governors, with the aim of promoting commerce and military security in relations with the Roman and Persian-Sasanian empires. Land surveys were conducted for purposes of taxation, and the information was compiled in *Ashkharagir madiank* (geographic records). In the meantime, as discussed below, Trdat and his supporters experimented with a new approach in the governance of Armenia[34] and opted for a complete political and cultural disengagement from the Sasanian empire. The next hundred years of Arshakuni rule witnessed a cultural metamorphosis.

One of the most significant changes introduced by Trdat the Great was the acceptance of Christianity as a state religion. The conventional narrative depicting the Armenian conversion to Christianity is mixed with facts and myths. As historian Leo (Arakel Babakhanian) has pointed out, the historiography of the Armenian people is replete with literature on the conversion to Christianity, but there is little credible material on the subject. A detailed discussion of the legendary aspects of the conversion is beyond the purview of this chapter. Suffice it to note that according to the conventional view, two apostles, Thaddeus and Bartholomew, journeyed to Edessa and Armenia to disseminate the new religion. Two centuries later, this view holds, Grigor Lusavorich (Gregory the Illuminator), the first supreme patriarch of the Armenian Church, carried out extensive work to further spread Christianity among the people and the nobility. After initial opposition, Trdat the Great, who is said to have owed his recovery from a near-fatal illness to a miracle, declared Christianity as the state religion and established the Armenian Apostolic Church.[35]

The historical reality, of course, was far more complex than the quasi-mythological narrative. Christianity had first spread to Syria and then into Cappadocia in Asia Minor. The new religion thus entered Greater Armenia from two directions. In the south, it was first established as a formal religion in Mtsbin in Mesopotamia and farther west with its center at Edessa (Urfa), the capital of the Osreone kingdom. As a large Armenian population resided in both cities, it is likely that they had converted to Christianity long before it reached the Armenian centers of Van and Artashat. The first king to accept Christianity was Abgar IX Ukama at Edessa in the second century. Assyrian priests, among them Bardatsan of Edessa, were instrumental in the spread of Christianity in Armenia; they and their Armenian supporters founded new schools to teach and preach the religion. Christianity continued to make inroads on the bordering areas from the region of Bitlis (Baghesh) and Mush (Taron) located west of Lake Van through the southern shores of the lake and to Van. According to Eusebius of Caesarea, an Armenian bishopric was established in the region of Van under Bishop Mehruzhan, who was most likely associated with the Artsruni house. This southern Armenian form of Christianity was oriented more toward the masses, espoused more democratic ecclesiastical principles and communal philosophy, and was therefore less amenable to rigid institutional hierarchy.[36]

Whether in time this southern variant of Armenian Christianity would have evolved into the rigidly hierarchical church that the Armenian Church eventually became is subject for debate, but it was the western, Greco-Roman form of Christianity, which entered Armenia by way of Cappadocia, that superseded the southern church and established its ecclesiastical hegemony in Armenia. This movement was led by Grigor Lusavorich, a member of the Armenian nobility of Parthian origin and educated at a Greek Christian school in Cappadocia. He is believed to have possessed considerable organizational skills, which along with his enormous wealth and political power enabled him and his supporters to suppress and surpass the Edessa-based Christian movement in southern Armenia. At his urging, Trdat IV converted to Christianity and officially declared it a state religion in 301 (or 314), a process that was highly politicized and polarized Armenian society as it inflamed profound hostilities at home and in foreign affairs.[37]

Two principal factors possibly contributed to the conversion. The first involved Armenian foreign policy objectives and the determination on the part of the Armenian government, now relying on Roman protectorate support, to establish a renewed Arshakuni dynastic rule independently of the Sasanian regime. The Armenian leaders had to consider the political repercussions of adopting Christianity as state religion. The Sasanians under Hormizd II and his successor, Shapur II, perceived the conversion to be a direct threat to their domestic and geopolitical interests. Significantly, despite his initial hostility to the Christian movements within his domain, the Roman emperor Diocletian (r. 284–305) consented to Christianity in Armenia at the time as a demonstration of opposition to the Sasanians, given Trdat's loyalty to him. So long as the Armenian leadership continued its anti-Sasanian policy as expressed in military arrangements and in religious matters, Rome—regardless of doctrinal complications the conversion created—continued to tolerate Armenian "independent" posturing vis-à-vis Persia.[38]

The conversion to Christianity also involved domestic considerations. As a monotheistic religion, Christianity provided the philosophical or ideological foundations for the centralization and strengthening of the monarchy, placing the king, as the only deputy of a single God, at the apex of the sociopolitical hierarchy. Trdat the Great and his supporters utilized the transition from polytheistic to monotheistic religious order to achieve greater political and economic power and centralization.[39] Trdat sought to advance the new religion but also to destroy the temple complexes, the old pantheistic pagan traditions, and the wealth associated with the temple economies, so as to check the chronic centrifugal tendencies among some of the nakharar houses scrambling for power and wealth. By eliminating the pagan temples, Trdat sought to create new loyalties to his regime based on the new ideology and its institutions. Those loyal would accept the new religion and recognize the new religious order and hierarchy sanctioned by the state; those rejecting Christianity would lose their privileges. The destruction of the pagan temples therefore represented more than the mere physical removal of old institutions from the Armenian culture; it also meant the destruction of the economies and of the elites associated with those economies, now replaced by supporters of Trdat the Great.

The government lent its unequivocal support for the newly emerging ecclesiastical organization, the church. Trdat granted Grigor Lusavorich vast territories encompassing as many as fifteen provinces, the equivalent of a kingdom. The adoption of Christianity as official policy enabled the church firmly to establish its powerful institutions in Armenia. Grigor Lusavorich led the effort to Christianize Armenian pagan traditions and relied on education and the military. He established schools to train the children of the *krmapet* (high priest) families for Christian priesthood but also as a military force in cooperation with the government to destroy the ancient pagan temples and the social, cultural, and economic organizational life sustaining them. He and his supporters pillaged and plundered the pagan temples and communities and carried off the loot—gold and silver—to finance the construction of churches and schools. He also confiscated the estates owned by the pagan temple economies. While Armenian pagan traditions were never completely eradicated, the Armenian state and the church cooperated to impose Christianity throughout the country. Churches replaced old pagan shrines in Ani and Vagharshapat; in the latter, the temple of Anahit was replaced by the Cathedral of Holy Echmiadzin, the Mother See of the Armenian Apostolic Church, with its catholicos as the supreme patriarch. Echmiadzin may be translated as the site where the only Begotten Son descended.[40]

The emerging church and its institutional hierarchy paralleled the existing socioeconomic hierarchy with its own feudatory estates and slaves. The office of the catholicos remained hereditary for some time, as initiated under the family of Grigor Lusavorich. Similar to the nakharar families and their pagan traditions, he established the catholicosate as a hereditary institution, which further strengthened his control over the church hierarchy as a dynasty. The bishopric functioned as a representative of the ecclesiastical landowning nakharardom. Bishops were appointed from among the nakharar clans, and the lower clergy from the azats. The church eventually prohibited the clergy from marrying but permitted eunuchs to enter service as celibate clergy.[41]

The conversion to Christianity also introduced reforms in matters of familial relations and marriage, although it did not fundamentally change the androcentric, patriarchal customs and norms. The Armenian Church, with the full support of the monarchy, formalized the institution of marriage and required that husband and wife legalize their union by vows adhering to the Christian doctrine. It also expressly prohibited the clergy from officiating at secret weddings. The church dictated that a person marry outside the immediate family, although it permitted a widow to marry with her brother-in-law. It found unacceptable the pre-Christian practices of polygamy and marriage within the family, a custom that had enabled the nakharar houses to hold on to their inheritances. When opposition to the church increased, the Council of Ashtashat in 365, under the auspices of Catholicos Nerses I Partev, condemned those nakharar houses that insisted on continuing pagan practices. For their part, the anti-Christian nakharar families refused to acknowledge the authority of the church in matters of family and finances and ignored the Ashtashat decision. Determined to strengthen its position in society, years later, in 447, at the Council of Shahapivan, the church approved several resolutions regarding the responsibilities of the higher clergy and the family. With respect to relations between husband and wife, the Shahapivan edict reaffirmed the legitimacy of patriarchal dominance at home by providing that the bride money paid by the husband to her parents granted him the right to exercise control over her.[42] Such edicts passed by the church revealed the persistence of pre-Christian customs long after the conversion.

Mindful of the reality that Christianity could not be imposed on the population through sheer military force and political pressure, the Armenian Church and Trdat the Great also relied on education to Christianize and transform the public's pagan cultural values and customs. Such measures were particularly necessary to counter the spread of Syriac, southern Christianity, which in fact remained popular among the Armenians in the Lake Van basin. Moreover, there was considerable opposition to the church among the pro-Persian nakharar houses. They viewed the conversion to Christianity as undermining relations with the neighboring empire. The Trdat-Grigor alliance had forced the opposition leadership underground but failed to destroy them completely, and they frequently rebelled against both the government and the church. In the meantime, the Armenian government and the church adopted a pro-West, pro-Hellenistic orientation. As the center of Armenian Christianity gravitated from the Lake Van basin to Vagharshapat and the Lake Sevan basin in the far north-northeastern edges of Armenia, the divisions between southern and northern nakharar dynasties and between the pro-West and pro-Persian parties crystallized. The reign of Trdat the Great ended in 330, leaving Armenia in total disarray. The failure to solve these problems, according to the traditional view, led Trdat to abdicate the throne and to choose the life of a monk shielded from the turbulence outside. Other historians believe that the pro-Persian nakharars assassinated him.[43]

In matters of geopolitics, the consolidation of monarchical power and the institutionalization of the church increasingly, and ironically, posed a serious political challenge to the successors of Trdat the Great when securing some form of balance between the Roman and Sasanian empires became of paramount importance. During the reign of Khosrov III (r. 330–338), who succeeded Trdat the Great, the Arshakunis, the nakharars, and the church were divided among pro-Roman, pro-Sasanian, and pro-neutrality factions. The centrifugal tendencies of these factions (e.g., the rebellions led by the *bteshkh* Bakur with Persian support against Khosrov) weakened the kingdom. The adoption of Christianity thus added a religious dimension to its already precarious geopolitical situation and internal affairs.[44]

The declaration of toleration for all religions including Christianity in the Edict of Milan in 313 by Constantine I (ruler of the West, 312–324; emperor, 324–337) and his adoption of Christianity strengthened Armenian Christianity. Constantine also established his eastern imperial capital at the small town of Byzantium on the Bosporus in 324 and renamed it Constantinople, thus setting the foundation for the Byzantine empire. Internal divisions plaguing Rome enabled the Sasanian king Shapur II

(r. 309–379), one of the longest-reigning monarchs in Persian history, to advance his armies westward across Mesopotamia and the Syrian desert and northward to Armenia. Clearly dissatisfied with the geopolitical situation created by the Nisibis treaty since 297, Shapur II launched his devastating military campaigns against Armenia and extended political support to the pro-Persian nakharars (e.g., Sanatruk in Paytakaran province and bteshkh Bakur in Aghtsn) to remove western influences. The Armenian monarchy's alignment with Rome involved palace intrigue and machinations against the opposition in the political and religious institutions. King Tiran (r. 338–350), supported by Emperor Constantius II, ordered the assassination of the grandson of Grigor Lusavorich, Catholicos Husik I (341–347 or 342–348), and the Syrian bishop Daniel. Years later, King Pap, who sought to weaken the church, sent Husik's grandson Nerses the Great into exile and ordered his assassination, but in retaliation Pap was assassinated as well.[45]

Meanwhile, the Roman emperor Julian and Shapur II were at war with each other. Julian died in 363, and his successor, the emperor Jovian, signed a treaty of peace, according to which he ceded western Armenia to Shapur II. The much-resented Treaty of Nisibis appeared to be finally nullified.[46] Having lost Rome's support and under constant attack by Shapur II, Arshak II (r. 350–368), Tiran's successor, ruled an Armenia mired in internal dissension and discontent. After negotiations and machinations, Arshak was taken to Persia and killed. Shapur II incorporated Armenia into the Sasanian empire and installed pro-Persian nakharars vassals. By then his military campaigns had caused the destruction of several major cities, including Ervandashat, Artashat, and Tigranakert.[47] As one historian has pointed out, "the Sasanians took the lion's share of Armenia, while the Romans had to be content with a small area mainly around Mount Ararat."[48]

The death of Shapur II in 379 created an opportunity for the resolution of the Roman-Sasanian conflicts through the partition of Armenia in 387 under the Treaty of Ekeghiats between the emperor Theodosius I (r. 379–395) and Shapur III. The boundary dividing Greater Armenia under this treaty ran from the east of Theodosiopolis (Karin; Erzerum) in the north, to the east of Martyropolis in the south, to the west of Nisibis in Mesopotamia, granting nearly 80 percent of Greater Armenia to Persia. Arshak III (r. 379–389) thus ruled as an Armenian "king" but also as a vassal for Byzantium and over a much smaller Armenia. Khosrov IV (r. 384–389, 417–418) ruled as a vassal for the Sasanians in Persian Armenia. After Arshak III's death in 389, Byzantium refused to appoint an Armenian king, effectively terminating the Arshakuni kingdom in Byzantine Armenia, although some members of the dynasty retained their nakharar houses.[49]

In Persian Armenia, the Arshakunis remained in power for several more years. During that time, under Vramshapuh (r. 389–417), in reaction to the partition of Armenia, they inaugurated another policy—the invention of the Armenian alphabet—which proved to be pivotal to the course of Armenian history and national identity. Both the crown (Vramshapuh) and the church (Catholicos Sahak) viewed the partition of Armenia as a formula for assimilation and as a loss of their respective juridical, political, and administrative sovereignty, with potentially fatal consequences for their institutional and financial survival.[50] The oral tradition, they believed, was insufficient for the demarcation of distinct national cultural identity. The church was particularly sensitive to this threat since paganism and Zoroastrianism had not been completely eradicated. Taking advantage of a relatively more tolerant political environment, they commissioned Mesrop Mashtots, a clergy, to develop an alphabet. The following years witnessed enormous efforts by learned religious leaders and scholars to translate Greek and Syriac Christian texts into Armenian and to strengthen the new national culture through Armenianization. The church gradually gained control over Armenian culture, literature, and education and, with the support of the state, instituted a Christian hegemonic, "totalizing discourse."[51] Armenian culture, identity, and history came to be viewed nearly exclusively through the prism of Christian theology.

Yet as with the adoption of Christianity, the development of the Armenian alphabet solved neither the problem of East-West rivalry nor domestic factional struggles. After Vramshapuh's death in 417, the Arshakuni dynasty in Persian Armenia survived for a decade longer, briefly under Khosrov IV, who returned to power from 417 to 418. He was succeeded by Shapuh (or Shapur, r. 418–422)—one of the sons of the Sasanian king Yazdgird I (r. 399–420)—followed by Vramshapuh's son Artashes (r. 422–428). In Ctesiphon, the Sasanian king Bahram V (r. 421–438), insecure in his role as monarch, viewed the growing Christian community within his domain as a direct threat to his rule and launched a massive campaign of persecution, which caused Christians to flee to the Byzantine empire. By then the position of the Armenian king vis-à-vis the nobles had considerably weakened as "pro-Persian" nakharars, for their own personal gain, pressed the Sasanian rulers to remove the Armenian king. In 428 the Sasanians did just that: They recalled the last Arshakuni king, Artashes, and ended the Armenian Arshakuni kingdom.[52] The *marzpanate* period followed (428–652), succeeded by two centuries of Arab domination (640–884).

ARMENIA UNDER SASANIAN MARZPANATE RULE

The Sasanians appointed their first *marzpan* (viceroy or governor), Vehmihrshapuh, to Armenia in 428, with both military and civilian (administrative, judicial, religious) authority.[53] The absence of an Armenian king at the center allowed the nakharars greater autonomy, although the Sasanian king and his representative viceroy held ultimate political power. In the early stages of marzpanate rule, the Sasanians were tolerant of local interests, but they remained intensely hostile toward the Armenian Church. It was not surprising, therefore, that a government determined to dominate a people would not tolerate the presence of a competing power, military, religious, or otherwise. As soon as he assumed power, the marzpan Vehmihrshapuh commenced a campaign to weaken the Armenian Church. He replaced Catholicos Sahak in 428 with the more pliable Syrian patriarchs, Brkisho (428–432) and Samuel (432–437), and imposed severe restrictions on the privileges enjoyed by the clergy, on the church finances, and on the uses of church estates. The primary cause of this ostensibly religion-driven policy originated in the Persian domestic political economy. The Sasanian monarchy had come under considerable pressure from the nobility in Persia to rely on outside sources for a larger share of state revenues. Keenly aware of the potential domestic political repercussions of financial problems, Bahram turned to Armenia for revenues, a policy that met stiff resistance among the Armenian secular and religious institutions. The geopolitical competition against the Byzantine empire only heightened the saliency of the Armeno-Persian conflict.

Armeno-Persian relations deteriorated rapidly with the accession of Yazdgird II (r. 439–457) and his famed Prime Minister Mihr-Narseh, who had served under Yazdgird I and Bahram. Yazdgird II intensified the campaign to destroy the Armenian Church. In 447 he dispatched Denshapuh as his plenipotentiary, ostensibly to supervise the population census. Soon, however, a series of edicts issued by Denshapuh made it obvious that he had been entrusted with powers far exceeding even those of the newly appointed marzpan Vasak Siuni. The first edict terminated the privilege of tax-free status the church had enjoyed since its establishment during the reign of Trdat the Great. Henceforth, clergy at all levels were required to pay the head tax. The second edict increased taxes across the board. Still another edict removed the authority of the catholicos as the head of the mets datavorutiun (supreme court) and granted it to the Persian *mogpet* (Zoroastrian religious leader).[54]

The Armenian Church and its supporters naturally viewed these policies as an all-out attack. The Sasanian leaders, whether staunchly Zoroastrian or not, had shown little tolerance for Christianity and attempted to impose their religion so as to establish their hegemonic rule in Armenia and to isolate it from Byzantine influences. The Armenian nakharars were again divided between pro-Roman/Byzantine and pro-Persian factions. Among the latter supporters, many had converted to Zoroastrianism in return for guarantees for lower taxes and other privileges.[55] Catholicos Hovsep I Hoghotsmetsi (437–452) and Sparapet Vardan

Mamikonian led the pro-Christian, pro-Byzantine, and vehemently anti-Sasanian nakharars against the marzpan, Vasak Siuni and his supporters. In 449–450 the anti-Sasanian nakharars readied their ranks for rebellion, with the expectation that the Byzantine military would come to their aid. To address the escalating crisis, an Armenian council at Artashat in 450 headed by Catholicos Hovsep I and the marzpan Vasak Siuni—despite their disagreements on a range of issues—formulated a statement to the Persian king declaring their loyalty to the Sasanian empire but also to Christianity. This declaration certainly represented a compromise between the pro-Persian and pro-Byzantine factions attending the conference. Not so easily satisfied, Yazdgird II ordered an Armenian delegation to Ctesiphon. Upon their arrival, he demanded immediate conversion to Zoroastrianism. Faced with certain death in case of refusal, the Armenian leaders decided to feign conversion. Immediately after their conversion was made public, some members of the entourage, especially the clergy, dispatched the urgent news to Armenia: Members of the Armenian delegation, among them Vardan Mamikonian, had accepted Zoroastrianism.[56]

Upon their return to Armenia, they were greeted with open rebellions organized by the church and pro-Byzantine nakharars. Vardan Mamikonian departed for Constantinople to seek military assistance rather than face further hostility at home. Vasak Siuni, fearful of losing control over the situation, proposed a secret plan to the catholicos to secure protection for ecclesiastical leaders and nakharars identified as anti-Sasanian. The church, according to Vasak Siuni's scheme, would mobilize further rebellions, and he, as the marzpan, would arrest the leaders ostensibly to put down the rebellions but in fact to place them in prison so as to ensure their and the nation's physical safety against the imminent retaliation by Yazdgird. Meanwhile, they would dispatch a petition to Constantinople for assistance.[57]

An Armenian delegation met with the Byzantine emperor Theodosius II, who listened attentively to the details of the crisis and promised to respond as soon as possible. While the Armenian delegation waited in suspense for his decision, Theodosius went on a hunting excursion on the banks of the Licos River, where his horse inexplicably kicked him, causing the emperor to fall into the river with a broken backbone. His death on July 28, 450, forced the Armenian delegation to wait for the coronation of his successor, Marcian, which took place on August 24. Unlike Theodosius, Marcian had extensive military experience, and wary of unnecessary military entanglements, he refused to commit his troops. To make matters worse, Marcian sent a secret message informing Yazdgird of his decision in the Armenian matter. By the time the Armenian delegation returned home, the unity forged among the nakharars and the clergy by Vasak Suini's secret plan had dissipated.[58]

Contrary to the conventional view the ensuing conflict, the Battle of Avarayr, was in fact a combination of a civil war and Sasanian military intervention rather than an exclusively Persian-Armenian war, as immortalized in Armenian memory. The pro-Persian nakharars criticized the pro-Byzantine groups for their naive reliance on Constantinople and opposed further seditious activities against Yazdgird. The pro-Byzantine nakharars insisted that the failure to act would render them infinitely more vulnerable to a Sasanian military campaign. The situation degenerated into chaos and mob action as anti-Sasanian groups, led by the virulently anti-Sasanian Vardan Mamikonian and the priest Ghevond Erets, sanctioned by the higher clergy, began to attack the Persian temples, in the process killing several of the temple officials. Vasak Siuni ordered cessation of all such anti-Sasanian activities and a speedy return to law and order. He and the pro-Persian nakharars insisted that rebellion against Persia at this point, when Yazdgird's army enjoyed peace at other fronts, would certainly invite the full brunt of his military retaliation, against which the Armenian military could defend neither itself nor Armenia. Not inclined to permit the pro-Christian, anti-Sasanian elite to monopolize policy through radicalization of politics, Vasak Siuni attacked the clergy and their supporters.[59]

The nakharar families themselves were divided between members who supported the rebellion and those who opposed it. Thus, for example, the head of the Khorkhoruni house allied with Vasak, but a minor Khorkhoruni prince sided with Vardan Mamikonian. In the Paluni house, the military general Varazshapuh allied with Vasak Siuni; Artak Paluni sided with Vardan. Vahan Amatuni supported Vasak, but Manen Amatuni, Vardan. Nor were the great houses of the Mamikonians and Siunis immune from such divisions. Babken and Bakur Siuni allied with Vardan, while Vahan Mamikonian, the sparapet of Lesser Armenia, sided with Vasak Siuni. Only members of the Bagratuni house did not exhibit such a division; all allied with Vasak Siuni.[60]

Critics of Vasak Siuni maintained that the marzpan, fearing for his own and family's safety, refused to support the rebellions and that his inability to manage the crisis led to the escalation of the conflict. Vasak Siuni was certainly concerned that a rebellion would leave him in the unenviable position of either mobilizing his forces to restore internal stability, and therefore to continue to serve Yadzgird, or else to accept failure, in which case the king would hold him directly accountable. Vasak Siuni chose the first option. As the reigning marzpan, his forces were far superior to those serving under Vardan, who, while officially still the commander, had become the subject of intense vilification. Without losing much time, Vasak resorted to dictatorial means to quell the opposition. He arrested several members of those nakharar houses that supported Catholicos

Hovsep and Vardan and took nearly all of their children hostage. He then moved to arrest the clergy, seized the military garrisons under Vardan's command, and forced the military personnel to leave the barracks. Vasak Siuni reported the situation to the Sasanian shah and warned that failure to intervene would lead to further instability, which in turn would disrupt commercial relations throughout the region and jeopardize the sources of revenues for the Sasanian royal treasury.[61]

By the closing days of the winter of 451, tensions between the parties had polarized Armenian society. As spring approached, the two camps prepared to commence their fratricidal military campaigns. In May Yazdgird II, informed of the impending conflict, ordered his troops to Her (Khoy) and Zarevand. News of the Persian advance hardened the divisions. The pro-Persian parties predictably sided with the Persian army, while the pro-Christian, pro-Byzantine parties moved to confront the enemy. In the middle of May, all forces converged at the town of Avarayr in Artaz province, and in early June, Persian and Armenian armies clashed. The troops under Vasak nearly decimated Vardan's army, estimated at about 9,000, although Eghishe, who is believed to be a contemporary Armenian priest and historian, gives the highly exaggerated figure of 66,000. As casualties mounted, soldiers on both sides fled the battlefield. The casualties included Sparapet Vardan Mamikonian, while several of the other military leaders were taken prisoner.[62] Although Iranian historiography on the Sasanian empire hardly mentions the Armenian-Sasanian conflicts, to this day the Battle of Avarayr represents a landmark in Armenian history, memorialized by Armenians worldwide as a moral victory in defending their faith.[63]

Armenian rebellions continued during the 460s to the 480s, spearheaded by Sparapet Vahan Mamikonian, a nephew of Vardan. In 481, an Armenian army unit seized Dvin and installed as governor Sahak Bagratuni, a brilliant military commander who, in contrast to members of the Bagratuni house in the 450s, had emerged as a leading figure in the anti-Sasanian rebellions. After the death of Yazdgird II in 484, the new Sasanian leader, Peroz, in an effort to avoid further bloodshed, appointed Vahan as the marzpan of Armenia in 485.[64]

The return to political and economic normalcy enabled (albeit briefly) the Armenian state and ecclesiastical leaders to rebuild the destroyed cities of Artashat and Vagharshapat and to address the consequences of decades of international and domestic conflicts. In 485, Catholicos Hovhannes I Mandakuni transferred the Mother See from Vagharshapat to the more secure environs of Dvin, that city regained its earlier religious and commercial significance.[65] Artashat again became a major center for international commerce. Encouraged by the peaceful relations with the new Sasanian leadership and Byzantium, Catholicos Babgen I Otmsetsi in 506 summoned the clergy to Dvin for a conference to examine various theological, social, and economic issues, including corruption within the church hierarchy and society at large. Members of elite families, some conferees complained, habitually used the local monasteries for private pleasures and festivities. Moreover, the church had yet to eradicate pagan traditions and customs, particularly polygamy and marriage within the family. In the meantime, the Sasanian king Kavat (r. 488–531), having subdued the domestic and foreign enemies on the eastern borders, redirected his military ambitions to Armenia, but upon his death in 531, his successor, Khosrov I Anushirvan (r. 531–579), signed a treaty of "perpetual peace" with the emperor Justinian I (r. 527–565).[66]

THE JUSTINIANIC REFORMS

Since the partition of 387 the civilian *Comes Armeniae* (Count of Armenia, the Roman equivalent of the Persian marzpans) had ruled Byzantine Armenia. Loosely administered by the Roman/Byzantine empire, Byzantine Armenia was divided into Armenia I in the north and Armenia II in the south, each administered by a governor (*praeses*) responsible to the imperial diocese (*vicarii praefectorum*) of Pontus, who in turn was responsible to the Praetorian Prefect of the East (*Praefectus praetorio Orientis*).Armenians retained some local autonomy as loyal subjects (they paid taxes and served in the military), and members of the nakharar families held offices in the Byzantine bureaucracies.[67] The next major threat to the Armenian social order, however, came not as a result of military engagements but under the guise of administrative and legal reforms.

The reforms initiated by the emperor Justinian in 527 introduced major changes into Byzantine-Armenian relations and Armenian society, changes that served to incorporate Armenia into the Byzantine empire. The first set of reforms involved the jurisdictional reorganization of the *dux* (provincial military commander) and *Comes Armeniae*, which were replaced by the more centralized military office of *magistri militum* (Masters of the Troops) in Armenia, headquartered at Theodosiopolis (Karin; Erzerum). This was followed by the *Novella XXXI* (March 18, 536), which created four separate administrative units as provinces. The Justinianic reforms were not limited to administrative and jurisdictional issues, however. A far more fundamental transformation occurred with the introduction of Roman inheritance laws into Armenian society. Under the traditional nakharar law, the land passed from father to son or to brother, and the line of succession excluded women. Feudal land ownership, as patronage, depended on military service, which excluded women and as a result prevented women from holding land.[68] Justinian viewed the eastern custom of *ozhit* (dowry) as payment for the purchase of the bride. In condemning the practice, he imposed the new inheritance law requiring that daughters be considered as equals to sons.

The Justinianic reforms in this area, though couched in humanitarian terms, were in fact intended to undermine the nakharar estates. Justinianic law enabled daughters to transfer their inheritance to foreign husbands, thereby leading to the fragmentation of Armenian clan ties and weakening the nakharar structure.[69] The renowned historian Nikoghayos Adonts comments:

> Like any native system, historically developed, and forming the bulwark against foreign aggressors, the *naxarar* [nakharar] system stood in the way of centralizing aims of the great imperialist. The demands of Justinian, like any other measures directed against the unity of the *naxarar* lands, would necessarily undercut the power of the princes which was based on their lands. In spite of his repeated affirmations, it is evident that a concern for the welfare of the country was the last motive which urged the Emperor toward reform . . . . What matters is not the fact that the reformer looks down on local culture; a contemptuous attitude toward the Orient and its culture was as characteristic of the ancient West as of the present one. We might think that the Armenian nation had, indeed, stagnated in some sort of disorderly and chaotic conditions and that Justinian had decided to lead it out of this confusion for the sake of the development and welfare of the Armenians. The true purpose of the bombastic style of the *Novellae* is to obscure the truth.[70]

Some nakharar families, including the Arshakuni house, at first rejected but were politically and economically too weak to resist the imposition of this law.[71]

As the traditional powers of the nakharar houses disintegrated, the unfolding international crises during the course of the next several decades only exacerbated the conditions in Byzantine and Persian Armenia. Preoccupied with inordinately expensive military operations in Mesopotamia and the Balkans, he soon withdrew. After falling ill, he consented to an armistice, which after his death was signed by Tiberius II Constantine with the Sasanian king Khosrov I in 578, reestablishing Sasanian rule over Persian Armenia. The overtures for peace notwithstanding, in 578 the Byzantine general Maurice (later emperor, 582–602) attacked the southern frontiers of Armenia and forced the deportation of nearly 10,000 Armenians to Cyprus. In 591 Armenia was again partitioned, when the Persian shah Khosrov II Parviz (r. 590–628), politically too weak at home, granted a considerable portion of Persian Armenia to Maurice, thus moving the Byzantine-Persian border farther east of the dividing line of 387. New rebellions against Byzantine rule divided the Armenian nakharars, as between Mushegh Mamikonian, who favored Byzantium, and Smbat Bagratuni, who led the opposition against its military presence on Armenian land.[72] In 637 the Sasanian empire collapsed when the capital, Ctesiphon, fell into the hands of the newly emerging Islamic empire.

THE ARAB INVASIONS AND OSTIKAN RULE

Arabs first invaded Armenia in 640, and by the late eighth century they had conquered most of the land. Arab domination in Armenia began first under the Umayyad caliphate centered at Damascus from about 650 to 750, followed by the Abbasids in Baghdad from 750 to 888. In 639 Theodore Rshtuni, appointed *ishkhan* (prince) and *curopalate* (governor) by the emperor Heraclius, had reunited Byzantine and Persian Armenias as both empires had been weakened after years of warfare.[73] The Arab armies of the governor of Syria and later Umayyad caliph Mu'awiyah (r. 661–680) captured Dvin in 640, and although Rshtuni successfully defended Vaspurakan, with no Byzantine or Persian military assistance forthcoming, he and the supporting nakharars were compelled to sign a peace agreement with him in 652 to prevent further destruction while preserving some degree of autonomy. According to the agreement, Armenia was exempted from taxes for the next three years, and thereafter it would pay according to its ability. In return for Mu'awiyah's concessions, Armenia was required to provide military forces to defend his dominion against Byzantium. This agreement, which appeared to have secured peace between Armenians and Arabs, yet again divided the Armenian leadership. Catholicos Nerses Tayetsi and some of the leading nakharars, including Mushegh Mamikonian, representing the pro-Byzantium faction, opposed the Rshtuni-Mu'awiyah accord and characterized it as "a covenant with death and an alliance with Hell."[74] In a sign of appreciation, Byzantium extended military support to Mushegh Mamikonian to defeat Rshtuni, now clearly seen as leading a pro-Caliphate faction.

The discord among the leadership was symptomatic of the power struggles between the most powerful noble houses: Bagratuni, Mamikonian, Gnuni, Kamsarakan, Artsruni, Amatuni, Siunik, and Rshtuni. Theodore Rshtuni, the ishkhan, failed to stabilize the situation, which was exacerbated by efforts of the Mamikonian house to reverse its own decline as a nakharar house of sparapets. Taking advantage of the succession crisis in the caliphate, the pro-Byzantine Mamikonians, Kamsarakans, and Gnunis cooperated with Byzantium to overthrow Rshtuni, who, after a brief withdrawal from power, returned with Mu'awiyah's military support and continued his rule until his death in 654. The Umayyads formally annexed Armenia in 701.[75]

The Umayyads reorganized Armenia as the province of al-Arminiya, comprised of a large part of Greater Armenia as well as Caucasian Albania and parts of Georgia, led by Muhammad ibn Marwan as the *ostikan* (the Muslim governor), headquartered at Dvin, the regional capital.[77] The caliphate stationed Arab forces in key cities, imposed Islamic law, and imprisoned opposing Armenian political and religious leaders, although under Islamic law the Armenian Church, as the leading spiritual institution, was generally treated with some leniency. As Arab rule grew repressive, pro-Byzantine nakharars began to organize rebellions against Marwan and requested Byzantium's support. Armenians rebelled before guarantees for military aid could be secured from Constantinople. The initial military successes in Vardanakert near the Arax River encouraged compatriots in other areas from Vanand to Vaspurakan to join in the rebellion. The Byzantine emperor Tiberius III (r. 698–705) agreed to appoint Smbat Bagratuni as curopalate of Tayk, despite the favorable disposition shown by Bagratuni nakharars toward the caliphate. The Umayyad response was swift; the Arab military invaded Tayk in 705, followed by another campaign in Nakhijevan, which culminated in the massacre of a large number of nakharars.[77] By then, however, the Umayyads were in decline, and their brutal reaction probably represented a desperate effort to save the empire.

The emergence of the Paulician movement as a heretic iconoclastic sect made matters worse for the Christian establishment in Armenia. This movement, believed to have its origins in Manicheanism founded by the Persian prophet Manes (ca. 216–276), underscored the north-south division of Armenia. The Arab occupation of Armenia provided the Paulicians with the political support they had never had. Encouraged by the presence of the Arab military, the Paulicians organized rebellions against the Armenian nobility and Byzantium. Together with Armenian Muslims and Armenian sun worshipers (*arevortik*) in cooperation with Arab sects, they became known as the *Shamsiyya al-Arman* in northern Syria. In 719 Catholicos Hovhannes III Odznetsi summoned an ecclesiastical council at Dvin to address the issue of heresy, and the council issued a condemnation of the Paulician movement. In 725–726 he called for another council at Manazkert concerning reconciliation between the Armenian and Syrian churches, one of the primary objectives being to address the growing popularity of the Paulicians. In the early ninth century, Paulician rebellions against the Armenian nobility and the Byzantine empire intensified. Having established the capital of their state at Tephrike, the Paulicians cooperated with the enemies of Byzantium, especially with the Arabs. In 872 the emperor Basil I attacked Tephrike and destroyed the Paulician army and state, forcing the Paulicians to escape southward to Syria and Egypt.[78]

The Abbasid revolution in Damascus in 750 ended the Umayyad caliphate and transferred the capital to Baghdad. The Abbasids distrusted the Armenian nakharars, particularly the two leading houses—the Bagratunis and the Mamikonians—for their pro-Umayyad and pro-Byzantine sentiments, respectively. Most of the Armenian public and leaders in turn held a deep hatred toward the Abbasids. The political situation rapidly degenerated into chaos, rebellion, and bloodshed. From 747 to 750 and again in 774–775, led by several nobles, particularly the pro-Byzantium Artavazd and Mushegh Mamikonian, Armenian rebellions in different regions attempted to overthrow Arab rule. Rebels expected Byzantium and the leading Bagratuni, Ashot, to support the movement, but the latter, considering the political and military situation hopelessly volatile, rejected the rebellions as too radical and counterproductive and withdrew his support. Grigor Mamikonian, ill disposed to allowing a Bagratuni to foil a movement led by his family, captured and blinded Ashot (hence his name, Ashot the Blind). The Armenian rebellion regained momentum as neutral nobles now sided with the anti-Abbasid forces. The turbulence and the bloodshed caused most Bagratuni leaders to espouse a conservative and circumspect political philosophy, in sharp contrast to the doctrinaire pro-Byzantium orientation of the Mamikonian and Kamsarakan houses. The Bagratunis henceforth adopted a realpolitik approach to domestic and foreign affairs.[79] The revolutionary movement collapsed when the Abbasids retaliated with brutal force; in the spring of 775, an army of 30,000 led by Amr ibn Ismail defeated the Armenians and killed most of the leading members of the nakharar houses, including Smbat Bagratuni, the son of Ashot the Blind, who had sided with the revolutionaries.

The increasing repression and financial difficulties (e.g., rising taxes, reduced circulation of silver) under the Abbasid caliph al-Mahdi (r. 775–785) considerably weakened the resolve of the survivors of the massacres of 775 and forced some nobles to emigrate to Byzantium. Among the principal nakharar houses, the Bagratunis, Artsrunis, and Siunis now cooperated with the caliphate and continued to rule their respective realms. The Bagratunis gained the confidence of the Abbasids and emerged as the leading nakharar family in Armenia.[80] Further, under Mahdi's second son, Harun al-Rashid (r. 786–809), the empire for the first time promoted the policy of Arab settlements throughout Armenia, which in turn led to fundamental demographic changes across the Armenian terrain. The Arab settlements became part of the East-West geopolitical competition, strategically encouraging the defense of the Arab frontiers against Byzantium until the Arab empire began to decline by the early ninth century.[81]

The demise of the Abbasids enabled the Bagratunis under Ashot Msaker (Meat Eater), the most prominent nakharar house, to reassert Armenian independent rule. In 806 Harun al-Rashid rewarded Ashot with the title of "Prince of Armenia" for his close relations with Baghdad. Immediately thereafter, Ashot carried out several military campaigns against

Zahap, a leader of the Kaysite (Kaysik) group, who had captured the region of Arsharunik and was poised to attack Taron. Equally troubling for Ashot Msaker was Zahap's compatriot Sevata, who had married Princess Arusyak Bagratuni for her wealth.[82] His good offices with the prominent noble houses and Baghdad enabled Ashot to institute effective administration of law and order. By the time he died in 826, he had strengthened the Bagratunis as one of the most respected nakharar houses in Armenia with enormous international prestige.

Upon Ashot's death Caliph al-Ma'mun (r. 813–833) elevated Ashot's eldest son, Bagarat Bagratuni, the leading Bagratuni in the region of Taron, to the post of "prince of princes" (patrik al-patarika), and appointed Bagarat's brother, Smbat, lord of Shirak, as the military commander. Like their father, Bagarat and Smbat maintained good offices with Baghdad, but political crises in the Abbasid capital, exacerbated by Arab, Persian, and Armenian attacks and counterattacks, led to an intensely hostile reaction by Caliph Zafar al-Mutawakkil (r. 847–861). He mobilized Muslims against Christians and, no longer considering Arab troops reliable, employed Turkish mercenary forces to reassert control over his domain. The Bagratunis, unable to check Armenian opposition to Mutawakkil, in a rare move joined with other nakharar families in organized rebellions. The joint Bagratuni and Artsruni military defeated the armies of Arab generals Ala Savafi and Musa ibn Zurara across the Lake Van basin from Vaspurakan to Taron, where also the much-feared Arab general Yusuf was killed.[83] Smbat Bagratuni opposed the rebellion in Taron. In 852, when one of Mutawakkil's ostikans, the Turkish general Bugha, invaded the region, Smbat cooperated and guided him through towns and to the forts of the nakharar families. Bagarat was captured and killed in the city of Samarra, followed by the capture of Smbat Bagratuni and a number of nakharars. Bagarat's sons, Ashot and Davit, and his brother Smbat Bagratuni were held captive in that city under Bugha and forced to apostatize. Smbat, who had collaborated with Bugha, died in prison in Samarra in 859/860. After some of the nobles were released in 858, they resumed their efforts, under the leadership of Ashot Bagratuni (Smbat's son), to free Armenia from Arab domination.[84]

Ashot subsequently established an alliance with Byzantium. Troubled by this development, the caliph al-Mu'tamid in 862 granted the title of "prince of princes" to Ashot and in 884 crowned him as King Ashot I. The Byzantine emperor Basil I (r. 867–886) countered by sending a crown to Ashot.[85] After four centuries since the collapse of the Arshakuni monarchy, the Armenian kingdom reemerged, and although Ashot I's reign was short-lived (he died in 890), the Bagratuni kingdom survived for the next two centuries.

Part II

Transformation and Transplantation

This page intentionally left blank

3

The Bagratuni Kingdom and Disintegration

The assassination of the caliph Zafar al-Mutawakkil in 861 and the ensuing internal turmoil in the Abbasid dynasty weakened Baghdad's influence in Armenia. The Byzantine Empire, capitalizing on the Abbasid decline, intensified its expansionist policy. The military victories and territorial conquests of Emperor Basil I against the Muslim East enhanced Armenia's relations with Constantinople. The absence of a direct threat from both empires set the stage for the establishment of a new Armenian kingdom by the Bagratuni dynasty. Ashot I was crowned King of Armenia (*Malik al-Arman*) in 885 with the blessings of Caliph al-Mu'tamid (r. 870–892), who, according to Hovhannes Draskhanakerttsi (catholicos from 897 to 925), sent "a royal crown . . . together with royal robes, gifts, honors, swift horses, weapons and ornaments."[1] Two years later, not prepared to lose influence in Bagratuni-Abbasid affairs, Emperor Basil I, founder of the Macedonian dynasty that ruled in Constantinople until 1057, also sent a crown to Ashot, indicating the significance Constantinople attached to the region.[2] Ashot I's rise to power inaugurated a new Armenian government under the Bagratuni dynasty, but the task of maintaining territorial and administrative unity across the land proved near impossible. Greater Armenia was divided into five major regions, four of which eventually emerged as minor kingdoms. The Bagratuni house, as the principal Armenian monarchy from 885 to 1064/5, maintained its supremacy over the northern and northwestern regions of the Lake Van basin. The Artsruni kingdom of Vaspurakan ruled across the eastern and southeastern lands of Lake Van (from 908 to 1019); the kingdom of Kars, farther north (from 961 to 1081); the kingdom of Lori, north of Lake Sevan (from 966 to 1100); and the kingdom of Siunik, southeast of Lake Sevan (from 966 to 1166). After nearly four centuries since the last independent Armenian monarchy collapsed in 428, the Bagratuni house, with great political skill and at times sheer luck amid turmoil and triumphs, revived the Armenian kingdom.

ASHOT I

Ashot I (r. 885–890) began his reign at a time when local conflicts among nakharars competing for power and wealth had destabilized the entire Armenian Plateau. With the support of the military, Ashot consolidated his rule over vast territories as he cajoled and coerced his followers and opponents to stabilize his dominion and assumed authority in managing the governmental apparatus and functions of administration, such as taxation, while the *ostikan*, or governor, of Arminiya served as overseer at Dvin.

Ashot's reign strengthened the monarchy through various networks of alliances but failed, largely because of its short duration, to create a united Armenian state with full sovereignty.[3] While the Bagratunis emerged as the principal nakharar house buttressed by the caliphate in Baghdad, the other nakharar families found it politically expedient— particularly since familial ties were involved—to cooperate with Ashot I when necessary. Three of Ashot's daughters had married into the leading nakharar houses: Sopi married the Artstruni prince Grigor-Derenik at Vaspurakan; Mariam married the Siunik lord Vasak Gabur; and another daughter married the Bagratuni prince Guaram at Kgharjk.[4]

Opposition to Bagratuni rule began to take shape in regions beyond Ashot's immediate control and coalesced around several issues that proved intractable. Of central import was the problem of political legitimacy, as the rise of the Bagratunis to the status of monarchy created a new configuration of power relations among the nakharar houses. Some of them, including the Siunik and Artsruni houses, despite their familial ties, only reluctantly accepted the legitimacy of the Bagratuni kingdom. They claimed that the Bagratunis had served as coronants during the Artashesian and Arshakuni eras and that while they rightly held these esteemed offices, they should not have arrogated to themselves the right to crown Bagratunis.[5] Having attained the status of royalty, the Bagratunis for their part expected the other nakharar houses to support them loyally, an expectation that clashed with Artsruni and Siunik political aspirations. Moreover, in order to strengthen their position, the Bagratuni leaders initially relied heavily on patronage and distributed privileges of vassalage in the form of estates (*gavars*) and honorary titles to members of their own dynasty, exacerbating the growing tensions among the nakharar houses.[6] Ashot I died in 890, and his death led to further deterioration in the Armenian polity.

The Bagratunis had little choice in determining the form of their government. Rather than inherit stable social and political structures with clearly delineated territorial boundaries and administrative jurisdiction, they confronted a political system embroiled in turmoil. Even after Ashot I consolidated power with the support of the church and some of the nobles, for strategic reasons he continued to rule from Bagaran, his power base, rather than transfer his court to Dvin, the administrative capital under the later Arshakunis.[7] Ashot could not immediately achieve a high degree of centralization of power and instead opted for a loosely organized union of princely states, a "feudal confederation," whereby the administration of affairs would be based on cooperation among functionally parallel offices in each region. The feudal lords of nakharar houses and officials thus retained their local autonomy and institutional prerogatives. Privileges derived from patronage, the traditional system of rewards and punishment, served as the cement for political order and unity. In cases when a nakharar leader violated the *uhkt* (oath of allegiance) and treaties of union—as in 903 when Prince Ashot of Siunik rejected the supremacy of the Bagratuni king Smbat I—the monarch retaliated by formally nullifying the prince's privileges of vassalage, including his rights to estates and honorary titles.[8]

SMBAT I

The reign of Smbat I (r. 890–914), Ashot I's son, proved to be a combination of successes and failures, as the new monarch struggled to balance domestic and external pressures. That his own uncle (Ashot's brother), Abas Bagratuni, the *sparapet* (commander of the army), schemed against Smbat's accession to the throne did not augur well. Smbat formally secured the Bagratuni throne in 890, when the caliphate sent a crown, delivered by none other than the *emir* (governor) of the caliph's vassal state in Azerbaijan, Muhammad Afshin of the Muslim Sajid dynasty. Following his father's pro-Byzantium policy, however, Smbat I preferred closer ties with the emperor Leo VI in hopes of securing total independence from the caliphate. The bilateral treaty signed by Smbat and Leo in 893 contributed to the economic growth of Armenia and further integrated the Bagratuni finances into the regional economy.[9] It was Smbat's misfortune that while the treaty signified amicable relations, it did not guarantee military support. Abas Bagratuni posed the first domestic challenge to Smbat's rule in part because he coveted the throne but also because he disagreed with his nephew's pro-Byzantine leanings. Before the conflict escalated into a seriously destabilizing affair, Catholicos Gevorg Garnetsi, as the supreme patriarch of the Armenian Church, intervened.

The principal foreign threat to Smbat's rule involved Muhammad Afshin, who sought to expand his domain under a unified Armeno-Azerbaijani military administrative system. Ostikan Muhammad Afshin had been appointed emir of Azerbaijan in 889/890, and although he had maintained good relations with the Bagratunis, shifting winds in Baghdad's foreign policy objectives, particularly in response to Smbat's commercial agreement of 893 with Byzantium, elicited an aggressive posturing toward the Armenian lands. As Muhammad Afshin prepared to invade Armenia, Smbat reacted with a two-pronged policy: He dispatched envoys to confer with Muhammad Afshin in hopes of preventing a conflict, while ordering a military force of an estimated 30,000 troops to halt an invasion. The governor of Azerbaijan called off the operation and met with Smbat to strengthen their old relations, although the Armenian king nevertheless continued to seek closer alliance with Leo VI.[10]

Smbat I cultivated peaceful relations with Muhammad Afshin so as to encourage Muslim merchants to travel through Armenia en route to Byzantium and to enrich Armenia's coffers. Trade between Byzantium and the Orient as facilitated by the "economic buffer" territories within Smbat I's domain contributed to the rapid local economic and urban development during this period. The enormous wealth accumulated by the ruling elite through international trade enabled them to build and adorn churches and palaces.[11]

Pockets of recurring crises, however, diverted energy and resources from the monarchy. In Vaspurakan, for example, local Artsruni lords Sargis-Ashot and Gagik Abumervan, nephews of Smbat I, contended for land and power. Smbat I favored Abumervan, causing Sargis-Ashot to solicit Muhammad Afshin's support against both. Negotiations led to the agreement that Muhammad Afshin would grant a crown to Sargis-Ashot, and the latter in turn would cooperate against Smbat. In the meantime, Ahmad Shaybani, the son of the Mesopotamian emir Issa ibn Shaikh, conquered the cities of Amid (Amida; Diarbekir) and Taron in 895. What followed after the battle for Taron must have amused Muhammad Afshin and military strategists in Baghdad and Constantinople. Shaybani gained control over Taron in part because of the support by the local opponents of Gagik Abumervan. King Smbat I, not willing so easily to lose the strategically important town in the southern flank of his domain, mobilized a force of 60,000 men to liberate Taron. Gagik Abumervan at first pretended to join Smbat's forces against Shaybani but suddenly defected and led his troops to the village of Tukh on the western shores of Lake Van, expecting to join forces with Shaybani. The latter, apparently informed of Abumervan's approaching army, had readied his troops and caught Abumervan by surprise. Shaybani's forces decimated the units under Abumervan, while those led by Smbat I deserted in large numbers. By the time the war ended, the Armenian military had lost 5,000 men, including Abumervan.[12]

Muhammad Afshin welcomed with a great sense of relief the news of the military disasters suffered by the Armenians at the hands of Shaybani. In preparation for another invasion of Armenia, Muhammad Afshin in 898 invited his erstwhile ally Sargis-Ashot to join in the campaign. Sargis-Ashot at first appeared ready for the task, but Smbat I interceded and convinced the lord of Vaspurakan to abandon the plan. The rewards for cooperation with Smbat seemed to outweigh the advantages sought in collusion with Muhammad Afshin at least for one obvious reason: Sargis-Ashot's principal competitor, Gagik Abumervan, was dead, and he, the leading Artsruni in Vaspurakan, could finally rule as the sole prince of Vaspurakan.[13]

When Muhammad Afshin launched the invasion from the north-northeast, Smbat I's army, recovering from the devastation sustained in the south, was hardly in a position to withstand another onslaught. Muhammad Afshin attacked Dvin, forcing Smbat I, the royal family, and the entire royal entourage to flee the capital in total chaos. After sacking Dvin, Muhammad Afshin's forces marched on Kars, where the Armenian queen had sought refuge with the royal treasury and several women from other nakharar families. The ensuing negotiations between Muhammad Afshin and Smbat I led to a peace treaty which required that the Armenian king, now relegated to a subordinate status, pay heavy taxes as well as send his son and heir apparent, Ashot, and his nephew Smbat as hostages to the court of the emir of Azerbaijan. He was also required to marry his niece to Muhammad Afshin. However, Muhammad Afshin died in 898 and did not enjoy the fruits of his victory.[14] Thus ended a period of turbulence and tribulations for the Bagratuni monarchy.

Nearly eight years of invasions and instability had diminished King Smbat I's less-than-enviable capabilities to defend his dominion. If Armenians welcomed Muhammad Afshin's death and expected stability in the region, they were soon to be disabused, for his brother, Yusuf ibn Abu Saj Devdad, the ostikan from 901 to 919 and 922 to 929, resumed his predecessor's aggressive policy. Yusuf planned to establish his own rule with greater autonomy and even total independence from Baghdad. When Caliph Ali al-Muktafi (r. 902–908) refused to entertain such notions of decentralization, Yusuf nevertheless pressed forward and invaded Smbat I's lands. Negotiations in 903 led to an unequal armistice, whereby in return for peace Yusuf demanded recognition of the supremacy of his rule and payment of tribute directly to him in addition to the taxes paid to Baghdad.

The Smbat-Yusuf armistice permitted several years of peace and stability, but its provisions weighed heavily on Armenian finances. Smbat I required that the nobles contribute to the tribute by surrendering one-fifth of their wealth. The nobles, finding the imposition quite unacceptable, responded by plotting to oust the king. The attempt failed largely because internal conflicts among the nakharar houses prevented a united front.[15]

Yusuf, himself gambling for regional supremacy, was hardly in a more magnanimous mood. Taking advantage of the weakened leadership in Baghdad under the new caliph Zafar al-Muktadir (r. 908–932), he began yet again to mobilize his forces against Armenia. In 908, Yusuf crowned Gagik Artsruni king of Vaspurakan and "King of All Armenians" (*Tagavor Amenayn Hayots*), and their combined armies invaded Bagratuni Armenia. Smbat sent Catholicos Hovhannes to negotiate a settlement with Yusuf, but to no avail. In fact, Yusuf held the catholicos hostage and in chains at Dvin. Smbat's urgent calls for assistance from the Byzantine military leaders in Constantinople and the caliph in Baghdad proved equally fruitless.[16]

The joint Yusuf-Artsruni military campaign against Smbat and across Armenia escalated in the summer of 909, as the Bagratuni monarch sought refuge from fort to fort. Members of other anti-Yusuf dynasties also fled their homes—for example, Prince Vasak of Gegharkunik in Siunik escaped with his brother Sahak and mother Mariam (the daughter of Ashot I).[17] Yusuf remained in control of Dvin during the winter and resumed the war in the spring of 910. In light of the sheer impotence of Smbat's military, Yusuf deemed it sufficient to rely on native forces under the command of King Gagik I Artsruni rather than engage his own troops. The war dragged on intermittently for the next three years. Smbat's military had disintegrated by early 914 as a result of death and desertion. He eventually surrendered and was beheaded on Yusuf's orders in Dvin. Smbat's death followed by persecutions, executions, forced conversions of Armenians to Islam, and overall destruction of agriculture and economy. The nakharars and the Armenian leaders in general reacted by efforts to reassert Armenian dominance and to reunify the country; accordingly, they supported Smbat I's son, Ashot II, as the new king.[18]

The question as to whether Gagik I Artsruni would support Armenian reunification or continue his alliance with Yusuf remained suspended in the balance. His support for Ashot II would be essential to bring forth a modicum of unity. In fact, while Smbat's military strength rapidly disintegrated beginning in 912, Gagik Artsruni, with sufficient self-confidence if not an exaggerated sense of self-importance, had contemplated shifting alliances against Yusuf, for, he had reasoned, the elimination of Smbat could provide him, as the King of All Armenians, the power and authority to rule all of Armenia from Vaspurakan independently of Yusuf. Gagik also expected, however, that Yusuf would turn against him immediately after removing Smbat.[19] Realistic assessment of the geopolitical situation in this case prevailed over personal ambition and self-glorification, and Gagik Artsruni threw his lot with Ashot II.

ASHOT II ERKAT

No sooner had Ashot II (r. 915–928/9) secured the throne than he launched successive military campaigns to consolidate power over his domain and commenced a new era of reconstruction in Greater Armenia, although like his predecessor his capabilities were severely tested by domestic and external threats. His first objective was to remove Yusuf and Arab military presence from his dominion, and with the support of his brother Abas and Gagik Artsruni of Vaspurakan, Ashot II liberated Bagratuni lands. He relied on piecemeal operations and guerrilla warfare tactics to launch surprise attacks on the Muslim armies stationed in urban centers and rural areas. Armenian commando units raided the forts and garrisons under Arab control, as in Bagrevand, Shirak, Gugark, and Tashirk. The battles quickly spread from the northern and southeastern regions, including Ani, Dvin, and Siunik, to the west and south in Vaspurakan and the Lake Van basin. His military successes earned him the title of *Erkat* (Iron) and so enhanced his prestige that most of the nakharar families—with the exception of his cousin, Ashot Shapuhian— forged alliances under his leadership.[20]

Such unity among the Armenian elite did not deter foreign invaders from Iberia at the southern slopes of the Caucasus Mountains in the north. In efforts to check potential vulnerabilities against Yusuf, Iberian forces invaded Armenia from the north and pushed as far south as the plains of Ararat, in the process destroying and plundering the land and people. According to the tenth-century Catholicos Hovhannes Draskhanakerttsi:

> They devastated many provinces and turned them into deserts, untrodden and barren, almost like a land through which men had never passed, and where the Son of Man had never dwelt. Thus, they turned the habitable places into wasteland . . . . Thus, through us the prophesy of Isaiah came to its fulfillment: 'Your country is desolate, your cities are burned by fire; strangers devour your land in your presence; it is made desolate, and over-thrown by foreign nations.'[21]

The destruction had a strategic purpose, as it sought to render a military march by Yusuf to Caucasian Iberia logistically unfeasible, if not absolutely impossible. The geopolitical situation was exacerbated when Ashot Shapuhian took advantage of the crisis to ally himself with Yusuf in exchange for coronation as king at Dvin.[22]

The successes registered by Ashot II and the international prestige gained in the process appeared to be unraveling when Byzantium, realizing the potential challenge Yusuf posed to its own security in the absence of an Armenian buffer, encouraged closer relations with Ashot II. Patriarch Nicholas Mysticos and Catholicos Hovhannes arranged a meeting in Constantinople for Ashot II to promote Byzantine-Armenian alliance and Christian unity against the Muslim invaders. Ashot II visited Constantinople in 914 and found the Byzantine military favorably disposed toward such a cooperation. He returned with Byzantine forces, but the latter soon withdrew before any direct engagement with the enemy.[23]

Ashot II began to restrengthen his position after two years (918–920) of wars with Ashot Shapuhian at Dvin and established his rule in Utik, Gardman, and all of western Siunik. In Siunik, he assisted Prince Vasak and his family to return home in Gegharkunik and subsequently launched a major military campaign to remove the Arabs and other Muslims from the region. Ashot II timed his Siunik campaign to take advantage of the political crisis experienced by Yusuf. The latter's political adventures and ambitions had eventually pitted him directly against the caliph al-Muktadir in Baghdad, whose forces, after a brief war in 918–919, arrested Yusuf and imprisoned him in Baghdad for four years. The removal of Yusuf as the archenemy certainly relieved the Armenian monarchy and its supporters. For Ashot Shabuhian, however, Yusuf's removal as a political force also meant the elimination of a protective shield against Ashot II. Unable to devise alternative means to maintain his position at Dvin, Ashot Shabuhian approached the Bagratuni king for reconciliation. Ashot II was the Bagratuni king but also represented the Armenian monarchy, he conceded. Ashot II appeared to have secured stability at home, and his position grew stronger when Sbuk, Yusuf's successor as ostikan, in part because of personal disposition but also as instructed by Baghdad, conferred the title of *shahanshah* (king of kings) upon him, further enhancing the legitimacy of the Bagratuni kingdom.[24]

SOCIAL STRUCTURE

The traditional Armenian social structure prevailed during the Bagratuni era. The monarchy represented the apex of power as a hereditary institution. The king was recognized as the *shahanshah* over his domain, encompassing both Christian and Muslim subjects, and his success or failure as a ruler rested mainly on his personal leadership qualities. Despite years of political upheaval, the social hierarchies, as inherited from the Arshakuni period, had survived. They consisted of the nakharar classes, the knights, the church, the military, urban workers, peasants, and slaves.[25] The royal court consisted of palace advisers and the royal ministries. The former comprised of the most loyal and prominent nobles and members of the Bagratuni dynasty who advised the king on matters of policy and administration. The royal ministries included the *sparapetutiun*, *hazarapetutiun*, *tagadir*, chief of the royal escort, administrator of the royal treasury and fortresses, and the high court.

The Bagratunis also revived the Armenian legal system and philosophy of jurisprudence as developed during the Arshakuni kingdom. The royal ministry of justice investigated and administered cases involving high crimes, offenses against the crown and royal offices, and cases between nakharars and the crown, while the lower courts under the governors of gavars and minor princes heard cases involving urban dwellers and peasants. Slaves had no access to the courts.[26] The Bagratuni judicial system consisted of civil and criminal law, which was governed by the same legal principles as under the previous Armenian kingdom. In civil cases, the principle of restitution applied, enabling the plaintiff to recover the material conditions enjoyed prior to the grievous act involved. In criminal cases, the royal ministry of justice or the lower offices under the nakharars and regional feudal lords heard and administered material and physical punishment, including revocation of privileges and honors, such as estates and titles granted by the monarchy, and corporal and capital punishment. In civil cases, the defendant assumed the burden of proof; in criminal cases, that obligation rested with the plaintiff.

Legal evidence consisted of confession, witness accounts, documents, and expert opinion. The legal philosophy of Mekhitar Gosh (1130-1213), author of the famed *Datastanagirk* (code of laws), reflected developments in Armenian jurisprudence during the Bagratuni and the Cilician eras. He maintained that representation should be limited to family members who would be most familiar with the parties involved. In theory, poor and rich had equal standing before the law, but in actual practice, the judicial system favored wealthier classes. Moreover, the legal system placed several restrictions, as for instance pertaining to witnesses: They had to be male, twenty-five years of age, of good standing in the community and knowledgeable about its affairs, and Christian in cases of involving Christians.[27]

Mekhitar Gosh also integrated in his legal philosophy issues related to family, marriage, property, and religion. The Bagratuni period, like its predecessors, restricted the rights of women in all aspects of public life, including legal matters. The Justinianic reforms had granted the right of inheritance to daughters but had not extended similar rights to other areas, as women were considered too emotional and too erratic in judgment. To Gosh, women inherently possessed no more than half the value of men. Most marriages were arranged by parents, and it was not uncommon for the bride and the groom to meet each other for the first time at the altar. The husband had to be older than his wife so as to control her effectively, yet if a man suffered from sexual impotence, his wife could decide to stay with him or else divorce him, in which case she could reclaim her *ozhit* (dowry). A wife, however, could not remarry without permission from her former husband, although no such restrictions were placed on him. Concerning domestic violence, Gosh maintained that the victimized woman could not leave her husband even if he caused severe bodily harm. She could, however, divorce him if he abandoned his Christian faith. The views expressed by Gosh reflected the concerns of the Armenian Church regarding marriages with foreigners, particularly Muslims, which had occurred with greater frequency since the Justinianic reforms and the Arab invasions. Such marriages, the church maintained, threatened the wealth and power of the nakharar houses and weakened the Armenian family both spiritually and materially, as it removed the individual and his or her inheritance from the Christian community.[28]

TRADE AND ECONOMY

Political stability at home and good relations with the major powers encouraged commercial relations, integrating the economy of Armenia with regional and wider international trade and financial networks. Trade relations expanded considerably with Byzantium, the caliphate, and the Far East, and economic growth led to rapid urbanization. Roads were constructed connecting principal commercial cities, such as Ani, Kars, and Dvin, with cities in Arab lands, Persia, the Caucasus, and on the shores of the Black Sea. The economies of smaller cities, such as Bagaran, Erevan, Koghb, Garni, and Talin, contained markets and shops for the distribution of agricultural goods both produced in nearby villages and imported.

During the Bargatuni era, about fifty cities existed. The population of large cities ranged from between 25,000 and 100,000, of medium size cities between 10,000 and 20,000, and of small towns from 3,000 to 9,000. In the largest cities—Ani, Kars, and Dvin—the population exceeded 100,000.[29] Medieval Armenian cities were similar to most cities in Muslim Asia at the time. Following the Persian tradition, they were made of three parts: *kuhenduz* (the citadel), *sharistan* (the city), and *rabad* (the suburbs). The ruling aristocracy lived in the *sharistan*, while the lower classes lived in the *rabad*. For example, the inner part of the city of Ani included the citadel and the palace, while most of the population lived outside of the walls of the city.[30] The ruling elite generally preferred to live in isolated and fortified communities and maintained minimum direct contact with their subjects. Feudal lords residing in the cities maintained military units for physical security and protection of property. They paid the soldiers for their services, which, in addition to imposing law and order, included supervision of laborers during construction, escorting tax collectors, and arresting and punishing the rebellious, disobedient, and delinquent.[31] The urban population also included the clergy. By the early eleventh century, the higher clergy, with the support of the monarchy, had gained enormous wealth and power. Catholicos Petros I Getadardz, who occupied the patri-archal throne from 1019 until the fall of Ani in 1058, is said to have owned and controlled as much land, serfs, farm animals, and money as most of the leading feudal lords, and he made sure the clergy served him loyally or else were defrocked.[32]

By the tenth century, agricultural economies no longer represented the sole bases for commerce and wealth, but growing urbanization also brought a host of social and economic problems. Towns and cities during this era witnessed the proliferation of artisans and laborers in metal and wood shops, carpenters, tailors, bakers, and producers of various manu-factured goods.[33] These production and market activities stimulated rapid economic development, which in turn led to the growth of the monopolies in the hands of elites, economic dislocations, and rampant corruption, as rich and poor sought through bribery and otherwise to take advantage of the opportunities offered by new and expanding markets. The wealth accumulated by the urban rich, landowners, and merchants during this period is believed to have stimulated early phases of capitalism in Armenia. The emergence of merchant classes with enormous capital accu-mulated in commerce posed a serious challenge to the old landowning feudal nakharar houses. The merchant classes, whose wealth was based on money rather than land, represented financial power independent of the feudal lords, whose wealth was based on land and therefore immov-able. Both sectors competed to shape the course of economy and policy.

The expansion of markets more closely integrated the urban and rural economies within each region, particularly as the ever-growing urban pop-ulation increased the demand for agricultural goods. Khans (commercial courtyards) or caravansaries (inns) in urban centers served as clearing-houses for goods delivered from rural areas and as places where local and traveling merchants exchanged goods, information, news, and gossip. Over time, however, the rural economies grew more dependent on and therefore more vulnerable to market fluctuations in the urban sector. The promise of jobs in the cities attracted more rural poor than the urban economies could sustain. Those who failed to secure jobs resorted to beggary, prostitution, thievery, and violence to survive. Employment entailed twelve or more hours of labor per day at the whim of the employer. Slaves of foreign origin (numbering in the thousands in the major cities) were required to work as laborers for seven years and to accept Christianity in order to gain their freedom. The refusal to convert would grant the owner authority to resell or keep the slave for free labor.[34]

Armenia exported a variety of manufactured goods and raw materials, including jewelry, metalwork, glassware, ceramics, and textiles from Dvin; silver from Sper; copper from Gugark; iron from Vaspurakan; horses and mules from Andzevatsik; the *tarekh* fish from Lake Van and the *surmahi* from the Kura and the Arax rivers; peaches, apricots, and pomegranates from the Arax and Vaspurakan valleys; wine from Dvin; and walnut wood and red dye (*kirmiz*) from the Araratian plains. Despite the rapid economic growth and development, the Bagratuni kingdom could not remedy certain institutional and structural deficiencies. The monarchy did not mint its own coins and failed to establish an integrated commerce across Greater Armenia. Nor was it able to institute protectionist policies to reduce the vulnerability of domestic markets and finances to fluctuations in international demand and political instability.[35]

Rapid economic development and urbanization beginning in the ninth century heightened the saliency of various social and economic issues and generated tensions among competing nakharar families, between the different sectors and social groupings, and between Armenians and their Muslim neighbors. These divisions created a polarized society between the urban mercantile classes and the rural economy dominated by "parafeudal Christian aristocracy surrounded by its traditional peasantry."[36] As the Paulician movement had attracted the lower classes between the sixth and ninth centuries, so did this polarization directly contribute to the strengthening of the Tondrakian movement. Named after the district of Tondrak near Lake Van, this religious sect opposed the rigid and elite-oriented feudal Armenian Church hierarchy and found support among the lower classes, leading to protests against both the church and the ruling elite.[37]

Despite the challenges posed at home, external relations appeared to favor the Bagratunis when Byzantium, concerned by the renewed relations between Ashot II and the Muslims, in 927 dispatched the Armenian general John Kurkuas (Hovhannes Gurgen) to instigate rebellion against the Armenian king and to capture Dvin. After a number of attempts Kurkuas failed to conquer the coveted city. Meanwhile, Yusuf, released from prison in Baghdad, returned to Azerbaijan, where, by sheer coincidence or conspiracy, Sbuk died immediately after Yusuf's arrival. The latter regained control over Azerbaijan and resumed his invasions, directed first mostly at Siunik and Vaspurakan and subsequently against Ashot II. The Bagratuni king and his supporters successfully, albeit briefly, defended his land, but palace intrigue and machinations by opposing nobles, some in cooperation with Byzantium and others with Yusuf, considerably weakened Ashot II.[38] Armenia was in a highly unstable state when, as fate would have it, in 929 both Ashot II and Yusuf died, and in the course of the following decade the caliphate in Baghdad declined.[39]

ASHOT III

It was under Ashot III (r. 952–977) that the Bagratuni dynasty became a dominant force in a more united Armenia, which at times included Dvin. Ashot III began his reign with the promulgation of administrative reforms, various social services (e.g., hospitals, sanatoria, and leprosariums), and major construction projects. In fact, his social programs earned him the title of *Voghormats* (Merciful), but his intentions encompassed broader considerations, most prominently the strengthening and centralization of authority under his rule. Accordingly, he reorganized and augmented the military and reinforced state patronage for the Armenian Church, thereby exerting a considerable influence in its affairs. More significantly, the nakharar houses regained certain key posts lost since the collapse the Arshakuni government, but, unlike the previous dynastic rule, four minor kingdoms in Greater Armenia contended for power and privilege. The title "lord of lords" referred to the heads of the principal nakharar houses in Vaspurakan, Siunik, Lori, and Kars, which were elevated to the status of kingdoms. As part of his overall reorganization in hopes of cultivating strong alliances with the regional elites, Ashot III in 961 granted the title of king of Kars to his brother Mushegh and in 966 the title of king of Tashir-Dzoraget (or Lori) to his youngest son Gurgen; he also elevated the principality of Siunik to the status of kingdom. Despite the division in territory and devolution of authority, Ashot III maintained a strong center at Ani.[40]

The emergence of the Artsruni kingdom of Vaspurakan in 908 had underscored the need for fundamental reforms in institutions and in relations between the Bagratuni monarchy and the Artsruni offices. In time, certainly by the 960s, the feudal confederal union established by Ashot I had evolved into a fairly integrated federation, which, on the one hand, formalized the stratification and distribution of power horizontally among the Bagratuni monarchy, the nakharar houses of the Artsrunis, and locally autonomous officials in each region, and on the other hand established closer relations vertically between the functionaries of the royal court and the local bureaucracies. The federal structure, cemented by *ukht* (oath of allegiance) and treaties, facilitated the integration of the emerging kingdoms of Kars and Lori in the 960s and Siunik in the 970s.[41] In addition, with the formation of the federation, the Bagratuni royal court appointed members of the other nakharar houses to leadership posts within the royal ministries so as to further integrate the political system. The Pahlavunis, for example, having replaced the Mamikonians as the more influential house, headed the sparapetutiun and kept the catholicosate within their family from 1065 until 1203 with only one exception.[42] The Royal Ministry of Justice, which under the Bagratunis had to take into account the other kingdoms of Vaspurakan, Siunik, Lori, and Kars, could not function effectively and independently of them in matters of law and order pertaining to society at large.[43] The structural reorganization implemented by Ashot III appeared to have achieved a certain degree of success in securing the loyalty of the nakharardoms in different regions. In 974, in response to threats from the Byzantine emperor John I Tzimisces (r. 969–976), the Bagratuni government called for the mobilization of forces, and the military of the kingdoms of Vaspurakan, Siunik, Lori, and Kars cooperated with the military command of Ashot III at Ani. By then, Ashot III had consolidated power as the king of Armenia and therefore with great magnanimity could show tolerance toward the lesser kingdoms.[44]

Among the numerous successes by Ashot III, no other feat has become as much a part of Armenian collective memory as the designation of Ani as the Bagratuni capital city.[45] Among the places most favored in Armenian historical memory, only Mount Ararat and the island of Aghtamar on Lake Van can with equal force give flight to Armenian nostalgia and imagination. In 961 Ashot III declared the city of Ani in Shirak province the new capital of Armenia for a number of reasons. Since their rise to power, the Bagratunis had not established an administrative, political, and economic center. As a result, different cities temporarily came to be associated with the monarchy. Bagaran had served as the capital during the reign of Ashot I; Shirakavan (Erazgavork), also on the western banks of the Akhurian River, served as the capital during the reigns of Smbat I and Ashot II, followed by Kars during the early years of Ashot III. The lack of a center as *the* Bagratuni capital signified the political disunity prevalent among the Bagratunis themselves but more important among the nakharar houses in general. Although the coronation of Ashot III had taken place at Kars in 953, he summoned the catholicos and the nobility to Ani in 961 not so much for a second coronation but rather for coronation as the "King of All Armenians."[46] The famed Matthew of Edessa, who lived in the early twelfth century, commented:

> On that day there was a formidable and large assembly in the city of Ani, which at this time was the capital of the Armenians. In this year [Ashot] . . . was anointed king as his ancestors had been anointed and occupied the throne of the former kings of the Armenian nation. There was great rejoicing throughout all Armenia, for the people witnessed the reestablishment of the royal throne of Armenia as it had existed among their

ancestors . . . . On this day he conducted a review of his troops comprising of one hundred thousand select men, [all of them] well-equipped, renowned in combat, and very valiant . . . . When all the surrounding peoples and all the kings of the nations, [i.e.,] the Abkhazes, Greeks, Babylonians, and Persians, heard this, they sent largess and expressions of friendship together with expensive gifts in recognition of the majesty of the Armenian kingdom.[47]

Amid festive ceremonies and military parades, Ashot launched at Ani one of the most prosperous periods of the Bagratuni kingdom. For material and intangible reasons, no other city possessed sufficient cultural clout or acquired as a cultivated image fitting for royalty as Ani. Dvin certainly could not serve such a purpose; it had remained under Muslim rule since the Arab conquests.[48]

Ani thus became one of the most important cities in Armenian history. The years following the coronation witnessed major construction projects, including palaces, military installations, churches, public paths, irrigation canals, and roads. The city, along with its suburbs, was a center of artisans of various crafts, commerce and finance, education and culture, while monasteries and churches dotted the landscape. Motivated largely by domestic political and economic considerations, Ashot III allied closely with the catholicosate, and the symbiotic relationship between the monarchy and the church enhanced the political legitimacy of the reigning king and the catholicos. Under the auspices of the Bagratuni monarchy and the catholicosate, churches were built in the region of Lake Sevan, Amberd, and Bjni; cathedrals in Kars, Argina, Ani, and Aghtamar; and monasteries in Tatev, Sanahin, Haghpat, Geghart, and Makaravank,[49] creating in Armenian culture the famous metaphoric, albeit exaggerated, claim of the "1001 churches of Ani." Contrary to the romanticized images, however, the city also had its poor population, most of whom resided in *storgetnya* (subterranean) Ani. Built in caverns by the river banks, *storgetnya* Ani consisted of rows of residential rooms, small churches, hotels, and cemeteries, all connected by underground roads and tunnels. By one estimate, such habitable caverns numbered more than 1,000 in the tenth century.[50]

In matters of foreign affairs, no other issue preoccupied Ashot III and the Armenian nakharar leadership as much as the resurgence of expansionist orientation in Byzantine. Constantinople viewed the decline of the caliphate as an invitation to invade the East. Led by generals Nicephorus Phocas and John Tzimisces, the Byzantine army scored military successes against the Arab forces and secured the eastern borders of the empire. Nicephorus Phocas became emperor in 963, but Tzimisces continued the military campaigns, conquered Cilicia after two years of war in 964 and 965, and succeeded Phocas as emperor in 969. While their forces expanded toward Arab lands, they also gained control over the region of Taron in

966, the region of Manazkert (Manzikert) four years later, and Melitene in 973. Only at Amid did the Byzantine army experience losses.

The decline of the caliphate and the Byzantine attention diverted to it enabled Ashot III further to strengthen the supremacy of the Bagratuni kingdom among the nakharar houses. By the time he died in 977, however, he had not solved several structural problems. The Bagratuni monarchy, its economic successes notwithstanding, failed to integrate the economies of the different regions across Greater Armenia into a single economy. Markets, finances, and wealth remained predominantly regional. Moreover, and related to the economic divisions, the Bagratuni kingdom could not assume automatic military support from the other nakharar houses, as recurring instability in intranational and international affairs magnified the fluidity of loyalties. An external threat against one nakharar house heightened the others' susceptibility to cooperation with foreign invaders, often sealed with incentives and bribery in various forms, such as military alliances and security and in special cases even grant of a crown and elevation to kingdom. These structural deficiencies and political concerns seemed insurmountable for the Bagratuni kingdom or for Armenia in general.

Smbat II (r. 977–989/90) succeeded his father, Ashot III, in Ani. The coronation took place on the same day the latter died in order to avert a succession crisis, particularly since Smbat feared that his uncle, the Bagratuni king Mushegh of Kars (r. 961–984), would intervene to block the ceremonies. Prior to his accession to the throne, Smbat II as the eldest son had since 950 served as co-ruler with King Ashot and had participated in the affairs of government. He had also cooperated with his younger brother Gurgen to promulgate a series of administrative reforms in the region of Tashir-Dzoraget (or Lori). During his early years on the throne, King Smbat was successful in cultivating mutual respect with the principal nakharar houses at Vaspurakan and Siunik, although tensions with the kingdom of Kars under Mushegh continued to pose a threat to his rule.[51]

Following the footsteps of his father, Smbat II oversaw large-scale construction projects that fueled rapid economic growth, which in turn enhanced Bagratuni military capabilities. Expanding commercial relations in the capital city of Ani pressed the city boundaries beyond those he inherited. The construction of the Mother Cathedral at Ani, along with other churches, began under his patronage and was completed during the reign of his brother and successor, Gagik I. Further, in order to strengthen the security of the capital, Smbat II oversaw the construction of additional fortresses and wider and higher city walls with double ramparts.[52] His accomplishments may be explained in part by his diplomatic dexterity in avoiding entanglements in regional and international conflicts, but at home he wished to leave no doubt that he was the king of Armenia and that sources of patronage emanated from him according to degrees of loyalty and goodwill.

While domestic politics clearly facilitated centralization of power under Smbat's rule, international struggles for power did not afford him the luxury of a peaceful reign. Byzantium was determined to establish its hegemony in the east, from Asia Minor to as far east as the Caucasus Mountains, and in the Middle East as far south as Egypt. In 966 Byzantium captured Taron, west of Lake Van, and in 1000, under the emperor Basil II (r. 976–1025), established its rule in Tayk, farther to the north. Constantinople's territorial aspirations directly clashed with those of both the Muslim Caliphate in the Middle East and the invading Seljuks from Central Asia.[53]

A crisis confronting Smbat II early in his reign involved the conflict between Basil II and Bardas Sclerus, one of the leaders of the opposition movement in the east based at Melitene, who had his own ambitions to become emperor. Sclerus was intensely hostile to Basil II and his military stationed in the Anti-Taurus. Smbat II at first attempted to remain neutral in their conflict, but the spreading hostilities so rapidly altered the geopolitical situation as to render moot any claims to neutrality. Subsequent events considerably undermined the power of both the Bagratuni and Artsruni houses. As the Byzantine military clashed with Sclerus in the western parts of Armenia, Muslim forces escalated their military campaigns toward Dvin and Ani. In retaliation for the seizure of a fortress in Shirak by Smbat II, his uncle, King Mushegh at Kars, urged the Persian Sallarid emir Abul Haijan (Ablhaj) of Dvin to attack Ani. The campaign surprised Smbat II and the Armenian military command, but as Abul Haijan's forces advanced to the Bagratuni capital in 982 and to nearby Horomos—the latter also famous for its church architecture—they were pushed back at Ayrarat by Abu Dulaf, the emir of Goghtn. Before the conflict escalated into a regional war, the *curopalate* (governor) David of Tayk (Tao) of the Iberian Bagratuni family intervened and reconciled Smbat II and Mushegh. The death in 990 of the Bagratuni monarch terminated the Ani-Kars reconciliation.[54]

David of Tayk had also supported Basil II during the first wave of rebellions by Bardas Sclerus between 976 and 979. The emperor had amply rewarded him, granting David the entire region extending from the western boundaries of the Bagratuni kingdom to the south and southwestern areas of Tayk, encompassing the *kleisura* (military district) of Khaldoharidz, the district of Theodosiopolis (Karin; Erzerum) and its fortress, and the provinces of Basean, Hark, and Apahunik, the latter including the city of Manazkert, at the time the center of the Kurdish Marwanid emirs, who had captured it from the Kaysites. David forced the withdrawal of the Marwanids from the region in 992–993 and, with the support of the Bagratuni kings at Ani, Kars, and Iberia, brought Armenians and Iberians to replace the Muslims.[55] David miscalculated Basil's reaction, however, when in 989/90 he supported the revolution against the emperor. Having quelled the movement, Basil II demanded that David sign an agreement providing for the return to Byzantium, upon the curopalate's death, all of the lands awarded to him in the aftermath of the earlier revolution in 976 to 979.

David died in 1000/01 under suspicious circumstances. Contemporary author Asoghik states that David died of old age on Easter day in the year 1000. The eleventh-century Armenian historian Aristakes Lastiverttsi and the twelfth-century chronicler Matteos Urhayetsi (Matthew of Edessa), however, maintain that certain members of the Georgian nobility who had been promised rewards by Basil II poisoned David during Holy Communion. Urhayetsi adds that David realized that he had been poisoned and took antidotes immediately after returning to his palace. Bishop Ilarios, with similar expectations for rewards either from Basil II or from the Georgian leaders, followed David to the palace soon thereafter. Finding him asleep, he placed a pillow over his mouth and suffocated him. The Byzantine emperor annexed David's territories in accordance with the arrangement of 990.[56]

KING GAGIK I AT ANI

Gagik I (r. 990–1017/20) enjoyed enormous power and prestige because of his personal capabilities but also because he inherited a prosperous economy and powerful military from his able predecessors. Gagik, ever masterful in the utilization of personalities and bureaucracies, cultivated close familial ties with the nakharar houses. He took for wife Princess Katramidé, daughter of King Vasak of Siunik. His daughter, Khushush, married King Senekerim (Senekerim-Hovhannes) Artsruni of Vaspurakan. Tigran Andzevatsi of the Artsruni house in Vaspurakan permitted his daughter Sofi to marry Vahram Pahlavuni, the nakharar house that led the sparapetutiun under the Bagratunis.[57] During Gagik's reign, no significant opposition appeared to his rule. The principal competitors against the Bagratunis, the Artsrunis of Vaspurakan, could not compete for hegemony over Armenia as they came under sustained attack by the Daylamites and Turkomans and accepted Byzantine protectorate. The kingdom of Siunik, weakened by invasions from the East, granted its lands to Gagik as protectorate. King Abas of Kars, Gagik's cousin, showed little interest in the struggle for power. Two other leaders, the king's nephew Abusahl of Kogovit and King Davit Anhoghin (the Landless) of Tashir-Dzoraget (Lori), who sought to establish their own independent kingdoms, posed the greatest challenge to Gagik but were eventually forced into submission. It was unfortunate for the Bagratuni kingdom that Gagik's death created a power vacuum and led to hostilities between his sons, Hovhannes-Smbat and Ashot.[58]

Both sons had been active in the affairs of state in various capacities, and immediately after their father died they became mired in a malicious struggle for power. The responsibility for the unfolding crisis rested to a large extent, if not solely, on Gagik's shoulders, for he had bequeathed the crown to both sons on equitable terms, in theory establishing a diarchical royalty, whereby each son would hold equal power and territory—an arrangement that in fact proved impracticable. The acrimonious affair eventually ended after the intensive mediation by Catholicos Petros I Getadardz and influential members of the nobility. Gagik's eldest son, Hovhannes-Smbat (r. 1017/20–1041), inherited the key territories including the capital Ani, Shirak, the plain of Ayrarat, and Aragatsotn, while the inheritance of his brother Ashot, now King Ashot IV (r. 1017/20–1041) with his capital at Talin, remained confined to peripheral lands but with the proviso that he succeed his brother and acquire the inheritance in its entirety after Hovhannes-Smbat's death.[59]

Unfortunately for Hovhannes-Smbat, Basil II turned his attention to Armenia and Georgia upon his conquest of Bulgaria in 1019. The following year Basil traveled to Theodosiopolis to survey his potential territorial acquisitions and demanded that the Bagratuni king grant him the key cities of Ani and Kars. Basil also launched a military campaign against Georgia, drawing Hovhannes-Smbat into the conflict on the side of the latter. Basil II defeated both forces and was posed to attack across the regions of Her and Shirak when, in the winter of 1021–1022, the Armenian king dispatched a delegation headed by Catholicos Petros I Getadardz to Trebizond to negotiate peace. Basil demanded that Hovhannes-Smbat in his will grant his entire domain to Byzantium. The Armenian delegation, under extreme pressure with instructions from Ani not to give occasion for disagreements, consented and agreed to bequeath Hovhannes-Smbat's crown and royal domain to the Byzantine emperor. Contemporary Armenians labeled the Trebizond Will as *gir korstutyan* (the "writ of loss").[60] This act gave rise to wide opposition to Hovhannes-Smbat, severely criticizing him for imposing such an accord upon the kingdom. Ashot IV and Catholicos Petros, who had served as his envoy in Trebizond, led the opposition, and the Bagratuni king reacted to the threat by resorting to force and arrests. Fearing for his life, Catholicos Petros fled to Vaspurakan in 1037, but a few years later he returned to the capital with the king's personal guarantees for his safety. Nevertheless, the authorities arrested the catholicos as he was entering Ani.[61]

No one was as perturbed by the Trebizond Will as Hovhannes-Smbat's brother Ashot IV. Despite their agreement, Ashot had refused to relinquish his aspirations to capture the throne of Ani and on occasion even resorted to military invasion and instigation of armed rebellion against his brother. The onerous ramifications of the Trebizond agreement for the Bagratuni kingdom were obvious. For Ashot, however, the gravity of the matter was intensely personal as the accord negated the succession agreement he had sealed with his brother in a rare mood of reconciliation. Ashot, adamantly insisting on his right to succession, traveled to Constantinople to petition for a reconsideration of the Trebizond Will and to Baghdad to secure military and diplomatic support from the caliphate. No evidence suggests that he succeeded in directing the interest of the caliphate to the matter; in Constantinople, the imperial government agreed to extend military support but only against the Muslim emirs who repeatedly invaded and seized Ashot's ever-shrinking territory. The political implications of such support against the emirs did not escape him; the Byzantine emperor sought to exploit the situation to contain the Muslim armies now advancing into the territories of Hovhannes-Smbat, the same lands promised to Basil II under the Trebizond Will. The emperor had in fact relegated Ashot IV to a mere holder of a buffer state, while continuing to recognize Hovhannes-Smbat as the king of Ani. Having exhausted all other means to win his father's throne, Ashot IV resorted to trickery. He dispatched news to Ani reporting his purportedly failing health and invited Hovhannes-Smbat to Talin to make fraternal amends. When his brother arrived, Ashot arrested him and ordered a vassal, Apirat Pahlavuni, to execute him. The latter refused and instead freed Hovhannes-Smbat. Soon thereafter, whether because of fate or foul play, both Hovhannes-Smbat and Ashot IV died in 1041. The former had no sons, and therefore the kingdom was left to Ashot's sixteen-year-old son Gagik. Ironically, Ashot was buried in Ani, the city he so intensely coveted but never ruled.[62]

Upon ascending to the throne at Ani, Gagik II (r. 1041/2–1045) found the Armenian leadership deeply divided on matters of foreign policy. In hopes of reconciliation, he released Catholicos Petros from prison. The Byzantine emperors Michael IV the Paphlagonian (r. 1034–1041) and Michael V the Calaphates (r. 1041–1042) demanded the Armenian territories, as stipulated by the Trebizond Will, but the pro-Gagik faction, led by Sparapet Vahram Pahlavuni, refused to acknowledge such an obligation. The anti-Gagik faction, headed by the regent *vestis* (steward) Sargis Haykazn of Siunik and with a strong western orientation favorable to Byzantium and personal aspirations to control Armenia, expressed concern that failure to comply with the terms of the Trebizond Will could lead to warfare.[63] In 1044 Gagik II was invited to Constantinople by Emperor

Constantine IX Monomachus (r. 1042–1055) for negotiations and placed under "honorable confinement"—that is, house arrest. Gagik at first refused to negotiate and insisted on upholding his sovereignty as the king of Armenia, saying: "I am lord (tēr) [ter] and king (t'agawor) [tagavor] of the realm of Armenia, and behold, I do not give my kingdom into your hands, because you fraudulently brought me to Constantinople."[64] As luck would have it, in 1044 large groups of foreigners, including Armenians, whose migration to the Byzantine capital dated at least as far back as 626, rioted against Constantine. He in turn expelled them from the capital. In no position to defy the emperor, Gagik finally consented to surrender his realm and in exchange received territory in Cappadocia.[65]

Catholicos Petros I Getadardz surrendered the city of Ani and the treasures of the Armenian Church to the Byzantine army in 1045. The catholicos and his nephew and successor Khachik II (1045–1060) were exiled to Constantinople. Byzantine governors ruled the city of Ani until its conquest by the Seljuk Sultan Alp Arslan. Seljuk invasions into Armenia had begun in the 1020s, and after they destroyed the Ghaznavid kingdom in Iran in 1040, they turned their attention to Ani, which they captured on August 16, 1064.[66]

Gagik moved the entire Bagratuni dynasty from Ani to Cappadocia where he found himself surrounded by Byzantine feudal lords and government officials hostile to Armenians in general and to members of Armenian royal families in particular. He did not completely sever his ties with Ani, however. His son Hovhannes married with the daughter of the newly appointed Greek governor at Ani but left the capital for Constantinople probably to plead for Gagik's return to the throne. Meanwhile the Seljuk Sultan Alp Aslan captured the city and removed the Byzantine officials from power. Gagik petitioned Alp Aslan for permission to return to Ani, a request which he was prepared to grant only if the Bagratuni king would accept the absolute sovereignty of his sultanate. Gagik refused but sent his grandson Ashot for further negotiations, but when Ashot arrived at Ani, he found the city in the hands of the Shaddadid emir Manuché who had either seized or purchased the city from Alp Aslan. Rather than negotiate with Ashot, the Shaddadid leader poisoned him, thus ending attempts by the Bagratunis to return to the throne of Ani. Gagik II, too, was murdered (probably poisoned) in a Byzantine prison or under house arrest in Cilicia in 1079.[67]

THE FALL OF KINGDOMS

The emigration of the Artsruni dynasty from Vaspurakan to Byzantium had begun as early as the 980s, decades prior to the Seljuk invasions. In

1016, when Turkish forces defeated the Artsruni army, Prince Davit, son of King Senekerim Artsruni of Vaspurakan, traveled to Constantinople to seek support in exchange for the lands he inherited. Emperor Basil II, intent on populating the buffer region of Cappadocia/Sebasteia (Sebastia, Sivas) with Christians already hostile to Muslim rule, signed an agreement with Davit in 1019, which provided that the latter would serve as the *strategos* (governor) of the Cappadocian theme. More than 14,000 people left their homes and sought refuge in Sebasteia,[68] including the nobility, government officials, and military leaders. In the meantime, Basil II transferred a large contingent of troops from the Bulgarian theater to Vaspurakan (Asprakania or Basprakania, under Byzantine rule) ostensibly to support the Artsruni kingdom, but instead in successive campaigns they attacked the regions of Taron, Manazkert in north of Lake Van, and Vaspurakan, a situation further exacerbated by subsequent Turkish-Seljuk invasions.[69]

After the fall of the kingdom of Ani, the Bagratuni branch at Kars, first established in 961 under Mushegh, the brother of Ashot III, assumed the leadership among the Bagratunis. Mushegh's successors had failed to strengthen the kingdom at Kars and repeatedly clashed with their kinsmen at Ani, Lori, and Siunik. The Seljuks invaded Kars in 1053/54 during the reign of Gagik-Abas II, but withdrew from the city under attack by the Byzantine army, which captured Kars in 1064. Seljuks resumed their attack on Kars after they seized Ani; they retook Kars in 1065. King Gagik-Abas II petitioned Byzantine Emperor Constantine X Ducas (r. 1059–1067) for support, and the emperor agreed to the transfer of the Bagratuni dynasty in Kars to Byzantine lands in Cilicia. The Bagratuni kingdom of Kars ended with the death of Gagik-Abas II in 1081.[70]

Likewise, the Bagratuni kingdom at Lori (or Tashir-Dzoraget) failed to maintain a strong military presence to fend off Byzantine and Seljuk invasions. King Gurgen, the younger brother of Ashot III and after whose name the kingdom was called Kyurikyan in local dialect, had survived the military campaigns of Emperor John I Tzimisces in the early 970s, but his son and successor Davit Anhoghin (r. 996–1048) remained in constant conflict with the neighboring Arabs and Irano-Kurds. Too arrogant because of his early military successes, in 1001 Davit rebelled against King Gagik I of Ani, who in response invaded Lori and seized large tracts of land from him—hence the "Landless" name attached to Davit.[71] Despite the tensions between the leaders at Ani and Lori, however, when in 1040 the Shaddadid emir Abuswar (Abu al-Aswar) of Dvin attacked Lori and it became quite obvious that Davit could not withstand the onslaught, King Hovhannes-Smbat of Ani, along with the kings of Siunik and Iberia, mobilized a force of 20,000 troops to defend Lori. Davit appreciated their assistance but was not willing to abandon his aspirations to win the throne of Ani. Immediately after the cessation of the conflict in Lori, he intervened in the succession struggle in Ani occasioned by the Trebizond Will. The ruling nakharar families in the Bagratuni capital made it clear to Davit that he should not interpret the succession crisis as an invitation to usurpation or invasion, but he nevertheless led two military campaigns into the region of Shirak, causing much death and destruction. His reign ended in 1048 in total disgrace, leaving behind in Lori a considerably weakened leadership. When Kyuriké I (r. 1048–1089) succeeded his father, the Seljuk invasions into Armenia had intensified. In 1064 Sultan Alp Aslan led his army into the land of Lori and, after much bloodshed and pillage, demanded Kyuriké's daughter for wife. The king of Lori refused at first, but further negotiations and mediation by the Abkhazian king Bagrat IV convinced him that the failure to grant his daughter's hand to Sultan Alp Aslan would aggravate the already grave situation. By then the Bagratuni kingdoms at Ani and Kars had collapsed, leaving the kingdom of Lori as the only Armenian stronghold.[72]

Kyuriké found support among the Byzantine leaders who, albeit briefly, adopted a favorable policy toward Lori to forestall further Seljuk invasions. Cooperation from Byzantium enabled Kyuriké to assume the symbolic leadership of the Armenian kingdom, although Constantinople recognized him as curopalate or governor rather than as a sovereign monarch. Nevertheless, Byzantium also permitted the catholicosal ordination of Bishop Barsegh of Shirak (Barsegh I Anetsi) in Ani and also granted Kyuriké the authority to mint his own silver and copper coins.[73] No sooner had he enjoyed some respite from internal and external difficulties than the Seljuk military victory against the Byzantine army at Manzikert in September 1071 altered the power configuration in the region, forcing the withdrawal of the Byzantine military. The kingdom of Lori collapsed in about 1100, and the kingdom Siunik, in 1166.

The last major Armenian kingdom in historic Armenia ended, as Byzantine and Seljuk invasions escalated. Aristakes Lastiverttsi, the eleventh-century cleric historian, commented on the Seljuk seizure of Mount Smbatay Berd (Smbat's Fortress) during the collapse of the Bagratuni kingdom:

Such is your wicked history, o mountain! Mountain whereon God was not pleased to dwell, mountain of blood, of invasion, and loss. It is impossible to call you a mountain. Rather, you were a mud pit in which the entire population of the country was lost . . . . Oh mountain! You were not fertilized by the dew of Heaven like [mount] Hermon, but with the fat and blood of the corpses which fell upon you. Oh mountain! You were not, like mount Sinai, a medium through which Moses spoke with God; no, you silenced many priests singing the psalms, [priests] who by their prayers were always conversing with God.[74]

This page intentionally left blank

4

The Cilician Kingdom, the Crusades, and the Invasions from the East

Cilicia (Kilikia or Giligia in Armenian), located on the northeastern corner of the Mediterranean Sea, first appeared in the Egyptian annals of the thirteenth century B.C. as Kedi (or Kode), and in the records of the Assyrian empire in the eighth century B.C. Waves of migration and invasions from the ages of the Hittites and Homer led to the emergence of communities inhabited by Aegean peoples mixed with local tribes such as the Cetae (Cietae), the Cannatae, and the Lalasseis. The name Cilicia refers to two regions with different physical attributes. Cilicia Pedias (Dashtayin Kilikia), as labeled by the Greeks, refers to the plains rich in agriculture, producing cereals, vines, and flax that stimulated the linen industry in the region. Cilicia Tracheia (Lernayin Kilikia) refers to the mountainous (also called "rough") region of Cilicia that, isolated from main commercial routes, lacked major towns and economic centers, except for ports and timber depots.[1]

The geostrategic position of Armenian Cilicia proved as significant as that of Greater Armenia in the East-West conflicts and competition for regional supremacy. The routes of Alexander the Great's military expansion toward the Middle East had passed through Cilicia and served equally well for Seleucid expansionist objectives. Partly because of the mountainous terrain, invading armies often devolved authority to local officials in Cilicia Tracheia, a practice frequently used by the Roman and Byzantine governments.[2] In the second half of the seventh century, the

Arab conquests expanded to the eastern part of Cilicia. Their control lasted well into the tenth century, followed by Byzantine domination. Armenians, including the nakharar houses, migrated to Cilicia in large numbers from Vaspurakan, Ani, and Kars as a result of recurring Arab-Seljuk-Byzantine invasions and counterattacks, fueled further by the defeat of the Byzantine military at the Battle of Manzikert (Manazkert) in 1071. Many Armenians escaped the destruction wrought upon them by Alp Arslan and sought a safe haven in Cilicia.[3] In 1065, for example, King Gagik of Kars surrendered his kingdom to Byzantium in return for safety in the Taurus Mountains.[4] Emperor Constantine Monomachus (r. 1042–55) resettled Armenians in the region of Cappadocia and encouraged them to settle in Cilicia as well.[5] By 1198 when Levon I was crowned as the first king of Armenian Cilicia, the international environment riven by intense conflicts between the Byzantine empire, the Seljuk sultanate of Rum, the Arab states, and the Crusaders restricted the foreign policy options available to the Armenian kingdom in Cilicia.[6]

As part of its grand geostrategic objectives, Byzantium sought to strengthen the Armenian leadership in Cilicia as a buffer between Constantinople and the Muslims.[7] This strategy assumed that Armenian society would be sufficiently monolithic and strong to serve such a purpose and would be amenable to Byzantine interests. As in Greater Armenia, however, the Armenian leadership was deeply divided between factions favoring either an eastern or western orientation; unlike in previous centuries, however, those insisting on closer ties with the West clearly dominated Cilician politics. Nevertheless, factional divisions gave rise to enormous political difficulties. As a result, throughout its three centuries of existence, the Cilician kingdom remained highly unstable internally and highly vulnerable to foreign forces.

Some Armenian lords entered into service for the Byzantine empire, as did the Haykazun and Natalinian princes, who assumed the responsibility of guarding Cilician lands bordering with the Arabs. Soon, however, unwilling to tolerate Byzantine domination, some of the leading Armenian nakharar families began to establish their own dominion based primarily on Armenian forces. Most notable among them was Pilartos Varazhnuni (Philaretus Brachamius) of Vaspurakan, who had served as a general in the Byzantine military under Emperor Romanos IV Diogenes (r. 1068–1071) during the Battle of Manzikert in 1071. Immediately after the Byzantine defeat, Pilartos Varazhnuni, in cooperation with Arab forces, established his short-lived warlord state (1078–1085) stretching from Malatya to Antioch and Edessa and centered on Marash. In the meantime, he either converted to Islam or pretended to have done so; but he clearly advocated pro-eastern, pro-Muslim, and anti-Crusader policies. The Armenian Church, which adamantly supported Byzantium and the Crusaders against the Muslims, condemned him. After Varazhnuni's death, a number of chieftancies emerged: Khoril at

Melitene, Toros at Edessa, Tatul at Marash, and Kogh Vasil at Kaysun.[8] Byzantium tolerated Pilartos Varazhnuni's and his successors' territorial ambitions as long as they could help contain Seljuk expansion. By the second half of the 1080s, however, although Seljuk military capability proved too overwhelming for the Armenians, two Armenian dynasties, the Rubenians (named after their first leader Ruben) based at Vahka in the north and the Hetumians (named after Hetum) based at Lampron in the west, had established a political base for expansion and to experiment with kingdom-building in Cilicia.[9] Equally important, Varazhnuni had inspired some Armenians who opposed the Armenian Church and were critical of the pro-Byzantine elite to cooperate more closely with the Arabs. Indeed, Armenian-Arab relations assumed particular significance approximately around this time when Muslim Armenians emerged as leaders in Fatimid Egypt. It was ironic that after the collapse of the Bagratuni kingdom in Greater Armenia in the 1040s and prior to the emergence of the Armenian kingdom in Cilicia in 1198, a Muslim Armenian dynasty would assume the reigns of government in Egypt.

THE FATIMID DYNASTY

Egypt was a peripheral province under the Umayyad and the Abbasid caliphates. Beginning in the middle of the ninth century, as the Abbasid caliphate showed signs of decline, slave soldiers assigned to Egypt by the Abbasids created their local dynasties that aspired to establish an independent empire of their own. The Tulunid dynasty of the famed governor Ahmad ibn Tulun led Egypt from 868 to 905, followed by the Ikhshidids from 935 to 969. In 969 the Fatimids, who traced their origins to Fatima, a daughter of the Prophet Muhammad, and belonged to the Shi'ite Isma'ili movement based in Tunisia, consolidated power in Egypt under a new caliphate, which lasted until 1171.[10] Like the Abbasid dynasty in Baghdad, it claimed to represent the true caliphate, with similar aspirations for expansion that clashed with Byzantine geopolitical objectives across the eastern shores of the Mediterranean. Nevertheless, despite the hostilities between Byzantium and its Muslim neighbors, Fatimid-Byzantine relations remained on friendly terms until the Fatimids sought to establish control over Syria and barred Byzantine merchants from markets in Egypt. In 975 the Emperor John I Tzimisces attacked Hamdanid Syria to remove the Fatimid army from the area. The Arab Hamdanid dynasty, named after Hamdan ibn Hamdun who posed a serious threat to the Abbasids in Baghdad until his family's cooptation by the caliph al-Mu'tadil into military service, beginning in 903 expanded its rule from Mosul to Aleppo, before it declined in 1004 largely as a result of the hostilities among the competing regional Buwayhid dynasty, Fatimid Egypt, and Byzantium.[11]

Fatimid-Byzantium relations improved somewhat in 987, after the Byzantine military had consolidated its control in Aleppo and Egypt had removed the restrictions on Byzantine merchants. Byzantine-Fatimid relations continued to oscillate between intense hostility, as in 995 when their forces clashed for control over Aleppo, and strategic alignment, as during the period from 1027 to 1071, when Seljuk attacks on Byzantine forces escalated.[12]

The emergence of the Fatimid Armenians in the latter part of the eleventh century was the culmination of cooperation between the Paulicians and Tondrakians, two movements that had challenged the authority of the Armenian Church and state, and the Arab conquerors.[13] As some Armenians had embraced Islam during the Arab conquest, they gradually had made inroads into the civilian bureaucracies and armed forces of the caliphate. Muslim Armenians began their political career in Fatimid Egypt in 1074, by which time an estimated 30,000 (and perhaps as high as 100,000) Armenians lived there. The earliest signs of political ambitions among Muslim Armenians appeared under Amir Aziz al-Dawla, Fatimid Muslim Armenian governor of Aleppo between 1016 and 1022, who sought to create his own government in Aleppo. He was assassinated by another Muslim Armenian, Abu'l Najm Badr al-Jamali, who later served as governor of Damascus. When Egypt was in political turmoil in the early 1070s, the Fatimid caliph al-Mustanshir called on Badr al-Jamali to restore stability in Egypt. Having accomplished his task and successfully defended Egypt against Seljuk Turks invading from the north, Badr al-Jamali was appointed *wazir* (vizier, prime minister) of the Fatimid government, which enabled him to establish the Jamali dynasty within the Fatimid dominion. Armenian wazirs ruled Fatimid Egypt for nearly ninety years.[14]

Badr al-Jamali ruled (from 1074 to 1094) through a tightly controlled military dictatorship, utilizing administrative centralization to strengthen the Egyptian economy and to integrate rural and urban financial and commercial relations. He enjoyed wide support among the Muslim Arabs for his efforts to restrengthen Egypt, but the fact that he also maintained his own Armenian military forces generated opposition from some Arab quarters against his "foreign" rule. His son, Abu'l-Qasim al-Afdal (1094–1121), continued his father's policies and organized his Armenian military unit, the Afdaliyya, named after him. He suffered a major defeat against the Crusaders in 1099, and although he retaliated in 1102, the Crusaders began to expand throughout the Middle East, including the conquest of Palestine, which at the time was under Fatimid rule. Relations between the Fatimid caliphate and the Armenian Church improved considerably when the Armenian Christian Prince Vahram (Bahram) Pahlavuni, son of Grigor Pahlavuni Magistros, served as Fatimid wazir from 1135 to 1137. Grigor Magistros had served as Byzantine Duke of Vaspurakan and Mesopotamia, and Emperor Constantine IX

Monomachus, having conquered Bagratuni Ani in 1045, ordered Grigor to defend his realm against the threat of local and invading Muslims. The last Armenian wazir, Ruzzik ibn Tala'i, briefly led the Fatimid government from 1161 to 1162 and was assassinated in 1163. His death was followed by years of power struggle and political turmoil, putting an end to the Armenian wazirate in Fatimid Egypt.[15] In 1169 the Ayyubid Salah ad-Din seized power and in 1171 removed the last Fatimid Shi'ite caliph. The Ayyubid dynasty ruled Egypt until 1250 and Syria from 1183 to 1260, during which period the Armenian Rubenian princes in Cilicia, having enjoyed sufficient domestic power and international prestige, established a kingdom in the region.

WARS OF LIBERATION

By 1100 the Rubenians commanded sufficient force and loyalty to emerge as the leading princely house and to weather the complexities arising from Byzantine, Seljuk, Arab, and Crusader conflicts. The Byzantine empire generally preferred to cooperate with the Hetumians, as the Rubenians, with the support of the Franks, agitated against Byzantium for total independence. In 1080 Ruben rebelled against Byzantine rule in northeastern Lernayin Kilikia and between 1080 and 1095 established his control over the territory. Ruben's son and successor, Constantine (1095–1102), consolidated power over the region centered at the fortress of Vahka and expanded his domain throughout Cilicia at the expense of Byzantines and Seljuks.[16]

The Crusaders appeared in the Middle East to "liberate" Christendom from Muhammedan forces.[17] Armenians in general welcomed them with open arms, and the Cilician monarchs even granted land and fortresses (as *beneficium*) to them in return for economic and military support. As the Crusaders expanded their influence in the region[18] and their military campaigns passed through Cilicia, and princes Constantine and Oshin, believing this opportunity would strengthen their position against the Seljuks, cooperated to reassert Christian dominion in the Middle East against the Muslim threat. Beginning in 1098 the Crusaders established their first state at Edessa (Urfa), followed by Antioch, Tripoli, and Jerusalem, the seat of the Crusader kingdom. Because of their proximity, these states greatly influenced the internal politics of the Armenian principalities, especially under the constant pressure of Byzantine emperor Alexius I Comnenus (r. 1081–1118) to regain control over Cilicia. Thereafter, the sons of Constantine, Toros and Levon, were engaged in constant struggles against the Crusaders and Byzantium to maintain their independence. Toros, continuing his father's balance-of-power policies, sought to cooperate with the Crusaders and the Byzantines while expanding his domain over Sis and Anazarba, "the seat of his barony."[19] Toros was successful in securing Cilician independence from both powers but failed to prevent further Seljuk attacks on eastern Cilicia. Despite their cooperation, the benefits accrued to Armenians in Cilicia in the early phases of the Crusader invasions proved ephemeral, as the Crusaders' intervention in Cilician affairs in fact weakened the Armenian leadership.

In the 1130s the Crusader principality of Antioch posed the greatest threat to Cilician Armenia, as Prince Raymond, the successor of Bohemund II, attempted to extend his control over southeastern Cilicia.[20] Unable to achieve his objective through military means, in 1136 he invited Prince Levon to Antioch, where he held the Armenian prince hostage and demanded the territories of Mamistra (Misis), Adana, and Sarvandikar in exchange for his release. Levon consented, but no sooner had he regained his freedom than he reconquered the lost lands.[21] Despite their conflicts, immediately thereafter Cilicia and Antioch agreed to cooperate against the common enemy, the Byzantine emperor John II Comnenus (r. 1118–1143). In 1137 the emperor captured the cities of Tarsus, Adana, Mamistra, and Anazarba, and as he prepared to attack the region of Vahka, the Antioch principality agreed to recognize Byzantine supremacy, a policy that isolated Levon against the Byzantine military campaigns. The Byzantine army captured Vahka in 1138, removed the last center of resistance at Raban, and took Levon and his family to Constantinople as prisoners. Levon died in captivity, but in 1142 his son Toros escaped to Cilicia to reorganize the Armenians for independence from Byzantium.[22] Soon thereafter the Armenian Church too established itself in the region. In 1147 the catholicosate seat was transferred from Tsovk, where it had been for more than thirty years, to the monastery of Hromkla (1147–1293) on the Euphrates, which at the time was within the jurisdiction of the Franks based at Edessa.[23]

The timing proved propitious. Byzantine Emperor Manuel I Comnenus (r. 1143–1180) was preoccupied with events on the European front, while Zangid troops under the leadership of Zangi, the founder of the Zangid dynasty (1127–1222), were strengthening their control over Mosul and Aleppo. They directed their expansion largely toward the south, although in the initial phases they seized Edessa in 1144. Two years later the Aleppine Zangid Nur al-Din (1146–1174), Zangi's son and successor, defeated the Crusader principality of Antioch and in 1154 advanced southward to Damascus and Egypt.[24] Nor did the Byzantine attempt under Andronicus Comnenus—with the complicity of Prince Oshin of Lampron—to reassert control over Cilicia prove successful, and in 1152 Toros defeated both in a critical battle near Mamistra. At the same time Sultan Mas'ud of Iconium (Konya) and Nur al-Din divided between themselves the Cilician territories under the Crusader state at Edessa. Mas'ud took Marash, Kaysun, Marzuban, and Aintab, while Nur al-Din took Guros, Azaz, Ravandan, Tel Bashir, and Tel Khalit.[25] By the time this phase of the military conflict with Byzantium had ceased, Antronicus had fled. Oshin was required to pay 40,000 Byzantine gold to regain his freedom as well as give his daughter in marriage to Toros's son, Hetum. For a short time Toros appeared to have secured a guarantee from Byzantium not to appoint a governor to Cilicia.[26] An attempt by Manuel I to recruit Mas'ud's support against the Rubenians proved fruitless. Prince Reynald of Châtillon of Antioch did capture some Cilician cities, but he subsequently refused to hand them over to Byzantium. Weary of Byzantine intentions, he instead agreed with Toros in 1155–1156 to attack Byzantine forces in Cilicia and Cyprus.

In 1158 Manuel I counterattacked and temporarily captured parts of Cilicia, and for a while it appeared that Cilicia would fall under Byzantine domination. The Seljuk threat at Konya and the principality of Antioch, however, was too crucial for Manuel to remain content with maintaining partial suzerainty over the region, and he went as far as soliciting the support of his former enemy Nur al-Din. Having failed in Konya, in 1164 Manuel solicited the support of Toros and Prince Bohemund III of Antioch (1163–1201) against both the Seljuks in Konya and Nur al-Din. Manuel I failed to sustain their cooperation, however. After the military alliance with Byzantium collapsed, Toros regained and maintained his independence until his death in 1169, succeeded by Ruben's short reign (1169–1170).[27] The military defeats suffered at the hands of the Konyan Seljuks at the Battle of Myriocephalum in 1176 forced Byzantium to withdraw its troops from Cilicia and northern Mesopotamia, thus creating an opportunity for the Rubenian and Hetumian houses to assert control. Despite their weakening hold on Cilicia, between the 1150s and the 1180s, the Byzantine governors (e.g., Andronicus in 1162; Constantine Calamanus in 1164), viewed the Rubenian princes as their subjects and tried to dominate the Cilician political scene. Beginning in the closing decades of the twelfth century, however, under the emperors Isaac II Angelus (r. 1185–1195) and Alexius III Angelus (r. 1195–1203), Byzantium entered its phase of long decline after the Crusaders sacked Constantinople in April 1204.[28]

Meanwhile, the struggle for power among the Rubenians led to the emergence of Mleh (1170–1175), one of Toros's brothers and said to have caused the murder of Ruben (Toros's son), as the uncontested leader of Cilicia. Mleh, whose relations with Toros had deteriorated in the mid-1160s, had served in the military of Nur al-Din. In 1172–1173, with Nur al-Din's blessings, Mleh defeated the Byzantine army in Cilicia, captured the cities of Adana, Mamistra, and Tarsus, and established Sis as the political and administrative center of Cilicia. Sis (modern Kozan), which Nur al-Din granted to Mleh for his loyalty and cooperation against the Crusaders and Byzantium, remained the Cilician capital until 1375. Mleh, however, failed to defeat the pro-Byzantine Hetumians at Lampron. In the spring of 1173 Bohemund III and the neighboring anti-Mleh barons mobilized forces to capture Mleh, and a year after Nur al-Din's death in 1174, the Hetumians, supported by the Armenian ecclesiastical leaders, conspired to kill him as punishment for his cooperation with the Muslim Nur al-Din. Mleh was succeeded by his nephew Ruben (1175–1187), who, to redress the murder of his uncle, killed the conspirators. He freed Adana and Tarsus from Byzantine rule, but, like his predecessor, he failed to unite Hetumian Lampron with Cilicia. His successor, Prince Levon, finally defeated the Hetumians and began the process of consolidating power over Cilicia as an independent state.[29]

The Crusaders, urged by Pope Innocent III (1198–1216), redoubled their efforts to maintain control over the Frankish states, especially in reaction to the military threat from Egypt by the Ayyubid Salah al-Din. Between 1185 and 1187 the latter had expanded his control northward to Damascus, Aleppo, Diarbekir, and Mayyafarqin, followed by Hattin, Acre, Galilee, Samaria, and Jerusalem. The Battle of Hattin (1187), where the Aquitainian king, Guy de Lusignan, had commanded the Frankish forces to their miserable defeat, proved a turning point, as much of the Frankish territories quickly fell to Salah al-Din.[30] Encouraged by his military successes against the Franks in the Arab countries, Salah al-Din launched a series of military campaigns against Cilicia but failed. His last offensive was aborted when he fell ill in Damascus and died on March 3, 1193. Nor was Bohemund III successful in defeating Prince Levon. In 1194, when Levon met with him ostensibly to negotiate the future status of Baghras (Gaston), Levon held him hostage and forced him to sign an agreement that provided for Bohemund's withdrawal from Baghras, the return of territories seized from Ruben, and the marriage of Bohemund's son, Raymond, with Levon's niece, Alice.[31]

Levon's military and political successes enhanced his international prestige, and on January 6, 1198, he was crowned as Levon I, King of Cilicia, accepting crowns from both the Byzantine emperor Alexius III Angelus (r. 1195–1203) and Holy Roman emperor Henry VI. The coronation took place at the cathedral in Tarsus. In attendance were the Armenian catholicos and a host of foreign dignitaries, including the papal envoy Conrad of Mainz, the Greek metropolitan of Tarsus, and the patriarch of Syrian Jacobites. Conrad of Mainz presented Levon "with the royal insignia, his crown having been brought from the Emperor Henry VI by the imperial chancellor, Conrad of Hildasheim."[32] Levon I thus revived the Armenian kingdom, albeit not in historic Armenia. In the absence of an Armenian kingdom in Greater Armenia, the Cilician kingdom came to represent the Armenian people. Armenians in their historic homeland in Erzerum, Sebastia, and Van and as far away as the Crimea recognized the Cilician kingdom.[33]

THE CILICIAN KINGDOM

Cilicia developed into an economically dynamic and prosperous society during the reign of Levon I. He cultivated close ties with commercial networks in Genoa and Venice and alliances with the Teutonic and Hospitaller Knights. Under Levon I, the kingdom minted its own gold and silver coins, one of the paramount privileges of sovereign rule. The geostrategic location of Cilicia on the northeastern corner of the Mediterranean Sea, its ports, roads, and rivers directly linked its economy with the centers of world trade (e.g., Genoa, Venice, France, Crimea) and markets throughout Asia, and the monarchy financed enormous infrastructural development. The various taxes collected from trade and domestic market transactions and transport brought immense wealth into the economy and for the king.[34] Levon maintained a considerable degree of independence from Byzantium and Rome despite their pressures to bring the Armenian king into their fold.

SOCIAL STRUCTURE

The Armenian social structure in Cilicia fundamentally reflected the feudal traditions and institutions as developed over the centuries in Greater Armenia.[35] At the apex of the hierarchy was the king and the royal court. Next were the nobility; however, in Cilician Armenia feudal lords and barons replaced the nakharars. The smaller landholders were granted the right to serve in the military as cavalry. A merchant capitalist class emerged in the urban centers. They were primarily engaged in trade, but the wealthier families also purchased lands. Of the 1 million total population in Cilicia, nearly 50 percent resided in urban areas, but the barons and aristocratic classes resided in mountain castles isolated from the towns. As in Greater Armenia, the mountainous terrain provided defenses locally, but the scattered communities of the nobility also encouraged centrifugal tendencies. Finally, the Armenian Church also acquired vast tracts of land, and by the thirteenth century the enormous wealth it accumulated in Cilicia enabled it effectively to exert a considerable influence on society and foreign policy.[36]

Two general socioeconomic classes developed in Armenian Cilicia: *azats* and *anazats*. The former was led first by the "lords" (or "princelings") and after the establishment of the kingdom, by the king. The feudal hierarchy consisted of secular and religious authorities and the landowning classes. The *anazats* were city and rural dwellers. The Armenian feudal system in Cilicia was largely built on the existing

Byzantine social structure and estates granted to the Armenian lords who had served as vassals with various military and administrative responsibilities in the Byzantine bureaucracies. After the establishment of the kingdom in 1198, the Armenian monarchs also relied on vast networks of patronage in the form of allotment (*benefice*) of lands (including fortresses, castles, forests, mines, ports) and distribution of wealth. Cilician political customs and administrative practices, as developed under the Armenian nakharar houses, included the appointment of the high-ranking nobility to hereditary offices and grants of fiefs in exchange for loyalty and military service.[37]

ADMINISTRATIVE STRUCTURE

The administrative structure of the royal court in the Cilician kingdom also resembled the structure found in Greater Armenia but with greater Byzanto-European cultural influences. The principal administrative offices included the *sparapet*, the *bail*, the *baillis royaux*, the chancellor, the senechal, and the *maksapet* (superintendent of custom houses). The *sparapet* (or *comes stabuli* or *constable* in the European tradition) performed similar functions as in Greater Armenia (e.g., the Mamikonians) but also had the added responsibilities of the *bdeshks* to guard the fortress towns along the borders of Cilicia. Unlike the Mamikonians, however, no single family monopolized the *sparapetutiun;* instead, the Cilician kings entrusted loyal princes with the office. The *bail* (custodian) specifically referred to individuals who served as custodians of the throne in times of vacancy or served as regents (*tagavorahayr*) for royal heirs. The royal custodian (*baillis royaux*) functioned as ambassador and represented the Cilician king in foreign countries. The offices of the chancellory and the seneschal performed similar functions as those in Greater Armenia.[38] Cilicia's geographical position as an international trade center with major port cities made the office of the *maksapet* one of the most important administrative institutions. It supervised a network of custom houses, bringing revenues from trade transactions at the ports as well as the transfer of goods on land and rivers. The kingdom's expanding economy and international economic ties also contributed to the development of its legal system.[39]

JURISPRUDENCE AND THE LEGAL SYSTEM

The legal structure in Cilician Armenia was shaped by Armenian secular and religious traditions, various Middle Eastern and Roman legal traditions, and Byzantine jurisprudence. The sources of law in Cilician Armenia included, for example, Assyrian law, the Latin Assizes of Antioch,[40] Roman law, Byzantine law, royal decrees issued by the Armenian kings, international treaties, church canons and decisions by church councils (e.g., the Sis Council of 1243) issued as official proclamations (*kondak*) by the catholicos, as well as the legal opinions and works by major jurist-philosophers, including Nerses Shnorhali, Mekhitar Gosh, Smbat Sparapet, and Kirakos Gantzaketsi.[41]

The legal structure consisted of two parallel secular and ecclesiastical judicial authorities, although the royal court and the monarchy always acted as the final arbiter. At the apex of the secular system was the high or royal court located at Sis. It exercised jurisdiction over cases involving, for example, international trade and financial disputes, inheritance rights within the royal family, administrative issues, authorization to construct fortresses and cities, taxation, criminal cases involving citizens of foreign countries, and capital punishment.[42]

Below the royal court was the court of princes, presided over by the "prince of princes"; it addressed disputes between the princes, barons, and the major feudal lords. This court also performed appellate functions, as it could confirm or reverse decisions by the lower courts. The latter heard cases involving ownership of private property, primogeniture, inheritance, adoption, debt and amortization of debt, dowry, marriage (age, religion, relations), and divorce. As the national economy and urban centers grew and trade became an essential source of revenue, Levon II (r. 1271–1289) established the *bail* courts (*bailia regis*) in the major cities and ports to resolve disputes between merchants and between foreign merchants and local citizens.[43]

The structure of the religious court was similar to that of the secular court system. At the apex was the court of the catholicosate led mainly by the court of the archbishop at Sis, followed by the bishopric courts. The archbishop of Sis, who also served as the royal chancellor, exercised jurisdiction over both civil and criminal law, particularly in cases between citizens and foreigners, and crimes by foreigners. The religious court had dual jurisdiction. It heard cases involving the clergy, disputes between Christian and non-Christian citizens, and offenses (*meghk*) committed against church canons and religious doctrines in general.[44] In certain legal areas, such as marriage, the religious courts shared responsibilities with their secular counterparts.

CILICIAN ARMENIAN CULTURE AND THE SILVER AGE

The invention of the Armenian alphabet in the fifth century under the Arshakuni dynasty in Greater Armenia had inaugurated the Golden Age.

During the twelfth century, referred to as the Silver Age, Armenian culture, now in Cilicia (beyond the historic Armenian homeland) experienced remarkable cultural developments in the cosmopolitan environment.[45] The commercial and diplomatic ties with the major trading centers in the West complemented the domestic advances in the sciences, theology, and philosophy by renowned scientists, philosophers, writers, poets, and painters. Among them were writers Catholicos Nerses Shnorhali (the Gracious, 1102–1173); his nephew and successor Grigor Tgha (ca. 1130–1193); Nerses Lambronatsi (Nerses of Lambron, 1153–1198); Hetum Patmich (Historian) of Korikos (thirteenth century), author of *La Flor des Estoires de la Terre d'Orient* in Old French for Pope Clement V (1305–1314); the chronicler Smbat the Constable (1208–1276), the brother of King Hetum I; the medical writer, Mekhitar Heratsi (Mekhitar of Khoy, ca. 1120–1200); the philosopher Vahram Rabuni (thirteenth century); the musicologists Toros Tapronts and Gevorg Skevratsi (thirteenth century); and the renowned miniaturists Grigor Mlichetsi (Krikor Mlijetsi) of Skevra (twelfth century), Toros Roslin of Hromkla (thirteenth century), and Sargis Pitsak (Sarkis Bidzag) of Sis (fourteenth century).[46]

Cilician cultural leaders maintained close ties with foreign cultures and introduced them to Armenians. For example, Grigor II Vkayaser (1065–1105) translated works from the Greek Orthodox Church into Armenian. Nerses Lambronatsi translated various Latin ecclesiastical rites. Armenian jurisprudence and philosophy also benefited from translations of various Latin, Greek, and Syriac secular and religious works. By the twelfth century, the Armenian Cilician kingdom had become home to some of the most productive Armenian religious and cultural institutions (e.g., scriptoria) as in Sis, Hromkla, Anazarba, Tarsus, Lambron, and Korikos.[47] It must have been possible to imagine that the losses suffered in Greater Armenia could be compensated for with productive work in the fortress-monasteries and cathedrals ensconced in the beautiful mountains and vales of Cilicia.

CILICIA BETWEEN EAST AND WEST

The Cilician kingdom confronted a host of military conflicts and diplomatic tensions as shaped by the geopolitical environment in which it conducted its domestic affairs. The foreign policy objectives of the kingdom included, in addition to commercial relations, the formation and reformulation of alliances with or against the Crusaders, Mamluks, Seljuk Turks, and Mongols, and control over strategic areas, such as the port city of Ayas, and Antioch, Baghras, and Payas.[48] These foreign policy issues were compounded by incessant internal tensions, particularly those pertaining to succession. Despite its access to the sea, the Cilician kingdom lacked effective institutional mechanisms to rectify the shortcomings of the Arshakuni and Bagratuni political systems. In fact, access to the sea appeared largely irrelevant to the internal dynamics of the clash between centrifugal and centripetal tendencies. The Mamluk invasions further complicated the regional conflicts, exacerbated the internal divisions, and ultimately led to collapse of the Cilician kingdom.

The Crusaders and the Seljuk posed the principal threat to the monarchy soon after its establishment. Armenian secular and religious leaders were fully aware of the political implications of accepting a crown from the Holy Roman emperor for the coronation of Levon I. In granting a royal crown, Pope Innocent III and his envoy Conrad of Mainz expected the Armenian monarchy to acknowledge the Pope as the supreme leader of Christendom, a papal policy objective since the First Crusades. Levon I, in his turn, granted lands to the Crusader orders; the Hospitallers received Seleucia, Norpert (Castellum Novum), and Camardias, and the Teutonic Knights, Amoudain and Haruniye.[49] Initially the interests of the Crusades and the Cilician kingdom coincided, as both sought to contain Seljuk and Byzantine expansionism.[50] To strengthen his ties with the West, Levon I and his supporters were willing, as a matter of formality, to "concede a 'special respect' to the pope as the successor of St. Peter."[51] The Armenian Church, however, vehemently opposed such foreign doctrinal encroachment on Armenian orthodoxy and religious cum national prerogatives, and widened the pro- and anti-Rome factional chasms (reminiscent of the pro- and anti-Persia factional struggles that had divided Greater Armenia centuries earlier).

In 1215 the Fourth Crusade attempted to strike against Salah al-Din's power in Egypt but the Ayyubid caliph refused to capitulate, and in their struggle for regional hegemony, both powers sought to expand their dominion across Cilicia. Salah al-Din had become a formidable regional force in control of both Egypt and Syria, but the Crusaders, having attacked Constantinople in 1204, felt confident of their military power to push farther east and south.[52] In efforts to reassert his control in regional geopolitics, Levon I, after much machination and maneuver, in 1216 succeeded in gaining control over Antioch by placing his grandson Ruben Raymond in power. Three years later, however, members of the local Antiochene nobility conspired to overthrow Ruben Raymond, while Seljuk troops invaded Cilicia, causing heavy Armenian losses and physical damage in some areas, such as Lampron. Seljuks took a number of Hetumian princes hostage, whose release Levon I secured only after submitting to Seljuk demands. Levon promised to surrender a number of fortresses as a ransom to the Seljuk Sultan, to provide 300 soldiers per annum, and to pay annual taxes.[53]

Levon I had been successful in ameliorating the tensions between the Rubenian and Hetumian houses, and after his death in 1219 the crown, except for intermittent attempts at usurpation, served as a center for cooperation between the two houses. Although Levon had appointed his daughter Zabel (Isabelle) as his successor, Ruben Raymond (his grand-nephew) conspired to usurp the crown, but the pro-Zabel barons swiftly imprisoned him. Zabel assumed the throne, under the care of the Hetumian regent (*tagavorahayr*) Constantine of Lampron. Constantine's efforts to strengthen ties with Antioch (through marriage of Philip of Antioch with Zabel) in alliance against the Seljuks failed when Philip, who held a condescending attitude toward all things Armenian and preferred to spend his time in Antioch, was murdered in 1224. Nevertheless, Constantine was successful in establishing the Hetumian kingdom in Cilicia by arranging Zabel's marriage with his son, Hetum, thus ending the hostility between the Rubenian and Hetumian houses.[54]

During the reign of Hetum I (r. 1226–1270), Cilicia witnessed rapid cultural and economic development but also constant threats to its security on three fronts: the Seljuk sultanate from the north, the Mamluks from the south, and the Mongols from the east.[55] Cilician foreign policy during the reign of Hetum I centered on defending the kingdom primarily against the Seljuks and secondarily against the Mamluks. Hetum initially allied with the Mongols to deter invasions by both enemies. In 1233 and again in 1245–1246, the Seljuks invaded Cilicia, while they clashed with the Mongols across the plain of Erzerum. Hetum sided with the Mongols and in return expected to win their alliance in future conflicts against the Seljuks. Immediately after the Mongolian army defeated the Seljuks at the Battle of Kose Dagh in 1243, Hetum I sent a delegation to establish a military alliance with the Great Khan Mongke. The preliminary diplomatic overtures followed in 1247 by a mission headed by Hetum's brother, the Constable Smbat, to Qaraqorum (Kara Korum), the capital of the great khan in Central Asia, in preparation for the Hetum-Mongke negotiations, which for political reasons were postponed until 1254.[56]

In 1247 some Georgian and Armenian princes of the Zakarian dynasty, who decades earlier had briefly established a "kingdom" in the region stretching from Ani to Mount Ararat with aspirations to recover all of the Bagratuni lands,[57] conspired to rebel against the Mongols, but their plans were foiled and the culprits captured and sent to Qaraqorum. Upon their return in 1249, they regrouped to organize the rebellion, but spies working for the Mongols again thwarted their plans. The Mongols retaliated with a destructive campaign against both Armenians and Georgians.[58]

In 1248 Hetum I also sent a delegation to the Crusaders at Cyprus to discuss Cilicia's participation in the planned invasion and liberation of Syria and Egypt from the Muslims, a situation that became all the more pressing in

1250, when the Mamluks overthrew the Ayyubid dynasty of Salah al-Din in Egypt.

Hetum I finally visited Qaraqorum in the spring of 1254 to formalize an alliance with the Great Khan Mongke.[59] The Qaraqorum treaty provided that

1. The signatories maintain mutual security assistance in times of war. Cilician Armenians would assist the Mongols in their military campaigns in Mesopotamia, Syria, and Palestine, while the Mongols agreed to defend the Armenian kingdom against the Seljuks of Konya, the Mamluks of Egypt, and the other surrounding Muslim neighbors;
2. The signatories maintain perpetual peace and friendship;
3. Mongol soldiers and officials enter Cilician territory only with the official approval of the Cilician monarchy; and
4. All former Cilician lands and cities, castles and fortresses, seized by others and now under Mongolian control be returned to the Cilician kingdom.[60]

This treaty aimed at establishing more than mere mutual security assistance. From Hetum's perspective, the alliance with the Mongols would protect the Cilician kingdom against Seljuk invasions. He also expected the alliance to provide opportunities for eastward expansion. He did not, however, view this seemingly pro-Mongol policy as necessarily entailing a complete shift in his pro-western policy orientation.

Mongke Khan died in 1259, and with him died the unity of the Mongol empire created by Genghis Khan, the great khan of khans. Hulagu Khan, the grandson of Genghis Khan and brother of Mongke, established the ilkhanate dynasty in Iran after a period of political instability. (The term ilkhanate is derived from il-khan, meaning sub-khanate, representing a subdivision within Genghis Khan's empire.)[61] Both signatories adhered to or ignored the Qaraqorum treaty as dictated by circumstances. At times the Mongols remained aloof from entangling conflicts that posed no direct threat to their interests, as during the armed clashes between Cilicia and the Seljuk sultanate of Konya. Nor did Hetum I provide assistance to Hulagu's military campaigns in 1258 to capture Baghdad, as the Cilician king saw no tangible benefits from the campaign. Yet when in 1259–1260 Hulagu invaded Syria, a campaign that also served Cilician interests, Armenian forces (by one estimate, consisting of 12,000 cavalry and 40,000 infantry) took part in the invasion. According to Arab historians, during their campaign for Aleppo Hetum's soldiers caused damage to a mosque and the markets in the city and killed several local people.[62]

It may be argued that the Qaraqorum treaty signified Hetum's political acumen in assessing the potential importance the Mongols would assume as an emerging power in the region. There was an inherent dilemma in that alliance, however. On the positive side, Cilicia's close association with the Mongols, especially in the military campaigns against the Mamluks in Aleppo, Damascus, and Egypt, served the interests of both Sis and Qaraqorum. Hetum I found an ally in the Mongols who could provide much-needed military support, while the Mongols enjoyed the confidence of the Cilician kingdom whose territory allowed access to the northeastern shores of the Mediterranean and served as a buffer or base for further expansion. The Cilician economy also benefited from expanding Sis-Qaraqorum bilateral trade relations.[63] On the negative side, Hetum I could play the "Mongol card" so long as the latter remained a powerful force in the region and could protect both Mongol *and* Armenian interests. A strong Mongol presence became all the more essential for the Armenian monarchy as the alliance intensified Cilicia's conflicts with the neighboring powers at a time when Armenian military capability alone could not defend its sovereignty. Mongol territorial ambitions included expansion to the important port cities on the eastern shores of the Mediterranean and therefore posed a direct challenge to both the Crusaders and the Mamluks, further burdening Cilicia's association with the Mongols.[64]

By the early 1260s it had become abundantly clear that the Mongols under Hulago could not, even with Armenian cooperation, withstand the onslaught of Mamluk forces. After his victory in Syria, Hulago had neglected his troops in the region, and his army suffered a major defeat at the hands of the Mamluk military at the Battle of Ayn Jalut in 1260. The Mamluks were in the process of removing the Ayyubid rulers, already weakened by repeated Mongol invasions, from their strongholds across the Middle East. The Mongol army in the meantime withdrew to Iran and became preoccupied with internal political upheavals. By the end of the thirteenth century, the inability of the Mongolian army to check the revolutionary forces at home had led to the disintegration of the empire before the world empire as envisioned by Mongol leaders could materialize. The division of the Mongolian empire thus left the Mamluks, who viewed themselves as the guardians of the *dar al-islam* (the Islamic lands) against all infidels (non-believers), in control of the Middle East. The vast empire pieced together by the Great Genghis Khan was divided into four states: the Chaghatay khanate in Transoxania, the Golden Horde across the northern steppes and Russia, the ilkhanate in Persia, and the Mongol dynasties in Mongolia and China.[65]

For the Armenian kingdom, the geopolitical situation further deteriorated as the Persian ilkhanate's wars with the Golden Horde left Cilicia to its own fate. The Mamluk Sultan Baybars (r. 1260–1277), despite the exchange of ambassadors with Cilicia and efforts by Hetum I to maintain peaceful relations, organized a series of military campaigns with the support of the Ayyubids in Hama and Homs in 1261 and 1262 against Antioch and Aleppo, where he was confronted by joint Armenian-Mongolian forces. Hetum subsequently led his own campaigns into Syria from 1262 to 1264 and dispatched a contingent to join the Mongol attack on al-Bira.[66] In 1266 he journeyed to Tabriz to negotiate military assistance from the ilkhanate, a move that elicited a major retaliatory campaign by Baybars. The latter mobilized a force of 30,000 men under the command of al-Mansur of Hama for a "pedagogical war" against Cilicia. The Mamluk troops, facing a force of no more than 15,000, killed thousands of Armenians, attacked several cities (Sis, Adana, Ayas, Tarsus), destroyed forts, and looted and ravaged much of Cilicia. The Mamluks killed one of Hetum's sons, Toros, and captured the other, Levon, along with Vasil Tatar, the son of Constable Smbat. The outcome of the conflict must have been quite obvious to Baybars, for he shifted his attention to the military operations against the Franks. The Armenian military was in total disarray, and Hetum had failed to secure a commitment from the ilkhanate for military support. In 1268 his envoys met with Baybars in Cairo to negotiate the terms of armistice with the hope of gaining Levon's freedom. Hetum agreed to surrender several fortresses and to pay tribute. Although the ilkhanate had refused to grant military aid to Hetum, it handed over Sunqur al-Ashqar, a friend of Baybars and who was captured in the previous Mongol-Mamluk military engagement, to be exchanged for Levon. Nevertheless, the military and diplomatic disasters led to Hetum's abdication in 1269; he died the following year.[67]

As the Mongols lost their influence in the Middle East, the Mamluks filled the power vacuum and increasingly posed a serious threat to Cilicia and the Crusaders' position in the region. The changing power configuration led the Crusaders and Hetum's son and successor, Levon II (1269–1289), to form an alliance against the Mamluks, which appeared to enhance Cilicia's geostrategic role. Levon II thus took a decisive turn to the West. The European powers, however, did not view Cilicia as an ally. In 1274 Levon II sent a delegation to the church council being held at Lyon, requesting military support against the neighboring Muslims, but the council did not respond favorably. European powers ignored repeated requests (in 1278, 1279, and 1282). Cilicia thus remained in a precarious situation, suspended in the regional balance of power between a Europe indifferent to its security considerations and the Mamluks, who viewed the avowedly anti-Mamluk kingdom as too European oriented and too anti-Muslim.[68]

In 1274–75 and 1276, the Mamluks, determined to abolish the Armenian kingdom altogether on their way to unite forces with the sultanate of Rum, invaded. They failed to conquer the country, however, and after the death of

Baybars in 1277, the region enjoyed a short period of peace between the Mamluks and the Armenians. Baybars's son and successor al-Said Berke Khan resumed the policy of unification with the sultanate of Rum and ordered an invasion of Cilicia. During the campaign Mamluk opposition groups clashed with his government in Cairo, and after a series of coups and countercoups, Sunqur al-Ashqar emerged as the Mamluk Sultan in Damascus in 1280. Prior to his own fall from power the following year, Sunqur launched a major military campaign against Aleppo, which drew in the Armenians and the Mongols, the latter hoping to reassert power in the region. The Mamluks, now under Sultan Sayf al-Din Qalawun, destroyed both armies and marched northward to Cilicia. In May 1285 Levon II, unable to win support from either the Mongols or the Europeans, accepted a treaty that imposed extremely harsh conditions on the Cilician economy.[69]

The peace treaty of 1285 between Levon II and Sayf al-Din Qalawun contained, in addition to a preamble, thirty articles. It promised peace and security for Cilicia so long as the kingdom fulfilled the following obligations:[70]

1. The Cilician kingdom would pay each year 500,000 dirhams in silver coins, 50 horses and mules of superior quality, 10,000 iron horseshoes with nails;
2. Levon II agreed to release all Muslim merchants in Cilician prisons regardless of their ethnicity and to return their properties, goods, animals, and slaves;
3. The Mamluk Sultan agreed to free all the Armenian diplomats, state officials, and merchants held captive with their goods in Egypt and Syria;
4. The Cilician kingdom agreed to permit free and safe transit through its borders all merchants and travelers from Iraq, Persia, Seljukid Rum (the eastern lands of the former Roman empire), and so on whose destination was one of the territories of the Mamluk Sultan;
5. Both parties agreed to transfer salvaged goods from capsized ships in their respective territorial waters to the state officials representing the country of the owner;
6. Levon II agreed not to build additional fortresses; and
7. The catholicos and all the Armenian clergy would agree to abide by the conditions of this treaty.[71]

Included also was a provision for extradition, stipulating that both parties would return all individuals (and all their belongings) found to have escaped from their (Mamluk or Cilician) lands to their respective state, except those Armenians who had converted to Islam and were residing in Mamluk territories, in which case all their belongings (but not the persons) would be returned to Cilicia. The treaty thus placed enormous emphasis on commercial relations, indicating the significance of the Cilician trade and economy in the region. The treaty also clearly attested to the diminution of Cilician independence, which in the wider scheme of Cilician history represented a qualitative change in the power relations between the two monarchies but also in the international status of the Cilician kingdom.

While the peace secured with the Mamluks for a brief period provided an opportunity to reinvigorate the Cilician commerce and economy and to rebuild the destroyed cities (Sis, Tarsus) and the major ports (Ayas), after Levon II's death in 1289 the Cilician kingdom never enjoyed political stability and security.[72] His eldest son and successor, Hetum II, was hardly prepared to lead the kingdom and generally exhibited weak character and indifference to the affairs of the monarchy. In order to strengthen his position, he arranged the marriage of two of his sisters into the royal families in Byzantium and Cyprus.[73] Relations through marriage, however, could not provide the physical security his kingdom so desperately needed in the increasingly hostile neighborhood.

The Mamluk threat intensified during Hetum's first reign (1289–1294) as Cairo launched a series of invasions against the Crusader states and Cilicia. Pressed by the military circumstances, Hetum II requested assistance from the ilkhanate, but the latter, absorbed in their own internal strife, were not favorably inclined. Hetum II also dispatched requests to Rome, England, and France, but European professions of solidarity with the Cilician cause did not translate into military support.[74] The Armenian kingdom clearly lacked the military capability to defend itself and the wherewithal to extricate itself from the situation. When by the end of 1291 the major Mamluk offensives against the Frankish army in Acre eliminated the last remaining Crusader forces in the Middle East, the Cilician kingdom found itself virtually alone in the region to confront the Mamluks. In June 1292 the Mamluks, under Qalawun's son Sultan al-Ashraf Khalil (r. 1290–1293), attacked Hromkla and took Catholicos Stepannos IV along with war booty and thousands of people as prisoners to Egypt. Like his grandfather, who had abdicated the throne after the military defeat in 1269, Hetum abdicated in 1293, and having converted to Catholicism, withdrew to a Franciscan monastery. After his brother Toros I's short reign (1293–1295), however, Hetum returned to power (1295–1297).[75] As one historian has noted, it is also possible that rather than fully abdicate, he placed Toros on the throne to ensure palace stability while he traveled to meet with the Ilkhan Ghazan (r. 1295–1304). Hetum II went to Maragha in 1295 to revive the Armeno-Mongol security alliance and, with Toros, to Constantinople the next year for a similar security arrangement with Byzantium. They stayed in the Byzantine capital for six months. In the meantime, one of their brothers, Smbat (r. 1297–1299), usurped the throne with the support of their discontented brothers, and with the tacit support of Catholicos Grigor and Pope Boniface VIII. Hetum and Toros, not permitted to enter Cilicia, journeyed back to Constantinople and thence to the ilkhanate to rally support for their safe return home and for Hetum's resumption of the throne. Smbat imprisoned both men at Caesaria in 1297 and ordered Toros strangled and Hetum blinded. In retaliation, Smbat himself was removed from power in 1298 by yet another brother, Constantine (Gosdantin) of Gaban.[76]

The fratricidal struggle for power and leadership instability in Cilicia rendered the weakening kingdom infinitely more vulnerable to invasions. To strengthen his position, Constantine I employed military force to neutralize the supporters of Smbat, but his brutal efforts to deal with opposition at home antagonized the nobility and distracted the kingdom from the external threats. The Mamluk attacks on Cilicia had continued during the 1290s, with Mamluk military leaders vacillating between immediate capture of strategic points (ports, cities, fortresses) and the grander scheme of total conquest. In the spring and summer of 1298, Malik al-Mansur invaded southern Cilicia. Some of his troops reached the port city of Ayas and pressed forward on the eastern banks of the Pyramos River northward to Sarvandikar and Marash. Hetum II, though nearly blind, took advantage of the military situation and with sufficient political support from the nobility overthrew Constantine and exiled both him and Smbat to Constantinople.[77]

Having eliminated the power struggle within his own family, Hetum exercised stronger control over policy during his third reign (1299–1307). In part responding to the Mamluk attack on Hromkla in 1292–1293 and in part determined to establish firm control over the church, he moved the catholicosate from Hromkla to Sis and installed the pro-Latin Grigor VII of Anavarza on the catholicosal throne. Further, in order to avoid future succession crises, in 1301 Hetum II appointed his nephew Levon III (the son of Toros), barely three years of age at the time, as co-ruler. For a brief period Cilicia enjoyed internal peace and stability, while Hetum pursued an activist foreign policy in support of the ilkhanate's invasions against the Mamluks. Despite the fact that the Ilkhan Ghazan had converted to Islam in 1295, Hetum supported his Syrian campaigns of 1299 and 1301 to 1303 and occupation of Damascus. In 1302 the Mamluks resumed their attacks on Cilicia for a number of reasons, including the military assistance Hetum II provided to the Mongols and his refusal to pay tribute to the Mamluks. The latter were further rewarded by the succession crisis unfolding in the ilkhanate after Ghazan's death in 1304, which, the Mamluks believed, would hinder future Mongolian military campaigns. During Ghazan's Syrian campaign, Hetum organized an effective defense force, which included a Mongol contingent, and contributed to the defeat of the Mamluk army.[78] The contemporary Arab historian al-Ayni commented on Hetum II's military policy: "The lord of Sis hated the Muslims in his heart for what they had done in his territory which had been taken from him, and for the destruction which had been laid waste, and for his men which they had killed, and for the raids which were recurring against his territory from the side of the Muslims. When he agreed to assist Ghazan, the lord of Sis came before Ghazan, and requested that he allow him to enter by *al-bāb al-sharqī* and to egress from *bāb al-jābiya*, and place the sword between the two gates, and avenge [himself] on the Muslims."[79]

Perhaps Levon III would have reformulated Cilician foreign policy in favor of closer ties with the Mamluks if he had lived longer and was given the opportunity to rule alone. But his reign was cut short while visiting, along with Hetum II (a Franciscan friar after his conversion) and other dignitaries, the ikhanate military command in Cilicia. The ilkhanate's conversion to Islam during the reign of Ghazan and the anti-Christian orientation of his successors troubled the Cilician leadership,[80] but in order to reconfirm their relations with the new government, Hetum, Levon, and their entourage traveled to Anazarba (Anavarza) in November 1307, only to be murdered by the amir or commander Bularghu. Sheer personal vanity had moved Bularghu to orchestrate the massacre. His hostility toward the Armenian leadership did not stem from the clash of abstract religious values. Rather, he had proposed the construction of a mosque in Adana; Hetum II had rejected the project and had criticized the amir in a letter to the brother and successor of Ghazan, Ilkhan Khar-Banda Öljeitü (r. 1304–1316), who in turn had chastised Bularghu. Infuriated by this humiliation, Bularghu ordered his men to kill the entire Armenian delegation, including Hetum and Levon. Thus abruptly ended the long and checkered reign of Hetum II and his young nephew.[81]

One of Hetum's brothers, Oshin, succeeded him and Levon III. His reign (1307–1320) witnessed intense internal political instability as Armenians debated how to respond to the rapidly changing external circumstances. Oshin wished to remain on good terms with the ilkhanate, which, he expected, could serve as a counterbalancing force against the persistent Mamluk threat. He also sought to cultivate close relations with the European powers, and accordingly in a series of councils (Sis 1307; Adana 1308, 1309, 1316) he and his supporters decided to recognize the pope in return for economic and military support. Predictably, the Armenian Church vehemently opposed this pro-Roman policy. For his part, Oshin failed to convince Rome of his own ability to implement unification with the Roman Catholic Church. Having failed to secure papal support for his beleaguered kingdom, in 1317 Oshin confiscated the properties of the Hospitallers in Cilicia. Pope John XXII in a letter advised reconciliation with the Armenian king, but the Hospitallers refused. In 1320 Oshin offered to reinstate their ownership in return for military support, but the Hospitallers again refused.[82]

By then, Ertugrul (ca. 1199–1280), the leader of a Turkish state near present-day Ankara, had strengthened his position against the Byzantine army. His son, Osman I, founder of the Ottoman (Osmanli) empire, expanded the domain. Osman's son, Orhan, captured the town of Bursa in 1326 and advanced to Gallipoli in 1345. Although his son, Murad, fell victim during the Battle of Kosovo in 1389, the victory secured soon thereafter by Bayazid, Murad's son, enabled the Ottomans to consolidate their rule in the Balkans. They appeared posed to conquer the Byzantine capital, Constantinople. The invasions by Timur Leng (Tamerlane), which began in 1382 from Transoxania and advanced to Moscow and to the Taurus Mountains, briefly arrested the Ottoman expansion when in July 1402 his forces dealt a devastating blow to Bayazid near Ankara.[83]

THE END OF THE CILICIAN KINGDOM

Unable to secure a reliable alliance with a Muslim power in the region, and oscillating between competing pro- and anti-West factions, the Cilician kingdom rapidly degenerated into chaos at home and paralysis in foreign policy. The magnitude of the crisis became evident during the Armenian ecclesiastical councils at Sis (1307) and Adana (1316) under the auspices of the Cilician catholicosate. Several barons and clergy at the Sis synod decided to unite with the Roman Catholic Church, and the Cilician government and church leaders attempted to impose their decisions on the Armenian Church. In 1311 Bishop Sargis of Jerusalem, vehemently opposing subordination to Rome, rebelled against the catholicosate and established his own independent church.[84] Taking advantage of the internal crisis in Cilicia, the Mamluks and the Turkomans of Konya attacked Cilicia, while palace intrigue and conspiracy led to the murder of Oshin in 1320.[85]

The reign of his son Levon IV (1320–1341) witnessed a significant change in the region's geopolitical configuration as the Mongol ilkhanate collapsed in 1336, removing even the possibility of a pro-Cilician leadership in the region. The death of the last ilkhan, Abu Sa'id, in 1335 and continued struggles for succession and power partitioned Persia and Mesopotamia into smaller states. The beginning of the Hundred Years War (1337–1453) in the West further isolated Cilicia.[86] In the 1320s (and with five to ten year intervals until 1375), the Mamluks launched a series of campaigns against Cilicia in part to capture the port city of Ayas. After the expulsion of the Crusaders from the Middle East, Ayas had gained in importance in East-West trade, as European merchants preferred to deal with the Christians there rather than with the Muslim Mamluks at Alexandria (who had only recently expelled the

Europeans from the region). Moreover, the customs duties on trade transactions at Ayas were considerably lower than those at Alexandria. The intensified competition between Alexandria and Ayas for European trade contributed to the Mamluk drive to conquer Cilicia and to capture Ayas, a policy achieved in 1322. The following year Levon IV was forced to sign a peace treaty at Cairo, which imposed heavy taxes on the Cilician kingdom. The Cairo treaty of 1323 provided that the Cilician kingdom pay to the Mamluks an annual tax of 1.2 million silver dirhams, 50 percent of the income derived from commercial transactions at Ayas, and 50 percent of the income from salt exports. The Mamluks, for their part, agreed to withdraw their troops from Cilicia and to rebuild the devastated infrastructure of the port city.[87]

The hostile environment enveloping Cilician foreign relations exerted a deleterious influence on the factional divisions at home. In reaction to the military defeats of 1322–23 against Mamluks, Levon IV pressed for a total alignment with the West. He tightened his grip on the political institutions by exiling or executing the anti-West officials, replacing them with members of the House of Lusignans at Cyprus. In order to solidify his relations with the Lusignans and thereby with the West, he also ordered the assassination of his own wife and married the Sicilian king Philip's daughter, the widowed queen of Cyprus. Having secured his position with a nobility favorable to his pro-western policies, in 1331 Levon IV sent his envoys to Europe to revive the Crusader missions.[88]

The Mamluk Sultan Nasir, the son of Baybars I, viewed Levon's policy as a clear violation of the spirit (if not the letter) of the Cairo treaty of 1323 and ordered Altun Bugha, the amir of Aleppo, to invade Cilicia. In 1336 and 1337 Altun Bugha's forces seized a number of key Cilician cities (Mamistra, Adana, Ayas, and Tarsus) and looted their wealth. Again defeated by the Mamluks, Levon IV dispatched a delegation to negotiate yet another peace treaty. Sultan Nasir imprisoned some of the Cilician delegates and insisted that the new treaty extend Mamluk jurisdiction over Ayas and the territory east of the Pyramos River. Levon IV also agreed to terminate relations with Rome and France, but soon thereafter, refusing to abide by this treaty, he entered into negotiations with the pope. Before the negotiations were completed, however, Levon IV was murdered, probably by nobles who opposed his pro-Latin orientation.[89]

By then, neither the Rubenian nor the Hetumian houses had legitimate inheritors to the Cilician crown. The line of succession passed to Hetum II's nephews in the family of Amaury de Lusignan of Cyprus. The Lusignan period proved highly unstable, as the new monarchy failed to establish a strong basis for political legitimacy. After two years on the throne, Guy de Lusignan (Constantine II [r. 1342–1344]) was killed in his palace at Adana along with 300 members of the French nobility serving him in Cilicia. Guy was succeeded by his cousin Constantine III (r. 1344–1362), during whose reign Mamluk-Turkoman invasions escalated, particularly in response to his military alliance with the European powers and promise to Pope Clement VI to secure the conversion of Cilicia to Catholicism. Constantine III's reign also had the added misfortune of confronting the Black Death (1347–1349).[90] The plague also decimated the Mamluk army. One third of the population in Egypt and Syria died from the plague. The Mamluk economy was devastated, and the military never recovered from its losses in manpower and wealth, especially since agricultural wealth was concentrated in the hands of the military elite.[91]

Successors to Constantine III followed in rapid order: Levon V (Lusignan) ruled from 1362 to 1364, followed by Peter I of Cyprus (r. 1367/8–1369), and Constantine IV (r. 1367–1373). Throughout this period the Lusignans had relied on the European powers, who, as before, on numerous occasions promised military support that never materialized. Also, despite their pro-western predilections, the Lusignans sought a peaceful modus vivendi with the Mamluks but failed. In compromises with the Mamluks, they surrendered parts of their domain, including Tarsus, and even agreed to surrender the kingdom in its entirety, on condition that the Mamluk government would guarantee their physical safety. These compromises antagonized the Armenian nobility, who held little respect for the "European" family in the first place. In 1373 Constantine IV was murdered and succeeded by Levon V, who returned to the throne to salvage the kingdom, a task that proved impossible.[92] He was the last monarch of the Armenian kingdom of Cilicia.

In 1375 the Mamluks invaded Cilicia and forced members of the Lusignan family to Cairo as prisoner, thus putting an end to the Cilician kingdom. The Turkoman Ramazanids gained control over Cilicia under Mamluk tutelage. After his release, Levon V traveled to Europe soliciting aid to rescue his kingdom from the Mamluks but to no avail. The Mamluks appointed Yakub Shah as governor at Sis, and Armenians migrated en masse to other regions for safe haven. Levon V died in Paris in November 1393 and was buried in St-Denis, but the title of Cilician kingdom survived through one of his relatives, King John I of Cyprus, and through him passed to the House of Savoy, which survived until the nineteenth century.[93]

Part III

Sultans, Tsars, and Tyrants

This page intentionally left blank

5

Armenia under Ottoman, Persian, and Russian Rule

Timur Leng or Tamerlane envisioned himself as a new Genghis Khan and sought to unite the post-Mongol successor states. During his reign of more than three decades from 1370 to 1405, Timur Leng's vast domain encompassed the entire region from his capital Samarqand to India, Iran, parts of historic Armenia, and Syria. In the spring of 1386, his forces marched from Tabriz to Siunik, captured Nakhijevan, and thereafter advanced to Erzerum and Georgia.[1] Discontent with Timurid rule eventually led to mass uprisings throughout the Caucasus, instigating another wave of invasions beginning in September 1399. In the long process of conquests and calamity, Timur Leng gained the support of Muslim elites, as he continued his conquests in the name of Islam until his death on February 18, 1405[2] the city of Van and most Armenian cities across the land were devastated.

In the meantime, individual states emerged that sought to control the local population. The formation of these states and their efforts to maintain a balance between nomadic warriors' independence at the local level and establishing a centralized and settled society set the stage for the Ottoman empire, which ruled these territories for the next 500 years. Two Turkoman dynasties, the Kara Koyunlu (Black Sheep) centered at Van and the Ak Koyunlu (White Sheep) at Diarbekir, replaced the Timurids and extended their power across Greater Armenia and Iran. Kara Yusuf, the leader of the Kara Koyunlu dynasty, established his reign in Armenia, Georgia, and Baghdad, and channeled local resources toward economic reconstruction. Eventually until internal dissension and successive invasions by the Ak Koyunlu leader Osman and Timur's son, Shah Rukh, weakened Kara Yusuf, who died in poor health in 1420.[3]

Kara Yusuf's successors, proclaiming themselves Shah-i Armen (King of Armenia), enlisted Armenians (e.g., Rustum, son of the Beshken Orbelian nakharar house of Siunik) among their advisers. One of Kara Yusuf's sons, Jihanshah, governor of Armenia and Tabriz (1437–1467),[4] after his initial brutalities subsided, appointed a number of Armenian nakharars (nobles) as "princes" of Siunik, Vayots Dzor, Artsakh (Karabagh), and Gugark. Jihanshah also granted permission to rebuild some of the churches and to reinstitute the catholicosate at Echmiadzin in 1441. The catholicosate of Sis had declined since the collapse of the Armenian kingdom in Cilicia, and the ecclesiastical assembly in 1441, which was attended by about 300 clergy and prominent Armenians, decided to return the catholicosate to Echmiadzin, its original location, away from the influences of the Roman Catholic Church. The assembly also elected Kirakos Virapetsi as catholicos, whose short tenure (1441–1443) was followed by the more able Grigor Jalalbekiants (1443–1465). The catholicosate of Sis retained its status as an independent see, the Great House of Cilicia (Metsi Tann Kilikio), as did the catholicosate of Aghtamar, which had been established in the twelfth century in opposition to the catholicosate of Echmiadzin; however, the Armenian ecclesiastical center had decidedly gravitated to Echmiadzin.[5]

THE ARMENIAN CHURCH REVIVED

In the absence of an Armenian government amid the political turbulence, no Armenian ecclesiastical center felt confident in its status and jurisdiction, and leadership and institutional insecurities bred jealousies and hostilities between the catholicosal seats. Historian Dickran Kouymjian writes: "Corruption and laxity were evident among some clergy in all the ecclesiastical centers of the Armenian Church during the fifteenth and sixteenth centuries. Considering the terror and destruction of the period, church leaders found it necessary once and for all to adjust themselves to dependency on non-Christian rulers."[6] Yet despite the difficulties, the church remained the only viable institution in Armenian communities. To prevent expropriation by Muslims, the nobility often found it prudent to donate properties to the church, which in turn strengthened the church. Its monasteries managed various educational complexes (e.g., the Tatev monastery in Siunik) and produced manuscripts and miniature paintings. Among the leading artists were Khachatur of Khizan in the fifteenth century and Hakob Jughayetsi (of Julfa) of the seventeenth century.[7]

The last two decades of the fourteenth century had witnessed rapid Ottoman territorial expansion from the reigns of Murad I (r. 1360–1389) and Bayazid I (r. 1389–1402) to the reign of Sultan Mehmed II the Conqueror (r. 1444–1446, 1451–1481). The Ottomans gained control over the port cities on the Black and the Mediterranean seas, and in 1453 they defeated the

Byzantine military and captured the much coveted city of Constantinople, the Byzantine capital. The Ottoman Sultans established a Muslim state in what had been the eastern frontiers of the old Roman Empire.[8]

Sultan Mehmed II resettled Armenian merchants and craftsmen from different parts of his expanding empire to Constantinople to revive the city's economy. By the end of the fifteenth century, there were an estimated 1,000 Armenian households in Constantinople, and political upheavals in the East led to the migration of thousands more to the city and its vicinity. In the meantime, according to traditional accounts, Mehmed is said to have set the foundation for what emerged as the *millet* system of religious communities, appointing in 1461 Bishop Hovakim of Bursa as patriarch for all Armenian subjects. The patriarchate of Constantinople represented the Armenian millet before the Ottoman government and assumed various administrative responsibilities in the Armenian communities, while the authority of the catholicosate of Cilicia diminished.[9]

Meanwhile, Armenia became a battleground between the Ottomans and the emerging Safavid empire (1502–1783) in Iran, as they struggled for regional supremacy, and their constant campaigns and countercampaigns led to westward migration by Armenians. The Ottoman Sultans Selim I (r. 1512–1520) and Suleyman I the Magnificent (r. 1520–1566) expanded the empire by land and sea. Selim defeated the Mamluk sultanate of Egypt and annexed parts of the Middle East (e.g., Cilicia, Syria, Jerusalem, Egypt). In addition to his conquests in Europe, Suleyman seized the entire area from Bitlis to Baghdad and Tabriz from the Safavids. The Ottoman army consolidated power across historic Armenian lands and beyond—from Sivas to Erzerum to Alashkert, Diarbekir, Van, Mosul, and Marash. The need for wider commercial relations with the West led, in 1563, to a treaty between Francis I of France and Suleyman I, which introduced the capitulations as a concession granting all Christian powers the right to conduct their commercial affairs in the Ottoman empire according to the laws of their home countries. This represented the earliest major concession by the Ottomans to the European powers. More than a century later, the Peace of Karlowitz (January 26, 1699), which concluded the war between the "Holy Alliance" led by the Pope against Turkey, also abolished tributes Europeans paid to the Ottoman Sultan.[10]

The Safavids had expanded their domain across the Caucasus and established their rule over the historic lands of Persian Armenia during the marzpanata period. Mired in internal strife, however, they failed to defend the territories under their control beyond Tabriz. Upon securing the throne, Sultan Murad III (r. 1574–1595) launched a series of military campaigns that lasted until 1590. The Ottoman army, about 200,000 strong, advanced to capture Tabriz in 1585. The new Safavid leader, Shah Abbas (r. 1588–1629), felt compelled to sign a peace treaty with Murad in 1590, surrendering Tabriz, Shirvan, and parts of eastern Armenia, Azerbaijan, and Georgia.

Soon thereafter, however, Shah Abbas moved his army northward deep into the Caucasus. While initially the Armenians in Jugha (Julfa), Agulis, and Meghri celebrated his arrival as a liberating force from Ottoman domination, his troops destroyed the land and ordered thousands of Armenians to abandon their communities and to march to Persia. No more than one-fifth survived the march. The survivors settled in New Julfa in the southern region of the capital city of Isfahan, south of the Zangi-Rud River. The Treaty of Zuhab (1639), signed by Sultan Murad IV and Shah Safi I, granted to the Ottomans Iraq (including Baghdad and Mosul) and a large part of historic Armenia—the vast territory stretching through the Armenian Plateau and encompassing the region of Lake Van, Bayazid, Kars, and Ardahan, as its eastern border—while Persia controlled Tabriz, Shirvan, and Erevan. The treaty thus divided historic Armenia between Turkish Armenia and Persian Armenia.[11]

The political economy of empire-building and the military conquest of such vast territories necessitated effective institutional mechanisms for the administrative and economic integration of nomadic tribes and sedentary communities of various cultures and religions. Neither the economic nor the military situation seemed conducive to their smooth incorporation into the Ottoman system. While western mercantilism encouraged economic expansion and development of industries for the acquisition of wealth and power by the state, the Ottoman political and economic elites relied mostly on agricultural production. By the sixteenth century, European markets were increasingly relying on money economy, while their Ottoman counterparts continued to use bartering and credit. As a result, the Ottoman economy grew vulnerable to European financial penetration. As the central government struggled to defend its realm, as in the clashes across Armenian lands bordering with Persia, beginning in the 1580s the injection of vast quantities of silver coins into the Ottoman economy from the Americas and Europe caused the depreciation of Ottoman silver.[12] Moreover, the central government sold the provincial governorships and local offices to the highest bidder and employed imperial administrators and tax-farmers to collect taxes— a practice that made the burden and prevalence of the economic corruption and political instability doubly unbearable for the people. Once in power, governors imposed heavy taxes on their subjects to recover the capital expended to win the office.[13] Further, they raided the towns and villages to accumulate wealth and to pay their taxes to the central government. As raids and wars destroyed the land and economy, Armenians migrated westward to Constantinople and to European countries such as Poland.[14]

In the late sixteenth century the economy and commerce began to improve and contributed to rapid increases in population in the Ottoman empire and the Mediterranean basin.[15] Political stability and economic revival led to the emergence of a new class of merchants, with commercial ties with Europe, India, and Russia, and set the foundations for the Armenian *amira* (business barons) class and the *esnafs* (guilds) of the eighteenth- and nineteenth-century Ottoman economy. Their occupations included such crafts as goldsmiths, shoemakers, and tailors. The Armenian communities in the Lake Van basin (especially Van city, Bitlis, Arjesh, and Varag) grew economically and culturally vibrant.[16]

In Persian Armenia, the Safavids established the two provinces of Chukhur-i Sa'd, encompassing Erevan and Nakhijevan, and Karabagh, which included Zangezur (Siunik) and Ganja. Each region was placed under a governor-general (*beglarbegi*).[17] Shah Abbas granted the Armenians the freedom to develop their own commercial networks with the outside world, which facilitated the growth of a new group of wealthy and powerful Armenian families. Likewise, the Armenian churches, including Echmiadzin, became closely linked with outside trade and financial relations.[18] The emergence of a wealthy Armenian elite with close ties to the church resembled the old symbiotic relationship between the nakharar houses and the church centuries earlier.

Commercial expansion and economic reconstruction in both Ottoman and Persian Armenia also encouraged cultural revival, as evinced by the development of scriptorium and monasteries as the Surb Karapet monastery in Mush and elsewhere. Beginning in the seventeenth century, as a result of economic growth and migrations from the eastern parts of the Ottoman empire, Constantinople became one of the most important cities for Armenians; unlike some of the other major cities in the empire, however, no Armenian quarter developed in the capital.[19] Further, commercial relations with Europe, Persia, and China influenced Armenian art. The printing of Armenian books was a product of the close ties between finance and culture for merchant markets. The first Armenian book was printed in 1641 in New Julfa. In 1666 the Armenian Bible was produced in Amsterdam by the printer Oskan, and the first press in Armenia was established at Echmiadzin in 1771, financed by an Armenian merchant living in India.[20]

As the Persian Armenian economy expanded, Armenians gradually developed close ties with the Russian economic sphere of influence, encouraged particularly by the improved status of Armenian merchants in St. Petersburg and Moscow. Thus, by the time Russian military expansionist activities reached the Caspian Sea and the Caucasus in the seventeenth century, the Persian Armenian communities had economic and cultural ties with the Christian power to the north. The growing Armenian economic and cultural orientation toward Russia became particularly pronounced as Armenians found themselves divided between the two Muslim empires. Nothing demonstrated the sentiments of the Armenian elite favoring Russia better than the richly decorated Almazi Throne that Armenian merchants presented to Tsar Alexei Mikhailovich in 1660. In return, the tsar granted them the right to monopolize particular sectors (e.g., silk) of Persian commerce in Russia, constructed a port on the Volga River to facilitate commerce, and permitted the construction of churches as well as the recruitment of Armenians for the state bureaucracies.[21]

As Armenian communities prospered, both secular and religious leaders sought to revive the Armenian sense of "nationhood" and even thought of plans to liberate the nation from Muslim domination. The church played a leading role in nearly all such endeavors. The catholicosate of the Mother See at Echmiadzin, at the time within the Safavid domain, became directly involved in Armenian liberation affairs and cooperated with the Armenian *meliks* (local feudal landlords and leaders) of Karabagh and Zangezur. The meliks, secure in their mountain fortresses, had maintained a culture of local independence, which readily transformed into liberation movements under propitious circumstances. In the sixteenth century, Catholicoses Stepanos V Salmastetsi (1545–1567) and Mikayel I Sebastatsi (1567–1576) had made repeated attempts to secure the support of the Roman Catholic Church and European governments for the liberation cause. In 1547 Catholicos Stepanos had summoned community leaders to a secret conference at Echmiadzin to devise plans to protect Armenians against further persecution and physical attacks. The conferees proposed that the catholicos travel to Europe to petition for political support to liberate the Armenians from Turkish and Persian control. Armenian ecclesiastical leaders and commercial magnates in European capitals met with leaders of the major powers, including the conference held by Catholicos Stepanos with the German emperor Charles II. The Armenian Church even went as far as pretending to accept unity with the Roman papacy, the sine qua non for papal engagement in Armenian affairs, but to no avail.

More than a century later, in 1678, Catholicos Hakob Jughayetsi (1655–1680) summoned the Armenian meliks to a secret meeting at Echmiadzin with similar plans. In a letter to the catholicos, Pope Alexander VII had promised support for liberation on condition that Echmiadzin recognize the supremacy of the Roman Catholic Church. By this time, however, Echmiadzin-Rome relations, coupled with matters pertaining to the finances of and corruption in the Armenian Church, in addition to jurisdictional issues, had become the source of tensions within Echmiadzin as well as between the Mother See, the catholicosate at Sis, and the patriarchates of Constantinople and Jerusalem. Nevertheless, the participants at the secret meeting sent a delegation to Constantinople that included the young and idealistic Israel Ori, whose solicitations for

European support, like similar attempts earlier, produced promises but little policy.[23]

Political instability and the power struggles among the Afghans, Afshars, Qajars, and Zands led to the fall of the Safavid empire in 1722 and to the emergence of the Qajars, who governed Persia for the next two centuries.[24] The prolonged political upheaval also caused a large number of Armenians to migrate to Tiflis, Moscow, and St. Petersburg, and their petitions for national liberation coincided with growing Russian interest in the Caucasus. The tsarist government capitalized on such appeals to pursue its geopolitical objectives. Peter I the Great (r. 1689–1725), who proclaimed himself "Emperor of All Russia," had maintained good relations with the Armenian community in Russia, but his immediate purpose in the Caucasus was to create a united front with the local population against Ottoman and Persian presence in the area.[25] Peter I seized the opportunity presented by the collapse of the Safavid government to launch in 1722 his southern military campaign into the Caucasus. Although Peter the Great abandoned his troops in the Caucasus in 1735, the Russian military's engagement in the region encouraged local Armenian chieftains, such as Davit Bek, to press for independence. Not to be outdone, the Ottoman army also invaded Safavid lands in the region, and in 1724 their combined attacks led to the partition of Transcaucasia, whereby the Ottomans established control over Armenia and Russia gained lands on the Caspian Sea.[26]

Russian expansionist policy resumed under Catherine the Great (r. 1762–1796), whose drive to bring the Black Sea and the Balkans into the Russian sphere of influence provoked a war with Turkey in 1768 and culminated in the favorable Treaty of Kuchuk Kainarji (July 1774). Under the treaty, Russia gained territory on the Black Sea coast and access to the Mediterranean through the Straits of Dardanelles. Although the western powers—particularly Britain and France—briefly cooperated with Russia against the Ottomans, by the late eighteenth century such cooperation appeared less sustainable as European industrial and colonial interests collided with Russian objectives from the Balkans to the Middle East and to the Caucasus. After the Russo-Ottoman wars of 1768 to 1774, Catherine the Great encouraged Armenians of Crimea to settle in the area of Rostov-on-Don, located on the banks of the Don River about thirty miles from the Sea of Azov.[27] The early phases of the "Great Game," which in the nineteenth century pitted the imperial powers against each other for power and prestige in the Caucasus and Central Asia, had begun.[28]

The Armenian community in Russia witnessed a period of economic and cultural revival under such prominent families as the Lazarians, who along with their counterparts in India (e.g., Joseph Emin [1726–1809]), continued to envision, and sought Russian protection for, an autonomous Armenia.[29] Two proposals were submitted for such a plan. The first, prepared by Archbishop Hovsep Arghutian, proposed the creation of an

Armenian kingdom with its capital at Vagharshapat. The king would be chosen by the Russian tsar and could be of Armenian or Russian origin; the Armenian king would possess the authority to maintain his own seal and mint his own currency. Armenia and Russia would sign commercial treaties, granting the former access to at least one port city on the Caspian Sea. The second proposal, drafted by Shahamir Shahamirian of India, proposed a republican form of government rather than a kingdom. Following the British system, it would be led by a prime minister and an "Armenian House" as the parliament. The Armenian government would maintain a permanent embassy at St. Petersburg. In matters of defense, Armenia and Russia would sign a mutual security pact, whereby Russia would maintain a force of 6,000 soldiers in Armenia, subject to gradual withdrawal over a twenty-year period. In times of war, Armenia would supply 6,000 soldiers to Russia. Russian merchants would have free access to Armenian markets for a fee comparable to taxes paid by local merchants. These two proposals reflected the two major intellectual currents among Armenians at the time. Arghutian's proposal represented the religious and feudal institutions and tradition and would revive the Armenian monarchy and the powers of the nakharar houses. Shahamirian's proposal, clearly influenced by the presence of the British East India Company in India, expressed the sentiments of the emerging bourgeois classes, who, as in Britain, would check the economic and political power of the aristocratic class and the monarchy through political liberalization and parliamentary democracy.[30] Would the Russian government be favorably inclined?

Beginning in April 1783, the Russian military formulated plans for a campaign across the Caucasus, which, with further discussions with the Georgians, culminated in the Treaty of Georgievsk (July 24, 1783), thereby establishing Russian protectorate over eastern Georgia. Catherine the Great made preparations for further military expeditions across the Caucasus, but in 1784, having signed a treaty with the Ottomans regarding the security of the Crimea, she reversed her decision, although plans for a Russian protectorate over an autonomous Armenia were not shelved. Although during the Russo-Turkish war of 1787-1792 Catherine the Great refused to become too heavily involved in the Caucasus, she escalated Russian involvement soon thereafter, certainly by 1795. The Russian and Persian empires now preferred peace and stability in the Caucasus so as to widen their trade relations. The growing French influence in Isfahan, however, foiled these plans, as Paris perceived Russo-Persian friendly relations as detrimental to its interests in the region and insisted on Ottoman-Persian cooperation against Russia. The death of Ali-Murat Khan, the chief Persian negotiator representing the Qajar leader Agha Mohammad Khan (r. 1743–1796), provided an opportunity for the opposition to terminate the Russo-Persian negotiations. In 1794 the Persian military launched a campaign to reinstate control over Tiflis and Eastern Armenia, which it accomplished in 1796, after massacres and much destruction (including the death of the famed Armenian troubadour Sayat Nova, 1762–1796).[31] The triangular Russo-Persian-Ottoman competition over the Caucasus increasingly involved the European powers, most notably Britain and France, each with its own imperial ambitions but with the common geostrategic objective of preventing any of the three powers from becoming too powerful in the region. In December 1800, Tsar Paul (r. 1796–1801) declared Georgia's annexation to the Russian empire, and in September 1801 Tsar Alexander I proclaimed direct incorporation of Georgia and territories in northern Armenia (e.g., Lori) into the Russian domain with plans to annex Erevan and Ganja. The Persian army, now firmly under Qajar rule, and with British and French military and economic support, retaliated, escalating the conflict into the Russo-Persian War (1804–1813). The local Armenians sided with the Russians as their liberators from Persian rule, and in May-July 1804 the Russian army under General Pavel Tsitsianov, commander of the Caucasus, captured Gumri and Erevan. Unable to defend the area, the Persian troops under Ibrahim Khan of Karabagh surrendered in the spring of 1805. The Russians were in control of Karabagh and Ganja when war with the Ottoman empire, on the one hand, and Napoleon's campaign across Europe, on the other, again weakened their resolve in the Caucasus. Responding to the Russian threat, France and Persia signed the Finkenstein treaty on May 4, 1807, whereby France promised military support to Persia against Russia, and Persia guaranteed free passage for French troops through its land to India in case of a war with England.[32]

The Russians had not gained total control over the conquered lands in the Caucasus, and there followed a series of treaties solidifying the boundaries among the three empires, with profound implications for the future of their Armenian inhabitants. The Treaty of Bucharest in 1812 concluded the Russo-Turkish war that had begun in 1806, establishing the Akhurian River as their border. The Persians, mired in their own military conflicts with Russia and faced with the possibility of further territorial losses, signed the Treaty of Gulistan in October 1813, which forced it to surrender, with the exception of Erevan and Nakhijevan, the area north of the Arax and Kura rivers, including Georgia, Karabagh, and Zangezur.[33] Unwilling to accept the defeat sustained under the treaty, immediately after the death of Tsar Alexander I and the Decembrist rebellion in 1825, the Persian crown Prince Abbas Mirza attacked Karabagh in 1826, instigating another Russo-Persian War (1826–1828), which let to yet another Persian defeat. Russia seized Sardarabad, Nakhijevan, Erevan, and Tabriz by October 1827, forcing Persia to negotiate a peace treaty. The Treaty of Turkmenchai (a village between Tabriz and Tehran), signed in February 1828, granted the khanates of Erevan and Nakhichevan to Russia, thereby establishing Russian control over all of Eastern Armenia with the new boundary set at the Arax River.[34]

Russian military successes in the Caucasus strengthened the empire's position in relations with the Ottoman empire. Ottoman territorial losses were symptomatic of its domestic economic decline, which had serious ramifications for its military capabilities. Western powers began to view the empire as the "Sick Man of Europe," and predictions of its immediate demise gave rise to the Eastern Question. Considering its territorial losses and inability to contain Russian imperial expansion across the Caucasus and the Balkans and potentially to the Mediterranean Sea and the Middle East, what regional configuration of power would replace the decrepit Muslim empire? And in that context, what could be expected of the role and aspirations of the various nationalities within the Ottoman empire? As discussed below, the increasingly volatile geopolitical situation in the empire heightened the urgency and unpredictability concerning such "questions" as the Armenian Question.[35] By the late nineteenth century, the Armenian Question emerged as an international issue, as a subcomponent of the Eastern Question.

THE EMERGENCE OF THE ARMENIAN QUESTION

The Treaty of Andrianople (1829) concluded the Russo-Turkish War of 1828–1829, granting Poti, Akhalkalak, and Akhaltsik to Russia, as well as the right to free passage through the Straits of Dardanelles and free access for Russian merchants to Ottoman markets. Article 13 of the treaty provided for the free exchange of population. Mass migration to Russian Armenia, involving 7,668 families, began in October 1829; nearly 14,047 families (between 90,000 and 100,000 individuals) moved to Russian Armenia. Under the treaty, Turkey also recognized the independence of Greece and the autonomous status of a member of regions, including Montenegro, Moldavia, and Serbia. British and French diplomatic pressure, however, forced Russia to return to Turkey the Western Armenian territories gained during the war (Kars, Ardahan, Bayazid, Erzerum, and their surrounding regions).[36] The geopolitical dynamics unfolding soon thereafter indicated that the Armenian Question had already become politicized at the international level.

In consolidating power over Armenia, Russia granted the status of the Armianskaia Oblast' (Haykakan Marz) to Erevan and Nakhijevan as an "autonomous" Armenian province between 1828 and 1840. As the Russian government pursued broader geopolitical objectives, it tightened its control over the ostensibly "autonomous" Armenian province. In March 1836, Tsar Nicholas I instituted the *Polozhenie* (statute), which restricted the activities of the Armenian Church in political matters and required that the catholicosate at Echmiadzin conduct its relations with the outside world through the Russian ministry of foreign affairs. With respect to the election of the catholicos, the government required that Armenians submit the names of two candidates to the tsar for his ultimate vote. In return, it granted certain privileges to the church, including inter alia freedom of worship, tax exemption, and local autonomy under the primacy of Echmiadzin. Russian authorities greatly appreciated the role of the church in Armenian community life and sought to utilize its influence to promote and protect Russian interests in the region.[37] Armenians in and outside Russian Armenia protested Russian control over the church as violating Armenian traditions; for instance, in 1840 Armenians in India petitioned Tsar Nicholas I to repeal the restrictions imposed on the church.[38]

Despite the political difficulties, Armenia experienced rapid development. Armenian economic growth and prosperity enhanced the loyalty of the business classes to the Russian empire. The emerging Armenian intelligentsia, influenced by various intellectual movements in Europe and Russia, became active in various aspects of Armenian community life. Those who were more radical challenged the Armenian traditional institutions (especially the church), customary practices, and power structures, and advocated transformation of Armenian culture along the lines of the European Enlightenment. Conservatives stressed the importance of traditional institutions in strengthening the communities and in revitalizing centuries-old traditions and culture. Both intellectual currents, however, sought the same ultimate objective: to revive Armenian national identity as an expression of their communities across the dispersion from the Caucasus to Constantinople and to Europe. Hence the proliferation of Armenian publications—for example, *Kovkas* (Caucasus), *Hiusisapail* (Northern Lights), *Meghu Hayastani* (Bee of Armenia), and *Masiats Aghavni* (Dove of Ararat)—debating the advantages and disadvantages of *grabar* (classical Armenian) and *ashkharabar* (vernacular), of religion and secularization, of tradition and modernization. Unlike the European experiences of the Enlightenment and modernization that required construction of new ideological edifices on more stable cultural foundations, the re-formation[39] of Armenian national identity necessitated the far more laborious task of construction or reconstruction of community identity, language, and culture destroyed by centuries of foreign invasions. The intellectual struggle to redefine and reformulate that national identity by the 1870s and 1880s shaped the modern Armenian worldview, the new Armenian Weltanschauung, with its derivative philosophical ideals and political ideologies. These advances in the Armenian experience, however, lacked the strong institutional and cultural bases necessary for sustainable *national* development commonly found among the attributes of the modern nation-state. The absence of an Armenian nation-state rendered the Armenian identity vulnerable to foreign subversion and even to extinction—a process already set in motion in Western Armenia.

THE MALIGNED REFORMS

Since the emergence of the Ottoman empire, over the years many Armenians had adopted the Turkish language, culture, and Islam to escape their second-class status within the ethno-religious administrative system, the *Ermeni millet* (or Armenian religious community).[40] Those who chose to maintain their national identity were required to pay heavy taxes, comply with orders regarding the *devshirme* (the forced collection of Christian children to serve in the Ottoman janissary corps),[41] and submit to numerous restrictions under imperial and religious laws. Added to the burdens of foreign imperial rule were the recurring attacks on Armenian towns and villages by Kurdish and Circassian bands. By the nineteenth century, widespread discontent with the "backwardness" of Ottoman society, rampant corruption, and chronic maladministration disrupted and paralyzed the economy and polity. Matters were made worse by pressures of European colonialism, as each empire arrogated to itself the right to "civilize" the Ottoman empire and the rest of the world, and as each pursued its geoeconomic objectives irrespective of their consequences for the local populations. The European powers viewed reforms toward political and economic liberalization as an integral component of political stability in the Ottoman empire. The Ottoman government at all levels frequently resorted to repressive measures to halt and reverse the process of imperial decline.

Sultan Abdul Mejid (r. 1839–1861), responding to domestic and European pressures for structural reforms, introduced the Tanzimat reforms in the Ottoman empire, which consisted of the Hatt-i Sherif of Gulhane (Noble Rescript of the Rose Chamber) declared on November 3, 1839, followed by the Hatt-i Humayun (Imperial Rescript) on February 18, 1856, in the aftermath of the Crimean War. Under these reforms, the sultan promised equality for all his subjects (Muslims and non-Muslims regardless of sect and creed) before the law, security of property and of life, elimination of arbitrary taxation, and modernization of the legal and administrative institutions. His Muslim subjects, however, viewed the principle of equality before the law for non-Muslims as a violation of "Islamic law and tradition."[42] Muslims continued to view the Ermeni millet with great suspicion, and their hostility toward the Armenians increased exponentially as society became polarized.[43] Further, these reforms required long-term commitment on the part of the sultan and the Ottoman state bureaucracies in general for effective institutionalization and implementation. Yet neither the political nor the economic conditions proved conducive for such a development. The sultan himself represented the epitome of arbitrary rule characteristic of "oriental despotic" sovereigns.[44]

As part of the promised reforms, the Sublime Porte (*Bab Ali*, the seat of the Ottoman government) in 1847 ratified the establishment of the Armenian

Spiritual Council (religious) and the Supreme Council (laymen), both under the directorship of the patriarchate at Constantinople. In 1863 the government also issued an imperial iradé (decree) ratifying the Armenian National Constitution.[45] The Constitution introduced democratically oriented principles in the functions and powers of Armenian institutions (e.g., the church) and social relations (e.g., *amira-esnaf* relations). The constitution provided for the creation of the General Assembly, consisting of ecclesiastical and lay members. The amira class, comprised of the wealthiest and most influential Armenian families in the Ottoman capital and Smyrna, had opposed the constitution and considered the *esnafs* or trade guilds and demands for fundamental reforms as a direct threat to the privileged position they had come to enjoy. Issues such as *amira-esnaf* relations, however, and the steps taken to resolve their conflicts through structural liberalization—which within a more democratic environment would have been viewed as an exercise in "good governance"—remained peripheral to the more ominous tensions and bloodshed between Muslims and Armenians, as demonstrated in the Zeitun rebellion of 1862 and the subsequent massacres.[46] Similarly, the Ottoman Constitution of 1876, promulgated by Sultan Abdul-Hamid II (r. 1876–1908/09), provided for a democratic system predicated on wider public participation in the political process and guaranteed various civil and political freedoms. The Ottoman sultanate, however, with its despotic institutional traditions and abusive bureaucracies, could not accommodate or tolerate demands for civil and administrative reforms even if it aimed for modernization.[47]

His Armenian subjects, totaling about 2 million, were dispersed throughout the provinces, but were mostly concentrated in their historic land (in the provinces of Bitlis, Diarbekir, Erzerum, Kharpert, Sivas, and Van), and Cilicia. Political reforms, if implemented, would require the restructuring of the system throughout the provinces and, the sultan feared, would eventually jeopardize the unity of his empire. The Sublime Porte appeared determined, especially after the Crimean war (1854–1856), to reverse the course of imperial decline. The war, however, placed heavy burdens on the Ottoman treasury and accelerated British and French involvement in the empire's financial affairs through the Ottoman Bank and the Public Debt Administration. Rather than implement the promised reforms, the government reacted by imposing more repressive measures and intensified persecution of groups and movements it deemed a threat to its rule. By the 1880s the increasingly oppressive political environment, coupled with economic stagnation, stimulated antigovernment activities by various groups, particularly by young intellectuals, including Armenians, trained in European universities. Some Armenians also organized self-defense societies for protection against atrocities.[48]

The internal difficulties were compounded by deepening British and French colonial domination,[49] the escalation of geopolitical competition among the major powers, and the proliferation of western-influenced political and increasingly organized opposition challenging the sultan's sovereignty.[50] In 1878, using the Russo-Turkish war (1877–1878) as a pretext, Sultan Abdul-Hamid suspended the constitution indefinitely and ended the Tanzimat period. Confronted by the twin evils of imperial decline in foreign relations, on the one hand, and growing internal instability, on the other, he reacted with malicious zeal to eradicate opposition to his rule. During the Russo-Turkish war, Patriarch Nerses Varzhapetian of Constantinople encouraged Armenians to support the sultan, but some Armenians in the eastern provinces viewed the war as an opportunity for Russian intervention and protection from the destruction wrought upon them at the hands of the local Turkish and Kurdish tribes. Across the border, Armenian volunteers served in the Russian military. Russian forces, led by generals M.T. Loris-Melikov and Hovhannes I.I. Lazarev, captured Kars in November 1877, while General A.A. Gukasov took Bayazid and Alashkert and in January 1878 marched toward Erzerum. In the meantime, Russian forces advancing across the Balkans had reached Adrianople (Edirne). To prevent further Russian advances to Constantinople, the Sublime Porte agreed to a peace treaty. The Armenian patriarchate petitioned the tsarist government to include in the peace treaty a provision granting Armenians administrative reforms in the six provinces.[51]

The Treaty of San Stefano (March 3, 1878), which concluded the war, required Ottoman recognition of the independence of the Balkan states and granted Russia in addition to Batum the Armenian districts of Ardahan, Alashkert, Bayazid, and Kars. Significantly, Article 16 of the treaty provided that prior to the withdrawal of Russian forces, the Sublime Porte ameliorate, "without further delay," conditions in the Armenian provinces and protect them against Kurdish and Circassian attacks.[52] The European powers, most prominently Britain, viewed this treaty as a Russian imposition of pan-Slavic designs on the Balkans and the Ottoman empire and demanded a congress of major powers to revise the Russian scheme. Fearing the domestic consequences of yet another military engagement, Tsar Alexander II (r. 1855–1881) agreed. Three months after the signing of the San Stefano treaty, Russian representatives met with the European powers at Berlin under the auspices of German Chancellor Otto von Bismarck.[53]

The British successfully maneuvered the Berlin negotiations to deprive Russia of some of its territorial and political gains at San Stefano. The Treaty of Berlin returned the Armenian districts of Alashkert and Bayazid to the sultan and, although requiring that the Sublime Porte introduce necessary reforms to secure the safety of the Armenians, it repealed San

Stefano's stipulated direct linkage between reforms and Russian with-drawal. Instead, under Article 61, the European powers assumed collec-tive responsibility for the Ottoman reforms, with the proviso that the Sublime Porte report its efforts to that end. Armenian protests to this insulting trivialization of their cause proved futile.[54]

While the European powers conferred in Berlin to reformulate the San Stefano treaty, British and Ottoman representatives met in secret to arrange for the defense of Ottoman territories against future Russian encroachments. The Cyprus Convention, signed between London and Constantinople, provided for British occupation of Cyprus "to balance Russian acquisitions in the Caucasus," and added that if Russia insisted on occupying Ottoman lands in the future, Britain would provide the sul-tan the military support necessary to defend his domain. In turn, the sultan, in cooperation with the British government, would earnestly seek to implement the reforms for the protection of his Christian subjects.[55] The reversal at Berlin notwithstanding, Armenians in general remained hope-ful that the major powers would consider their cause.

THE EMERGENCE OF ARMENIAN NATIONALISM

The emergence of modern Armenian nationalism in the nineteenth century stemmed from a number of factors.[56] Eric Hobsbawm attributes the rise of national consciousness in various groups to their growing sense of a distinct cultural, linguistic, and, therefore, ethnic identity. He explains that as a result of the "multiplication of potential 'unhistorical nations,' ethnicity and language became the central, increasingly the decisive or even the only cri-teria of potential nationhood."[57] The development of modern Armenian nationalism in the nineteenth century in Turkish and Russian Armenia was no exception; it took place within the context of the emergence of influential bourgeoisies divided along ethnic (e.g., Arab, Kurdish) lines.[58] During the early part of the century, Armenian nationalism appeared in the form of cul-tural reawakening, although by the end of the century, it had evolved into armed revolutionary struggle in reaction to oppressive Ottoman rule. Armenian nationalism benefited enormously from the importation of European and Russian philosophies of nationalism and socialism. The Armenian cultural reawakening involved the reassertion of national iden-tity as distinct from neighboring cultures and, paradoxically, the integration of western principles and values espousing liberation, nation-building, and state-building.[59] The Mekhitarist Order, a Catholic order, represented one of the first steps toward the revival of Armenian culture. Among its members were Mekhitar Sebastatsi (1676–1749), founder of the order on the island of Saint Lazarus in Venice in 1717); Mikayel Chamchian (1738–1832) author of the classic *Hayots patmutiun* (History of Armenia); Father Ghevond Alishan (1820–1902), author of *Sisakan* (About Sis), *Hushikk Hayrenyats Hayots* (Memories of the Armenian Fatherland), *Hayastan haraj kan zlineln Hayastan* (Armenia before becoming Armenia), and the monumental *Hayapatum* (History of Armenia); Edvard Hurmuzian (poet and translator, 1799–1876); and Arsen Bagratuni (1790–1866), author of *Hayk diutsazn* (Hayk the Hero).[60] Mekhitar Sebastatsi, a religious leader, sought to revive the Armenian language and literature through the publication of the master-pieces in Armenian classical literature.[61] The movement was eventually led by a new generation of intellectuals, some of whom with training in European universities. They were heavily influenced by the European Enlightenment, various French and Russian revolutionary thoughts, and like their Russian counterparts, they were engaged in the struggles for self-definition and modernization as a nation and as individuals.[62] This "renais-sance generation," usually defined as the period between the 1850s and 1880s, advocated not only reforms within the Ottoman political system but also within Armenian institutions and society. The Armenian Church as the dominant institution, they argued, had for too long exercised monopoly over Armenian arts and letters, and its conservative nature, including its insistence on employing the *grabar* (classical) language, had prevented an Armenian enlightenment. The similarly conservative orientation of the Ottoman system merely reaffirmed the traditionalist proclivities of the Armenian Church, society, and customs. Armenian modernists emphasized liberalization and secularization of Armenian culture and endeavored to lead the transition from the classical to the vernacular Armenian language.[63]

A number of institutions served as the springboard for the Armenian enlightenment. The nineteenth century witnessed the founding of the Lazarian Academy (or Jemaran) in Moscow in 1815, the Martasirakan school in Calcutta in 1821, the Nersisian College in Tiflis in 1830, and the Gevorgian Jemaran in Echmiadzin in 1874, along with a score of other edu-cational institutions throughout Western (Turkish) and Eastern (Russian) Armenia. These institutions, especially the Lazarian and Nersisian colleges, worked closely to develop the vernacular Armenian language and became active in the translations of European works into Armenian as a way of dis-seminating the philosophies of the Renaissance and Enlightenment while promoting literacy and liberation across the Armenian communities.

The nineteenth century produced such intellectual giants as Khachatur Abovian (1805–1848), author of the monumental novel, *Verk Hayastani* (Wounds of Armenia); Mkrtich Peshiktashlian (playwright and poet, 1828–1868); Raffi (Hakob Melik-Hakobian, novelist, 1835–1888); Hovhannes Hisarian (writer, archaeologist, 1827–1916); Rafayel Patkanian (Kamar Katiba, poet, 1830–1892); Nahapet (Nahabed) Rusinian (linguist, 1819–1876); and Krikor Odian (Grigor Otian) (lawyer, 1834–1887). The last two were among

the authors of the Armenian National Constitution of 1863; Odian also participated in the formulation of the Ottoman Constitution of 1876. There were the
clergy as well: Nerses Ashtaraketsi (1770–1857), prelate of Tiflis (later catholicos at Echmiadzin, 1843–1857); Mkrtich Khrimian "Hayrik" (Father)
(1820–1907), patriarch of Constantinople and subsequently catholicos at
Echmiadzin, 1892–1907); one of Khrimian's prominent disciples, teacher and
priest Garegin Srvantsdiants (1840–1892); and Tlkatintsi (Hovhannes
Harutiunian, 1860–1915), whose literary works, similar to those of Khrimian's
and Srvantsdiants's, idealized Armenian provincial and village life.[64]

Cultural reawakening also included advances in physical sciences.
Armenian scientists had in general left their homeland because of the political
and economic conditions and sought education and training in foreign lands.
Among the leading scientists were Andreas E. Artsruni (1847–1898), Harutyun
Abelyants (1849–1921), and Hovhannes Adamyan (1879–1932). Educated at
the Nersisian College, Abelyants continued his training in chemistry at universities in Heidelberg and Zurich, where he also became a professor of chemistry. Adamyan developed a technology for color television and held patents in
Germany (1907) and Russia (1908).[65] Armenian scientists made advances in
cosmology as well. In the 1840s an observatory was built on the St. Lazarus
island in Venice, where Armenian scientists such as Khoren Sinanian studied
cosmic structures, planets, and Halley's comet. H. Parseghyan published the
Principles of Astrology and *Comets* in Constantinople in 1880 and 1885, respectively. These publications delved into such controversial issues as the transition from the Ptolemaic to the Copernican heliocentric view and, in the case of
Nazaret Taghavaryan (1862–1915), theories of Darwinism and evolutionism.
Taghavaryan was educated in Paris and founded the scientific periodical
Gitakan Sharzhum [Scientific Movement] in Constantinople in 1885.[66]

The repressive governments under Sultan Abdul Hamid and Tsar
Alexander III (r. 1881–1894), coupled with European diplomacy of decep-
tion at the Treaty of Berlin, caused gradual shifts in the philosophies of
Khrimian, Srvandztiants, Raffi, and Patkanian from Armenian nationalism
as a cultural reawakening to nationalism as an armed revolutionary movement. Armenian literary movements and cultural nationalism developed
into emancipatory and revolutionary nationalism. The transmutation of
the San Stefano treaty into the Berlin treaty proved a significant transition
in Armenian self-perception and strategic thinking for purposes of defense,
as the Ottoman government failed to introduce effective reforms. As
Turkish hostilities intensified, some Armenians responded by arming
themselves rather than continuing to rely on outside powers for protection.
Such groups included the Black Cross Society at Van (established in 1878)
and the Protectors of the Fatherland in Erzerum (1881). Organized political
parties espousing nationalist ideologies and revolutionary strategies
emerged in the 1880s: the Armenakan Party in 1885 in Van, the Hnchakian

(Bell) Revolutionary Party in 1887 in Geneva, and the Hay Heghapokhakan Dashnaktsutiun (Armenian Revolutionary Federation, ARF) in 1890 in Tiflis.[67] Despite their ideological differences and modus operandi, these parties, but most prominently the Dashnaktsutiun, cooperated with the Young Turks in opposition to Sultan Abdul Hamid and agreed on the common objective of protecting the physical security of their communities. A key contributing element in this transition was "the absence of a 'bourgeois' nationalism"; as a result, "a radical nationalism of the intelligentsia linked the future of all Armenians regardless of class or country in a common, sacrificial struggle."[68]

INTO THE CAULDRON OF NATIONALISMS

By the late nineteenth century, the explosive admixture of national struggles for liberal reforms and outright independence, first in the Balkans on the west and subsequently by some Armenians in historic Armenia in the east, as well as Turkish movements opposing Sultan Abdul Hamid, created a perilous environment of Turkish nationalist chauvinism, paranoia, and mutual hostilities. The Armenian nationalist movement was a part of the wider phenomenon of nationalisms, including Turkish and Arab, that had emerged throughout the Ottoman empire. The Ottoman government sought to eradicate such threats to the system and frequently imprisoned their leaders.

The government arrested Armenian community leaders and intellectuals suspected of conspiracies against the Sublime Porte. Government-sanctioned, organized and unorganized wholesale massacres began in the region of Sasun in 1894. The notorious Hamidiyé regiments, Kurdish troops armed and organized by Sultan Abdul Hamid, attacked Armenian towns, massacred thousands of inhabitants, and destroyed homes and lands. Some of the major massacres occurred at Sasun in August-September 1894; Trebizond, Urfa, and Erzerum in October 1895; and Diarbekir, Arabkir, Kharpert, and Kayseri in November 1895. Additional massacres took place during the second half of 1896. The massacres claimed more than 100,000 (and by some estimates about 300,000) Armenian lives before they ended in late 1896.[69] Sultan Abdul Hamid became known as the "Red Sultan."

By then conditions in Russian Armenia had deteriorated as well. The assassination of Tsar Alexander II by the Russian terrorist group "Will of the People" (Norodnaia Volia) in March 1881 ended decades of Russo-Armenian cooperation. Tsar Alexander III showed little tolerance for Armenian national aspirations in political and economic matters. In contrast to his predecessors but very similar to the Ottoman Sultan, he viewed his Armenian subjects as a threat to Russian unity and therefore insisted on uncompromising policies of "Russification" (obrusenie) through cultural assimilation and the institutionalization of Russian administration.[70] These objectives to some extent had been accomplished in practice since the incorporation of the Caucasus into the Russian empire in the early nineteenth century, but Alexander III particularly emphasized cultural (including linguistic) Russification so as to bring Armenian schools under direct Russian control. Russian Armenians, considering the tsar merely another Sultan Abdul Hamid in Russian garb, mobilized opposition against his rule through revolutionary movements.

Most Armenians in the Russian empire worked on the land; a relatively small number was engaged in commerce and various crafts and industries. By the end of the 1880s, agricultural production led to the development of key industries in the production of vodka, cognac, and wine. The advent of industrialization in the late nineteenth century in Russia and across the region created opportunities for economic development and modernization but also led to widespread economic inequalities and dislocation. The Armenian liberal intelligentsia class, influenced by the intellectual currents in Russia and beyond, became active in various aspects of Armenian community life. The more radicals challenged the Armenian traditional institutions (especially the church), customary practices, and structures of power, and advocated a fundamental transformation of Armenian culture to embrace modern (i.e., western) values. These intellectual movements sought to revive Armenian national identity according to their ideological principles and political posture from the Caucasus to Constantinople and to Europe. Their activities also led to the proliferation of Armenian daily and weekly newspapers, debating the advantages and disadvantages of religion and secularization, of tradition and modernization.[71] Although most of these papers had a short lifespan, they severely criticized the tsarist regime and Russian policy toward the Caucasus, reported daily on events transpiring in both empires, and drew parallels between the "Red Sultan" and the "Red Tsar."[72]

Beginning in July 1903, when Tsar Nicholas II (r. 1894–1917) confiscated Armenian church properties, Armenian-Russian relations proved a critical testing ground for the organizational mettle of the Hnchakian party and the Dashnaktsutiun (ARF), and a turning point in their political alignments, as they participated in various forms of anti-tsarist and anti-Russian activities.[73] Khrimian Hayrik (catholicos at Echmiadzin, 1892–1906) outright rejected the confiscation order. The Dashnaktsutiun and the other revolutionary organizations, which until then had criticized the Armenian Church as a conservative institution and for its opposition to revolutionary movements, supported the catholicosate and demanded the return of the church properties. In Ottoman and Russian Armenia, the Armenian Church had maintained a comfortable distance between itself and the emancipatory groups; however, after the confiscation of properties, the church, particularly under Khrimian's leadership, welcomed the activism of the revolutionary parties, especially by the Dashnaktsutiun, the leading Armenian party in the region.[74]

The Armenian revolutionary movement became closely associated with the general anti-tsarist rebellions against the Russian government during the "First Russian Revolution" of 1905.[75] Demonstrations, labor strikes, and violence spread throughout the Russian empire, including the Caucasus. Workers and peasants demanded better living conditions. Nascent revolutionary cells established underground presses, and mobilized the public against the tsarist regime. The tsarist government reacted by repressive campaigns against the revolutionaries, as in the cities of Lori and Alexandropol (Gumri) and in the neighboring regions, where Armenian peasants and workers continued their armed clashes with government troops.[76]

The tsarist policy of confiscation of the Armenian Church properties led to ideological and political realignments among the Armenian revolutionary movements and between them and the Armenian people. The 1905 revolution further crystallized their alignments. These two crises called upon the Armenian organizations that had participated in and led the nationalist movements in Turkish Armenia to protect the nation's interests in Russian Armenia. The most influential among the political organizations was the Dashnaktsutiun, while some members of the Hnchakian Party increasingly identified themselves with the Marxist-oriented Social Democrat and Social Revolutionaries (successors to the Norodnaia Volia) and subsequently with the Mensheviks and Bolsheviks. Internal divisions within both the Armenakan and Hnchakian parties by the closing days of the nineteenth century had weakened their organizations and led to the loss of popular support. The Armenakans had become closely associated with the political and economic interests of the upper classes, while the Hnchakians, albeit engaged in armed self-defense in certain areas, in general remained preoccupied with the theoretical and international dimensions of socialism. The Armenian masses, especially the peasants, viewed both parties as being too removed from their everyday concerns for physical safety and economic security. The Dashnaktsutiun, however, put a premium on active self-defense and became involved in international socialism only secondarily and certainly not as an adherent to orthodox "scientific socialism" à la Marx. Since its inception, the party maintained a pragmatic approach toward western imperialism and capitalism. The Dashnaktsutiun leaders were familiar with the works of past and contemporary leading radical intelligentsia, including Dmitrii I. Pisarev (1840–1868), Mikhail Bakunin (1817–1876), Louis-Auguste Blanqui (1805–1881), Jean Jaurès (1859–1914), Georgi Plekhanov (1856–1918), Rosa Luxemburg (1871–1919), Henri Van Kol (1852–1925), and Karl Kautsky (1854–1938).[77] Some of them had even commented on the Armenian question. For example, in October 1896, Rosa Luxemburg wrote in the *Sächsische Arbeiter-Zeitung* (German Social Democratic paper in Dresden) that the west had to support Armenians in their demands for liberation from the Turkish yoke as well as their aspirations for statehood.[78] In 1905, were the Armenian political parties in Turkish and Russian Armenia prepared for such challenges?

In 1905 Tsar Nicholas II took a number of steps to stabilize the situation in the Caucasus. He appointed the more Armenophile Count Illarion I. Vorontsov-Dashkov as viceroy of the Caucasus to reestablish law and order and, on August 1, 1905, returned the confiscated church properties.[79] The tsar also issued the October Manifesto (October 17, 1905) approving the creation of the Russian Duma.[80] Although the Duma, which included several liberal and radical Armenians, promised to be a representative body, the tsar showed little tolerance for radical and reformist movements in the institution. On June 3, 1907, he dissolved the Duma and subsequently introduced laws that favored greater representation for the wealthy classes. Most of the middle class supported the tsarist regime so long as it promised political and economic stability. Persecution of Armenian revolutionaries continued, however, in 1912, including, the imprisonment of many members of the Dashnaktsutiun, although after trials in 1912 some of them were released from prison.[81]

THE YOUNG TURK REVOLUTION

The political instability in the Russian empire that challenged the legitimacy of Tsar Nicholas II paralleled the crisis of political legitimacy in the Ottoman Empire that undermined the authority of Sultan Abdul Hamid II. By the early part of 1908, the sultan could no longer check opposition forces, and in July the Young Turk revolution forced him to reinstitute the Constitution of 1876 but forced him to abdicate the throne in 1909. The Young Turk government promised political and economic liberalization, a representative government based on free elections, freedom of religion, and equality among the millets. A democratically oriented leadership in Constantinople, Armenians hoped, could take necessary measures to ameliorate the conditions in the empire in general and in the Armenian provinces in particular. Armenians and foreign observers expected conditions to improve. Hopes for the new era proved ephemeral, however, as the extremist factions among the ranks of the Young Turk leadership pressed for a strong central government, one that would consolidate power and rectify the deficiencies in foreign relations and domestic priorities. The more radical, nationalist Turks within the movement feared that the implementation of political and administrative reforms could potentially contribute to imperial decline, the nationalist leadership within the Ittihad ve Terakki Jemiyeti (Committee of Union and Progress, CUP)—also referred to as Ittihadists—established a dictatorial regime and propagated the ideologies of pan-Turkism/pan-Turanism and military modernization to bolster the legitimacy of their rule. Ittihadist party ideologues such as Mehmed Ziya Gokalp (1876–1924), pan-Turkist author and member of the CUP; Yusuf Akchura (1876–1933), founder of the journal *Türk Yurdu* (Turkish Homeland); and Tekin Alp (1883–1961), pan-Turkist nationalist, disseminated publications urging the Turkish masses to envision a new Turkey exclusively for the Turks, a Turkey whose cultural ties with all Turkic peoples from Constantinople to Central Asia could revive the Golden Age of Osman.[82]

No sooner had the Young Turk revolution appeared to have succeeded removing Sultan Abdul Hamid than crises in the Balkans and wider military disasters challenged the legitimacy of the new government.[83] Less than a year after the revolution, in April 1909, as reactionary, counterrevolutionary forces attempted to recapture Constantinople, massacres broke out in the Cilician town of Adana and neighboring villages, leading to the death of approximately 20,000 Armenians.[84] In 1908, taking advantage of the revolutionary situation, Austria annexed Bosnia and Herzegovina, Bulgaria declared independence, and Crete declared its union with Greece. A succession of military disasters thereafter undermined the credibility of the Young Turk government. In September 1911 the successful Italian campaign to conquer Tripolitania (Libya) and the Balkan wars of 1912–1913 threatened to dissolve the empire, as Turkey lost its European territories except Adrianople, Scutari, and Janina.[85]

By 1913 the extremist faction of the Ittihadist leaders, finding further territorial losses intolerable, was prepared to take over the reins of power. On January 23, 1913, a military clique led by Ismail Enver launched a coup against the government of the more liberal political party Hurriyet ve Itilaf (Freedom and Association) and established a military regime that ruled the empire until its demise by the end of World War I. The military coup resulted in the murder of several leading government officials, including Minister of War Nazim Pasha, the grand vizier Mehmed Kiamil Pasha, and other members of his cabinet.[86] The repeated military disasters in the preceding decades, they believed, had exposed fundamental weaknesses in political leadership and military organization; therefore, as a first step to consolidating their dictatorial rule, the Ittihadists dismissed the officials associated with the sultan from their posts and appointed party loyalists. The Ittihadist regime thus became dominated by the ultranationalist triumvirate of Mehmed Talaat as the minister of interior, Ismail Enver as the minister of war, and Ahmed Jemal as the minister of marines and commander of the Fourth Army in Syria. Moreover, the pro-German faction led by Enver emphasized military modernization and invited a German military mission, headed by General Otto Liman von Sanders, which arrived at Constantinople in December 1913, to effectuate further improvements.[87] The convergence of the ideology and politics of pan-Turkism and militarism culminated in a national catastrophe of unprecedented proportions for the empire's Armenian subjects.

6

The Armenian Genocide

After years of neglect, beginning in 1913 the Russian government redirected its attention to the Armenian Question in order to exert a greater influence on the increasingly pro-German Ittihadist leadership in Constantinople. The rapidly escalating tensions among the European powers convinced Russian authorities of the urgency to engage in Ottoman affairs so as not to permit Britain, France, and especially Germany wider involvement in matters of Ottoman political economy. While the Turkish-German alliance solidified, Count Illarion I. Vorontsov-Dashkov, reportedly at the urging of Catholicos Gevorg V Surenyants (1911–1930) of the Mother See at Echmiadzin, advised Tsar Nicholas II to revive the Armenian Question and to improve relations with the Armenians. Foreign Minister Sergei Sazonov was accordingly instructed to promise the catholicos Russian support for reforms in the Ottoman Empire. These efforts led to the "Final Reform Plan" of February 8, 1914, which was signed between Russia and Turkey and supported by the western powers.[1] The plan provided for the creation of two large provinces, one comprised of the Trebizond, Sivas, and Erzerum *vilayets* (provinces) and the other consisting of the Van, Bitlis, Kharpert, and Diarbekir provinces. It also provided for the appointment of a European inspector-general for each province.[2] Grand Vizier Said Halim, elated by the conclusion of the negotiations, reportedly sacrificed two sheep and two donated by the Russian chargé d'affaires, Konstantin Gulkevich, to celebrate the "epoch-making event."[3] The reform act, Gulkevich declared, marked "the dawn of a new and happier era in the history of the Armenian people!"[4]

The Ottoman Armenians responded with mixed reactions to the reform plan. Although, as decades earlier, most welcomed such initiatives on the part of the major powers interested in their plight, many Armenian leaders viewed with great trepidation this ostensibly humanitarian engagement in Ottoman affairs on behalf of their nation.[5] In February 1914 Rostom (Stepan Zorian), a founding member of the Dashnaktsutiun, in a letter to Simon Vratsian, a prominent member of the party, expressed grave concerns regarding the Ittihadists' willingness to allow such a fundamental restructuring and the European powers and Russia serving as protectors of the Armenians. Rostom commented prophetically that the reform negotiations under way in Constantinople represented no more than diplomatic theatrics, which could be easily dismissed as irrelevant except for their deleterious consequences for the Armenian people as they could result in a new round of persecutions and massacres.[6] Nevertheless, in the middle of 1914, Major Nicolai Hoff of Norway assumed office as the inspector-general at Van, and Louis Westenenk of the Netherlands was expected to arrive at Erzerum soon thereafter.

Perhaps the Young Turk government signed the agreement under German pressure to buy time for certain policy considerations, but the fanatically nationalist Ittihadist regime would not long tolerate such a plan, although initially they concealed their resentment toward foreign intervention.[7] Jemal Pasha commented in his memoirs: "Just as it was our chief aim to annul the Capitulations . . ., so in the matter of Armenian reform we desired to release ourselves from the Agreement which Russian pressure had imposed upon us."[8] The Turkish government responded to the combined external and internal challenges by defining the Armenian people within the empire—for decades the beneficiaries of various cultural and commercial ties with foreign institutions—as the principal internal threat. Accordingly, the wartime policy of the Young Turk regime targeted the entire Armenian population.

If Armenians expected the Reform Act of February 8 to lead to administrative and economic reforms to ameliorate their condition, unfolding events soon disillusioned them. The outbreak of World War I certainly dashed all such hopes. On July 28 Austria, with German support, declared war on Serbia, setting in rapid motion the mobilization of forces across Europe. Germany declared war on Russia on August 1 and on France on August 3, followed by a declaration of war by Great Britain on Germany on August 4. On August 2 the Young Turk regime concluded a secret military alliance with Germany against the Entente Powers and commenced general mobilization for the war.[9]

The war provided the Young Turk government with the opportunity to augment the scope of its Turkification scheme from mere cultural conversion to the physical elimination of its Armenian subjects, although the latter were not the only victims. The Young Turks' nationalist and religious hostilities toward Christian subjects combined with the economic conditions in general and in the eastern provinces in particular rendered the situation extremely oppressive for the Armenians. When World War I broke out, the Turkish government and Turkish masses in general vented their collective outrage and nationalist chauvinism against the Armenians, who, the Turks were convinced, had become instruments of foreign subversion conspiring against the Ottoman government but who could not elicit European military support, as demonstrated time and again. The history of the British reaction to the San Stefano treaty and the Russian acquiescence in British demands to revise it at the Berlin conference, in addition to western indifference to the massacres since the 1890s, had amply demonstrated that the major powers directly involved in the regional geopolitical competition and diplomatic endeavors would show no particular concern about the security of the Armenians.[10]

The Young Turk regime introduced two policies related to the war that also prepared the grounds for the unfolding genocidal scheme: military conscription as mobilization for the war and the abrogation of the Capitulations. As the Turkish government commenced general mobilization for war in late July, the Dashnaktsutiun party convened its Eighth General Congress (July 23–August 2) in the city of Erzerum.[11] There the Ittihadist representatives, led by Behaeddin Shakir, the chief of the Teshkilat-i Mahsusa (Special Organization), sought guarantees from the Dashnaktsutiun that, if Turkey entered the war, the party would mobilize Armenians in the Caucasus to rebel against Russia and thereby facilitate Turkish advances across the Russian frontier.[12] The Dashnaktsutiun rejected this strategy, instead proposing that Turkey remain neutral. If the country opted for war, however, party leaders maintained, the Armenians in each empire would loyally serve their respective governments.[13] The Ittihadists found this response quite unsatisfactory,[14] for it implied that a political organization such as the Dashnaktsutiun, with close ties to Russian Armenians, could incite insubordination against the Young Turks at an opportune moment.

MASSACRES AND DEPORTATIONS

Zeitun and Erzerum experienced the initial phase of the physical attacks on the Armenian population. When the *seferberlik* (mobilization) commenced requiring registration for military service, local Armenian men, fearing wholesale attacks on their families, were reluctant to comply with government orders, although objectors to military service were threatened with death. In the regions of Zeitun, Ali Haidar Bey, the *mutessarif* (county governor) of Marash, began to mobilize the local Muslims against the Armenians, whom he hated. For nearly a month, the Muslims engaged in a campaign of pillage and destruction. On about August 31, 1914, Haidar Bey arrived at Zeitun with 600 troops to confer with Armenians there. Ostensibly concerned that the refusal by the Armenians in Zeitun to serve in the military could set a precedent for Armenians in the neighboring towns, the government imprisoned about 50 Armenian leaders.[15]

At the same time, the province of Erzerum witnessed increasing political repression and economic hardship. Local authorities in Erzerum city arrested two Armenian leaders, E. Aknuni (Khachatur Malumian) and Vahan Minakhorian; Aknuni was exiled to Constantinople, and Minakhorian to Samsun. Moreover, the commerce and economy of Erzerum plummeted into depression, as discriminatory business and taxation policies nearly paralyzed Armenian enterprises, while mounted irregular *chete* bands (comprised of criminals released from prisons) and Kurdish bands routinely attacked Armenian peasants. If the more superstitious among Armenians were convinced that the darkness brought on them for two minutes by the eclipse of the sun on August 21 foreshadowed a calamitous winter, they certainly could not have imagined the magnitude and gravity of the catastrophe awaiting them.[16] Because of the geostrategic significance of the plain of Erzerum, the Ottoman army dispatched a large contingent to the area to defend the frontier against a potential Russian invasion. Soon thereafter about 100,000 Turkish troops were stationed in the region of Erzerum. Additional Turkish military forces moved to Kharpert in preparation for transfer further east, while between 8,000 and 10,000 troops were assembled in Arjesh and the plain of Abagha north of Van. The burden of service and provisions fell mostly on the local Armenian peasants, and at the same time the government commenced search and seizure operations for weapons and army deserters in the Armenian communities. The release of criminals from prisons beginning in October for the express purpose of organizing and arming them only intensified the hostilities. In October and November, under the pretext of searching for weapons and capturing escapees from military service, Turkish soldiers and chete bands pillaged and plundered the villages near Erzerum city. Armenians suspected that the Turkish government required conscription into military service in order to render the Armenian towns and villages defenseless against such attacks.[17]

On September 10 the Young Turk regime formally notified all foreign embassies of its decision to abrogate the Capitulations on October 1.[18] A few days later the Sublime Porte closed the Dardanelles, abrogated the Capitulations on the specified day, entered the war in alliance with Germany on October 30, and issued a proclamation of *jihad* (holy war) on November 14 against all Christian infidels.[19] The unilateral abrogation of the Capitulations signified Turkish nationalist aspirations for independence from foreign intervention. Having disposed of the Capitulations, the Ittihadists also removed any legal pretensions on the part of foreign powers to intervene in the domestic affairs of the empire, a consideration all the more significant as deportations and massacres were in progress on the eastern frontier of the empire. The Young Turk triumvirate was prepared to eradicate the Armenian Question.

The conscription brought about 1.6 million able-bodied males to military service, leaving behind more than an estimated 1 million families without sources of labor and income and further exacerbating the country's economic crisis.[20] Inflation (in some cases as high as 50 percent), shortage of goods, lack of money, and decline of public confidence in the government's financial policy had already devastated the economy, with the intricate web of domestic and foreign banking arrangements and commercial investments further complicating the problems. Economic depression coupled with national fanaticism led to repressive measures against foreign institutions and investments. The government also terminated all communications with the outside world, except cipher telegrams for official use.[21] The Young Turk leadership, distrustful of Christians, decided to rely on Muslims for the war effort, although, at least according to one source, an estimated 150,000 Armenian soldiers were serving in the military by October.[22] Armenian men, first from 20 to 45 years of age and subsequently from 15 to 20 and 45 to 60, were drafted into military service. As the military mobilization for the war gained momentum, the government also mobilized chete bands to attack Armenian towns and villages.[23] Rather than allowing them to serve as soldiers, however, the Armenians were disarmed and used in labor battalions to build roads and to haul carts.[24]

In October 1914 the Turkish 37th Division had moved eastward to reinforce the Turkish army on the Caucasian front. Subsequent military offensives and counteroffensives by Russian and Turkish forces across the region heightened the physical vulnerability of the Armenian inhabitants. Russian military strategists believed that the Ottoman Third Army stationed in Erzerum and led by General Hasan Izzet Pasha would lack sufficient capability to launch an effective offensive against Kars and beyond. Izzet Pasha, for his part, also considered his army incapable of a significant offensive, but he also estimated that the Russian troops were not prepared to mount a sustainable defense.[25] His assessment appeared deceptively accurate, for after an initial advance toward Erzerum in mid-December 1914, the Russian army withdrew from the region. Turkish troops reacted by attacking the Armenians in a number of villages and forcing them out of their houses, as in Dzitogh, located about fifteen miles north of Erzerum.[26] Further, sporadic attacks against Armenians increased in frequency beginning in early November 1914 in Sivas province, as in the region of Shabin-Karahisar, and spread to Van, Bitlis, Diarbekir, and Kharpert. As the government prepared for further confrontations on the Russo-Turkish front, it issued an imperial rescript on December 16, 1914, that nullified the Reform Act of

February 8.[27] "We live on a volcano," commented the Danish missionary Maria Jacobsen in her diary.[28]

In Van city, local prominent Armenians, such as Aram Manukian (Sergei Hovhannisian, 1879–1919), one of the principal Dashnakist leaders there, sought to calm the public—Armenian and Turk alike—through negotiations with the governor. The futility of such efforts became apparent when, in November, the Armenians across the province, from Adiljavaz (Adiljevaz, Aljavaz) and Arjesh on the northern shores of Lake Van, to Gevash (Gavash) and Karjkan (Garjgan) on the southern shores, to the valley of Hayots Dzor south of Van city, and as far south as Shatakh, became the targets of escalating government repression, searches for weapons and for deserters, and official and unofficial extortions. The ensuing clashes between the Turkish military and the Armenians dissipated any hopes for peace and security.[29]

In early November the Turkish forces under Izzet Pasha stationed near the Arax River were ordered to move against the Russian army and were successful in their advance for most of the month. Despite the harsh weather in December, Minister of War Enver launched his Sarikamish campaign, a major offensive against Russia. Referred to as Napoleonlik (Little Napoleon) because of his grandiose schemes in imitation of the great strategist and emperor Napoleon Bonaparte, Enver led an army of about 95,000 troops against the Russian force of 65,000 troops on the Caucasus front. The Sarikamish battle was fought on December 29, 1914; after initial successes, Enver's military offensive ended in total disaster. The Turkish divisions were annihilated during the first week of January 1915, and by the middle of the month no more than 18,000 had survived. The Russian army figures totaled 16,000 killed and wounded. Enver's inadequate logistical preparation, the perilous conditions of winter, and Russian military strategy destroyed the Turkish forces. Enver returned to Constantinople having suffered a humiliating military defeat.[30]

Back in the capital, Enver praised the loyalty and bravery of the Ottoman Armenian soldiers during his failed campaign.[31] He intimated to Patriarch Zaven Der Yeghiayan that "had it not been for an unauthorized maneuver executed by a certain Sergeant Major Hovhannes, he would have been taken captive." Enver "promoted Hovhannes to the rank of Captain on the spot."[32] Enver attempted but failed to conceal the humiliating truth about his military fiasco at Sarikamish. Soon thereafter rumors spread that an opposition clique, most likely led by Jemal Pasha, conspired to remove him from power. Jemal was known for his opposition to Enver's close ties with the German military, and as the pro-German faction led by Enver consolidated power in the military, Jemal was in November 1914 appointed commander of the Ottoman Fourth Army centered at Damascus with the objective of removing the British from Egypt.[33]

On November 3, 1914, the British government gained total control over Egypt, and on November 4 it terminated Turkish sovereignty over the island of Cyprus, proclaiming it a "Crown colony," followed on December 17, 1914, by the abrogation of Turkish sovereignty in Egypt. The British replaced the pro-Ottoman khedive, Abbas Hilmi II, by Prince Hussein Kamil Pasha, Hilmi's uncle, and proclaimed him the new sultan of Egypt. British policy in the eastern Mediterranean clashed directly with Germany's eastern geopolitical designs, for, as the German ambassador in the Ottoman capital, Hans von Wangenheim, explained, while his government preferred to avoid Turkish conquest of Egyptian or Russian territories, "as that would make adjustment more difficult," Germany also sought to strengthen Turkey so as to prevent it from absorption into the Russian or English empires.[34]

Jemal's Egyptian campaign proved as disastrous as Enver's. In early November the British army launched an offensive against Turkish strongholds at the Persian Gulf and within a month advanced to control Basra. Losses on the battlefield in the Caucasus and Mesopotamia placed Jemal's Fourth Army under severe pressure to register a military success. His military campaign to conquer the Sinai Peninsula and the Suez Canal escalated during the second half of January 1915. By then, however, the British had deployed about 70,000 troops in Egypt against the advancing Turkish forces of 20,000. British and French surveillance aircraft detected their movements, and the British forces offered an insurmountable defense. Within weeks the Turkish army suffered humiliation in this offensive as well.[35]

Mismanagement and misfortunes on the battlefield jeopardized the political legitimacy of the Ittihadist triumvirate, who had justified their January 1913 military coup as saving the empire from further humiliation experienced in the Balkans. The Ittihadist leaders, now suspecting their own institutions and supporters, friends and foes alike, of collusion in conspiracies against their rule, unleashed their nationalist, fanatical outrage, immeasurably intensified by wartime hostilities toward the European powers, against the unarmed Armenians.[36] As the optimism in the early days of Turkey's entry into the war was replaced by military defeats in December 1914 and January 1915, hostilities toward Armenians escalated.[37]

Events unfolding across the eastern provinces of the Ottoman Empire gave Armenians cause for little hope for their physical safety. The Young Turk regime relied on anti-Christian propaganda in the form of jihad to mobilize the Turkish masses with fanatical nationalism and hostility toward the Armenian, Assyrian, and Greek communities. The Ittihadists were intensely scornful toward religion and religious leaders and institutions. As U.S. Ambassador Henry Morgenthau commented in his *Story*, "Practically all of them were atheists, with no more respect for

Mohammedanism than for Christianity, and with them the one motive was cold-blooded, calculating state policy."[38] Contrary to the conventional view that the Young Turks committed a genocide against the Armenians because the latter refused to convert to Islam, they merely used religion as an instrument of propaganda to mobilize the Muslim masses against the Armenians for political, territorial, and economic gains. The jihad was directed at the European powers and against the Armenians.[39] In Kharpert, for example, the local economy rested primarily on agricultural production, although several modern businesses, such as the Singer Sewing Machine Company, had been operating for years. The Singer factory operated nearly 150 machines before it closed its doors after its local Armenian agent was deported in July 1915. A significant proportion of businesses—merchants, carpenters, bankers, doctors, dentists, lawyers—were owned by Armenians, and it was estimated that as much as 95 percent of the deposits in the banks belonged to Armenians.[40] Like Sultan Abdul Hamid II before them, the Young Turk leaders viewed with profound suspicion the close relationship between western business and missionary communities and the Armenians, and they sought to terminate all such ties to prevent what they considered interference in internal affairs and threats to national sovereignty.

For the Young Turk leadership, the principles of national sovereignty and territorial integrity were particularly sensitive in the aftermath of the ill-fated Sarikamish and Sinai campaigns, which had heightened their vulnerability to a growing domestic political opposition.[41] In fact, the triumvirate of Enver, Talaat, and Jemal began to suffer from a crisis of political legitimacy, as fear of failure, national humiliation, and even physical attacks created an acute sense of political and personal insecurity. Paranoid delusions of imagined attacks from all quarters were further exacerbated by the end of January 1915 by rumors of conspiracies to oust them from power. For example, rumors spread of a plan prepared under the leadership of Prince Sabaeddin in Paris and Athens against the regime.[42] Determined to remain in power and further consolidate power, the Ittihadists accelerated their attacks on Armenians, whom they viewed as a potential source for a coup. Armenian political organizations, the Ittihadists reasoned, had colluded with them to overthrow the despised Sultan Abdul Hamid, and there could be no assurances that the same Armenian organizations would not now conspire with new opposition groups against them. Beginning in February 1915, the Young Turks ordered the removal of all Armenian officials in Constantinople from their government posts, followed by the closing of *Azatamart*, the main Dashnaktsutiun newspaper in the capital.[43]

During a conference on February 14 at the Nuri Osmaniye headquarters in Constantinople, the Committee of Union and Progress (CUP)

Central Committee decided to shoulder the responsibility of "freeing the fatherland of the aspirations of this cursed race" and to put an end to the Armenian Question during the war.[44] The CUP leaders in attendance included Talaat, Enver, the famous poet and party ideologue Ziya Gokalp, Minister of Trade Mehmed Javid, Dr. Behaeddin Shakir, Minister of Education Midhad Shukri, Dr. Mehmed Nazim, and Hussein Jahid (editor of the CUP organ *Tanin*). The CUP wished to create a brighter future for the Turkish nation and accordingly granted the government wide authority to eliminate all Armenians living in Turkey.[45] The Ittihadist regime thus responded to the combined forces of real and imagined external and internal threats by defining the Armenian people within the empire as the principal internal threat and by declaring total war against the Armenians. It ordered the removal of the entire Armenian population, ostensibly as a matter of military security.

WAR AND GENOCIDE

By the end of January 1915, the Turkish military had commenced attacks on Armenians in the Turkish-Russian-Persian frontiers near Lake Urmia and the Zeitun-Marash-Aintab region in eastern Cilicia. Since September of 1914, the Turkish and Russian military campaigns had created thousands of refugees and led to the massacre of Armenians by the Turkish troops and local Turks and Kurds in several towns across the Caucasus region and stretching to Lake Urmia. In one instance, local Turks and Kurds led by Khan Simko viewed a Russian evacuation from the region of Urmia as a sign of weakness and ambushed the Armenian, Nestorian, and Persian refugees marching from the town of Urmia to Dilman and Tabriz inside Persia. Russian General Chernozubov dispatched General Tovmas Nazarbekov (Nazarbekian) to take control of Khoy, Dilman, and Kotur, while Chernozubov himself, ordered by General Yudenich to reassert Russian command in the area, advanced from Julfa to Tabriz and occupied the city.[46]

The eastern region of Cilicia had already become mired in political and military crises. Decades of official and unofficial persecution of Armenians there had led them to mistrust government officialdom and Turks in general. It was not surprising therefore that at the outbreak of the war, most Armenians in the region hoped for an Allied victory so as to secure a degree of autonomy.[47] The Turkish government, for its part, suspected Allied military engagements in the region, such as a bombardment by a French warship off the Gulf of Alexandretta in early January 1915, which heavily damaged the railway in the area, as providing an opportunity for Armenian collusion with the invading armies. The authorities arrested several hundred Armenians in Dort Yol and Hasan Beyli and forced them to rebuild the railway. The government subsequently ordered the arrest of the prominent Armenians in Dort Yol and transferred them to Adana for trial. On February 14 armed forces surrounded Dort Yol and demanded the surrender of all Armenian men over the age of twelve. Nearly 1,600 Armenian men were gathered and forced to march to Entili (Intili), where they were ordered to labor and were subjected to brutalities by the gendarmes; subsequently, most were murdered. The small numbers of survivors were permitted to return to Dort Yol. Upon their return, however, they and their families were deported to Aleppo and thence to Hama or Ras ul-Ain. After this group, the entire Armenian population of Dort Yol, totaling about 20,000 persons, was soon deported to Aleppo.[48]

Meanwhile, General Fakri Pasha and *kaimakam* (district governor) Husein Husni led 3,000 soldiers into Zeitun to thwart any rebellious activities against government orders to mobilize.[49] Government oppression in Zeitun intensified under the pretext of suppressing Armenian revolutionaries. Pierre Briquet, serving on the staff of St. Paul's Institute of Tarsus, noted: "It is obvious that the Government are trying to get a case against the Zeitounlis, so as to be able to exterminate them at their pleasure and yet justify themselves in the eyes of the world."[50] In late February, the county governor of Marash, Mustafa Ahmed Mumtaz, successor of Ali Haidar Bey, entered Zeitun with between 2,000 and 3,000 troops and arrested Armenian political and religious leaders, intellectuals, and members of the wealthier classes. Minister of War Enver warned that Armenian violation of the law and killing of any Muslim would instigate massacres. As noted earlier, some Armenians in Zeitun, fearing massacres, had armed themselves, and during skirmishes from April 4 to April 8, about 300 Armenian leaders were imprisoned in Zeitun and Marash and deported. Mass deportations from Zeitun also began during the week of April 4; within the next three weeks nearly 20,000 Armenians were deported from the area. Divided into two caravans, one was deported westward to Sultaniye in the Anatolian desert and the other southward to Deir el-Zor in the Syrian desert. By May between 20,000 and 30,000 Turkish soldiers had been stationed in the region of Zeitun. The fighting continued in the nearby mountains, while the city was emptied of its Armenian population. Soon thousands of Muslim *muhajirs* (refugees) from the Balkans—who after the Balkan wars of 1912–1913 had been transported to Cilicia—occupied the houses owned but now evacuated by Armenians.[51]

Armenian political and religious leaders appealed to the authorities to alleviate the dangerous situation. In March 1915 Catholicos Sahak Khapayan (Sahag Khabayan) of the Great House of Cilicia at Sis appealed to Jemal Pasha to provide for the physical safety of the Armenian deserters. Jemal replied that those loyal to the government would be guaranteed protection and that only the deserters would be subject to government measures. The catholicos also expressed his apprehensions about the conditions in Zeitun in a letter to Jelal Bey, the governor of Aleppo vilayet. Despite such appeals, however, under the pretext of searching for arms, the authorities arrested some of the notable Armenians, while Turks and Kurds raided and plundered the Armenian communities, razed their houses to the ground, and killed the inhabitants.[52]

By the middle of April, as the scope of arrests widened exponentially and the pace accelerated, Catholicos Gevorg V, the supreme patriarch of the Armenian Apostolic Church at the Holy See of Echmiadzin, appealed to foreign powers to use their good offices with Constantinople to cease the persecutions.[53] On April 23 a group of Armenian leaders in Constantinople, including members of the Ottoman parliament Krikor Zohrab and Vartkes (Hovhannes Serengulian), met at the Armenian patriarchate and decided to convey to the Sublime Porte their concerns regarding the gravity of the situation.[54]

The following day, on April 24, in response to the Allied campaign at Gallipoli, soldiers were stationed throughout Constantinople. During the night of April 24–25, the government arrested and exiled more than 200 Armenian community leaders, followed by an additional 600 Armenians immediately thereafter. Most were sent to the predominantly Muslim town of Ayash west of Angora city, others to Changri, located in Kastamuni province and between the cities of Angora and Kastamuni, and farther east to Chorum in northern Angora province. The government's campaigns against the Armenians continued unabated: within weeks, for example, 600 were arrested and deported in Erzerum, 500 in Sivas, 100 in Izmid, 80 in Adabazar, 50 in Shabin-Karahisar, 40 in Banderma, and 20 in Diarbekir.[55] Whether the Allied campaign at Gallipoli instigated the wholesale arrests of the Armenians in Constantinople is subject to debate,[56] but Minister of War Enver justified these measures on grounds that Armenian revolutionaries and Russian Armenians had attacked government officials and buildings in Van. The fact that Armenians sided with the Russians, Enver maintained, led to the security measures taken in Constantinople as Turkish authorities, fearful of a similar collusion by the Dashnaktsutiun in the capital, deported the city's leading Armenians.[57]

The Gallipoli campaign, which began on March 18, 1915, as Allied heavy artillery fired at the forts of Chanakkale and Hamidiye, provided one of the rare opportunities at this early stage in the war that perhaps, if successful, could have prevented further deportations and massacres. The Russian military command had proposed the Allied attack on the Dardanelles so as to diffuse the pressure in the Caucasus when Enver's forces were attacking the Russian front in December 1914. The British military leaders, who favored the removal of Turkey from the war, supported the plan, and the military defeats sustained by Turkey in the Caucasus, Cairo, and Mesopotamia strengthened British resolve.[58] On April 25 the Allied troops successfully landed at Helles and Anzac, but the operation led to disastrous results and withdrawal eight months later.[59] The Turkish military success assuaged the growing public opposition to the Turko-German alliance, fortified Enver's pro-German faction in the CUP, and enhanced the regime's political legitimacy. The Allied defeat strengthened the Turkish resolve to free themselves from the European powers. U.S. Ambassador Morgenthau commented: "New Turkey, freed from European tutelage, celebrated its national rebirth by murdering not far from a million of its own subjects."[60] Similarly, Lewis Einstein, then serving as a special agent at the U.S. embassy in Constantinople, noted that no sooner had the Turks regained their confidence at the Dardanelles than they seized the "opportunity to destroy the Armenians, who were the real victims of the naval failure."[61]

In the meantime, the anti-Armenian propaganda campaign by the Special Organization escalated, as did the mass arrests and deportations.[62] In May 1915 Mounted irregular chete bands, organized as instruments of government policy, assisted the state bureaucracies and the military in the implementation of the deportations and massacres. Despair and desperation enveloped the Armenian communities throughout the Ottoman empire. The Armenians had been referred to disdainfully as *giavurs* (infidels), but now they were accused of collaborating with the enemy.[63] In early May Halil Bey, Enver's uncle, led a Turkish force of 10,000 to oust the Russians from Urmia and Dilman in Persia, in the process destroying Armenian villages.[64] The Turkish army overran the Russians and forced them to withdraw from Dilman. Within a few days a successful counteroffensive by General Nazarbekov forced the Turkish army to retreat to Van. After a few weeks of losses, Halil withdrew to Bitlis. Meanwhile, the Russian forces registered successes in the Urmia-Dilman-Tabriz region and, led by General Trukhin, moved to Beghrikale near the northeastern tip of Lake Van and toward the Murat Su (Lower Euphrates) valley north of Lake Van. The campaign was coordinated with Nazarbekov, who advanced from Dilman to Bashkale, arriving on May 7. By then the Turkish troops and Kurdish irregulars had abandoned the northern shores of Lake Van. General Trukhin and the Armenian volunteer units, led by General Andranik (Ozanian), advanced toward Van and after a month of heavy fighting entered the city on May 19.[65] In June, the Russians captured Arjesh, Adiljevaz, and prepared to move to Malazkert. Trukhin and the Armenian units forced the withdrawal of Turkish soldiers from Shatakh and Mukus and moved to Sairt, from where Halil Bey and his remaining Turkish and Kurdish troops, arriving from the Van region, had reorganized themselves yet again and moved to Bitlis.[66] The Russian military campaigns across the region and occupation of Van enabled the Armenians to form a government, under the leadership of Aram Manukian, in that ancient city at the heart of historic Armenia. In the midst of the death and destruction unfolding in towns and villages across their ancient land, Armenians unfolded the Armenian flag above the Citadel of Van and expectations soared. The Russian military, as the downtrodden Armenians in the eastern provinces had always expected, had liberated them from Turkish rule.

Armenians hoped that the Russian military successes and support would strengthen their hand in European capitals. In May 1915 a secret document titled "The Petrograd Plan," submitted to the Russian embassies in London and Paris by Dr. Hakob Zavriev, assistant commissioner of the Russian government in Van, summarized the conditions for the creation of an autonomous Armenia within the Ottoman Empire after the war. The plan proposed, for example, that the borders of postwar Armenia include the six provinces of Van, Erzerum, Kharpert, Sivas, Bitlis, and Diarbekir as well as Cilicia with access to the Mediterranean. Also, Russia, England, and France would agree to provide protection for Armenia. Zavriev delivered a copy to Boghos Nubar, appointed by the catholicos in 1912 to head the Armenian National Delegation to secure European support for the Armenians in the Ottoman empire.[67] Boghos Nubar praised the plan since (unlike the Agreement of February 8, 1914) it proposed the unification of Cilicia with the six Armenian provinces.[68] Representatives of the Allied governments, however, thought proposals for such a plan too premature at this juncture; the task at hand was to ensure victory.

During the month of May thousands of Armenians were deported from various parts of Cilicia, including Sis, Hasan Beyli, Enzerli, Furnuz, and Tundajak. Some of them were sent to Konia, others to Aleppo. Thousands of refugees were scattered from Aleppo to the desert towns of Deir el-Zor, Rakka, and Baghdad.[69] In the meantime, massacres occurred in Baiburt, Khnus, Erzerum, and Mamakhatun (Derjan). In Baiburt, the Armenian prelate and several other community leaders were murdered, and the town was completely emptied of its Armenian population. By early June, an estimated 174,000 Armenians were made refugees, removed from their homes in various parts of their historic homeland. By then about 70,000 Armenians had been massacred.[70]

On May 24 the Allied Powers issued a joint declaration condemning the deportations and massacres committed by the Turkish government against the Armenians. The declaration warned that the Allied governments "will hold personally responsible [for] these crimes all members of the Ottoman government and those of their agents who are implicated in such massacres."[71] Rather than be deterred by such declarations, the Young Turk regime strongly protested the Allied action as violating Turkish national sovereignty, and in turn adopted, on May 29, the "Temporary Law of Deportation," which granted the military vast authority to implement the wholesale deportation of the Armenian people. In a memorandum to the grand vizier, Minister of Interior Talaat maintained that war conditions necessitated the deportations, as Armenians in general and their "rebellious elements" in particular posed a threat to the Ottoman army.[72] The central government subsequently formed the Commission on Abandoned Property for the purpose of confiscating properties left behind by the deported Armenians.[73]

Although the Allied declaration represented a strong condemnation of the Turkish atrocities against the Armenians, its purpose extended beyond humanitarian considerations. The Russian military successes on the eastern front in the Caucasus could be utilized for propaganda purposes to bolster British efforts to control the Dardanelles as well as to marshal domestic support for the war effort. Some Armenian leaders, however, undoubtedly encouraged by the favorable turn of events in Van, failed to assess the broader significance of the declaration. Boghos Nubar Pasha commented with satisfaction that the Allies "seriously" considered the Armenian cause and appeared "ready to offer us their complete cooperation."[74] He perhaps voiced the sentiments of most Armenians, but a more accurate assessment of the geopolitical and military situation and the political will of the Allied Powers would suggest otherwise. In a letter dated May 28, 1915, Levon Meguerditchian wrote to Boghos Nubar: "Unfortunately, at the moment, we cannot rely upon the Allies for their help, since they have focused their attention on Gallipoli."[75] Given the predominance of geopolitical expediency over humanitarian considerations, as evinced in the history of the western engagement in Ottoman affairs in general and in Armenian affairs in particular since the early nineteenth century, it was unrealistic to assume that the European powers would become so heavily involved in rendering assistance to the Armenians as to divert resources from the main theaters of war. The first dragoman of the French Embassy in Constantinople intimated to Boghos Nubar that the declaration of May 24 was like pouring oil on fire. In fact, Krikor Zohrab and Vartkes, both deputies to the Ottoman parliament, were arrested in Constantinople the following day and later sent to Diarbekir to be tried by the court martial. They were murdered on the road to their trial.[76]

Despite the Allies' joint declaration, on May 26 Armenians were arrested en masse in major cities and their properties were pillaged and plundered. For example, in Erzerum city, as the Armenian population prepared for deportation, Turkish and Kurdish mobs attacked Armenian shops and neighborhoods. In the meantime, Behaeddin Shakir visited

Erzerum to strengthen the ties between the local Special Organization and the central committee and ordered the full-scale formation of chete bands.[77] Turkish soldiers in Erzerum killed Sedrak Pastermajian, a vice president of the local branch of the Ottoman Bank and brother of Garegin Pastermajian (Armen Karo), former member of the Ottoman parliament. The murder of Aristakes Ter Harutiunian, the local priest at the village of Odz (Ots), followed.[78]

Beginning in June 1915, the wholesale deportations and massacres escalated markedly throughout the Armenian provinces. Between 10,000 and 15,000 Armenians were deported from towns and villages across the northern and eastern regions of the province of Erzerum in the first week of June. The deportation from the major cities began between June 7 and 11 in Erzinjan, home to 3,000 Armenian families, followed by three additional caravans totaling between 20,000 and 25,000 persons from neighboring areas. Approximately 25,000 Armenians from the region of Erzinjan were killed on their way to Kharpert, where the first caravan of 3,000 had already left for Malatia en route to Ras ul-Ain.[79] Some of the main roads for the deportations converged at Kharpert (Mamuret ul-Aziz), which was referred to as "the Slaughterhouse Province,"[80] as refugees from Trebizond, Sivas, Erzerum, Baiburt, Erzinjan, Kghi, Agn, Arabkir and elsewhere marched by Mezre and Kharpert (Harput) city. As they passed through Kharpert, refugees were allowed to stay in "camps" at the Armenian cemeteries nearby. Those still fit to march continued their journey to Diarbekir and Mardin, to Severek and Veran Shehir, while the rest died of illness and starvation or were massacred.

In Trebizond province, the bombardment by Russian cruisers of the port city of Kerasund (Giresun) on April 20, 1915, had heightened hostilities toward the Armenians. The previous day, the government had conducted extensive search and seizure operations for weapons and deserters throughout the city of Trebizond and the neighboring villages. Unable to unearth a significant number of weapons and deserters, the authorities had arrested the leading community figures accused of hiding weapons. Subsequently, several Armenian houses were torched. On June 25, the authorities issued a proclamation ordering the Armenians of Trebizond city to deliver, within five days, their properties to the government and to prepare for their journey to the interior on July 1. The declaration promised that Armenians could reclaim their goods upon their return at the conclusion of the war. On the morning of July 1 the first caravan began to march out of Trebizond city; within a few days 6,000 Armenians had become refugees. A week later most of the Armenian population was removed from the city, a large number of them murdered soon after they passed the town of Gumushkhane.[81]

In the cities of Kerasund and Samsun, the deportations began on June 27. In Kerasund 200 families out of 400 converted to Islam to avoid deportation.[82] No sooner had the first caravan, consisting of 1,200 people—nearly half of the Armenian population in the town—began its march than the men and the elderly were separated from the group and murdered in the nearby hills. The surviving refugees, mostly women and children, continued to Tamzara and Shabin-Karahisar.

In the middle of June the leading Armenian figures in Sivas city, including a professor at the American college, were arrested. Within a few days nearly 1,000 were in prison after the authorities conducted full-scale weapons searches.[83] On June 26, after an incident of resistance,[84] deportations began in Marsovan, followed by the deportations in Amasia and Zile to the south and in Gemerek farther southwest of Sivas city.[85] The mass arrests in Sivas city and its environs quickly filled the prisons.[86] Some of those arrested were killed immediately upon imprisonment and were replaced by new prisoners. Inquiries by Bishop Gnel Galemkiarian regarding the cause and purpose of these arrests elicited a simple response from the governor of Sivas province, Ahmad Muammer: The Armenians in Shabin-Karahisar were in rebellion, and in order to prevent Turkish massacres against the local Armenians, it was preferable to imprison them for their own safety. Mass arrests continued in a number of towns, including Amasia, Marsovan, and Tokat.[87]

In Shabin-Karahisar and the nearby Armenian villages, the Armenians had been disarmed by the second week of April 1915; one of those villages, Burk (Purk), in southwest of Shabin-Karahisar, was completely destroyed and its Armenian inhabitants deported. On June 1, as the government began to arrest the Armenian community leaders in Shabin-Karahisar, the Armenians responded by organizing for self-defense and on June 16 sought refuge within the nearby fortress. As in Van, Zeitun, and Sasun, the Armenians of Shabin-Karahisar resorted to arms and defended themselves for nearly a month until July 12, when Turkish troops finally entered the fortress and crushed the resistance. Most of the Armenian men were killed there. The women and children were forced to walk to the nearby towns, where some of them were killed and the small number of survivors converted to Islam.[88]

The conditions in Kharpert province followed the similar pattern as elsewhere. Beginning on May 1, 1915, the situation in Kharpert, Mezre, Hiusenig, Malatia, Perchench, and the surrounding villages had turned chaotic, as many shops and houses were looted and destroyed. Mass arrests in the city of Kharpert began in the middle of May, and in early June most of the arrested and imprisoned Armenian men were killed. Of those arrested, 800 were taken to the nearby mountain of Heroghli on June 24 and executed, while 300 Armenian men were murdered in Pertag. In the city of Kharpert, rumors that the 2,000 Armenian soldiers laboring in the *amele taburi* (labor battalions) were to depart for Aleppo to work on road construction evoked panic. The soldiers marched out of the city on July 1, and the next day the first wave of refugees, between 2,000 and 3,000 Armenians, were forcibly walked out of Kharpert, Mezre, and Hiusenig on their journey south to Urfa, Ras ul-Ain, and Deir el-Zor. Over the next several days a second and larger convoy of 6,000 Armenians left Kharpert.[89] Viewing the events in the streets, American evangelist missionary Tacy Atkinson noted in her diary: "What an awful sight. People shoved out of their houses, the doors nailed, and they were piled into oxcarts or on donkeys and many on foot. Police and gendarmes armed, shoving them along."[90]

Contrary to the claims by the Young Turk regime that the "deportations" were emergency measures necessitated by wartime security, there were no military threats to the province of Angora (Ankara) when the mass deportations and massacres began there. Its Armenian community was one of the most assimilated into the Turkish political culture, but its members met a similar fate as their compatriots in the eastern provinces. In late July, under direct orders from the Ittihadist Miralay Halil Rejayi Bey, the commander of the Fifth Army Corps headquartered at Ankara, notices were posted throughout the city of Kesaria announcing the removal within ten days of all the Armenians, with the exception of Catholics. Similar notices in Talas announced the deportation date to be within five days. And on August 5 the first caravan of Armenians marched out of Kesaria. The combined total number of Armenians deported from Kesaria and Talas was about 20,000. Only a small number chose conversion to Islam.[91] According to the government directive, the stores of the deported were to be closed and kept under government seal, while the sale of all movable goods would be supervised by local authorities. As soon as the mass deportations commenced, however, the Armenian neighborhoods were pillaged and plundered. Accused of conspiracy to favor Russian support for a military liberation of Armenians in the Ottoman empire, Bishop Pehrikian was subsequently deported, together with a caravan of hundreds of refugees, and murdered along with several other prominent figures.[92] Caravans of refugees marched to Aleppo, Ras ul-Ain, and Deir el-Zor.[93]

The region of Konia became a central station for refugees arriving by rail and land from the western and northern provinces. Refugees from the west came from as far away as Adrianople (Edirne) and Rodosto (Tekirdagh) in the province of Adrianople, from Izmid and Adabazar, Brusa and Eskishehir, on their way to Afion Karahisar and Konia. At times, as the ever-increasing number of caravans converged at Konia, between 40,000 and 50,000 refugees were pressed into thousands of tents within and on the outskirts of the city. By mid-July, the authorities had begun to deport the Armenians from Konia to Aleppo.[94] During the first two weeks of September, thousands of refugees from towns and villages in the *sanjak* (county) of Izmid, the province of Brusa, and the city of Angora joined the 11,000–16,000 refugees from Afion Karahisar on their march to the south and southeast. They gathered along the railway tracks with refugees from Eskishehir (12,000 to 15,000 refugees), Alayund (5,000), Chai (2,000), for some 200 miles to Konia to be joined by 5,000 to 10,000 additional refugees in cattle trucks if fortunate, but mostly on foot to Bozanti and thence to the Syrian desert.[95]

Those close to the Turko-Russian front were able to escape to the Caucasus. Near the end of 1915 approximately 170,000 had passed through Igdir, the first major town on the Russian side, while more than 18,000 refugees had passed through Kars and an equal number moved to Julfa. The entire region between Igdir and Echmiadzin, a distance of nearly 19 miles, was covered with refugees seeking safety. About 20,000 refugees remained in Igdir, 35,000 in Echmiadzin, and 20,000 in Erevan. By early 1916, an estimated 300,000 refugees had sought refuge in the Caucasus. An estimated 40,000 Armenians died during their journey to the Caucasus. Starvation and disease led to the death of 340 to 400 refugees per day.[96]

The enormity of the deportations as implemented since early 1915 indicated a vast administrative mechanism for the systematic destruction of the Armenian people in their historic homeland. The process of deportations and massacres culminated in the annihilation of the Armenian nation as it had existed for centuries across the Armenian Plateau. Morgenthau estimated that between April and October 1915, nearly 1.2 million Armenians were deported from their homeland to the Syrian desert, the primary destination for the refugees. Aleppo served as the clearinghouse for the Armenian refugees from Anatolia on their way to the desert.[97] By one estimate, the total number of Armenian refugees converged at Deir el-Zor reached as high as 350,000.[98] U.S. Consul Jesse Jackson reported from Aleppo that by August 15, 1915, more than 500,000 Armenians had been killed. In November he commented on the severity of treatment the surviving refugees received at the hands of "hostile tribesman" and escorting soldiers, and estimated that those who survived constituted no more than 15 percent of the total 1 million lives lost.[99]

When the victorious Allied powers signed the Mudros Armistice on October 30, 1918, which concluded the war with Turkey, the defeated Young Turk regime collapsed and some of its leaders fled the country. Turkish Pan-Turkish aspirations appeared to have come to an end. The Allied Powers organized a new government headed by Grand Vizier Damad Ferid Pasha, while keeping Sultan Mehmed VI on the throne. The postwar Ottoman parliament repealed the Temporary Law of Deportations on November 4, 1918, and under Allied pressure commenced the trials of the perpetrators of the genocide. Found guilty by the military tribunals, some of the Ittihadist leaders were sentenced to death in absentia.[100]

Part IV

Independence, Modernization, and Globalization

This page intentionally left blank

7

The Republic of Armenia:
The First Republic

The unfolding genocidal policies of the Young Turks forced about 300,000 Western Armenians to seek refuge in the Caucasus across the Russian frontier. By early 1916, 30,000 refugees had converged at Alexandropol (Gumri) alone, and as more refugees poured into the region the magnitude of the human catastrophe became patently clear to local Russian and Armenian officials. The region lacked the basic necessities to sustain life, reported a local Armenian clergy to Catholicos Gevorg V Surenyants at Echmiadzin.[1] To address the crisis, the Russian government approved a conference of prominent Eastern Armenians to meet in May, on the condition that the delegates limit their deliberations to relief efforts. The conference produced little assistance for the refugees, but it provided an opportunity for leading Armenians to assess the national crisis and the future direction of the nation. Nothing could have been more surprising at this point in Armenian history than the accelerating pace of developments that led to the reemergence of an Armenian state in the region after a millennium since the fall of the Bagratunis in Greater Armenia and more than five centuries since the collapse of the Cilician government.

REVOLUTIONARY RUSSIA

Despite the recent history of repressive rule in Russian Armenia, particularly since Tsar Alexander III, Armenians maintained a favorable attitude toward Russia regarding the empire's geopolitical objectives in the Caucasus and engagement in Armenian affairs. The tsarist government's positive responses to the Armenian plight, as demonstrated in the negotiations for the 1914 reforms in Ottoman Armenia and the military support in Van in 1915, reaffirmed the belief held widely among Armenians in the Ottoman empire that Russian geopolitical interests would lead to more direct involvement in the region. The tsarist regime retained its repressive rule over Russian Armenia, but Armenians in the eastern provinces of the Ottoman empire had come to rely on the same tsarist government for diplomatic and, in times of war, for military support against Turkish atrocities. The maliciously abnormal geopolitical conditions created by the Young Turk genocidal policies did not afford Armenian leaders in the Caucasus—even the very few capable ones—the luxury of diplomatic dexterity to cultivate good relations with the neighboring powers. The antitsarist political upheavals emanating from St. Petersburg and Moscow and the turbulence and bloodshed in Transcauasia exacerbated the situation for the Armenians.

The Russian revolutionary movement forced the last Romanov tsar, Nicholas II, to abdicate the throne on March 15, 1917, and installed the Provisional Government led by the more democratically oriented Prince Georgy E. Lvov as prime minister; Pavel Milyukov, foreign minister; Aleksandr Guchkov, war minister; Aleksandr Kerenski, justice minister, and others. Despite their apprehensions regarding the revolutionary movement, and very much like their compatriots in the Ottoman Empire during the Young Turk revolution in 1908, Armenians welcomed the March Revolution with expectations for political democratization and economic modernization.[2] Local peasants' and workers' councils (soviets) were established in anticipation of the formation of a representative government with the requisite institutional mechanisms for expansive participatory democracy. The Provisional Government promised democratic reforms but avoided issues of nationality and territory, insisting instead that the All-Russian Constituent Assembly would address such issues after the upcoming elections.[3] In this environment of optimism, in April 1917 Catholicos Gevorg V issued an encyclical urging the Armenian communities to respect the rights of women to political participation in national affairs and their rights to vote for and to be elected into offices. Women's involvement in various facets of political and economic affairs, Gevorg V averred, was essential for development and progress. He noted that the Armenian Church for centuries had recognized the equality of men and women but that foreign cultural influences had led to a transmutation of Armenian culture, thereby undermining the relationship between the church and the community.[4]

The peoples of the Caucasus, who had often accused the tsarist government of too frequently relying on divide-and-conquer strategies, soon realized that they themselves were in fact divided along lines of nationality, each led by its own political organizations and motivated by its own territorial claims. Declarations of Transcaucasian brotherhood and unity thus proved transitory, as the collapse of the tsarist regime exposed the contradictory interests of the Armenian, Georgian, and Muslim peoples. For most Armenians, the fundamental issues pertaining to the physical survival of Turkish Armenia and the military resources needed to strengthen Russian Armenia had relegated intra-Caucasus relations to a secondary concern at best. The Armenian political parties, among them the Dashnaktsutiun, Hay Zhoghovrdakan Kusaktsutyun (Armenian Democratic Party), the Armenian Social Democrats, and the Social Revolutionaries, proposed different platforms for the envisioned post-Romanov Armenia, but for now their disagreements over details could be overlooked. All concurred that, in the absence of concrete support from the Allied Powers, Armenia would rely on Russian military protection if the latter were so inclined.

Georgian and Muslim views were not as clear, however. Some of the leading Georgian Mensheviks, such as Noi (Noah) Zhordania, for example, initially opposed nationalist aspirations as "a weapon of the bourgeoisie" and advocated incorporation of the Caucasus into a single Russian republic. Other Georgians insisted on some form of national autonomy and the creation of a more democratic government than conceivable under Russian domination. The leading Muslim Musavat (Equality) Party championed wider aspirations, as encapsulated in the slogan "Turkism, Islamism, and Modernism." The party advocated a return to the "golden age" of Islam and the revival of Islamic unity transcending all territorial and sectoral borders. Some of the leading members of the Musavat also accepted integration into a Transcaucasian federative republic, proposed at the Transcaucasian Conference of Muslims held at Baku in April 1917, so long as it would respect local or national autonomy and the security of Muslims. Russo-Turkish relations ultimately determined the general outcome of the regional conflicts. Another Transcaucasian conference later in the year established the Transcaucasian Federation with its Commissariat as the executive body and the Seim as the legislative body.[5]

The creation of an integrative Transcaucasian federation was premised on the assumption that a consensus of coalitions existed among the various political groups with mutually compatible interests and objectives and that local conditions were conducive to equality in administration and economy. Yet the interests were essentially and inextricably national in orientation and collided against each other and with Russian national priorities. The latter, as for centuries under the tsarist regime, continued to view the Caucasus as a mere territorial buffer with the Ottoman Empire, its principal rival in the region, and unreservedly subordinated its

Caucasian relations to the wider pressing needs of war and peace. Neither the Petrograd Provisional Government nor the Bolshevik opposition could for long conceal the widening gap between the rhetoric and reality of Russian policy toward the region. Matters were made infinitely worse for the Russian empire and its Armenian subjects when the Bolshevik opposition seized power in November 1917.

The Bolshevik Revolution ushered in a new cadre of leaders, headed by Vladimir I. Lenin, who had criticized Lvov and Kerenski for their involvement in the "imperialistic war." Upon assuming power, the new cabinet, the Council of People's Commissars (Sovnarkom), chaired by Lenin, issued the "Declaration of Peoples' Rights," which, in addition to guarantees for political and economic equality and development, also promised national self-determination and the right to secede. Proclamations of democratic principles notwithstanding, the Sovnarkom in fact opposed self-determination in the Russian periphery and would not countenance centrifugal proclivities by the nationalities.[6] The Bolshevik obfuscation of intent could have served the Armenians well, for the latter sought national autonomy for Eastern and Western Armenia but within a Russian federative structure that could provide a security shield against the Ottoman army and Turkism. The Bolsheviks and Dashnaktsutiun—both products of revolutionary movements—could even cooperate in security and political matters. But in practice the Bolshevik scheme for "self-determination" deepened Armenian distrust toward the party, for that policy would mean the withdrawal of Russian forces from the occupied territories in Western Armenia, which in turn could result in the occupation by the Turkish forces and their advance into the Caucasus. Indeed, even such ardent Bolsheviks as Stepan Shahumyan understood the deleterious implications of "self-determination" for Armenians at this perilous juncture.[7]

With the exception of a small number of Bolshevik sympathizers, people in the Caucasus—Armenians, Georgians, and Muslims alike—vehemently opposed the Bolshevik seizure of power and their policies toward the region. A Transcaucasian conference, meeting on November 24, 1917, to address issues concerning the altered relation with Russia, created an interim administrative body, the Transcaucasian Commissariat, until the conclusion of the elections to the All-Russian Constituent Assembly. That assembly met on January 18, 1918, only to be routed by the Bolsheviks.[8]

While the delegates were preparing for the Constituent Assembly, General M.A. Przhevalskii, Russian Commander of the Caucasus Front, received a proposal for truce from General Mehmed Vehib Pasha. General Vyshinskii of the Caucasus Army traveled to Erzinjan, where on December 18, 1917, he signed the truce, which provided for the immediate cessation of hostilities, establishment of a neutral zone between the Turkish and Russian armies, exchange of information with respect to military training on both sides of the demilitarized zone, termination of transfer of Turkish soldiers to the Mesopotamian front, enforcement of Kurdish compliance with the truce, and advance communication of "modification or abrogation of the truce."[9] The demoralized Russian army was prepared to leave the war.

WAR AND REPUBLIC

The military situation in Western Armenia deteriorated as the Russian army began to withdraw. The Western Armenian Bureau, the executive committee of the Western Armenian Council comprised of representatives of Armenian political parties, convened a meeting in December and established a defense council to organize Armenian military units to replace the Russian forces in protecting Western Armenia. The Armenian soldiers, totaling no more than 20,000, were now responsible for defending the 250-mile stretch from Erzinjan to Van.[10] By January 1918 the Erzinjan Truce was in the process of dissolution as Kurdish attacks on the Armenian soldiers continued unchecked. On February 1 Vehib Pasha, claiming that Armenian "bands" were killing Muslims in the Russian zone, issued an ultimatum and moved Turkish forces across the neutral zone. Bolshevik declarations of "peace at any price" seemed to have encouraged the Turkish command to advance, and Colonel Kiazim Karabekir, undoubtedly apprised of the Russo-German peace overtures, soon captured Erzinjan, thus securing his prestige under the banner of Pan-Turkism across the Ottoman Empire and among the Caucasian Muslims.[11] Under the Russo-German Treaty of Brest-Litovsk, signed on March 3, 1918, and ratified on March 15, the Bolsheviks agreed to accept "peace at any price," to withdraw from the provinces of Eastern Anatolia and return them to Turkey (Article IV), and "to demobilize and dissolve the Armenian bands" in Russia and in the occupied Turkish provinces (Article I[5]).[12]

Meanwhile, Karabekir's army, having completed its offensive on Erzinjan, advanced farther eastward and captured Erzerum on March 12. Within a day the Turkish army was in control of the city and continued its march to Merdenek and Ardahan. The Armenian military defeat was repeated at several fronts, such as Van, Khnus, and Alashkert in early April 1918. Turkish troops advanced to Kars and Batum and captured the latter city within hours on April 14. General Tovmas Nazarbekian continued to defend Kars, and an emergency conference held at Alexandropol agreed to continue its defense for as long as possible. The defense of Kars did not last long, however.[13]

What transpired next reflected the prevalence of *realpolitik* thought among the Georgian leaders for which their Armenian counterparts proved no match. Akakii I. Chkhenkeli, acting as head of state of the

Transcaucasian Federation even before official confirmation of his government on April 26, 1918, ordered Nazarbekian to evacuate Kars. On April 23
Chkhenkeli in a secret communication had notified General Vehib that
the terms of Brest-Litovsk were now acceptable for the resumption of
negotiations for peace and that he had issued orders to cease all hostilities
and to commence withdrawal from Kars and the rest of Western
Armenia. As refugees fled from the Kars region across the Akhurian
River to Erevan, Turkish forces captured Kars on April 25–26. Once
Chkhenkeli's communications with Turkish authorities became known to
the Armenian leaders in Tiflis and Erevan, the Dashnaktsutiun called for
his resignation, and Aleksandr Khatisian, Hovhannes Kachaznuni, and
Avetik Sahakian withdrew from his cabinet. The Georgian Mensheviks
argued that Transcaucasian cooperation was necessary to maintain
regional unity and, expressing their own opposition to Chkhenkeli, proposed Kachaznuni to head the Transcaucasian government. Yet the
Dashnakist leaders, believing that Turkey would view Kachaznuni's
appointment as the rise of a "war cabinet," declined the offer and instead
decided to retain membership in Chkhenkeli's cabinet.[14]

Having achieved a major military and diplomatic victory, Turkey offered
to resume the peace negotiations at Batum. Chkhenkeli accepted the invitation and the Transcaucasian delegation departed for Batum with the clear
objective of officially accepting the Brest-Litovsk treaty as a condition for
peace. On May 11, 1918, during the opening session of the conference, Halil
Bey Ottoman Minister of Justia representing his government at Batum,
surprised the participants by declaring that since conditions had changed
during the past month, the Brest-Litovsk Treaty would no longer serve as
the basis for the peace negotiations. He demanded the surrender to Turkey
of Batum, Alexandropol, Akhalkalak, Shirak, and Echmiadzin, as well as
control over the Alexandropol-Kars and Alexandropol-Julfa rail lines.
Events on the battlefields hardly necessitated such demands, for the
Turkish forces proceeded to extend their control over these regions. While
at Batum, however, General Otto von Lossow, present at the conference as
one of the two German observers, had secretly agreed with the Georgian
delegates to meet in Poti in preparation for the Georgian declaration of
independence. The Georgians, concurring with von Lossow, considered
secession from the Transcaucasian Federation and independence under
German protection preferable to Turkish occupation. Germany, with interests in the Batum-Baku oil line and other natural resources (e.g., copper and
manganese), agreed to provide military and economic assistance to independent Georgia.[15]

On May 26, during its final session, the Transcaucasian Seim adopted
the Georgian resolution to dissolve itself, and within hours the Georgian
National Council declared independence. The following day the Muslim

National Council met in Tiflis and declared the independence of "Eastern and Southern Transcaucasia," followed by a declaration of the formation of the Republic of Azerbaijan on May 28. The Armenian leadership was divided on the issue of independence. When the National Council met on May 26, the Social Revolutionaries opposed independence, for it would expose the isolated Armenian state to Turkish attacks. The Social Democrats and the Armenian Democratic Party, however, faced with the inescapable realities, supported independence. The Dashnaktsutiun was also divided. Avetis Aharonian, Ruben Ter Minasian, and Artashes Babalian opposed independence, but Simon Vratsian and Khachatur Karjikian favored such a move. During a meeting in Tiflis, Khatisian and Kachaznuni agreed that under the circumstances Armenian preferences notwithstanding the National Council had no alternative but to opt for independence and establish a *modus vivendi* with Turkey. On May 28 the National Council agreed to send Khatisian and Kachaznuni to Batum to negotiate peace with Turkey. The following day, in an emergency meeting, the Dashnakist leaders agreed to declare the independence of the Republic of Armenia and appointed Kachaznuni minister-president. On May 30 in the midst of rapidly unfolding and confusing events the council issued its proclamation without mentioning the words "independence" or "republic."[16]

THE FIRST GOVERNMENT

The leaders of the nascent Armenian republic were hardly prepared for the task of organizing a new government. As is often the case with leaders of revolutionary movements, with the exception of a handful of individuals (e.g., Khatisian, who had served as mayor of Tiflis),[17] the emerging Armenian leaders had little or no experience in the management of government. The land they now hoped to govern lacked nearly all essential ingredients for a viable republic. Both the government and the population it was to govern lacked sufficient money, food, and military capability. About 50 percent of its people were war refugees in abject poverty. Nearly 60 percent of its territory was under foreign occupation. The town of Erevan, the designated capital of the new republic, had no particular appeal to the more cosmopolitan Armenian intellectuals and businessmen in Tiflis. Some even refused to move there. As historian Richard Pipes has commented, "No territory of the old Russian Empire had suffered greater losses from the First World War, and none was placed in a more desperate situation by the empire's disintegration."[18]

While in Batum the Armenian delegates were negotiating peace with Turkey, Turkish forces had moved on three fronts: southward from Alexandropol to Sardarapat (Sardarabad), eastward to Karakilisa, and southeastward to Bash Abaran. The Armenian defenses under General Nazarbekian resisted the Turkish advance between Karakilisa and Dilijan. General Dro (Drastamat Kanayan) defended the route from Hamamlu to Bash Abaran to Erevan, while General Movses Silikian defended the road to Sardarabad. As Turkish forces were driven back on all three fronts, Armenians insisted on marching to Alexandropol and on to Kars. Yet the National Council, calculating that the limited supplies of ammunition could not sustain a prolonged conflict, ordered the Armenian forces to halt the advance. The Batum delegation had secured a peace agreement.[19]

On June 4, 1918, the Armenian delegation at Batum signed the "Treaty of Peace and Friendship between the Imperial Ottoman Government and the Republic of Armenia" and its supplementary agreements, setting the new boundaries between the two nations and the conditions for the conduct of their bilateral relations.[20] Additional agreements notwithstanding Armenians and Turks clashed in the region of Pambak; by the middle of July Turkish troops rapidly approached Erevan and stationed cannons four miles from the city and Echmiadzin.[21]

The National Council formed the new government with the intention of creating a coalition cabinet headed by Kachaznuni. Unable to bring together a coalition government, however, the council permitted the new premier to form his cabinet independently of party affiliation. In early July, after much bickering, the Armenian leaders finally agreed to relocate the government seat from Tiflis to Erevan, and on July 19, under most inauspicious circumstances amidst death and destruction, the new Armenian government entered Erevan to resume leadership of the nation after centuries of state dormancy.[22]

On August 1, 1918, the Armenian Khorhurd (legislative body) held its first session, and on August 3 Kachaznuni presented the general outlines of his government's program. The Armenian state, he noted, lacked the fundamental ingredients of political economy, and it had to build anew institutions of public administration, of law and order, of health and welfare. The new government had to address the issues of refugees and their survival amid homelessness, hunger, and unsanitary conditions. Disarmament of the population was particularly vexing. Some, including Minister of Internal Affairs Aram Manukian, argued in favor of total disarmament of the populace as a necessary step toward establishing law and order. Others, however, contended that a people who had experienced turmoil and treachery for years would not comply with orders to surrender their arms, and insisted instead on allowing the armed population to contribute to the defense of the nation.[23]

In Constantinople, the government of Ahmed Izzet Pasha, having replaced the Young Turk regime, signed the Mudros Armistice on October 30, 1918, prior to the German surrender on November 11. With respect to

Armenia, the armistice provided for the evacuation of the Ottoman troops from the Caucasus and northern Persia (Iran), the demobilization of the Ottoman troops except in areas that required maintenance of law and order, and the release of imprisoned Armenians. The Allies would occupy Baku and Batum. At the Mudros conference, while the Allies insisted on Turkish evacuation of Transcaucasia, they were mainly concerned with maintaining access to the Dardanelles and the Black Sea.[24] The Turkish delegation was temporarily successful in keeping the province of Kars and sections of the Batum province as well as in delinking Cilicia from the historic Armenian provinces. In November, as provided by the Mudros Armistice, Turkey completed its withdrawal from the Erevan *guberniia* (province), British troops occupied Baku, and General George F. Milne's Army of the Black Sea established its headquarters at Constantinople. The Allied authorities now stationed in the Ottoman capital were to command the occupying forces in Anatolia and the Caucasus.[25]

WITH THE WESTERN POWERS IN PARIS

On December 8, 1918, the Armenian delegation, headed by Avetis Aharonian, left Erevan for the long-awaited Paris Peace Conference. The delegation arrived at Paris on February 4, 1919, only to learn that the Allied Powers had excluded the Republic of Armenia from the official list of participant states. Further complicating matters was the presence of Boghos Nubar Pasha as president of the Armenian National Delegation. As the official representative of the republic, Aharonian represented what may be termed the minimalist position with respect to his government's objectives at Paris. He had instructions to win Allied support for Armenian control over Eastern and Western Armenian provinces, with a corridor to ports on the Black Sea. Extension of Armenian borders to Trebizond and Cilicia seemed unrealistic for so weak a government heading so devastated a country. Boghos Nubar represented the maximalist position. The existing small republic, he and his supporters contended, was not established in the historic lands of Armenia. Instead, they argued, the boundaries of the republic should be extended not only to the six provinces but also to Cilicia.[26] The true Armenia would embrace the Armenian heartland and would have access to the Mediterranean, thus eliminating the potential threats of coercion and blockage strangulating its economy. Despite their differences, for the sake of unified representation both men agreed to function as the "Delegation of Integral Armenia."[27]

The Armenian delegation in Paris was encouraged by the favorable official and public sentiments expressed in western capitals. As early as January 1918, President Woodrow Wilson in his Fourteen Points had outlined his support regarding the Ottoman subjects. The American Commission to Negotiate Peace (formerly the Inquiry) proposed an Armenian state whose boundaries would include not only historic Armenia and the republic, but also Cilicia, Trebizond, Akhaltsik (Akhaltskha), and Akhalkalak. The Western Asian Division even recommended inclusion of Karabagh and Alexandretta. The British proposal concurred, as indicated in an official memorandum dated February 7, 1919. When Aharonian and Nubar Pasha met with the Council of Ten (Supreme Allied Council) on February 26, they presented the Armenian case along similar lines. Disagreements among France, Italy, and Britain soon weakened the Armenian position, as the European powers struggled to protect their interests after the expected partition of the Ottoman lands and in the Middle East. With the exception of protecting the Baku-Batum pipeline, the British showed no interest in greater involvement in the Caucasus; in March 1919 they prepared to withdraw from the region and announced July 15 as the withdrawal date, later postponed until August 15.[28]

That political and economic support from the western powers would not be forthcoming any time soon should have been obvious to the Armenian delegation by the simple fact that they refused to extend formal recognition to the republic. Even the most ardent advocate of self-determination, President Wilson, withheld recognition on grounds that the prevailing circumstances did not permit such a step at that time. Recognition of that republic, the western powers feared, would invite unacceptable political, economic, and military obligations. The Turkish government found support among the Allied military officials (most notably Rear Admiral Mark L. Bristol, senior American naval officer) stationed in Constantinople, who opposed Armenian claims to statehood and rejected proposals to extend Armenian boundaries to the Mediterranean or the Black Sea. The protection of Armenia, they argued, would require enormous military capability for the complete occupation of the Ottoman Empire. None of the major powers showed any willingness to shoulder such responsibilities. Britain, the only power that possessed the necessary military force in the region, was already preparing for withdrawal from the Caucasus.[29] Could the Republic of Armenia survive without the protection of a major power?

BETWEEN GEORGIA AND AZERBAIJAN

In late 1918 the Georgian military had restrengthened its position in northern Lori, but the local Armenian population requested unification with Armenia. Disagreements over such territorial issues escalated hostilities into open warfare. Beginning on December 14, Armenian troops advanced toward

Vorontsovka and the regions of Haghpat and Akhova. After the initial successful advance, Dro's forces launched a major offensive toward Tiflis. The
warring parties finally agreed to a truce mediated by the Allied Powers. On
December 31, when the hostilities ceased, the Armenian forces were in control of the region south of the Khram River. Between January 9 and 17, 1919,
the negotiations for a peaceful settlement led to the creation of the neutral
zone at Borchalu under British supervision, while Georgia retained soldiers in
Akhalkalak.[30] Armenia and Georgia also sought to contain recurring clashes
with the neighboring Muslims. Both governments attempted to develop
functional bases for bilateral cooperation, and in March 1919 they agreed to
create a joint commission on transportation, while the finance ministries
worked toward a common monetary union. These projects were curtailed,
however, when tensions resurfaced both at home and in international forums,
such as the conferences of the Second International at Berne (February-May
1919), where both delegations could not conceal their differences under the
cloak of conciliatory pronouncements.[31]

Nor were relations between Armenia and Azerbaijan more peaceful. As
the Muslims gained control over Baku and Ganja (Gandzak; Elisavetpol,
the temporary capital), they aimed at extending their rule over Karabagh
and Zangezur where close relations with the Ottoman army strengthened
their position vis-à-vis Armenians in both regions. Despite Turkish-Azeri
demands for submission, by September the Armenians were prepared to
resist by force.[32] Yet they were no match for the combined Muslim forces
who marched to Shushi in early October. Only in the mountains of
Zangezur (encompassing the districts of Sisian, Goris, Ghapan, and
Meghri), the troops under General Antranik Ozanian offered a stiff resistance, but here too soon shortages in supplies and ammunition required
help from the Erevan government. The Kachaznuni government pursued
two seemingly contradictory policies regarding the region: In diplomatic
discussions with Turkish officials, it tried to distance itself from the conflicts in Karabagh and Zangezur. Yet it also claimed jurisdiction over the
area and contended that territorial detachment from Armenia would vio-
late Armenian national sovereignty and unity. As in the case of Armeno-
Georgian hostilities, British mediation temporarily restored order.[33]

Armenians expected British intercession to tilt the balance of power in
their favor, but soon they would be disillusioned. As noted, the British
were concerned primarily with gaining access to oil supplies via the Baku-
Batum pipeline, and they considered the Muslim leadership with Turkish
support far more reliable as a political and military force in the region.
While emphasizing that the Paris Peace Conference would finally resolve
the existing territorial disputes in the Caucasus, on December 28, 1918,
General William Thomson sanctioned the establishment of a government
in Azerbaijan, headed by Khan Khoiskii as the legal authority in

Azerbaijan, thereby informally extending British recognition to the Republic of Azerbaijan. The situation for Armenians took a particularly alarming turn when on January 15, 1919, Thomson also approved the appointment of Khosrov Bek Sultanov as provisional governor-general of Mountainous Karabagh and Zangezur. The Armenians in the region were all too familiar with Sultanov's virulently anti-Armenian policies in cooperation with the Ottoman forces and his pan-Turkic aspirations. General Thomson rejected Armenian appeals to prevent Sultanov's governorship in Karabagh, and insisted on the immediate restoration of law and order.[34]

Order and stability, however, would not ameliorate the deteriorating economic conditions for Armenians within and without the republic. While the gradual clarification and formation of party coalitions began to establish some semblance of institutional normalcy in the Khorhurd, masses of refugees and the population in general needed housing, food, medical attention, and other necessities of life the destroyed economy could ill afford. The enormity of the difficulties notwithstanding, the Kachaznuni government began the process of reconstructing the country's economic infrastructure.[35] The government, with meager public and private funds, encouraged factory operations, built hospitals, surveyed the land for resources, rebuilt the communication system, and launched "Armenianization" campaigns in bureaucracies and educational institutions. These achievements, however, could not conceal the tensions within the government.

One of the most serious issues in early 1919 was the role of the Dashnaktsutiun as the leading political party and its relations with the government. The more conservative members (e.g., Kachaznuni) argued that having founded the republic, now the party Bureau, the organization's highest decision-making body, must relinquish direct control over government operations. The cabinet, they argued, should first and foremost be directly responsible to the Khorhurd rather than to the bureau, while the latter worked closely with party members in the parliament. The more radical factions within the party rejected these arguments. They complained that, once in power, the Dashnakist government had virtually ignored the revolutionary tenets of the party and had adopted an accommodative posture toward the bourgeoisie who not long ago had condemned and cast derision on the revolutionary activities of the Dashnaktsutiun. The Khorhurd was even more polarized between the Dashnakist-Armenian Democratic majority and the Social Revolution-Social Democrat opposition. The former stressed that the priorities of national security and physical survival demanded immediate decisions with respect to the Muslim population rather than become mired in parliamentary procedures and debates. The opposition, however, emphasized the need to cultivate interethnic confidence through caution and compromise as Armenia had remained virtually isolated from the outside world.[36]

The coiled webs of diplomatic, economic, and geostrategic considerations compounded the burden of isolation. The only possible ally in the region,

Russia, was mired in civil war between the White and Red armies. The coiled webs of diplomatic, economic, and geostrategic considerations compounded the burden of isolation. Armenia sought to maintain relations with the competing forces in Russia, but the Armed Forces of South Russia under the command of Lieutenant General Anton Denikin seemed the best alternative because of its proximity and support for Armenians in territories under its control. Closer association with it, however, would elicit the traditional Russophobic reactions from London and Paris as well as the other western capitals at a time when the success of the Armenian delegation at the peace conference depended in large part on its ability to convince western representatives of Armenia's reliability as a "democratic" republic. A turn to the White or Red Russians would perhaps benefit Armenia in the short run, but both sought the revival of the Russian empire. While it was clear that neither London nor Paris would tolerate Bolshevik supremacy, policymakers in both capitals were divided with respect to the White Army. The situation seemed hopeless for the Erevan government. Despite repeated Allied assurances that issues of moral weight would receive favorable attention at Paris, the conference offered no such solutions.[37]

The Armenian government faced a serious dilemma in relations with Turkey, where two competing forces—one in Constantinople under the sultan and another in Ankara under Mustafa Kemal—made bilateral relations difficult. In this case, however, the Armenian people, after enduring massacres and destruction, would have found it virtually impossible to contemplate reconciliation and normalization of relations with a divided or united Turkey.[38] The sultanate in Constantinople merely expressed its sorrow at the recent "incidents" under the government of the Ittihadists (Committee of Union and Progress) and promised that such violations would never occur again. The Nationalists in Ankara blamed the Armenians directly for the bloodshed and refused even to recognize the Armenian presence in their historic homeland. In March 1919 Major General Kiazim Karabekir thus promised to reassert Turkish control over the *sanjaks* (counties) of Kars, Ardahan, and Batum, and marched toward Armenia. Kemal and Karabekir were prepared to unite against Constantinople and all foreign (including Armenian) intervention in the Ottoman Empire. They particularly deplored officials in the capital who so readily acquiesced in Allied orders that threatened Turkish lands and interests, especially with respect to the extension of Armenian borders to the six provinces. When the Erzerum Congress led by Kemal met on July 23, 1919, at the famed Sanasarian Academy to declare national unity and the defense of the Turkish homeland against outside threats, Kemal had broken official ties with Constantinople. In its stead, he found a powerful, albeit temporary, ally in Russia, where the Bolshevik leaders welcomed Nationalist cooperation to eliminate Allied influence in Turkey and to control events in the Caucasus.[39]

After a year of independence, the Erevan government had begun to adjust to the difficulties in foreign policy and the daily struggle to organize the nation's economy. Intensive diplomatic efforts were necessary to attain a modicum of representation at the peace conference, while territorial disputes with the neighboring nations remained as explosive as ever. On the home front, economic and infrastructural development at home registered some successes, but the historically "natural" division of the nation between Turkish Armenians and Russian Armenians intensified tensions between the political parties. In an attempt to bridge that gap between the two, the cabinet of the acting premier Aleksandr Khatisian adopted two policies, both of symbolic nature but fraught with enormous legal and military implications. On May 26, in preparation for the first anniversary of the republic's independence, the cabinet adopted the Act of United Armenia which proclaimed the "official unification of Western Armenia and the Republic of Armenia. This act was followed (on May 27) by the formation of a twelve-member Western-Armenian bloc in the Khorhurd. Clearly, the Act expressed Armenian aspirations for the creation of a single Armenia. Could the Western-Armenian bloc in the parliament translate such desires into policy? On the day of the anniversary, Armenians greeted both acts with jubilation and a sense of national triumph.[40]

THE KHATISIAN GOVERNMENT

The first national parliamentary elections were held on June 21 to 23, 1919. The Social Democrats who early on realized they could not muster sufficient votes and the Armenian Democratic party boycotted them. The Democrats, who at the time of the proclamation of the Act had supported the initiative, shifted their position on account of intra-party disagreements. They also noted, however, that the legal authority to issue a declaration of such import resided in the parliament, not in the cabinet. Of the 260,000 votes, Dashnaktsutiun received 230,772 votes (88.95 percent, 72 of the 80 seats), while the Social Revolutionary party received 13,289 votes (5.12 percent, 4 seats). The Khorhurd named Aleksandr Khatisian as head of the provisional cabinet until the legislators reconvened on August 1. On August 5 the Khorhrdaran (parliament) confirmed the election of Khatisian as minister-president, and on August 10, the new cabinet.[41] On that date Khatisian presented his government's program to the Khorhrdaran (parliament). He stressed that the pro-western posture adopted since independence continued to constitute a key component in Armenian foreign policy. At home, his government would intensify the institutionalization of "Armenianization" programs (e.g., through eliminating Russian bureaucratic traditions), establish new national and local state organizations to address various social and economic issues, lower indirect taxes, and promote foreign direct investments. It was not surprising that the Social Revolutionary party, which held seats in the parliament, and Social Democrat party, which did not, criticized these programs and raised a host of questions not addressed by the premier. Would the government, for example, support Armenian integration into a federative structure with Russia? To what extent would the government allow foreign capital to penetrate the republic's economy, thereby rendering it dependent "on imperialist powers" and vulnerable to "colonial exploitation"? Khatisian also faced an increasingly divided the Dashnakist party. The Western Armenian members resented the Russian cultural influence in the governmental administrative agencies, while the Eastern Armenians—heavily influenced by that same culture— advocated pro-Russian policies. The more radical wing of the party (most prominently Ruben Ter Minasian) was convinced that "parliamentarism" and democratic ideals could prove detrimental to the sovereignty and survival of the republic at this critical point.[42]

The ideological-political controversies and tensions aside, by the second half of 1919, the government bureaucracies had achieved some degree of structural and functional constancy, although their political legitimacy waxed and waned depending on the domestic and international circumstances. The Ministry of Internal Affairs proved most controversial, as it shouldered the responsibilities of both internal security and law and order. The political parties, including the Dashnaktsutiun, frequently criticized the ministry for its failure to combat bureaucratic corruption and instability to provide sufficient security for the villagers beyond Erevan and for the transportation of goods. Structural reforms and greater decentralization were necessary to institute accountability and democratization, the critics argued. The Khatisian government and the Khorhrdaran took several steps in an effort to remedy the situation. In May 1919 the cabinet had authorized the ministry to organize Zemstvos (local assemblies), and in January 1920 the nation held its first local elections. The public elected the district (*gavarak*) assemblies, and the latter subsequently elected the county (*gavar*) assemblies. The Ministry of Judicial Affairs, created by the Khorhurd in December 1918, replaced the oppressive tsarist court system. At the apex of the judicial hierarchy rested the supreme court, the Tserakuit (Senate). Below it was the Datastanakan Palat (Palace of Justice) with appellate functions, followed by the shrjanayin dataran (circuit courts) and small claims courts. One of the ministry's major tasks was to transform the deeply ingrained public distrust of the tsarist courts into public confidence in the Armenian courts. It sought to improve the legal procedures governing criminal investigations and required the use of the Armenian language in all criminal proceedings.[43] On March 15, 1920, Armenians witnessed the nation's first trial by jury. As historian Richard Hovannisian describes most aptly: "The newspapers hailed the trial as a judicial milestone, and in the courtroom Chilingarian and Khatisian spoke of its significance in the evolution of a democratic republic. The actual legal proceedings were awkward and even amusing, as the prosecutor, public defender, and judges of the tribunal groped for the appropriate Armenian terms, but there was above all a sense of exhilaration, for after centuries of submission to the courts and discriminatory regulations of alien powers, the Armenians had succeeded in introducing the jury system in their national language."[44]

The responsibilities of the ministries of provisions and of finance were equally daunting but far more dispiriting. During its short life, the Ministry of Provisions administered the government-owned depots and the distribution of food and fuel as well as goods procured through foreign aid programs to meet, with the Ministry of Welfare, the needs of more than 580,000 refugees. Charges of rampant corruption in late 1919, however, led to its termination in January 1920. The Ministry of Finance struggled to maintain monetary stability and to check inflationary pressures. While the economy registered some minor improvements (e.g., in exports), the nation's financial health remained directly tied to the issue of international recognition of the republic as a sovereign entity. In the absence of such recognition, financial centers in Europe and the United States were reluctant to expend their resources. The Ministry of Education assumed responsibilities for maintaining all educational institutions, including some previously within the jurisdiction of the catholicosate at Echmiadzin. Under the existing economic conditions, the Armenian Church could not finance its school operations, which, along with other schools in the republic, became state institutions.[45]

The Armenian government lacked the ability to address a range of foreign policy issues, all which demanded resources beyond its capabilities. The rapidly changing international situation only made matters worse. The British withdrawal from the Caucasus and the matter of Allied recognition of the republic as a sovereign state underscored the potency of this reality. As the date for the British withdrawal neared, debate regarding mandatory responsibilities intensified, particularly on issues surrounding the repatriation of Western Armenians to their native land. The European powers determined that the United States, which claimed no territorial ambitions in the Caucasus, was best suited for such a role. The Armenian government expected the United States to extend recognition to the republic and to serve as the mandatory power securing the protection of Armenia. The Supreme Council had decided in June 1919 to postpone a final decision on the mandate question until the Wilson administration could state whether it would accept a mandate in parts of the former Ottoman empire. The Wilson administration, however, would respond only after Senate ratification of the German peace treaty and U.S. membership in the League of Nations. In the meantime, debates raged on in different quarters as to whether the United States could accept the mandate over Armenia and the extent to which U.S. foreign policy could promote humanitarian causes in conjunction with commercial considerations.[46]

To investigate matters, the Wilson administration sent two missions to the Ottoman lands. In March 1919 the administration secured the approval of the European powers to dispatch an Allied commission of inquiry (the King-Crane Commission) to survey issues involving the separation of nations from the Ottoman empire. After the commission traveled throughout the region during August, its members supported the joint-mandate approach. The King-Crane report stated that the Armenians could not be entrusted to Turkish rule and that a separate Armenia was necessary to secure their survival and to prevent further massacres by the Turks. The commission noted that the boundaries of the Armenian state should extend to parts of Trebizond, Erzerum, Bitlis, and Van (those areas under Russian control in 1916–1917), but Armenian territorial aspirations aside, Sivas, Kharpert, and Cilicia should be part of Anatolia. In case of failure in management, future negotiations would determine the status of these territories under Armenian rule. The report, submitted to the Wilson administration on September 27, 1919, was simply shelved.[47]

Wilson also appointed General James C. Harbord to head a mission to the Ottoman empire and the Caucasus in order to examine the feasibility of accepting mandatory responsibilities. The Harbord mission (September–October 1919) presented its report to the administration on November 12, 1919. It proposed to implement the unitary model advocated by Caleb Gates, president of Robert College, and Admiral Bristol, whereby a single mandatory would supervise the entire area from Constantinople to the Caucasus. Such a mandate would require an army of 59,000 soldiers and a five-year budget of over $756 million. The report included a list of fourteen reasons for and thirteen reasons against a U.S. mandate. The reasons favoring a mandate stressed the humanitarian bases for such a policy but offered little tangible benefits for the United States. Point 7 noted that "the building of railroads would offer opportunities to our capital," and Point 13 cautioned that "better millions for a mandate than billions for future wars." The reasons against a mandate, however, acknowledged the domestic and international complexities arising from deepening U.S. involvement in the region. Despite the overall favorable tone of the full report vis-à-vis Armenia and Armenians, it raised serious questions regarding the political, economic, and geostrategic feasibility of a U.S. mandate. The Harbord report also was shelved and was not submitted to the Senate until April 1920.[48]

The mandate issue remained inextricably intertwined with the Treaty of Versailles, U.S. participation in the League of Nations, and U.S. deployment of military forces in Armenia. In congressional debates, the proponents for a U.S. mandate underscored humanitarian and moral responsibilities for justice and peace. Mobilization of political support at home for an expansive U.S. role, however, required far greater and systematic efforts. Neither Wilson nor the Armenophile organizations were prepared for such a task.[49] By the time Wilson finally launched his speaking tour across the country in September to campaign for membership in the League, much valuable time had passed. The opponents of the mandate, led by Senator Henry Cabot Lodge, appeared on firmer ground; it was far easier to convince the American public that the United States must not become involved in additional "entangling alliances" and must not assume obligations abroad diverting resources needed at home. Policymakers in Washington preferred to avoid the difficult issues of mandate and recognition and found it more acceptable to send to Armenia surplus wheat left in the silos of the United States Grain Corporation.

The Armenian government dispatched Hovhannes Kachaznuni to the United States in October 1919, who, along with the Armenian Plenipotentiary Garegin Pastermajian (Armen Garo) in Washington, lobbied for economic support for the beleaguered republic. A few weeks later, General Hakob Bagratuni arrived in the United States with instructions from the Armenian Paris delegation to solicit military assistance. The Armenian missions headed by the former prime minister and General Bagratuni were received with much enthusiasm and optimism by Armenians and sympathetic societies, but by then it had become amply clear that U.S. officials in Washington would not translate such sympathies into actual policy. On November 19, 1919, the Senate rejected the Versailles Treaty, and on December 9, the United States officially withdrew from the peace conference. After the lengthy congressional debates and the tour by the Armenian mission in 1919, the republic received about 8 percent or $4.81 million worth of wheat of the total $57.78 million congressional allocation worldwide.[50]

MILITARY MATTERS AND CILICIA

Armenians welcomed outside assistance to alleviate the deplorable conditions in the republic. Military security, however, required more than piecemeal distribution of surplus wheat and clothes. For a while, as the United States debated the mandate issue and Britain withdrew from the Caucasus, the French appeared to be favorably disposed to engage in Cilicia, having contributed to the repatriation of Armenians from the Middle East to Cilicia. French policy in Cilicia, however, not only de facto delinked the region from the Republic of Armenia but also failed to provide the necessary support for the establishment of an Armenian state there. Despite their wartime policy of arming and training volunteer units (the Armenian region), like their British counterparts in the Caucasus, the French favored a strong military in the region and soon sought ways to cultivate friendly contacts with the Kemalist Nationalist Turks. In late

November 1919, François Georges-Picot met with Mustafa Kemal in Sivas, and during the two-day conference he attempted to convince Kemal that French intentions toward Turkey lacked the colonialist pretensions so characteristic of British policy. His government would negotiate commercial ventures, facilitate improvements in the Turkish military, and protect minorities. Kemal responded that the French military occupation of Cilicia was a most critical obstacle toward greater cooperation between the two nations and that so long as the French army remained on Turkish territory the Nationalist troops were ready to sacrifice their lives for the unity and liberation of their country.[51] Turkish Nationalists commenced their attacks on French military posts in Cilicia and eventually forced their withdrawal from the region beginning in early 1920. Its military failures notwithstanding, the French military had enabled the Kemalists to establish their military supremacy in Cilicia. The French, like the other Allied Powers, believed that a strong Kemalist army could serve as a buffer against Bolshevik expansionism.

The resolution of Armenian issues whether in Cilicia or the Caucasus ultimately depended on the outcome of the Russian civil war. The British Foreign Office emphasized the necessity of securing a buffer zone between revolutionary Russia and its southern neighbors and accordingly advocated recognition of the republics in the Caucasus to contain the spread of Bolshevism. This policy would entail substantial expenditures in economic and military assistance regardless if it favored one or all three republics. The War Office, however, stressed that British support for Denikin's army would incur fewer obligations for the task.[52] The Allied Supreme Council heard both British arguments on January 19, 1920, and after a contentious deliberation, it approved the transfer of ammunition and food to the three Transcaucasian republics. The Supreme Council, which had granted recognition to Azerbaijan and Georgia on January 10, finally agreed to extend recognition to the Republic of Armenia during its January 19 session. U.S. recognition followed on April 23, after two months of vacillation. Significantly, Allied recognition came nearly two years after the declaration of the Republic of Armenia in May 1918.[53]

LONDON, SAN REMO, AND SÈVRES

By April 1920 Armenian hopes for a united state inclusive of Sivas, Kharpert, Diarbekir, and Cilicia appeared quite unrealistic. The Turkish Nationalist army was in a stronger position than during the war and seemed determined to gain control Cilicia. At the London Conference (February 12 to April 10, 1920), in preparing the treaty with Turkey, Britain and the other European powers saw no need to make major alterations regarding Armenia except to provide the existing Armenian state access to a port on the Black Sea. A corridor to Batum as an international port would be feasible if the League of Nations assumed supervisory responsibilities. Having agreed on the impossibility of "Greater Armenia," the conference formed a commission to examine the remaining Armenian territorial issues. In mid-February the commission heard the Armenian delegation, headed by Avetis Aharonian and Boghos Nubar Pasha, with mixed results. The delegation was encouraged, however, by the French ambassador's promise that France "would never abandon the Armenians" in Cilicia and would secure for Armenia access to the sea.[54]

Before completing the Turkish treaty, the London Conference took a number of positive steps but failed to provide clear guidelines regarding their actual implementation. With respect to protection of minorities and war reparations, the conference insisted on including in the treaty provisions for the protection of minority rights and required that the Turkish government restore Armenian goods and properties and nullify the Law of Abandoned Properties. The conference, however, limited its claims to indemnification for Allied expenditures, thus ignoring the issue of reparations for Armenian victims since the outbreak of war.[55] Its successes and failures aside, a central feature of the London Conference was that the Allied Powers resorted to maneuvering the League of Nations into addressing those issues that they were not willing to resolve. They received a positive response from Secretary-General Eric Drummond confirming the willingness of the League to examine the proposal that it assume the responsibilities of a mandate for Armenia but with the understanding that the organization could not quickly develop the institutional mechanisms necessary for such a task. The Allied Conference at London promised to resume the negotiations at San Remo in April.

The San Remo Conference (April 19–26, 1920) finalized the authorization of the mandates but, preoccupied with matters pertaining to the control of oilfields in the Middle East, it paid scant attention to the Armenian question. Under the existing conditions, the Allied Powers could not include provisions they could not implement. Accordingly, they reiterated the necessity of the League's involvement to address the Armenian issue. Yet it was also clear that the League could not act effectively in this area without the moral, financial, and military support of the Allied Powers. On April 20, after calculations of costs and benefits on the extent of military involvement required in the Ottoman territories and Armenia, the Allies proposed to the Wilson administration that the United States directly participate in sharing the burden of Armenian security. Armenia's boundaries would remain unchanged until such time as Wilson either accepted the mandate or intervened as an arbiter.[56]

The peace treaty was finally presented to Turkey on May 11, 1920. Its provisions included, inter alia, Turkey's recognition of Armenian independence, submission of proposal to Wilson that he draw the international boundaries of Armenia, nullification of the Abandoned Properties Law and transfer of properties thus acquired to their rightful owners, and prosecution of persons responsible for the massacres. Turkish condemnation of the humiliating treaty was not surprising. Nevertheless, on July 22, 1920, Turkey agreed to sign the treaty and to send a delegation to Sèvres. By then, however, the constant attacks by the Bolshevik, Azerbaijani, and Turkish forces had so enervated the Armenian government as to render its physical survival highly unsustainable.[57]

THE BUREAU GOVERNMENT

In September 1919, during a secret meeting in Erevan, the Armenian Bolsheviks had organized the Armenian Committee (Armenkom) within the structure of the Russian Communist Party. Unlike in Baku, Bolshevism had not yet established a strong foothold in the country. In 1919 there were about 500 Bolsheviks in all of Armenia, and they lacked any significant organizational apparatus for mass agitation and mobilization, except in the region of Alexandropol. To avert radicalization of Bolshevism, the Dashnakist government at first resorted to co-optation and allowed Bolshevik sympathizers to hold jobs in government and schools.[58] In January 1920 the Bolsheviks formed the Armenian Communist Party.[59] The Dashnakist government for its part became less tolerant after January. While the nation was celebrating the long-awaited Allied recognition of the republic, the Bolsheviks launched a massive propaganda campaign vilifying the Allied Powers and their Dashnakist "collaborators" in Erevan. The latter responded by arresting several Bolshevik activists and by expelling others from the country. These tensions culminated in the "May uprising" in Alexandropol, where for two weeks the Bolsheviks threatened to take over the city as a first step toward overthrowing the Erevan government.[60]

In addition, relations between Armenia and Azerbaijan had escalated into armed clashes again. In February 1920, after a lukewarm attempt at negotiations, the British-appointed governor-general Mountainous Karabagh and Zangezur, Khosrov Bek Sultanov mobilized Azerbaijani forces from Baku to Karabagh. Armenian units under the direction of Hovakim Stepanian and Arsen Mikayelian responded by preparing their own battle plans in Karabagh, while General Garegin Nzhdeh (Garegin Ter Harutunian) organized his troops in Zangezur, gaining control over eastern Zangezur by the end of March. In Karabagh, however, Azerbaijani forces sacked Shushi and nearly thirty villages nearby. The Armenian troops under Dro could not withstand the combined powers of the Red and Azerbaijani armies and their Turkish supporters. Between May 22 and

24, after consultation with Nzhdeh, Dro withdrew to Zangezur. Two days later the Tenth Assembly of Karabagh declared the Sovietization of Karabagh.[61]

Local Armenian leaders in different parts of Armenia criticized the Erevan government and its officials in Karabagh for their disastrous policies. The loss of Karabagh posed as much a threat to the Republic of Armenia as the Turkish forces amassing on its western front. After the loss of Karabagh, the Erevan government could no longer afford such accommodationist policies, as the Red Army's advance had emboldened the Armenian Bolsheviks. In Erevan, the Bureau of Dashnaktsutiun decided to replace the more moderate Khatisian by the Bureau Government headed by Hamazasp Ohandjanian as prime minister and Ruben Ter-Minasian as minister of internal and military affairs. After confirming the new cabinet on May 5, 1920, the Khorhrdaran recessed for a month. The Dashnakist government resorted to force to suppress and contain the Bolshevik uprising in Alexandropol, but Revkom-organized rebellions continued to flare in other areas, such as Kars, Sarikamish, Bayazid, Dilijan, and Shamshadin.[62]

Having seemingly crushed the Bolshevik rebellions, the Bureau Government resumed the onerous task of constructing and strengthening the nation's economy and administrative agencies, and in the process it also stressed the Armenianization of civilian and military institutions. Armenianization revived the Armenian culture and language on the independent soil of Armenia; the nation could finally repair its mutilated identity if not pacify its tormented soul. The Bureau Government also considered the question of citizenship, electoral reforms and civic participation, demarcation of local administrative jurisdictions, distribution and ownership of land, bureaucratic reforms to eliminate corruption, and improvements in land and water communication networks. The failure to resolve the economic crisis as a result of the Azerbaijani blockade and oil shortages, however, severely impaired virtually all government programs and paralyzed the nation's economy. The government perforce continued to negotiate concessional terms for contracts with domestic and foreign enterprises and launched a major campaign, headed by Khatisian, for the "Independence Loan" (supplemented by the "Gold Fund") throughout the diasporan communities.[63]

During the summer of 1920, the Bureau Government tried to recover from the crisis of the May uprising and commenced military operations in several troubled areas to insure internal stability. It ordered the military to stabilize the Zangibasar region and to secure the communication lines. A similar military campaign began in Peniak, northeast of Olti, to control the coal fields, and by late June Armenian forces had occupied Peniak and a large part of Olti, within reach of Erzerum across the border. Emboldened by the military successes in Zangibasar and Olti, the hard-liners in the Bureau Government argued that further military action was necessary now toward Vedibasar and Sharur-Nakhijevan in the south and southeast to liquidate pockets of

Turkish-Azerbaijani militia units and to secure the transportation lines with Persia. By mid-July Armenian forces had accomplished their objective across Vedibasar and reached the city of Bash-Norashen, followed by a determined offensive toward Shahtaght, which they captured on July 25, and moved farther south across Nakhijevan. Three days later, however, the Armenian advance was suddenly halted, as Red Army troops arrived in Nakhijevan with military assistance for the local Muslim militia and gold for the Turkish Nationalists. Having defeated the White Army of General Denikin and in control of Azerbaijan, the Red Army rapidly advanced to Karabagh, Zangezur, and Nakhijevan. Nonetheless, the Armenian military successes in Vedibasar, Bash-Norashen, and Shahtaght inspired confidence in the Bureau Government even among the skeptics in the Khorhrdaran.[64]

Confidence earned at home did not translate into confidence in foreign policy priorities abroad. On June 1, 1920, the U.S. Senate defeated a resolution on the mandate question, followed by a similar decision by the House of Representatives two days later. Having failed in the mandate issue, Armenian organizations, such as the American Committee for the Independence of Armenia (ACIA), stressed direct economic and military aid as an alternative. Both the Wilson administration and Congress, however, were reluctant to extend such aid. In fact, while Wilson accepted the responsibility of preparing Armenia's boundaries, he did not create a boundary commission until July, which commenced its work in August, after the Treaty of Sèvres was signed.[65] The commission, led by Professor William Westermann, within a month completed its task and delivered its report to the State Department on September 28. According to the report, which reiterated the position of the Allied powers, Wilson "could transfer any or all of the territories of Van, Bitlis, Erzerum, and Trebizond, require the demilitarization of any adjacent Turkish territory, and provide for Armenia free access to the sea."[66] Kharpert would be excluded from the proposed boundaries of Armenia. Nevertheless, Armenians were satisfied that the boundaries as proposed incorporated the three provinces of Van, Bitlis, and Erzerum as well as Trebizond with guarantees for access to the Black Sea on the westernmost border located east of the port city of Kerasund (Girasun). Wilson did not send his boundary decision to the American Ambassador in Paris, Hugh C. Wallace, until November 24, 1920, who relayed it to the Supreme Council in early December. By then, however, the situation in the Republic of Armenia had changed so radically as to render the proposed boundaries irrelevant.[67]

GENERAL KARABEKIR TO KARS AND ALEXANDROPOL

On September 13, 1920, General Karabekir's troops had begun advancing eastward from Olti to Peniak and Akundir, followed by the invasion of Sarikamish on September 28 in preparation for the capture of Kars. On

October 4 the Armenian interparty assembly issued a declaration, signed by the Dashnaktsutiun, the Armenian Democratic party, Ramkavar, Hnchakian, Socialist Revolutionary, and Social Democratic parties, urging Armenians to unite for the defense of the fatherland against yet another Turkish offensive. Government appeals to the public to defend the republic went unheeded.[68] The herculean military success at Sardarabad in 1918 could not be replicated in late 1920. The persistent economic depression and insecurity at home, years of destruction and genocidal bloodshed at the hands of the Turkish government, the wide discrepancies between the humanitarian proclamations disseminated from western capitals and their actual policies, the Kemalist military and diplomatic victories, and the collusion between the Red Army and the Kemalists all had enervated the Armenian public and their leaders and drained their will to fight. Despite recent successes on the battlefield, public morale could not be maintained for long as the chronic military clashes continued unabated.

Confident that the Allied Powers would not intervene, on October 27 Karabekir moved his troops to capture Kars, while combined Turkish-Kurdish forces conquered the region from Igdir to Surmalu. On October 30 Turkish troops captured Kars with little Armenian opposition,[69] and immediately thereafter Karabekir advanced toward Alexandropol. On November 7 Ohandjanian sued for peace and agreed to accept the conditions set by Karabekir for a truce: the nullification of the Sèvres treaty by the Armenian government. His exchanges for proposals and counterproposals notwithstanding, Ohandjanian failed to stall the Turkish attack on Alexandropol, which resumed on November 11. By November 15 Armenian defenses around the city had evaporated, as had defenses in Surmalu and Sharur-Nakhijevan, a situation exacerbated now by the Georgian advance as well to Jalal-oghli, Bzovdal, and Shahali. The Armenian government was ready to accept the terms of armistice as demanded by Karabekir, and an Armenian delegation led by Khatisian arrived at Alexandropol to sign the agreement.[70]

Writing from Alexandropol on the chaotic situation created by Karabekir's invasion, Prelate Artak Smbatyants of the Armenian Apostolic Church reported to the catholicosate at Echmiadzin that the Turkish military had destroyed entire villages and churches in the region as well as the local economy. The crisis had exacerbated local social problems, and neither civil nor religious leaders paid much heed to civility and morality. No authority commanded sufficient power and legitimacy to stop the bloodshed and the rampant corruption. If left unchecked, Smbatyants warned, the clergy themselves would ransack the church treasuries and cause further hostilities within the communities. Unable to address the crises, he offered his resignation as prelate and urged Catholicos Gevorg V to appoint a bishop with a wider authority and more effective personal capabilities.[71]

THE LAST GOVERNMENT

By late November the military situation for the Erevan government had deteriorated beyond repair. The Bureau of the Dashnaktsutiun appointed socialist Simon Vratsian as the new prime minister in the hope that under him Soviet Russia would more favorably regard relations with Armenia. On November 23 the Khorhrdaran confirmed Vratsian as the new head of government. The following day Khatisian led a delegation to Alexandropol to conclude the peace treaty with Karabekir. Although his military campaigns during the past several weeks had de facto nullified the Sèvres treaty, Karabekir nevertheless demanded a formal declaration by the Armenian government to that effect.[72] On November 26 Khatisian delivered the Armenian declaration to Karabekir, acknowledging that the republic "is disavowing the Treaty of Sèvres."[73]

During a private conversation with Khatisian, Karabekir expressed his amusement at the Armenian territorial aspirations of uniting the republic with historic Armenian lands, as expressed by the Aharonian-Nubar Pasha delegation in Paris and Khatisian himself. "If the Armenians claimed all these territories while they were sitting defeated in Alexandropol, there was no telling what would be left of Turkey if they had been sitting in Van." Karabekir then lectured Khatisian on Armenian and Turkish history. The Armenians, he noted, arrived in Anatolia centuries after the development of the indigenous Turkish culture. "The brilliant Urartian civilization was Turanian, and the inscriptions at Van, Karabekir revealed, pertained not to the Armenian people but to the Turanian tribes of Urartu." During invasions in the eleventh century, Sultan Alp Arslan had conquered Byzantine lands, but, Karabekir asserted, "he had come across no Armenians, whose social and political order, if ever having existed, had long since vanished." "The Armenians were insignificant in that history," Karabekir averred.[74]

Meanwhile, in Erevan, Vratsian and Boris V. Legran, Soviet Plenipotentiary to the Caucasus, negotiated the sovietization of the republic. Only the Red Army possessed sufficient capability to prevent Karabekir's forces from capturing Erevan, and Vratsian, left with no alternative, accepted Russian rule in the republic, albeit with great trepidation and resentment. On November 29 the Armenian Military Revolutionary Committee (*Revkom*) declared the sovietization of Armenia.[75] The Bureau of the Dashnaktsutiun appointed Minister of Military Affairs Dro to negotiate the transition to Soviet rule and to sign the treaty with Karabekir. On December 1 the Armenian Khorhrdaran voted in favor of sovietization, and on December 2 Armenia was formally declared a "socialist soviet republic,"[76] with guarantees of immunity for the Dashnakist leaders. Despite the change in government, the Khatisian-Karabekir negotiations in Alexandropol continued, culminating in the Treaty of Alexandropol on December 3, which nullified the Sèvres treaty. Significantly, neither the Sèvres nor the Alexandropole treaty has been ratified.

The provisional Revolutionary Committee (Heghkom), comprised of five Communists and two Dashnakists and headed by Sarkis Kasian, began to impose sovietization policies with brutal force. On December 28, 1920, the government ordered the nationalization of all arable land in Armenia and the next year devised a specific plan to redistribute it to the peasants. Far more violent were the egregiously ruthless tactics to eliminate the Dashnaktsutiun. Despite the immunity guaranteed to the Dashnakists associated with the Republic of Armenia, in January 1921 the new government arrested and forced into exile about 560 of the Armenian military leaders, among them Generals Tovmas Nazarbekian and Movses Silikian, followed in early February by the imprisonment of former Prime Minister Hovhannes Kachaznuni.[77]

Armenia was not sovietized without resistance. Officials in the new Soviet regime were too impatient to consolidate power, and some old-hand Armenian Bolsheviks, such as Avis Nurijanian, who had participated in the May uprising, sought quick revenge. Armenians soon realized that the new Soviet order imposed on them through the Revkom and the secret police, or Cheka, could be as brutal as any Russian tsarist rule in recent memory. For Western Armenians, the Dashnakist republic had at least provided a haven from the Turkish yoke, but Soviet repressive rule now appeared to be a mere continuation of the persecution and plunder they had experienced in the Ottoman empire. Mass discontent, mobilized by the Dashnaktsutiun, led to armed rebellion against the Soviet regime on February 18, 1921, forcing the Revkom's withdrawal from Erevan.[78] Vratsian led the Salvation Committee of the Fatherland in the liberated regions. Upon entering Erevan, the Salvation Committee liberated the imprisoned from the Cheka jails.[79] As historian Ronald Suny has noted, "When the Cheka prisons were opened, a scene of horror greeted the liberators. Seventy-five bodies were discovered, hacked by axes. Among the dead were the Dashnakist heroes, Hamazasp (Srvandztian) and Colonel Dmitrii Korganov, shot [on] February 1, 1921."[80] The Dashnakists reacted by imprisoning and executing some Bolsheviks.

In April, after imposing Soviet rule in Georgia, the Red Army recaptured Erevan, while the Salvation Committee created "Mountainous Armenia" in Zangezur. Negotiations between the Soviet government in Erevan and Zangezur led to the surrender of the region to the Red Army but with guarantees that it remain part of Armenia. In July 1921 Vratsian and the other leaders of Mountainous Armenia moved to Persia, and on September 30 Soviet Russia and Armenia signed a treaty proclaiming unity.[81]

8

The Leninist-Stalinist Legacy: Seventy Years of Soviet Rule

The rebellion led by the Dashnaktsutiun in February 1921 against Soviet rule failed. After the Bolsheviks recaptured Erevan and the reins of power in April, the new government, led by Aleksandr Miasnikyan, imposed virtual dictatorial rule. By mid-1921 most of the anti-Bolshevik leaders had been liquidated: imprisoned, exiled, or killed. As the new Communist government in Erevan consolidated power, it also ensured Armenia's subordination to Moscow's rule. The Soviet government for its part was confronted with the onerous task of reconstructing the governmental machinery and the economic system.[1] It was under these conditions that the post-independence government in Armenia formally entered into the ostensibly "federal" structure with the Russian Soviet Federated Socialist Republic in September 1921. The seventy-year history of Soviet imperial rule in Armenia was divided into five phases, each reflecting the policy priorities of the leadership in the Kremlin until economic stagnation and political paralysis led to its demise.

LENIN AND THE NEP EXPERIMENT

As the Communist Party of Armenia was engaged in the establishment of the new socialist structures, Lenin had reversed his initial policy of total nationalization of the economy and opted for New Economic Policy (NEP, or state capitalism). Under the NEP, Moscow returned expropriated enterprises to their previous owners but retained exclusive control over the "commanding heights" economic sectors such as finance, transportation, utilities, and heavy industries. During this period, the Armenian economy was primarily an agricultural economy, with little prospects for rapid industrial development. The city of Erevan had a population of about 65,000 in the middle of 1920s, many of whom were survivors of the genocide. Nearly 80 to 90 percent of the populace lived in the rural areas, and urban workers (or the proletariat, in Marxist parlance) constituted no more than 13 percent of the population.[2]

The Communist Party in Armenia confronted the unenviable task of building an industrial infrastructure out of the agricultural economy. Allocated according to family size and production capacity, peasant landholdings consisted of three types: independent households, individual households within the village commune, and collective farms.[3] The crucial problem, however, was not the form of land allocation but the scarcity of land itself. Nor did the Armenian peasants, especially the Western Armenian refugees, show much inclination to work within the agricultural cooperative structures. In order to address the economic crisis, the Armenian leadership, headed by Miasnikyan, embraced the proposal by Joseph Stalin, General Secretary of the Communist Party from April 1922 to December 1952, and Gregory Sergo Ordjonikidze, Stalin's close ally who headed *Kavkazskoe Biuro* (*Kavbiuro*, Caucasian Bureau) and orchestrated the Bolshevik takeover in Georgia in 1921, to integrate the economies of the Caucasian republics—Armenia, Georgia, and Azerbaijan.[4] Immediately after they seized power, the Communists placed the foreign trade policies of the three republics under a single authority, as they did with the railroads in the region. Moscow subsequently removed trade barriers between the three republics; however, the next two years witnessed intensive negotiations on the part of the leaders in the republics and in Moscow to determine the boundaries of the republics.

Under the NEP, Moscow experimented with some degree of reliberalization of the economy, but no such experimentation was tolerated in the realm of government and politics. Miasnikyan advised party leaders in Erevan to permit some flexibility in local administration and in matters concerning the intelligentsia and the bourgeoisie. Only the Communist Party could claim legitimate rule throughout the system, and in the early 1920s all opposition or "counterrevolutionary" parties were abolished. Given the unstable economic condition in Armenia, its government favored revival of the Transcaucasian federal arrangement abandoned in 1918, and on March 12, 1921, the three republics created the Federal Union of Soviet Socialist Republics of Transcaucasia.[5] Further, the Communist government in Moscow sought to resolve amicably issues related to the Armenian-Turkish border and signed the Treaty of Moscow (March 16, 1921) and the Treaty of Kars (October 13, 1921) with the Kemalists. Soviet Russia, like the western powers before, was not disposed to antagonizing Turkey and the Muslims within the Soviet empire on behalf of the Armenian interests.[6]

The administrative structure of Armenia comprised of thirty-three districts (*gavarak*) divided among eight counties (*gavar*), with separate administrative status granted to Erevan, Alexandropol (Leninakan after 1924; now Gumri), and Nor Bayazid. The constitution also provided for the separation of church and state. Under the Soviet constitution, Moscow retained absolute authority over the conduct of foreign and national security policies, the formulation of the Soviet budget and implementation of economic policies, administration of transportation and communication networks and of the legal system, and the direction of all policies with respect to natural resources, education, religion, health, labor, and the mass media.[7]

Although Communists accounted for no more than 1 percent of the population in Armenia, the Communist Party maintained control over Armenian organizational activities through its agencies of repression and fear. These included the Red Army, the Armenian Cheka, the local police, as well as the Komsomol (the Communist Youth Union)—all geared toward, on the one hand, the imposition of national conformity to Soviet unity across the empire and, on the other hand, the institutionalization of *korenizatsiia* (rooting or nativization), the process of localization of sovietization through the employment of Armenians in the national bureaucracies and the use of the Armenian language in state agencies. The Communist Party, under the leadership of such Bolshevik loyalists as Ashot Hovhannisyan, Hayk Hovsepyan, and Haykaz Kostanyan, insisted on the sovietization of virtually all aspects of Armenian life, including the church and the intelligentsia, with little tolerance for deviations from the dictates of Communist rule.[8]

Armenia had to rely on primitive infrastructures for transportation and communication, and it lacked rudimentary industrial bases. The economy therefore depended heavily on agricultural production, which in turn depended on weather and other natural conditions. In 1922, for instance, locusts caused enormous damage to crops in the region of Zangezur. The following year, expecting a similar crisis, Armenian peasants in large numbers abandoned the land altogether. The fact that in the meantime the Communist government confiscated all private lands further exacerbated the situation for the peasants.[9] Despite the magnitude of the difficulties, the economy nevertheless registered some advances in irrigation and hydroelectric projects; for example, the Shirak and Sardarabad canals were put into operation in 1925 and 1932, respectively.

By the late 1920s Communist industrial policy was yet to produce positive results. State-owned factories were built in Leninakan, and during the period 1922 to 1928 employment in industry and transport increased from 4,941 to 20,361 workers. During the second half of the 1920s, the total value of industrial production did not exceed 71.5 percent of the 1914 level, and nationwide unemployment persisted. In Erevan alone, for example, the unemployment level was estimated to be as high as 50 percent of the labor force.[10] The Communist government encouraged the development of consumer and state cooperatives but stressed rapid industrialization with various sectors of heavy industry and chemical production. Cooperatives included the Haykoop, a consumer cooperative union already established during the republic, and the Armentorg engaged in external commerce. By 1928, as the state expanded its domain across different economic sectors, the share of private trade had declined from 46.4 percent in 1925 to 36.7 percent.[11] The government's initial policies aimed at the infrastructural, industrial, and financial integration of the Soviet economy across the enormous territory now under Soviet control.

In the name of national unity, the Communist Party "solved" the territorial issues, which had caused so many difficulties for the Republic of Armenia, through fiat on July 5, 1921. Lori was added to Soviet Armenia, while Karabagh and Nakhijevan were given to Azerbaijan.[12] The Caucasian Bureau of the Communist Party, which included Stalin, Orjonikidize, Nariman Narimanov (the chairman of the first Communist government in Azerbaijan), Miasnikyan, and Sergei Kirov (deputy chairman of Kavbiuro), rendered the final decision regarding Karabagh during a meeting in Tiflis on July 5, 1921. On July 4, the conferees favored the unification of Karabagh with Armenia and decided to hold a referendum on the matter. Narimanov protested and insisted that the case be presented to the Central Committee in Moscow. The following day, during the second meeting, the bureau reversed its decision and without further debate decided that peace between Muslims and Christians as well as the economic ties between Karabagh and Azerbaijan necessitated that Karabagh be "left within the borders of Azerbaijan with the city of Shushi as the center of this Autonomous Region."[13]

The conflict over Karabagh did not end until July 1, 1923, when Baku accepted Karabagh as an autonomous region with its administrative center at Stepanakert (Khankend, Vararakn). Moscow had appointed Asad Karaiev as the Communist leader in Karabagh while the boundaries were being determined. The borders promulgated under him did not provide a corridor between Karabagh and Armenia on the west, an area that consisted of Lachin (Abdaljar), Kelbajar, and Kedabek. Large numbers of Armenians had been removed from this region and from the northern part of Karabagh (Shamkhor, Khanlar, Dashkesan, and Shahumyan), where they had constituted as much as 90 percent of the population. When the first congress of the Soviet Autonomous Region of Karabagh convened in November 1923, 116 of the deputies were Armenians, and 16 Azerbaijanis.

In July 1924 the Central Committee of the Communist Party of Azerbaijan adopted the constitution for Karabagh, which kept the region within the Azerbaijan Soviet Socialist Republic for the next seven decades.[14]

The economic difficulties aside, Armenia in the 1920s and 1930s registered significant, albeit quantitatively limited, accomplishments in cultural development. In 1925, the Institute of Science and Art (renamed the Academy of Sciences) was established in Erevan. Among the luminaries were historians Hakob Manandyan (1873–1952) and Leo (Arakel Babakhanian, 1860–1935), linguists Hachia Ajaryan (1876–1953) and Manuk Abeghyan (1865–1944), writers Avetik Isahakyan (1875–1957) and Eghishe Charents (1897–1937), and musician Alksandr Spendiarov or Spendiaryan (1871–1928).Their works were published and supported by the state, as historian Ronald Suny has noted, "with all the advantages and disadvantages such an arrangement implies."[15]

THE STALINIST REGIME, 1928–1953

After Lenin's death in January 1924, political and economic conditions deteriorated rapidly as Stalin consolidated power in opposition to the more moderate Communists. By 1928 he terminated the NEP and launched rapid industrialization and collectivization campaigns across the nation to combat "peasant backwardness."[16] In the process, Moscow insisted on absolute orthodoxy along the lines of Stalinist dogma objectives. Many Armenian Communist leaders who criticized this sharp turn against the peasants were quickly removed from positions of power despite their strong credentials as loyal Bolsheviks. The government sent students to the farms to introduce the new policy for agricultural collectivization (Armenian: koltntesutyunner, literally, collective economies; Russian: kolkhozy). Resistance, unorganized or organized (as in the case of Daralagiaz), led to police crackdowns, and a large number of peasants were removed from their lands and exiled to Siberia. While the state collectives took control of peasant economy, farmers en masse migrated to the cities for industrial jobs. Industrial production in Armenia, as specified by the Communist government in Moscow, concentrated on chemical production and production of nonferrous metals. According to official statistics, industrial production between 1928 and 1940 rose by about eight times "as a result of the construction of about one hundred large industrial enterprises. In addition, the share of industrial production in the gross national product (GNP) increased from 23 percent in 1923 to 78 percent in 1940."[17] By the late 1930s industrial production accounted for 62 percent of total national production, and industrial workers constituted 31.2 percent of the population. In the economic sphere, the transition to Soviet "command economy" and industrialization required enormous human sacrifices on the part of the Armenian population in general and the peasantry in particular.

Despite the promises for and the sacrifices made in the name of industrialization and modernization, Armenia's economy remained underdeveloped for the duration of Stalin's era. The established factories served mainly to complement the production processes linked to the other republics, and the local economy failed to develop its own infrastructural base necessary for a comprehensive development. Armenia lacked sufficient communications and transportation networks to build a modern economy, even when its industrial output was higher than the agricultural sector.[18]

The political situation proved equally tragic. Stalinism placed a premium on loyalty to Stalin himself and the propagation of the cult of personality. The main strategy to achieve that objective was the elevation of loyalists to key positions within the party and bureaucratic hierarchies while eliminating all real or potential opposition to the Stalinist order. One early Stalinist loyalists was Aghasi Khanjyan, who once in power as the first secretary of the Communist Party in Erevan sought to undermine the Leninist Bolsheviks. In 1936, having "committed suicide," he himself became a victim of Stalin's purges of 1936 to 1938, however, under the ruthless machinations of Stalin's henchman in the Caucasus, Lavrenti Beria.[19] The Communist leadership in Erevan was quickly transformed from Leninist- to Stalinist-oriented "socialism" under the unusually long tenure of Grigor Harutyunyan, a Beria protégé, from 1937 to 1953. The Great Purges brought in a new generation of Communist leaders with a strong sense of loyalty to Stalin, and in the process they "ended any pretension by regional or republic leaders to autonomy from the center."[20]

Soviet unity, however, manifested itself most virulently in the form of Russification campaigns launched by the Stalinist regime. The latter viewed national identity as a threat to the Soviet Union. The "New Soviet Man" was expected to transcend boundaries of national identity and to supplant it with patriotism toward the Soviet Union, while Russian culture and language assumed a superior status among those of the nationalities within the empire. Armenian literary giants (e.g., Raffi, Rafayel Patkanian, Charents) were vilified as "nationalists." In fact, all expressions of criticisms against the Communist regime in Armenia were denounced as "Dashnakism."[21]

THE SOVIET REGIME AGAINST THE ARMENIAN CHURCH

A similarly severe attack was launched against the Armenian Church. Communist ideology, in the tradition of orthodox Marxism, viewed religion as the "opium of the masses" and sought to eradicate all religious influences on Armenian education, culture, and language. In a memorandum dated August 10, 1923, and classified as strictly confidential, a special internal security committee reported to the Communist Party leadership in Erevan that the Armenian Apostolic Church represented the ideology and interests of the bourgeoisie and that the clergy maintained close ties with the Dashnakists in Armenia and the diaspora. The memorandum identified a number of clergy in Iran, among them Bishop Nerses Melik-Tangyan, as cooperating closely with the Dashnakists to undermine the proletarian revolution. In Armenia, the memorandum noted, nearly 1,115 clergy in 850 churches remained under the influence of the Dashnakist ideology and sought to revive Christian life in the republic. The higher clergy, the memorandum emphasized, maintained ties with the western imperialist powers and the diasporan communities, most notably the United States and England. The document also pointed to two factions within the church: conservative traditionalists and reformists. The former adhered to the customs of orthodoxy and rejected interjections of Communist values, while the reformists were more inclined to embrace Communism. In fact, the memorandum noted, the clergy permitted Dashnak leaders to hold meetings in churches and monasteries at Echmiadzin, Sevan, Alexandropol, Ghamarlu, Oshakan, Lori, and Shahnazar, where the clergy worked with local Dashnakist cells, kept the party pamphlets and documents in fireproof safes, and continued their struggle against Communism. The memorandum underscored the imperative of combating the anti-Communist disposition of the Armenian Church and recommended that the Communist leadership find the means to exploit the existing economic hardships and ideological divisions within the church, systematically and scientifically to challenge the church hierarchy and its followers, and to employ various propaganda strategies through the press and local committees to undermine the church. A similar memorandum in February 1924 reiterated the urgency to sow conflict and division within the church by employing secret informants among the discontented.[22]

In early 1924 the Armenian Christmas, which according to tradition is observed in January rather than December, provided an opportunity for such a campaign against the church. In the Siuniats diocese, for instance, the local Komsomols at the town of Goris held meetings in early January to organize antichurch demonstrations during the Holy Mass planned at the Vorotan River that ran through the town. Prelate Bishop Artak Smbatyants expressed his concerns to the local authorities and requested several guards so as to prevent disorderly conduct by the Komsomols. On Christmas day, hundreds of parishioners closed their shops to attend Holy Mass, and as the procession marched by the Communist Party offices in the city, the local Cheka chief and Komsomol youths armed with guns and farm instruments attacked the churchgoers. Bishop Smbatyants communicated his protests to the local authorities for their failure to provide guards. He maintained that the attack appeared to have been planned in advance and that government officials stood by and watched. This barbaric attack, Bishop Smbatyants wrote, represented the party policy toward the Armenian Church, as similar instances had occurred in other towns and villages, where the culprits had gone unpunished. Centuries of such barbarous attacks, the bishop stressed, whether by the Mongols, the Seljuks, and the Arabs, have failed to destroy the Armenian Church. Referring to the Armenian struggle for religious freedom in the fifth century against the imposition of Zoroastrianism, he concluded that the events on Christmas day reminded the parishioners the significance of protecting the church against the modern variant of the Persian Yazdgird and his Armenian collaborator Vasaks of the very same Siuniats region. The Communist Party regional office of Zangezur, clearly perturbed by his acerbic tone, in a letter accused the bishop of provocative lies and exaggerations. The attack was not premeditated, the letter noted, but was merely the act of a single person. In fact, the letter added, the Soviet government should not be equated with the Mongols and the Seljuks, for Soviet policy sought to improve the economic lot of the masses rather than engage in barbaric acts.[23] As the accusations on both sides continued, Communist Party officials considered Bishop Smbatyants a threat to the Soviet regime.

The Soviet regime did not eliminate the Armenian Church but instead preferred to impose total control over the catholicosal seat at Echmiadzin, a policy reminiscent of the *Polozhenie* instituted by Tsar Nicholas I in 1836, which restricted the activities of the catholicosate. The Communist leadership in Moscow pursued a similar policy toward Echmiadzin but with the added ideological justification to support its hegemonic rule. An Armenian Communist, S. Surgunyan, commented in the Tiflis daily *Proletar* in 1938 that the clergy represented a cadre of thieves and liars who preached about fantastic tales labeled miracles as performed by imaginary people called saints who promised salvation in an imaginary place called heaven. In so doing, Surgunyan added, the Armenian clergy for centuries had impeded progress toward enlightenment and scientific thought, while serving the interests of the repressive institutions of such governments as the tsarist regime and the Dashnaktsutiun. The Communist revolutionaries led by Lenin, Surgunyan argued, struggled against the church, and the current government had to be vigilant to prevent the clergy from encroaching on the enlightened ways of the Communist proletariat.[24]

Beginning in early 1929, all religious freedoms were officially suspended, and heavy taxes were imposed on churches, including Echmiadzin. Failure to comply led to confiscation of land, animals, agricultural tools, vehicles, and even treasured sacred vessels. During the late 1920s and the 1930s, especially at the height of the Stalinist purges, Armenian

Communist Party leaders Haykaz Kostanyan, Aghasi Khanjyan, and Hayk Amatuni exiled several priests to Siberia and converted some churches to theaters, clubs, and warehouses. Khanjyan, who led the party in Armenia from 1930 to 1936, accused the Dashnaktsutiun of manipulating the Armenian Church to undermine Soviet Armenia. "Monks were forbidden to leave Echmiadzin in monastic garb or to talk to the people. No one could go to Echmiadzin without police permission."[25] Catholicos Gevorg V Surenyants, who had vehemently opposed Communist rule, died in May 1930 and was succeeded in November 1932 by the more pro-Moscow Archbishop of Erevan, Khoren I Muradbekyan. Catholicos Khoren did not survive the Great Purges of 1936 to 1938, however, and his death, on April 6, 1938, is believed to have been ordered by the secret police.[26]

The case of Bishop Artak Smbatyants illustrates the brutality of the Soviet regime against the Armenian Church. Smbatyants had graduated from the Nersisian Academy in Tiflis in 1894 and subsequently the Gevorgian Seminary of Echmiadzin, where he was ordained into priesthood in 1902. He was elevated to bishophood in November 1922, a year and a half after the final removal of the Dashnakist government. Beginning in 1910, he had assumed various administrative responsibilities within the church and played a leading role in relief assistance in the region of Gumri (Alexandropol) for the refugees fleeing the genocide in Western Armenia. Smbatyants served as prelate of the Shirak and Ararat dioceses from 1922 to 1935 and 1935 to 1937, respectively. By then, however, the Stalinist regime had launched its major offensive against all religious institutions, which culminated in the closing of nearly all churches in Soviet Armenia, with the exception of the Mother See at Echmiadzin. Smbatyants protested the government's repressive policies toward the church and the confiscation of its properties. As early as 1923, he compiled a list of the sacred vessels and other treasured valuables at the Tatev monastery for safekeeping at Echmiadzin, since, he noted in a letter to Catholicos Gevorg V, the political situation required precautionary measures to protect the church and its properties. In a letter dated January 29, 1929, for example, he petitioned the interior commissariat of the republic to be more lenient with respect to the heavy taxation imposed on the church and the clergy. Appointed in 1934 as a representative of the catholicos in Erevan, Bishop Smbatyants in numerous communications with the Communist Party at the capital pleaded for the reinstitution of the church's ecclesiastical authority and for an end to the religious and political persecutions. On April 13, 1937, the Communist authorities, under direct orders from the internal security chief in Erevan, arrested the bishop at the Echmiadzin monastery. The warrant for his arrest listed possession of nationalist literature (eighteen books).[27] After trials began on April 14, 1937, the internal security court found him guilty of propagating nationalist and anti-Soviet ideologies in his sermons and public statements, illegally preparing candles, and raising funds to assist the families of his collaborators now in exile or in prison.[28] On August 31, 1937, the court sentenced the bishop to death, despite repeated pleas by Catholicos Khoren I to the Communist leadership in Erevan for his release. At 2:00 o'clock in the early morning of September 3, a firing squad executed Bishop Smbatyants in an Erevan Cheka prison.[29]

The hardship endured under Stalin notwithstanding, World War II, referred to as the Great Patriotic War in the Soviet Union, accelerated Armenia's integration into the Soviet industrial networks and seemed to have strengthened Armenian loyalty to the system. Soviet Armenian contribution to the war effort ranged from the enlistment of thousands of nurses to about 500,000 soldiers serving in combat. The war claimed more than 25 million Soviet lives, including an estimated 175,000 Armenians.[30] After Catholicos Khoren's death in 1938, the Soviet government left the pontifical seat at Echmiadzin vacant for the next seven years. In 1945, with the participation of Catholicos Garegin I Hovsepian of the Cilician See at Antelias, Gevorg VI Chorekchyan was elected Catholicos of All Armenians at Echmiadzin. Gevorg VI whom the Communist Party utilized for purposes of propaganda cooperated with the Communist regime in support of the Western Armenian question and the repatriation policy in 1946–1947. The Communist government in turn permitted the reopening of the Gevorgian Jemaran (Academy) in 1948 and encouraged closer relations between Echmiadzin and the diaspora communities.[31]

STALINIST GEOPOLITICS AND THE ARMENIAN DIASPORA

Despite political and economic difficulties, two issues appeared to provide an opportunity for cooperation between Moscow and Armenians in the post-World War II period. The first involved territorial claims, including reannexation of Kars and Ardahan to Armenia, which would require renegotiation of the Treaty of Kars (1921), and Karabagh. While Stalin's motives can be debated, for Armenians at home and abroad the reemergence of the issue as an international question revived hopes for territorial, albeit partial, unification.[32] In 1945 Grigor Harutyunyan, the First Secretary of the Communist Party in Armenia from 1937 to 1953, submitted a proposal to Stalin to reunify Karabagh with Armenia. Harutyunyan sent a similar petition in 1949. Both attempts failed to convince the Kremlin of the urgency to rectify the situation in Karabagh.[33] The second issue concerned the repatriation (*nergaght*) of Armenians to Soviet Armenia. Stalin sought to draw diasporan Armenians to Soviet Armenia to replenish the labor force devastated during World War II and to improve relations with the Armenian communities abroad.[34]

By then Armenians had migrated or returned to Soviet Armenia in three phases. The first wave, from 1921 to 1925, involved about 25,000

Armenian *hayrenadartsner* (repatriates), most of whom arrived from the Middle East (Syria, Iraq, and Iran), France, and Greece. During the second wave (1926 to 1936), approximately 10,000 Armenians repatriated, mostly from Bulgaria, Greece, and France. It is likely that the worldwide economic depression contributed to this phase of repatriation. Although the third phase proved shortest, from 1946 to 1948, it nevertheless resulted in the repatriation of between 70,000 and 100,000 Armenians, the highest number since the collapse of the republic in 1921.[35] Armenians repatriated during this phase came from the Middle East (the first group was from Beirut, Lebanon), Bulgaria, France, and the United States.

The experiences of the repatriates varied depending on their personal and familial circumstances, but two contradictory views have emerged regarding their condition. Soviet Armenian historians, largely reflecting the views of the Communist Party, maintained that native Armenians welcomed their repatriating compatriots with open arms. The government built new schools, hospitals, and shops, and set aside large tracts of land for the construction of about 40,000 units to house the repatriates. According to this view, the repatriates had finally found spiritual solace in the bosom of the motherland and, with Stalin's blessings, began to enjoy the fruits of socialism and participated in the political process. The opposing view held that life was not so easy for the repatriates. There were hardly any government services for their well-being, some had to build their own houses, and an unknown number were sent to the villages for hard labor and others to Siberia. The native Armenians generally resented the large influx of foreigners that added to the existing economic and financial difficulties immediately after the war. The economic paralysis and political repression of postwar Soviet Armenia could hardly provide the repatriates an environment conducive to assimilation. The advent of the Cold War virtually froze relations between Soviet Armenia and the diaspora, and the worldwide East-West ideological polarization erected the Iron Curtain through Armenia as well. Stalin's cosmetic rapprochement with Armenians was reversed, and attacks on Armenian intellectuals and institutions resumed.

World War II severely affected the republic's economy; according to one estimate, by 1946 the GNP declined by about 7 percent of the 1940 level. The economy recovered rapidly in part due to the growing heavy industry sector in machine production and the creation of more than forty industrial companies.[36] By the time Stalin died in March 1953, Soviet Armenia had established an industrial base that the Republic of Armenia never had, but it lacked the privileges of sovereignty in domestic and international politics. Stalin's policies left behind a Russified Armenian language, a terrorized and a traumatized public, and a national political culture and economy dominated by the secret police and the Communist Party elite with little regard for the well-being of the population.

KHRUSHCHEV, DE-STALINIZATION,
AND REFORMS, 1953–1964

The new leadership under Nikita Khrushchev sought to disassociate itself from the brutalities committed during Stalin's rule. The first signs of reforms and a more relaxed political environment for Armenia appeared in 1954, when the Politburo sent Anastas Mikoyan, the leading Armenian official in Moscow, to Erevan to repair relations and remove the Stalinist antinational policies imposed on Armenian cultural activities. Thus, for example, the government made the works of formerly banned authors (e.g., Raffi and Charents) again available to the public.[37] This era of reform was formally enunciated by Khrushchev at the Twentieth Party Congress in February 1956. He condemned the excesses of Stalinism and the "cult of personality" and promised to improve political and economic conditions, especially for the agricultural sector.

A number of nascent intellectual movements supported Khrushchev in his efforts toward de-Stalinization. One of the earliest reform-oriented groups emerged at Akademgorodok (Academic City), founded in 1957 at the outskirts of the Russian city of Novosibirsk on the Ob River. Located in western Siberia far from the political centers at Moscow and Leningrad (again St. Petersburg), Akademgorodok served as an intellectual hub for younger artists, scientists, and scholars who, disillusioned with the rigidities of the political system and its ideology of communism, experimented with unorthodox ideas. The principal scholars engaged in the new enterprise included Mikhail Lavrentev, one of the city's founders, Abel Aganbegyan, and Tatyana Zaslavskaya.[38] Khrushchev's reforms attempted to remove national leaders who were closely associated with Stalinism, but during the next two decades, the Armenian Communist Party under the three successive leaders—Suren Tovmasyan (1953–1960), Iakov Zarobyan (1960–1966), and Anton Kochinyan (1966–1974)—continued to be dominated by the old guard. It should be pointed out, however, that de-Stalinization did not necessarily mean political "liberalization." The Red Army crushed the Hungarian rebellion during the same year that Khrushchev gave his de-Stalinization speech.[39] The Hungarian message could not have escaped the attention of the Armenians in Erevan.

Nor did the Soviet regime relax its onslaught against the Armenian Church and culture, and by the early 1950s, a crisis of profound import developed within the Armenian communities, first between the Mother See of Echmiadzin and the Great House of Cilicia seated at Antelias, Beirut, Lebanon, and then throughout the Armenian communities across the diaspora. The attacks on the intelligentsia in Soviet Armenia were complemented by a renewed propaganda campaign against the Armenian Church at home and in the diasporan communities. The death of Catholicos

Gevorg VI in May 1954 led to the election of Catholicos Vazgen I Baljian in October 1955. Although he improved relations between Soviet Armenia and some sectors in diasporan communities, he was instrumental, with the support of the Soviet authorities and the anti-Dashnaktsutiun parties in the Middle East, in Communist efforts to prevent the election of the next catholicos of Cilicia at Antelias. The Catholicosate of Echmiadzin sought to influence the election in order to enthrone a candidate who would be more amenable to Soviet geopolitical interests. Although in the ensuing political maneuvers and crisis the election, set for February 14, 1956, was at the last minute postponed for a few days, it nevertheless took place on February 20, with the Prelate of Aleppo, Bishop Zareh Payaslian, elevated to the catholicosal throne of the Great House of Cilicia. His ordination took place on September 2, 1956, at the Cathedral of Surb Grigor Lusavorich. The Soviet regime failed, but the crisis deeply divided the diasporan communities along ideological lines between pro-Soviet (Hnchakians and Ramkavars) and anti-Soviet (Dashnaktsutiun) parties.[40]

By the late 1950s the Armenian economy was beginning to be transformed from agriculture to industrialization and urbanization. In the early 1950s, about 50 percent of the labor force worked in agriculture; by the early 1970s the agricultural sector constituted no more than 20 percent of the labor force. Industrial production increased by an annual average of 9.9 percent, and by the mid-1970s it was "335 times greater than it had been in 1913."[41] The advantages gained in the 1960s did not necessarily improve conditions for the Armenian population, however. The economy still lacked a strong base for consumer economy, misuse of political and economic power led to rampant corruption, and the "second economy"—with all its deleterious implications for the public commonweal—became a permanent fixture.[42]

At the third session of its Fifth Conference in March 1960, the Supreme Soviet of Armenia paid particular attention to the economic problems. The post-Stalinist environment of reforms encouraged the deputies to criticize openly the various sectors of administration in the republic. As usual, those taking the floor first praised the Communist Party leadership in Erevan and Moscow for their successes in generating economic development in the industrial and agricultural sectors. They then presented a scathing evaluation of the performance of various bureaucracies and of the general economic situation. Addressing the floor, deputy Anton Kochinyan from Eghegnadzor, who a few years later became the leader of the Armenian Communist Party, reminded the chamber of the devastated and poor country the Soviets inherited from the first republic in 1921 and, after praising the Communist Party for its accomplishments since then,[43] he complained about the mismanagement and wastefulness of the existing budgetary process. For example, he noted that far too many construction projects (roads, sewerage, housing, schools) had been launched, and none could receive adequate funding or administrative attention. He noted that even where construction projects received sufficient funding, the inferior quality of workmanship and the unreasonably long duration of construction made such projects doubly expensive. Delays in completion compromised the structural integrity of sections already built, which in turn required additional funds to prevent further deterioration. Despite the huge sums allocated for beautification, the streets in Erevan, Leninakan, and other cities remained filthy, lacked proper maintenance, and in general looked unpleasant. The combination of such problems, he added, not only impeded economic development but also created unsanitary conditions and serious environmental crises in general. Kochinyan concluded his lengthy speech with the recommendation that the local policymakers and administrators institute major reforms so as to generate economic growth in a healthier environment.[44] Other deputies echoed his observations. Further, as part of the proposed reforms, some members also advocated the introduction of laws granting citizens the right to recall officials in the local soviets who failed to fulfill their obligations to their constituent communities of workers and farmers. A similar law had been adopted by the Supreme Soviet of Armenia in 1959 for the right to recall deputies to the Supreme Soviet of the republic.[45] The political and economic reforms introduced under Khrushchev promised to improve the Soviet system at all levels of government and society. His promises notwithstanding, Khrushchev's policies, especially in the area of agricultural production, largely failed, and the conservative members of the Politburo ousted him from power in October 1964. The Politburo appointed his protégé, Leonid Brezhnev, party first secretary.

BREZHNEV AND THE CRISIS OF LEGITIMACY, 1964–1982

Even if Khrushchev's reforms encouraged greater tolerance for expressions of national aspirations, such activities were confined to the ideological boundaries as determined by the Communist Party leaders in Moscow and Erevan. The Armenian intellectual community tried constantly to keep issues related to the Armenian language, culture, religion, and territories on the national agenda in both capitals. No event showed the revival of Armenian nationalism with greater force than the mass demonstrations in Erevan on April 24, 1965, commemorating the fiftieth anniversary of the genocide.[46] During the mass demonstrations Armenians demanded the reunification of the historic Armenian territories (occupied by Turkey) with Armenia. While during the April demonstrations Moscow and

Erevan refrained from using military force, the Kremlin soon replaced the Armenian leader, Iakov Zarobyan, by the more "reliable" Kochinyan. The latter insisted on preventing future public outpouring of such "local nationalist" sentiments but permitted the construction of the Genocide Monument at Tsitsernakaberd (Dzidzernagapert), which was completed in November 1967. The Communist government also permitted the construction of the memorial complex dedicated to the Battle of Sardarabad of 1918, which opened in May 1968 on the site of the battleground.[47]

The Communist Party nevertheless failed to uproot the underground nationalist movements, such as the National Unity Party, which advocated the reunification of Karabagh, Nakhijevan, and Western Armenia with Armenia. In June 1965 thirteen Armenian intellectuals, including the novelist Bagrat Ulubabyan, who served as the head of the Writers' Union in Karabagh for more than two decades, submitted yet another petition to Moscow calling for the unification of Karabagh with Armenia. Moscow responded by attempting to suppress such demands. In 1966 Armenians intellectuals in Erevan also urged unification; subsequently, Armenians in Karabagh petitioned the government in Erevan to address the matter. The petition enumerated the fundamental grievances against Azerbaijani rule: "Our situation is worse than it has ever been . . . . Our honour is soiled, our dignity and our rights are flouted." Moscow and Erevan refused to enter negotiations on the matter, and in 1968 violent clashes took place between Armenians and Azerbaijanis in Stepanakert.[48]

Coincidentally, the "Prague Spring" of 1968 in Czechoslovakia and the removal of the reformist Communist Party leader Alexander Dubchek clearly indicated that Moscow would not tolerate deviationism in the Soviet bloc.[49] Although some Armenian nationalist leaders were imprisoned and executed, by the middle of the 1970s it was virtually impossible to eliminate all such movements. In 1974 the Kremlin entrusted Karen Demirchyan with the responsibility of addressing local problems, particularly eradication of corruption, reinvigoration of the economy, and control of nationalism.[50] In a similar vein, Heydar Aliyev, head of the Communist Party in Azerbaijan, and Boris Gevorgov, an Armenian member of the Central Committee of the Azerbaijani Communist Party, assumed a more direct role in suppressing Armenian demands regarding Karabagh. In a speech at a session of the Regional Committee of Mountainous Karabagh in 1975, Gevorgov accused the Armenian intellectuals engaged in the Karabagh movement as holding "nationalist" sentiments and urged the committee to reject demands for the unification of Karabagh with Armenia as mere "Dashnakist propaganda."[51] Further petitions to the Brezhnev government continued to prove futile, despite Armenian protests.

Armenian nationalism also found expression in anti-Soviet and secessionist movements. Stepan Zatikyan organized the secret National Unity

Party (NUP) in 1967, which emerged in the 1970s as one of the principal nationalist organizations in the Soviet Union. The NUP demanded the reunification of the historic Armenian lands, including Western Armenia, Nakhijevan, and Karabagh. In January 1974 Razmik Zohrapyan, a member of the NUP, burned Lenin's picture in the Lenin Square (now Republic Square) in Erevan in protest of Soviet totalitarian rule. That year, the Soviet government arrested several NUP members. In January 1977 the group was accessed of setting off a bomb in the Moscow Pervomaiskaia metro station, killing seven people and wounding thirty-seven. The Soviet secret service reportedly foiled plans by the same group for a second explosion at Moscow's Kursk railroad station in October. The government executed three Armenians (Zatikyan, Hakob Stepanyan, and Zaven Paghtasaryan) accused of the bombing in January and the attempted attack in October. In February 1980 the New Armenian Resistance bombed the Soviet Office of Information in Paris in retaliation.[52]

Despite its various shortcomings and repressive rule, Soviet Armenia registered significant social and cultural advances. The republic boasted a literacy rate of about 98 percent and 13 institutions of higher education with 57,900 students as well as 1,371 schools with 592,000 students.[53] Moreover, a number of literary figures, most prominently the poets Hovannes Shiraz (1915–1984) and Paruyr Sevak (1924–1971), produced enormously popular works and perhaps even shaped the quality of the cultural and political discourse in Armenia and abroad. They struggled to liberate Armenian culture and literature from the dictates of the Communist Party in Moscow and Erevan and to cultivate a more authentic sense of Armenian identity—a worldview that directly clashed with the Kremlin's ideology of sovietization, de-nationalization, and de-territorialization.[54] While Russification and sovietization failed in the republic, Armenian parents, especially among the elite, encouraged their children to master the Russian language so as "to improve the chances of admission to a university in Moscow and Leningrad."[55]

In efforts to "modernize" Armenia, the Soviet government sought to remove obstacles in Armenian traditions and customs to the modernization of family structure. Armenian women particularly benefited from the liberalizing effects of educational and employment opportunities. Further, Soviet law demanded mutual consent for marriage, prohibited dowry, and criminalized rape.[56] The Soviets also encouraged women, based on the quota system, to hold political office; as a result, by 1990 women made up 30 percent of members in the Armenian Supreme Soviet or parliament. Only a few women, however, gained membership in the Politburo, Ekaterina Furtseva (1957–1961) being the most famous. Modernization and equality in law did not necessarily bring about modernization and equality in local culture and customs. While the Soviet system enabled Armenian women to fuse the responsibilities of employment and motherhood, in fact they continued to shoulder a disproportionately large share of the responsibilities in household labor.

These improvements notwithstanding, the Soviet leadership under Brezhnev refused to employ Khrushchev's more pragmatic approach to the economy and society at large. Although the economy had improved somewhat since the 1950s, the Brezhnev government encouraged a culture of corruption, whereby the informal economy permeated all aspects of society. Armenia's economy remained underdeveloped with no significant advances beyond servicing the Soviet republics. For instance, in 1970 "Armenia produced 42 million pairs of stockings and socks, about 60 million items of linen and underwear, and 10.3 million pairs of shoes. The production of consumer goods and commodities grew significantly, and Armenian production was able to meet a considerable part of the demand of the Soviet consumer goods market."[57] Production of socks and shoes however could hardly enable Armenia to achieve modern technological capabilities with competitive advantages within and beyond the boundaries of the Soviet Union. The economic problems were further complicated by the fact that Armenia's economy could not experience liberalization and technological modernization so long as the Communist Party maintained its monopoly over the Soviet political economy. The Communist elite rejected calls for political liberalization and self-criticism. The younger generation, however, trained and educated in the Khrushchev era of de-Stalinization, believed in the desirability and even inevitability of fundamental changes in Soviet institutions. Statements such as "everything has grown rotten" and "we can't go on living this way" were heard with increasing frequency in private conversations among younger bureaucrats. Such criticism of the Soviet system, however, did not consider the challenges associated with the nationalities, as most Soviet leaders in the mid-1980s continued to assume that the New Soviet Man had overcome parochial identities.[58] Equally important, economic stagnation and political repression, now combined with leadership instability inside the Kremlin, unleashed centrifugal forces that at first appeared as demands for structural reforms but subsequently led to secessionist movements. After Brezhnev's death in November 1982, leadership instability in Moscow magnified the existing political and economic structural deficiencies. Yuri V. Andropov, Brezhnev's successor, died in office in February 1984. Konstantin U. Chernenko, who succeeded Andropov at the age of seventy-two, also died in office the following year. As Mikhail Gorbachev, the new Communist leader at the Soviet helm, observed in his memoirs years later, "The very system was dying away; its sluggish senile blood no longer contained any vital juices."[59]

GORBACHEV'S GLASNOST AND PERESTROIKA, 1985–1991

Upon assuming power in March 1985, Gorbachev and his close advisers— Leonid Abalkin, Abel Aganbegyan, and Nikolai Petrakov—experimented with ideologically unorthodox policies in hopes of invigorating the Soviet economy. Yet such a course, their Communist conservatives at the Kremlin cautioned, could undermine the very political system they aimed to rescue. Gorbachev surrounded himself with advisers, such as Aganbegyan and Tatyana Zaslavskaya, author of the now-famous "Novosibirsk Report" in 1983, who advocated radical economic and political reforms in order to strengthen the Soviet system. The report criticized the Stalinist model as sheer anachronism and proposed "a qualitative restructuring"—*perestroika* (restructuring).[60] The advent of *glasnost* (openness) and perestroika led to fundamental questions regarding the ideological foundations as well as the structural arrangements of the Soviet regime.[61] The emergence of Gorbachev as the Communist Party leader in Moscow and his policies encouraged greater freedom.

Although Gorbachev, like his predecessors, was not inclined to entertain separatist sentiments or demands for redrawing of interrepublic boundaries, Armenian nationalism had already been radicalized and transformed into a powerful popular force in spite of Soviet policies and priorities. Most Armenians demanded less Russian political and cultural influences and pressed for the Armenianization of Armenia, which at first entailed democratization and greater local autonomy. For example, School No. 183 in Erevan, radically altered its educational curriculum in order to revive Armenian culture. "In other republics," one observer wrote in the early 1990s, "people dreamed about revamping their schools; here people were doing it." School No. 183 was "more than a center of cultural renaissance—it [was] a hotbed of political rebellion."[62]

Moscow's inadequate responses to the Chernobyl disaster in 1986—when a nuclear power plant reactor exploded and its fallout contaminated large parts of Ukraine, Belarus, and Russia, causing the resettlement of more than 336,000 people—and to the earthquake in Armenia in 1988, which, according to official data, claimed at least 25,000 lives, destroyed fifty-eight villages, and severely damaged twenty-one cities and regions, including hundreds of educational and cultural institutions and more than 200 manufacturing facilities—only served to amplify the ineptitude of the Communist leadership and to galvanize the opposition forces.[63] Gorbachev's public pronouncements for glasnost and perestroika gave rise to expectations, but the continuation of the disastrous military engagement in Afghanistan begun under Brezhnev in 1979, the failure to improve relations with the satellite states in eastern Europe, and the failure to eradicate the ills of maladministration and corruption further diminished the already tenuous and increasingly attenuated legitimacy of the Communist Party. Thus, a combination of factors—including the Stalinist legacy, mismanagement, and corruption—rent the system beyond repair.[64]

The western economies, from West Germany to the United States, had proved far more successful in their capacity to modernize and to adapt to the rapid globalization of markets and finance, while the Soviet bloc economies lagged behind despite the enormous human sacrifices since the accelerated industrialization policies under Stalin. Gorbachev believed that through glasnost and perestroika the Soviet economy could overcome "everything that was holding back development."[65] The Kremlin, according to his plan, would guide political and economic liberalization through public mobilization, the economy would lean toward market socialism, price liberalization, and a certain degree of private ownership, while scientific and technological modernization would facilitate economic growth. In his speech at the plenum of the Communist Party's Central Committee in January 1987, Gorbachev called for democratization and the institution of free elections. The speech was followed by the release of political prisoners, in demonstration of good faith.[66]

Beginning in the summer of 1987, Gorbachev's promises for democratization were put to the test. Crimean Tartars, who had been forced into exile to Uzbekistan by Stalin in 1944, demanded permission to return to their homeland. The Kremlin for decades had rejected such claims and refused to permit public debate on the matter, and in July 1987, when the Tartars held a protest demonstration at the Red Square, their demands went unheeded.

In addition, divisions within the party also became more visible. In October 1987 the removal of Boris Yeltsin from the Politburo signified a deeper divisions within the Kremlin than publicly recognized. By 1988 centrifugal tendencies in nearly all areas of the Soviet polity began to transform the political and economic structures, placing enormous pressure on Gorbachev to press for greater democratization. Yet Gorbachev and the Kremlin policymakers failed to gauge accurately the velocity and the trajectory of the public mood and continued to believe that their implementation of glasnost and perestroika would reform the system. As Gorbachev has noted, "We talked not about revolution, but about *improving the system*. Then we believed in such a possibility."[67]

Moreover, in addition to the problems of instituting a more open and democratic system, economic stagnation and political paralysis prevented Gorbachev from building a more viable system. In fact, the problems confronting Gorbachev necessitated a complete ideological, cultural, and institutional overhaul, which neither he nor his hard-line Communist colleagues would countenance. The events rapidly unfolding across the Soviet bloc made it obvious that the existing institutional mechanisms could not accommodate transformations of such magnitude and could not absorb the shocks of further economic and political disorder. The Chernobyl nuclear meltdown in 1986 and the secrecy imposed by the Communist leadership and bureaucracies regarding the catastrophe amplified the urgent need for liberalization at all levels and spheres of government. Thus, a number of closely intertwined factors led to the crisis in the Soviet Union, including economic stagnation, political atrophy, and secessionist movements in the republics.[68]

The growing secessionist movements represented an integral part of the various social and psychological consequencs of the hardship endured as a result of the economic stagnation and of the civil crisis experienced as a result of political atrophy. In Soviet Armenia, while some Armenians called for a declaration of independence, the ruling Communist elite remained hesitant at best. The Armenian National Movement (Hayots Hamazgayin Sharzhum) led the opposition to the Soviet regime. Headed by such intellectuals as Levon Ter Petrosyan engaged in the Karabagh movement, the Armenian National Movement, initially known as the Pan-Armenian National Movement, sought to represent all Armenian interests, with particular attention to the crisis unfolding in Karabagh. Indeed, beginning in 1988 and for the next two years, events in that Armenian enclave within Azerbaijan became closely intertwined with developments in Armenia proper.

Prior to the escalation of the conflict in Karabagh, in 1987 Armenian political and intellectual leaders petitioned the Kremlin for the annexation of the region, but after failed appeals, Armenians in Stepanakert and Erevan took their cause to the streets. Armenians in Karabagh numbered about 145,450, or 76.9 percent of the population, while Azerbaijanis numbered 40,668 (21.5 percent). Years of discrimination and repression in the dual structures of Soviet and Azerbaijani control, coupled with economic stagnation, had left the Armenians miserable and hopeless.[69] On February 20, 1988, the Soviet of People's Deputies of Karabagh voted in favor of reunification with Armenia, and in doing so it in effect nullified the decision rendered under Stalin on July 5, 1921.[70] The vote was followed by mass demonstrations in Erevan during the next week, when in successive decisions first Demirchyan, the head of the Communist Party in Armenia, and then the Kremlin vetoed the February 20 decision.[71] The Communist leadership in Moscow, according to former Prime Minister Nikolai Ryzhkov, considered the Karabagh Committee as a manifestation of "nationalist extremism" that radicalized the opposition toward the Kremlin.[72] On February 21 Azerbaijanis attacked Armenians in the town of Gadrut in Karabagh. No sooner had Gorbachev calmed the two sides with promises for negotiations than on February 28 a pogrom was launched against the Armenian inhabitants in the Azerbaijani cities of Sumgait, Baladzhary, and Kirovabad.[73] After three days of mass murder, which claimed the lives of thirty people, the Soviet military intervened to put an end to the bloodshed. During the pogrom, in one instance as an Azerbaijani mob rushed through the streets, an Armenian woman attempted to escape but was "chased down by a gang wielding bicycle chains, knives, and hatchets.

The Azerbaijanis came, all dressed in black . . . . They went through every building, looking for Armenians and shouting slogans—'Death to Armenians,' 'We'll annihilate all the Armenians. Get them out of here.'"[74] While not all Azerbaijanis supported such violence and some even protected their Armenian neighbors, the collective historical memories of the genocide colored the Armenian perception of the massacres as a repeat of the bloodshed and suffering their parents and grandparents had experienced at the hands of the Turks in the Ottoman empire. The local Azerbaijani police participated in the looting and murder, while firefighters and ambulances refused to lend assistance to the Armenian families.[75]

The Kremlin initially claimed to pursue a balanced approach to the crisis but failed to act immediately. The declaration in late March 1988 by the Politburo in Moscow that the Karabagh Committee acted illegally, on the one hand, and the policy directive by Politburo member Yegor Ligachev rejecting calls for boundary reforms, on the other, only fueled further resentment and hostilities in Armenia and Karabagh, leading to mass demonstrations demanding their unification. Communist Party leaders in Moscow during the preceding three years had received 500 letters from Armenians expressing their discontent regarding conditions in Karabagh, but the Kremlin considered the Karabagh question as potentially triggering a "domino" effect, with unpalatable ramifications across the Soviet Union. Beginning in May 1988, the Karabagh Committee in Erevan and the Krunk (Crane) Committee in Stepanakert led the popular movement for greater autonomy from Moscow. (The Karabagh Committee included Levon Ter Petrosyan, Vazgen Manukyan, Ashot Manucharyan, and other intellectuals and activists.)[76] On May 28, 1988, on the seventieth anniversary of the independence of the first republic in 1918, the Association for National Self-Determination organized a mass rally, when about 50,000 people waved the banned tricolor of the 1918 republic and demanded official recognition of the day as a national holiday.[77] Gorbachev commented at a Politburo meeting in early July 1988 that "reviewing boundaries is unrealistic; that would mean going down a disastrous path, and not only in these regions."[78] A few days later, on July 19, he noted that in the case of the clashes between Armenians and Azerbaijanis "passions are to some extent running out of control. There appear slogans of anti-socialist, anti-Soviet, and anti-Russian character."[79]

Matters deteriorated further when the Nineteenth Party Conference, mired in accusations of abuses of power in the selection of delegates, failed to offer a workable alternative or a solution to the Karabagh conflict. Armenian protests at the Zvartnots airport near Erevan escalated into a brief armed clash with the Soviet military. While anti-Soviet sentiments heightened, the Karabagh Committee held a mass demonstration in September explicitly demanding independence. It intended to pressure the

Communist leadership in Erevan criticize openly to the Kremlin's Karabagh policy.[80] Gorbachev insisted that the Soviet government could not permit conflicts in the republics to jeopardize the Soviet system. The inability of the central government to remedy the situation, however, further intensified hostility towards the authorities at all levels of government, contributing to the erosion of the political legitimacy of the Communist leadership.[81] By the end of 1988, Armenians in both Armenia and Karabagh were convinced that national independence represented the only option to address the various political, economic, social, and environmental crises.[82]

Yet, the diasporan political organizations initially opposed the independence movement led by the Armenian National Movement. It was indeed ironic that the Dashnaktsutiun—the political party that since the Bolshevik takeover of the first republic had for seven decades advocated Armenian independence and unification of historic Armenian lands— together with the Hnchakian and Ramkavar parties issued a joint declaration in October 1988 urging compatriots in Armenia not to secede from the Soviet Union. The Dashnaktsutiun, maintained that secession from the Soviet Union at this point would jeopardize the security of Armenia and that the potential threat posed by Turkey and its ideology of pan-Turkism necessitated Russian protection. The Dashnaktsutiun believed that under Gorbachev's leadership the Kremlin would facilitate a negotiated resolution of the crises enveloping both Armenia and Karabagh, and the party insisted on cooperation with Suren Harutyunyan (who succeeded Demirchyan in 1988 as the Communist party leader in Erevan) and Gorbachev.[83] The Dashnakist party leadership, whose political activities for decades had been excluded from Soviet society, clearly failed to appreciate the power of the pro-democracy and pro-independence movement.[84]

In reaction to the rising challenge against their rule, the Communist leaders in Moscow and Erevan in December 1988 declared martial law and arrested members of the Karabagh Committee. In January 1989 the Supreme Soviet of the Soviet Union placed Karabagh under the direct administration of Moscow but left the region within Azerbaijan. The Kremlin appointed Arkady Volsky as the "regional governor" directly accountable to Moscow.[85] This policy neither redefined the status of Karabagh nor granted Armenians authority in the region's administrative affairs. It merely promised greater attention to the protection of the Armenians against official and unofficial discrimination and against persecution and oppression by Azerbaijanis. Armenians complained to Gorbachev that the implementation of the new system failed to meet their demands as the familiar process of the Azerbaijanization of Karabagh accelerated. "The sounder and more just solution," the Armenians argued, would have been to reunify Karabagh with Armenia.[86] These demands grew into mass demonstrations in May 1989 for the release of the Karabagh Committee members from prison and for the lifting of the martial law. To pacify the Armenians, the Communist government made some concessions: it released the Karabagh Committee members from prison, granted authority for celebration of May 28 as a holiday, and permitted the use of the tricolor flag of the 1918 republic. Mass demonstrations continued in Karabagh, and in August 1989 Karabagh Armenians elected the Armenian National Council, which declared the secession of Karabagh from Azerbaijan and its reunification with Armenia.[87]

On November 28, 1989, Moscow removed Volsky and installed a military administration under the control of General Vladislav Safonov, whose patently favorable attitude toward Baku met intense Armenian opposition.[88] Armenians greeted this policy with another wave of demonstrations in Erevan and Stepanakert, the capital of Karabagh, and on December 1, the Armenian Supreme Soviet in Erevan declared the reunification of Karabagh. This act was followed by the nullification of Article VI of the Soviet Constitution and the renaming of Armenia as the Republic of Armenia.[89] Images of the Karabagh conflict and Armenian soldiers on military armored tanks victoriously waving the tricolor flashed on television screens worldwide, captivating the hearts and imagination of the diasporan Armenians.

THE DIASPORAN COMMUNITIES

Two traditional views on Soviet Armenia prevailed in the diasporan communities before the 1980s. The Dashnaktsutiun continued its opposition to the Soviet regime and viewed itself as the principal legitimate leader for the revival of an independent and united Armenia (encompassing historic and Soviet Armenia). The Ramkavar Liberal Democratic Party and the Hnchakian Socialist Democratic Party, on the other hand, embraced Soviet Armenia as the only viable "homeland"; under the existing circumstances, their sympathizers maintained, the preservation of culture and identity required close ties with Armenia even if within the Soviet system. Yet, as noted above, the three parties issued a joint declaration in 1988 urging their compatriots in Armenia not to abandon the Soviet Union. Since 1921, when the Red Army crushed the February rebellion, the Dashnaktsutiun had viewed itself as the lone fulcrum among the Armenian political parties sustaining the vision of an independent Armenia. It would not therefore accept a secondary role in a movement that sought to accomplish the very same objective that the party believed it was destined to accomplish. In the end, the diasporan communities, including the Dashnaktsutiun, Hnchakian, and Ramkavar parties, failed to gauge accurately the internal dynamics propelling Soviet Armenia toward independence. Although

Soviet Armenians had held the parties in great esteem, the joint declaration undermined the party's legitimacy in the eyes of their compatriots in the homeland.

Such debates among parties hundreds and in some cases thousands of miles away from Armenia gained political and economic significance because of the growing size and wealth of the diasporan communities. In the mid-1980s, there were about 3 million Armenians in Soviet Armenia and an estimated 1.61 million resided in the other Soviet republics, Russia being home to 360,000. The Armenian communities in the United States and Canada totaled between 800,000 and 1 million, of which more than 600,000 lived in the state of California, and 45,000 in Canada. In Europe, that figure was about 300,000, of which 200,000 lived in France and 10,000 in Great Britain. In the Middle East, the Armenian communities totaled about 550,000, of which about 100,000 were in Syria, 200,000 in Lebanon, and 200,000 in Iran. In Latin America, the Armenian community totaled about 120,000, the largest being in Argentina (80,000).[90]

The diasporan communities, after an initial shock, responded with enormous energy to the political shifts in Armenia and Karabagh beginning in February 1988 and the earthquake in December later that year. Armenian organizations across the diasporan communities collected humanitarian assistance for earthquake survivors in the affected cities of Spitak, Gumri (Leninakan), Vanadzor (Kirovakan), and Gugard.[91] Non-Armenian and diasporan experts in various fields traveled to Armenia to offer their services. Armenian organizations of different ideological leanings in diasporan communities that, with the exception of commemorating the genocide, seldom agreed on other issues, cooperated in matters pertaining to humanitarian assistance. The three principal diasporan political organizations, the Dashnaktsutiun, the Ramkavars, and the Hnchakians, along with their affiliates mobilized to assist the survivors. Soon the parties also, albeit belatedly, changed their position and supported independence. In 1991 construction companies from other parts of the Soviet Union constructed new buildings using "prefabricated concrete—much like the ones that collapsed so disastrously in the quake."[92] Soviet Armenia literally and metaphorically had become a "disaster zone."

THE END OF SOVIET ARMENIA

Gorbachev and his close economic advisers sought to decentralize the Soviet system to render it more conducive to reforms and market economy. They failed to ameliorate the economic situation, particularly the shortages in basic consumer goods, low wages, and miserable working conditions. Labor strikes, especially in the coal industry, protested hazardous working conditions, poor and unsafe housing, and deteriorating general social infrastructure.[93] By 1990 the results of Gorbachev's glasnost and perestroika policies had not been impressive, and the political situation clearly demanded close attention by the Kremlin. An effort in 1988 to introduce private enterprises had failed largely because local government and party apparatchiks had refused to relinquish their privileges and patronage in local economies. Nonetheless, on March 6, 1990, the Soviet parliament voted in favor (350 to 3) of privatizing small businesses to encourage new entrepreneurship while protecting the right to own private properties without fear of intrusion by local officials. A week later, on March 13, by a vote of 1,771 to 264 (with 74 abstentions) the parliament decided to amend the constitution in order to permit private ownership; by a vote of 1,817 to 133 (with 61 abstentions) it ratified the creation of a new presidency; and on March 14, by a vote of 1,542 to 368 (with 76 abstentions) it elected Gorbachev as president of the Soviet Union for a five-year term. A few days later, on March 18, local elections were held throughout the Soviet Union. The Communist Party lost in a number of cities throughout the country, including Moscow, Leningrad, and Kiev.[94]

The fact remained that by any standards perestroika failed to improve the living standards of the ordinary citizens. Experts such as Vladimir A. Tikhonov, president of the Union of Soviet Socialist Republics cooperatives, warned that failure to rectify the situation would have catastrophic consequences for the economy. Real GNP dropped by 4 to 5 percent in 1989 and by about 9 percent by early 1991. The economy appeared to be on the verge of financial meltdown as the government's finances spiraled out of control, the budget deficit (approximately 165 billion rubles in 1990) grew rapidly, and its credit rating reached its lowest levels. In order to improve the nation's credit rating, Gorbachev belatedly introduced a new economic package inaugurating liberalization of prices and trade.[95]

Gorbachev's experimentation with economic liberalization and joint ventures with western companies to stimulate wider trade relations for hard currency failed to improve the economy and merely amplified the structural deficiencies of the economic system. They drove home the point that the inferior quality of Soviet consumer goods could not compete with western products in international markets. Clearly, the Soviet economy could no longer be governed according to the principles of Marxism-Leninism; but what would replace them? Gorbachev's economic adviser, Nikolai Petrakov, encouraged him to press forward for full market economy in order to avert financial instability. Yet such advice and initiatives proved insufficient to reinvigorate the economy. The Soviet finances could not improve so long as the ruble was not convertible and the Soviet Union remained excluded from western international economic activities. Equally important, strategies proposed by Petrakov necessitated immediate measures by fiat rather than by relying on the party organization and bureaucracies. Gorbachev found himself in the unenviable position of attempting to balance economic liberalization with political stability. He could implement Petrakov's plan, but the conservatives would resist its implementation. Although for a while in 1990 Gorbachev seemed to win the political support of some members of the Soviet parliament, such alliances did not enhance his standing in economic matters, least of all among the administrative bureaucracies that proved inimical to liberalization.[96]

Beginning in early 1990, systemic paralysis, combined with the resurgence of nationalism across the Soviet Union, appeared too intractable to be remedied through normal channels of bureaucracy and legislation. In January 1990 the Supreme Soviet of Armenia had declared the supremacy of Armenian law to laws imposed by Moscow and claimed its own right to veto laws instituted by the Soviet regime.[97] The Baltic states in 1989 had declared Latvian, Estonian, and Lithuanian the official languages of their respective societies.[98] On March 11, 1990, the Lithuanian parliament declared its independence from Moscow and elected Vytautus Landsbergis, a music professor and leader of a grassroots movement, as president. The Kremlin condemned the declaration as "illegitimate and invalid," and although tensions between Moscow and Vilnius remained high for some time, the fact that Gorbachev demanded protection for national industries in Lithuania revealed his unwillingness to employ military force to halt secession—a fundamental shift from the brutal measures exercised under Khrushchev in Hungary in 1956 and Brezhnev in Czechoslovakia in 1968. Conservatives interpreted Gorbachev's failure to force an end to the secessionist process in Lithuania as an indication that his policies were doomed to fail. On March 30, 1990, the Estonian parliament declared independence from Moscow, but Estonians planned the disengagement to take place in phases of negotiations during the following three to five years. Other republics also began to discuss independence from the Soviet Union. In June 1990 Russia, the center of Soviet political power, declared its own sovereignty from the Soviet state.[99] By the end of the year, more than one in four among the Soviet population considered the disintegration of the Soviet Union inevitable.[100] By 1991 "the parade of sovereignties," as political scientist Mark Beissinger has noted, "universalized a situation of dual power (*dvoevlastie*) in which relations between lower-level and higher-level institutions of territorial governance throughout the ethnofederal hierarchy grew ambiguous and contested."[101]

In Erevan, Suren Harutyunyan, Communist Party chief in Armenia from 1988 to 1990, promised to take immediate steps to eradicate corruption, to address the environmental crisis by halting the operation of the nuclear plant in Armenia, and to convert the party's vacation homes into health and service centers. Unable to accommodate demands for fundamental democratic restructuring and for a favorable resolution of the Karabagh conflict, in April 1990 Harutyunyan resigned from his post. The parliamentary elections of that year rejected—for the first time since the Bolshevik seizure of power seventy years earlier—a Communist candidate, Vladimir Movsesyan, and ended Communist rule. Instead, the ANM and the coalition it led emerged as the majority, electing Levon Ter Petrosyan as president of the Soviet Armenian Supreme Soviet, with Vazgen Manukyan as his prime minister. The election results encouraged wider opposition to the Soviet regime. In August the new government, led by Ter Petrosyan, announced its intention to secede from the Soviet Union and began to introduce political and economic liberalization reforms.[102]

The conflict in Karabagh had by now escalated into a war. Armenian soldiers initially faced overwhelming opposition from combined Russian and Azerbaijani forces, but the attempted coup by the so-called Emergency Committee against Gorbachev in Moscow in August 1991 and the subsequent collapse of the Soviet military enabled the Armenian troops to gain strategic advantages on the battlefield. Further, in the absence of a powerful force both sides acted as independent, sovereign states. According to a Helsinki Watch report, during the spring and summer of 1991 in order to establish "law and order," Azerbaijani Special Function Militia Troops (OMON) with the support of Soviet Army troops introduced a "passport regime" and "arms check regime" known as Operation Ring throughout the Armenian villages in southern Karabagh and the districts of Khanlar and Shahumyan to the north. The OMON arrested hundreds of Armenian men, deported thousands, and emptied more than twenty villages. Helsinki Watch reported that the operation was "carried out with an unprecedented degree of violence and a systematic violation of human rights."[103]

Meanwhile, in response to the waves of opposition to Russian rule, Russian nationalism, long thought to have disappeared in the Soviet Union along with nationalism in the other republics reemerged with a vengeance, as manifested in the antinationalities rhetoric. Russian nationalists demonstrated in the streets of Moscow and other cities demanding the reinstitution of the Russian tsardom of the invincible old Mother Russia to stem the tide of anti-Russian movements spreading across the Soviet Union.[104]

Events in Moscow pressed Armenia and the other Soviet republics to formalize their independence, although the question of sovereignty was not resolved until the second half of 1991. Although the August coup failed, it nevertheless signaled the demise of the Soviet Union and rendered all efforts by Gorbachev to save the union irrelevant. In the meantime, the Supreme Soviet in Erevan authorized a public referendum on the independence of the republic. In September 1991 an overwhelming majority of Armenians with a great sense of optimism voted for independence from the Soviet Union, and the new parliament declared Armenia a sovereign and independent state. In October, having won the presidency with 83 percent of the popular vote, Ter Petrosyan, of the Armenian National Movement, was elected as the first president of the newly independent Republic of Armenia. By late December, as more republics declared independence, the Soviet regime, which had ruled Armenia for seven decades but was now rent beyond repair, finally collapsed.[105] In December 1991 the official *Rossiiskaia gazeta* (Russian newspaper) of the Russian parliament declared: "The former union is no more. And much more important, no one needs it."[106] Lenin's statue in the main square named after him at the heart of Erevan was toppled and the headless statue was removed to the courtyard of the National Gallery. The square was renamed the Republic Square. In December, the Belovezhsk accords, initiated by the leaders of Russia, Ukraine, and Belarus, and subsequently joined by most of the constituent republics, established the Commonwealth of Independent States (CIS) as the successor to the Soviet Union and confirmed their status as independent states, thereby nullifying the 1922 treaty that had legally formed the Soviet Union.

Armenian nationalist, secessionist groups that had remained peripheral rapidly gained in popularity by the late 1980s as economic mismanagement and the government's failure to address the crisis unleashed by the earthquake in December 1988, combined with the bloodshed in Karabagh, heightened Armenians' sense of physical insecurity. The tensions between the Soviet ideology of proletarian culture and the national political, economic, and cultural realities could not have been more obvious. For Armenians, the earthquake in December 1988 symbolized the disintegration of the Soviet Union. By the time the Soviet Union collapsed, the Armenian communities were deeply divided because of the memory of the bloodshed during the Bolshevik seizure of power in Erevan, the Stalinist legacy, and the Cold War ideological conflicts. Yet, with rare exceptions, the new generations of Armenians born in the diaspora were unfamiliar with the culture left behind in the land of their forebears in historic Armenia. Would the independence that the Republic of Armenia regained revive Armenian culture in diasporan communities? Would the republic itself become an economically and culturally vibrant society?

9

Independence and Democracy: The Second Republic

Armenians worldwide greeted the independence regained by the Republic of Armenia with great fanfare and jubilation. Seven decades of Soviet hegemonic rule had come to an end, and Armenian expectations and imaginations soared high. National sovereignty strengthened national pride, and Armenians once more considered themselves as belonging to the community of nation-states. And the Republic of Armenia had much to be proud of, for it had built a modern country, even if under the shadow of the Stalinist legacy. Clearly the newly independent republic in 1991 appeared infinitesimally different from the society that had fallen to the Bolsheviks in 1921. Soon after independence, however, it became apparent that domestic systemic deficiencies would not permit the immediate introduction of political and economic policies predicated on principles of democratization and liberalization. The obsolete institutions, bureaucratic customs, and the political culture as developed under the Communist Party hindered the transition from the centrally planned system to a more decentralized, democratic polity. Moreover, the absence of the interrepublic industrial networks as developed during the Soviet era posed a serious challenge to the emerging Armenian economy. The republic hardly possessed the infrastructure necessary for independent economic development and long-term financial stability. The deplorable conditions inherited from the Soviet regime in the aftermath of the earthquake in 1988 and the military conflict in Karabagh further exacerbated the situation. President Levon Ter Petrosyan sought to enlist the support of the diasporan communities to ameliorate the conditions, but widespread corruption, poverty, unemployment, and irreconcilable disagreements on foreign policy (e.g., Karabagh) undermined the legitimacy of the government and led to his resignation in 1998. The government of Robert Kocharyan, the second president since independence, hoped to develop a more balanced approach to domestic and foreign policy issues, particularly in relations with the diaspora. By 2000, conditions appeared to be improving somewhat, albeit slowly. The Soviet regime had failed to develop democratic institutions even decades after Stalin's death, but Armenians were determined to create and cultivate them in the new atmosphere of long-awaited freedom and heretofore untapped potentials and opportunities.

THE TER PETROSYAN GOVERNMENT

The collapse of the highly centralized regime and the transition to independence required the institutionalization of democracy and therefore a complete rearrangement of the political structure and a metamorphosis of political culture. The newly independent state faced enormous challenges in nearly all aspects of political economy. Expectations for a system based on principles of political and market liberalization could not be disengaged from the geopolitical and economic realities on the ground as inherited from the Soviets; moreover, the new republic was mired in the military crisis in neighboring Karabagh.

The task of institution building required a viable constitution, which was adopted by a national referendum in July 1995. The newly independent government, emulating the western tradition, established three branches of government: executive, legislative, and judiciary. Within the executive branch, the presidency represents the chief of state while the prime minister is head of government. The president is elected by popular vote for a five-year term. He appoints the prime minister, who in turn appoints the members of the cabinet, the Council of Ministers. The legislative branch, the National Assembly, or Azgayin Zhoghov, is unicameral, consisting of 131 members elected by popular vote for four-year terms. The judicial system is headed by the Constitutional Court composed of nine members. The presidency, as developed under Ter Petrosyan since 1991, emerged as the most powerful office. The National Assembly has oscillated between loyalty to the president and paralysis because of internal factional divisions and has failed to institutionalize effective means to check and balance presidential authority. The Constitutional Court has thus far failed to gain independence from political leaders and politics; as a result, it has lacked a sufficient degree of credibility and legitimacy necessary for a democratic society.

In forming his new government, President Ter Petrosyan sought to establish close relations with the large diasporan communities, especially those in the United States, and invited a number of diasporan Armenians to serve in ministerial posts and as close advisers. These included: Raffi K. Hovannisian, the first minister of foreign affairs of the post-Soviet republic; Sebouh Tashjian, minister of energy; Vardan Oskanian, deputy minister of foreign affairs and later minister of foreign affairs; Gerard J. Libaridian, senior adviser to the president and secretary of the Security Council and later deputy minister of foreign affairs; and Matthew Der Manuelian, chief of the North American diplomatic desk.[1] Despite the difficult conditions in the republic, the entire nation at home and across the diaspora was ready to serve the homeland, to give concrete shape to its dedication to the imagined independent republic that it had yearned for, from a far, for decades, to transform long-held aspirations into realities. The first term of the Ter Petrosyan government had begun with exhilarating energy, albeit in the midst of crises.

The economic situation was the first issue that the new government had to address, and the problems proved particularly pernicious. After the collapse of the Soviet Union the debates on economic policy centered on alternatives between "shock therapy" and "gradualism" in the transition from the Communist system to free market economy. The Ter Petrosyan government sought to balance the two approaches. As a constituent member of the empire, Armenia had been a part of the Soviet interdependent budgetary, manufacturing, and trade networks. The disintegration of these relations forced the republic to face the daunting task of becoming competitive in international trade and to secure foreign investments, at a time when Turkey and Azerbaijan had imposed an economic blockade on the country. The lack of natural resources and a large domestic market, combined with a general sense of political and economic insecurity, discouraged foreign investments.

The nation's economy was extraordinarily distressful during the first three years after independence. Observers warned that it faced the danger of sliding into a depression. In fact, Armenia's economy experienced a financial meltdown. The nation's industrial output dropped by nearly 64 percent between 1988 and 1993, while gross domestic product (GDP) declined by 50 percent and energy production by 60 percent. In the meantime, hyperinflation as a result of price liberalization sharply increased prices more than thirteen times between 1991 and 1993, and they continued to increase for the rest of the decade. The excise tax of 25 percent on imported oil further contributed to the inflationary pressures. The economic crisis significantly lowered the standard of living for a large sector of the population. In late 1992 the average pay for employees was estimated at about $25 per month, yet a family of four required at minimum about $200 a month for a decent livelihood. According to a 1996 survey conducted by the Ministry of Statistics (currently the National Statistical Service), 55 percent of the population in Armenia considered themselves poor, 28 percent very poor, and more than 10 percent extremely poor. The severe economic difficulties led to budgetary imbalances. Budget revenues fell to mere 15 percent of GDP in the period 1992 to 1994, as the tax base nearly collapsed, and, making matters worse, shrinking state expenditures caused a severe drop (nearly 50 percent from 1992 to 1996) in public social programs.[2]

In efforts to disengage the nation's economy from the institutions inherited from the Soviet regime, the Ter Petrosyan government relied on privatization and price liberalization policies, effectively ending price controls by October 1994. This was combined with the privatization of kolkhoz (collective farms) and sovkhoz (state farms) lands, and nearly 70 percent of state-owned apartments were privatized by early 1996. In 1992 Pavel Khaltakchyan, head of the Committee of Privatization and Management of State Property, identified three stages for the process of privatization, which he expected to be completed within ten years. The first stage involved the privatization of the food and light industries, followed by the transportation industry, and finally by the heavy industry. The state would retain control over strategic industrial sectors for national security purposes. The government's economic liberalization policies were supported by $65 million in assistance from the European Bank for Reconstruction and Development in 1995 for structural market reforms beginning the following year.[3]

A policy issue that required greatest attention was the 1988 earthquake regions of Spitak and Gumri. The Ter Petrosyan government failed to introduce a viable reconstruction program, and as late as December 1993, according to official reports no more than between 30 and 40 percent of the initial plans for reconstruction had been implemented, although unofficial sources placed the figure at 20 percent. The government, with Russian and diasporan assistance, had planned to construct houses, schools, and hospitals, but scarcity of funds limited the nation's construction capacity to 30 percent of its potential, of which only a small portion was allocated to the earthquake zone. Nearly 58,000 families lacked permanent housing and 400,000 people required some form of relief assistance.[4]

Further, an estimated 334,000 Armenian refugees had fled the bloodshed in Azerbaijan, constituting nearly 10 percent of the population in Armenia by the end of 1993. Of these refugees, about 130,000 received some form of international humanitarian assistance, which covered approximately 30 percent of their basic needs. About 100,000 were housed in 300 communal facilities, living in what one UN representative referred to as "atrocious" conditions. Taken together, the earthquake of 1988 and the war in Karabagh had left about 30 percent of the population in Armenia homeless.[5] The deteriorating educational system fueled additional concerns regarding the health of the economy and the future of the republic as government funding dropped by more than 50 percent since independence. The monthly salary for teachers in secondary education was no more than $20.[6] The economic difficulties compelled Ter Petrosyan to turn to the diasporan communities for assistance, but he was aware of the dilemma that his reliance on diaspora would create. Would the Ter Petrosyan government feel obligated to permit diasporan Armenians a voice in policymaking?

The complexities involved in Armenia-diaspora relations became apparent soon after the initial period of triumphant jubilation. The Ter Petrosyan government insisted on the priority of economically and diplomatically strengthening the republic and considered the diasporan communities as a source for financial and technological support. Particularly essential was the financial support extended to Armenia during its worst economic crisis between 1991 and 1994. Armenian churches and charitable organizations across the diaspora donated millions of dollars' worth of supplies, ranging from blankets to medical equipments. For example, assistance by the United Armenian Fund included the Winter Fuel Project in 1993 worth $21 million, plus clothing, construction materials, books, computers, medical instruments, and pharmaceuticals, with the total value of nearly $60 million for the period from 1990 to 1993.[7]

While the two diasporan political parties, the Hnchakians and the Ramkavars, and their associate organizations more or less cooperated with Ter Petrosyan, fundamental differences emerged by 1993 between his government and the Hay Heghapokhakan Dashnaktsutiun (Armenian Revolutionary Federation, ARF) on matters pertaining to Karabagh and the Armenian Genocide. The Dashnaktsutiun demanded either direct reunification of Karabagh with Armenia or Erevan's formal recognition of Karabagh's independent status. The Dashnaktsutiun underscored the close relationship between Turkish recognition of the genocide and the territorial issues of the Armenian lands under Turkish control and Nakhijevan under Azerbaijani control, on one hand, and the conflict in Karabagh, on the other. In contrast, Ter Petrosyan and the Armenian National Movement insisted on the physical security of Armenia as their immediate objective; concerns regarding the sovereignty of Karabagh were secondary. In an interview, Ter Petrosyan stated that no more than 10 percent of the diasporan community opposed his government. He attributed the tensions between Armenia and the diaspora to misperceptions and misunderstanding. "There will always be a mutual lack of understanding and trust," he emphasized, "so long as the Diaspora leadership does not come to terms with the reality that policy is determined here, on this land." Further, he noted, the diasporan opposition believed it had been "deprived of its just place of power." However, Ter Petrosyan argued, the diasporan leaders had failed to assess accurately the situation in Armenia and in the early stages of the anti-Soviet movement "the Diaspora kept its distance from the movement . . . . They did not understand it, didn't participate in it certainly, and finally adopted a negative stance." The diasporan communities, he maintained, "have remained within the confines of the Armenian community, in a manifestation of the ghetto mentality." In fact, he concluded, while the diasporan communities propagated various interpretations of his policies, the political and economic realities were that policy decisions pertaining to Karabagh and relations with Russia and Turkey "often depended on very simple realities: How many tons of wheat are in our stores, how many bullets we have, how many cisterns of diesel fuel are available to our tanks."[8]

During his tour of the United States in August 1994, Ter Petrosyan met with President Bill Clinton, Secretary of State Warren Christopher, Secretary of Defense Anthony Perry, and several members of Congress to discuss economic aid and the Karabagh crisis. Visiting the Armenian community in Detroit, he summarized Armenia's foreign policy. Concerning national security, he stressed the importance of a "balanced foreign policy" toward Russia, Turkey, and Iran. He pointed out that given the domestic and external difficulties, it was essential that Armenia's foreign policy in this toughest of neighborhoods be based on realism and prudence. Having gained independence for the second time in this century, he maintained, the current government of Armenia could not allow the loss of the hard-won independence. The pursuit of a peaceful resolution of the conflict, however, the president noted, would most likely require certain compromises by both parties, including a willingness on Armenians' part to withdraw from territories captured beyond Karabagh proper. The government of Azerbaijan had acknowledged its inability to achieve its objectives through military force and realized that the military option was no longer viable. Therefore, he added, it was in Armenia's best interest to negotiate a comprehensive plan for the peaceful resolution of this conflict now before it escalated into a war of far greater magnitude than thus far witnessed.

The Dashnaktsutiun reacted with intense hostility toward Ter Petrosyan's statement. He in turn accused the party of terrorist and other illegal activities to overthrow the government and issued a decree on December 28, 1994, to close the operations of the party in Erevan and its affiliate organizations and to arrest their leaders. This heavy-handed reaction to political opposition not only reminded the nation of the

Stalinist legacy of Soviet dictatorial rule but also violated both domestic and international human rights law. In 1992 the Armenian government had become a signatory to various international human rights instruments, including the United Nations Charter, the Universal Declaration of Human Rights, and the International Covenant on Civil and Political Rights, all of which prohibit such repressive measures against individuals and political organizations.

These political and economic, domestic and international challenges only intensified after the reelection in 1996. Perhaps the first fundamental problem involved the accusation that at least in some parts of the country the electoral process was rigged. As protest demonstrations spread, the situation could have spiraled into bloodshed, but the military reacted to the postelection violence by dispatching tanks to the streets of Erevan, further undermining the legitimacy of the regime. Ter Petrosyan therefore came under severe criticism at home and in the diasporan communities for his government's authoritarian measures, as in 1994, to silence the opposition.

The economic difficulties amplified the problem of political legitimacy. The fact that the "shadow economy" or the black market represented an estimated 35 to 40 percent of the nation's GDP accentuated the ties between corruption and the political system. The new leadership, however, sought to encourage the development of free market economy and to win the confidence of international investors, as indicated by the appointment of a number of cabinet members who had served as ambassadors to western capitals. For example, the newly appointed prime minister, Armen Sargisyan, had held the post of ambassador to London. Alexander Arzumanyan, appointed minister of foreign affairs, was ambassador to Washington and subsequently to the United Nations. Minister of Trade and Tourism Garnik Nanagulyan was ambassador to Ottawa. In the absence of adequate domestic resources, international trade remained the only avenue to economic growth, and the extent to which the nation's economy could improve its trade balance remained a significant question. The trade deficit rose from $178 million in 1994 to $565 million, or 30 percent of GDP, in 1996, and to $672 million in 1998. The nation's foreign debt increased from 31 percent of GDP in 1994 to 41.8 percent in 1997. Although that figure dropped slightly to 38.1 in 1998, it nevertheless indicated severe imbalances in productive output.[9] Had Ter Petrosyan been the head of a large, economically advanced country, his government perhaps could have relied on various instruments of foreign policy to alleviate the domestic economic and political pressures. The republic, however, is too small and too weak to exert any significant influence through bilateral relations, not to mention on the world political economy.

In the area of foreign policy, the crisis in Karabagh dominated Ter Petrosyan's national agenda, with enormous ramifications for his government's political legitimacy and economic performance. As a result of the Karabagh conflict, Baku and Ankara imposed an economic blockade on Karabagh and Armenia, nearly strangulating both. For years Karabagh lacked adequate food supplies, fuel, running water, electricity, sanitation facilities, and communication facilities. According to Helsinki Watch, during the period of its investigation (April 1992), most towns, including Stepanakert, were "at a standstill: no schools, shops, or workplaces operated, food was scarce, and the primary daily activity was fetching water" from twelve springs. Further, because of the conflict, the Ter Petrosyan government had to spend between 10 and 15 percent of the national budget revenues on defense.[10] Defense expenditures accounted for 2.2 percent of GDP in 1992 and increased to 4.1 percent in 1995, stabilizing at an average of about 3.5 percent GDP per year before his resignation in 1998.[11]

In the early stages of the war in Karabagh, each side expected a quick military victory and therefore was less amenable to a negotiated resolution. The Armenian forces registered successes on the battlefield, as in Khojali in March 1992 and the strategically situated town of Shushi in the south in May, which enabled them to secure the Lachin corridor that linked Karabagh and Armenia. Armenian successes led to the downfall of President Ayaz Mutalibov in Baku, who within weeks organized an attempt to regain power but, after failing, fled the country. Abulfaz Elchibey succeeded Mutalibov but was himself forced to resign by a military faction led by Colonel Suret Huseynov in June 1993, followed by the consolidation of power by the former KGB chief in Azerbaijan, Heydar Aliyev. Although Karabagh forces continued to gain further territory, as in the region of Kelbajar in the north in March 1993, the political reality was that the international community did not extend legal recognition to Karabagh as a sovereign nation-state. On the contrary, in April 1993 the UN Security Council adopted Resolution 822 condemning the Armenian offensive in the Kelbajar district and maintained that the said aggression violated the territorial integrity of Azerbaijan. Similarly, in July 1993, after the Armenian forces captured the town of Agdam, the UN Security Council passed Resolution 853, repeating its condemnation of Armenian use of force. The Security Council resolutions stressed the need to resolve the conflict through peaceful means.[12]

By early 1994, because of sheer exhaustion and the enormity of human suffering and bloodshed, both parties agreed to negotiate. The crisis, though far from being resolved, ceased on May 12, 1994, with the signing of the Bishkek Protocol in Kyrgyzstan under Russian auspices. By then, the Armenian-Karabagh forces controlled more than 15 percent of territory within Azerbaijan. The war had claimed more than 20,000 lives and caused hundreds of thousands of Armenians and Azerbaijanis to become refugees.[13] After two years of vacillation, Russian mediation drew Moscow closer to Armenia for strategic reasons largely in response to the engagement of western multinational corporations with Baku in cultivating the Caspian oilfields. Also, since Armenian and Azerbaijani membership in the Conference on Security and Co-operation in Europe in early 1992 enabled the latter to play, through the Minsk Group, a direct role in the mediation of the conflict, Russia deemed it essential to reassert its presence in its traditional sphere of influence.[14] Azerbaijan continued to reject Karabagh's claim to sovereignty as a violation of its own territorial integrity both by the secessionists in Karabagh and by the government of Armenia. The latter maintained that it had no territorial aspirations but would insist on defending Karabagh's right to self-determination. In fact, Erevan argued, the economic blockade imposed on Armenia by Turkey and Azerbaijan necessitated close ties with Karabagh in security and economic matters. Moreover, the hostile environment compelled the leadership in Erevan to continue to rely on Russia for military security, with Russian soldiers guarding the 214-miles-long Armenian-Turkish border.[15]

The broader issues concerning the political and economic difficulties confronting Karabagh and their implications for Ter Petrosyan's foreign policy objectives were obvious. His government sought to balance between the demands of the military conflict in Karabagh with Armenia's own national interests. The early part of 1994 witnessed a number of diplomatic initiatives to address the economic crisis. While in Paris in January 1994, President of the Armenian National Assembly, Babgen Ararktsyan, emphasized that the republic's domestic political and economic conditions were inextricably tied to the Karabagh crisis. In Germany, he noted that the Armenian government would welcome German technical assistance to reactivate the Metsamor nuclear plant. The European Community, he maintained in his speech before the European Parliament, must appreciate his nation's improved performance in democratization and human rights as well as economic reforms, and the lack of such progress in Azerbaijan. The European Community, he added, would have to acknowledge the urgency of its own involvement in the resolution of the Karabagh conflict.[16]

Such diplomatic initiatives with western European countries notwithstanding, Erevan considered relations with Russia of paramount strategic import both in the context of bilateral ties and within the Commonwealth of Independent States. Yet particularly troubling for Armenia were Russian nationalist, xenophobic attitudes and Communist old-guard visions of resuscitating the Soviet Union. For example, in March 1996 the Russian State Duma adopted two resolutions, sponsored by the Communist Party of Russia and other parties, denouncing the Belovezhsk accords of December 1991, which had established the CIS as the successor to the Soviet Union. President Boris Yeltsin immediately ridiculed the resolutions as "scandalous" and instructed Foreign Minister Yevgenii Primakov to communicate to foreign states and international organizations his government's opposition to the resolutions and to assure them that Russia would continue normal relations with the international community and meet its international obligations. Ter Petrosyan, at the time meeting with President Saparmurad Niyazov in Turkmenistan, severely criticized the resolutions as a challenge to Armenia's sovereignty. Negotiations with Niyazov led to bilateral agreements for the restructuring of Erevan's $34 million debt to Turkmenistan for the delivery of natural gas.[17]

Not surprisingly, Erevan's relations with Ankara proved extremely contentious. Driven in large part by the economic difficulties of nation- and state-building, the Ter Petrosyan government was prepared to establish diplomatic and commercial ties with Turkey. The geopolitical imperatives as dictated by the neighboring and major powers, on the one hand, and diasporan politics, on the other, delineated the parameters of Ter Petrosyan's policy options regarding Turkey and matters pertaining to the Armenian Genocide. Contrary to predictions in the early 1990s that the collapse of the Soviet Union would diminish Turkey's geostrategic significance as an ally within the North Atlantic Treaty Organization because that country no longer served as a shield against Soviet expansionism, Turkish foreign policy remained important for the United States, one of Ankara's principal allies since the 1920s, and even gained in significance for Israel, whose security concerns with respect to Muslim fundamentalism led to close ties with Turkey. The United States and Turkey had maintained good, albeit at times contentious, relations for nearly two centuries, and they had not permitted issues such as the Armenian Genocide to jeopardize their commercial and security ties, as demonstrated by the fact that the U.S. Department of State intervened on behalf of Turkey to prevent the production of Franz Werfel's *Forty Days of Musa Dagh* (a masterful novel based on the Armenian Genocide) by MGM Studios in 1935—that is, before the creation of NATO in 1949.[18] During the Cold War, Turkey received billions of dollars in U.S. economic and military aid, and since the collapse of the Soviet Union it has continued to exert considerable influence in Washington.

In developing bilateral ties with Turkey, the Ter Petrosyan government had to address two issues of immediate concern: Would he insist that Turkey accept responsibility for the genocide as a precondition for the normalization of relations? Would he disassociate his government from the conflict in Karabagh in order to improve relations with Turkey? Further complicating the situation was the Armenian-Turkish border inherited from the Soviet-Turkish treaty of 1921. Would the newly independent government revive Armenian claims to the historic homeland now in eastern Turkey? The Ter Petrosyan government was hardly in a position to resolve these questions in a manner favorable to Armenia. Their resolution would require the vast accouterments of military power and economic strength, an unrealistic scenario even under the best of circumstances. Instead, Ter Petrosyan opted for an Armenian-Turkish rapprochement, with hopes that Armenians and Turks could overcome their historical animosities. As he sought to develop ties with Turkey, Ter Petrosyan placed a premium on first revitalizing Armenia's economy. Issues related to the genocide and the sovereignty of Karabagh, his government maintained, could be addressed only after Armenia acquired sufficient economic and diplomatic strength. Accordingly, Ter Petrosyan urged Armenian diasporan communities to moderate their stance on the international recognition of the genocide, a policy that was denounced most vocally by the Dashnaktsutiun.[19]

Under President Turgut Ozal (1989–1993), Turkey viewed the collapse of the USSR as an opportunity to expand its relations with the former Soviet republics. His government hoped to see Russia neutralized in the Caucasus, which would enhance Turkey's role in the region. Seizing the moment, Volkan Vural, the Turkish ambassador to Moscow, visited Erevan in April 1991 to negotiate bilateral agreements. The Ozal government also initiated the Black Sea Economic Cooperation (BSEC), a regional arrangement to encourage commercial ties. At the Istanbul Summit in June 1992, government leaders from eleven countries, including Armenia, established the BSEC, with its headquarters in Istanbul, and its charter entered into force on May 1, 1999.[20] Discussions were also under way between Erevan and Ankara in 1991 for Armenia to gain access to the Trebizond port on the Black Sea. As the war in Karabagh escalated during the same year, Ozal strengthened his alliance with and extended military support to Azerbaijani president Ayaz Mutalibov. Ozal issued open threats toward Armenia in early 1993 and stationed forces on the Armenian border ostensibly to control Kurdish revolutionary activities; in September 1993, under his successor President Suleyman Demirel, at least two Turkish aircraft flying in Armenian airspace were reported by the defense ministry of Armenia.[21] Nevertheless, Turkey refrained from overt participation in the Karabagh war perhaps largely because of its cautious approach not to provoke a military clash with Russia, which in turn could potentially have drawn NATO into the conflict. Russian Army Chief of Staff General Shaposhnikov reportedly "warned that if Turkey entered in militarily, the conflict could risk turning into World War III."[22] As one analyst has correctly noted, "The Turkish and Russian positions in the mid-1990s were resonant of the imperial chess-playing attitudes of earlier centuries."[23]

The geopolitical situation in the region led to close ties between Iran and Armenia, and Iran provided much-needed economic support for Armenia, the junior partner. Their bilateral relations included agreements on energy, transportation, finance, and cultural relations. Iran's exports to Armenia increased from $14 million in 1993 to $82 million in 1995; that figure increased to $125 million in 1996.[24] At a time when Armenia desperately needed economic support, Iran provided an important political ally and an avenue for economic development (if not survival) against the Turkish-Azeri economic blockade. For Iran, itself the subject of U.S. sanctions, closer relations with Armenia offered an opportunity to expand its economic and political influence vis-à-vis its major competitors in the region, Turkey and Russia. In 1995 the Iran-Armenia Energy Program was established to encourage economic development, and in 1996 Iran began construction of electric lines to Armenia. Armenia's Minister of Trade and Tourism, Vahan Melkonyan, and Iran's Ambassador to Armenia Hamid Reza Nikkar Esfahani discussed development of the Iran-Armenia gas pipeline, while Armenia's Foreign Minister Vahan Papazyan and Deputy Foreign Minister of Iran Mahmud Vayezi met in Erevan to negotiate expansion of bilateral economic ties and regional stability. These bilateral talks continued in 1997 in Tehran, where President Mohammad Khatami, Bijan Namdar Zanganeh (Minister of Oil), and Hoseyn Namazi (Minister of Economy and Finance), met with leading Armenian officials. Cultural relations complemented economic and political relations. In July 1996, while the ministers focused on bilateral commercial ties, Catholicos Garegin I Sarkissian, Ambassador Esfahani, and Vayezi met at Echmiadzin to discuss promotion of cultural and educational relations between Iran and Armenia.[25]

One of the most fundamental decisions made by Ter Petrosyan concerned the Armenian Church. After the death of Catholicos Vazgen I in 1995, Ter Petrosyan invited Catholicos Karekin II Sarkissian of the catholicosate of Cilicia (Antelias, Lebanon) to the catholicosal throne of the Mother See at Echmiadzin. He was elected as Catholicos Garegin I of All Armenians in April 1995. In Antelias he was succeeded by Catholicos Aram I Keshishian. The Armenian communities of the Cilician prelacies, which are also closely associated with the Dashnaktsutiun, considered Ter Petrosyan's invitation to Garegin II to head the Mother See a few months after the arrest of the Dashnakist leaders in Armenia as a Machiavellean ploy *par excellence* to sow divisions within the party and the communities associated with the Cilician catholicosate throughout the diaspora. In matters of policy, the Armenian Church at Echmiadzin closely supported the government, as had been the case in Armenian history for centuries.

In January 1996 Catholicos Garegin I visited the United States and Canada. He had served as prelate of the eastern United States and Canada

in the mid-1970s, prior to his appointment in 1977 as coadjutor by
Catholicos Khoren I Paroyan of the Great House of Cilicia, and he succeeded Khoren I after the latter's death in 1983. During his tour of North
America, both the Cilician and Echmiadzin communities—whose intra-
communal tensions in the United States extend at least as far back as the
assassination of Archbishop Ghevond Durian in December 1933—held
serious reservations regarding Garegin I's transition from catholicos of the
former to catholicos of the latter. The Cilician community considered him
a traitor, while the Echmiadzin community viewed his transformation
with grave suspicion. By the end of his tour Catholicos Garegin I appeared
to have gained the confidence of both communities, although no public
opinion surveys exist to verify that fact. In addition to visiting the
Armenian communities and leaders, Garegin I also met with President Bill
Clinton at the White House, with Governor George Pataki of New York,
and with Mayor Willie Brown of San Francisco.

Garegin I's visit to the United States gave rise to rumors in the
Armenian communities that his visit, a few months after his election as
Catholicos of All Armenians, signified an initiative on the part of both
catholicoi to end the jurisdictional divisions across the diaspora. In his
messages to the communities, Garegin I encourage the public to think
about the "new era in Armenian history [which] heralds a new era for the
church." He further emphasized that "an administrative division that was
caused by an old world order does not need to continue under today's
political conditions."[26] Nevertheless, speculations regarding unification of
the two churches during his reign proved premature. In March 1999
Catholicos Garegin I also visited Pope John Paul II. After his death in June,
Garegin I was succeeded by Catholicos Garegin II Nersisyan, who was
consecrated as the Supreme Patriarch of All Armenians at Echmiadzin in
November 1999.

KARABAGH AGAIN

That the Karabagh conflict had become an integral part of Armenian politics was reconfirmed when in March 1997 Ter Petrosyan appointed
Kocharyan prime minister; he was succeeded in Karabagh by the first foreign minister of Karabagh, Arkady Ghukasyan. The appointment of
Kocharyan as Armenia's prime minister had broad ramifications for its
domestic politics and foreign policy. At the time bringing Kocharyan and
by extension Karabagh into future negotiations regarding the region's status might have seemed a valid strategic move. Soon thereafter, however,
geopolitical and economic considerations in the "tough neighborhood"
of the Caucasus appeared to have compelled Ter Petrosyan to shift his

position on the Karabagh question. The Lisbon summit of the OSCE in December 1996 proved pivotal. The declaration issued at Lisbon, which reaffirmed the Azerbaijani position but reportedly without consultation with Erevan or Stepanakert, accepted the principle of the territorial integrity of Azerbaijan, while permitting Karabagh autonomy within Azerbaijan. In other words, the Lisbon declaration rejected Armenian claims to national independence for Karabagh as a sovereign nation-state or as a reintegrated constituent region of the Republic of Armenia. The Ter Petrosyan government changed its policy from rejecting the Lisbon declaration to a potential compromise. In September 1997, during a televised press conference, he referred to the available options regarding Karabagh and proposed to accept the piecemeal approach to the negotiations as proposed by the Minsk Group.[27] He maintained that the status quo no longer appeared tenable, nor was Erevan in a position to extend formal recognition to Karabagh as a sovereign government. Further, he noted, a comprehensive or "package" solution—whereby Karabagh would return to Baku all the conquered territories, with the exception of the Lachin corridor, while the blockade imposed on Armenia would be lifted, international peacekeeping forces would be deployed at the Karabagh-Azerbaijan border, and the refugees would return home—was not practicable. Given that both Karabagh and Azerbaijan had rejected the package approach, Ter Petrosyan argued, the resolution of the Karabagh conflict required a step-by-step process in determining the status of the region, a proposal that had been accepted by Azerbaijan. In essence, this latter approach would forced Karabagh to return all the lands it had gained during the war, except perhaps the Lachin corridor, while Karabagh itself would be granted an autonomous status under the jurisdiction of Azerbaijan.[28]

The Copenhagen conference in December 1997 further solidified Ter Petrosyan's step-by-step policy implying "self-rule" for Karabagh as favored by the Minsk Group. Ter Petrosyan's position assumed a positive response from the Azerbaijani president Heydar Aliyev and showed unrealistic confidence in Baku's willingness to negotiate as equal partners. Would the Azerbaijani civilian leadership and the military command permit self rule for Armenians in Karabagh? Would an agreement at the negotiating table regarding the Lachin corridor in fact guarantee the region's security against future Azerbaijani attacks? The ensuing crisis between Ter Petrosyan and his supporters, on one hand, and the opposition including Arkady Ghukasyan and Kocharyan, on the other, revealed deep divisions at the highest levels of governments in Erevan and Stepanakert. By the end of January 1998, the tensions had paralyzed the Ter Petrosyan government as rumors spread of an imminent military takeover. The situation deteriorated further with news of assassination attempts against a

number of government officials and the resignation of some key supporters of Ter Petrosyan. Foreign Minister Arzumanyan resigned on February 2,
followed by chairman of the Central Bank, Bagrat Asatryan. The final collapse of the government came when more than forty ANM members in
the National Assembly, including Speaker Ara Sahakyan, withdrew from
the party. Most of them sided with the Union of Erkrapah faction, the
group representing the veterans of the Karabagh war and led by the
defense minister, Vazgen Sargsyan.[29]

Ter Petrosyan's willingness to compromise on the status of Karabagh
and the strongly negative reaction to it among his close advisers and by
different groups in Armenia and the diaspora defined the political
parameters of the debate. Opponents to this policy shift included Prime
Minister Kocharyan, Interior Minister Serge Sargsyan, and Defense
Minister Vazgen Sargsyan, the former two who had led the war against
Azerbaijan. Ter Petrosyan may have sought a practicable resolution
considering the geopolitical realities confronting Erevan, but the
Armenian blood spelled for Karabagh after seventy years of Azerbaijani
rule was too fresh to be subjected to political compromises. Although
for those in the decision-making circles in Erevan opting for a compromise represented a rational policy, the emotional content of the issue
would not permit the leadership the luxury of such options. Further, by
1997 Ter Petrosyan had lost political credibility in various areas of
domestic policy. He had arrested the Dashnaktsutiun leaders in 1994,
the elections in 1996 were rigged, corruption permeated the entire system, and his government had failed to ameliorate the economic situation. These tensions were exacerbated by the foreign policy crisis after
the Lisbon summit, which inevitably undermined the legitimacy of Ter
Petrosyan's political leadership. Prime Minister Kocharyan and some
members of the cabinet forced Ter Petrosyan's resignation in February
1998.[30]

By the time Ter Petrosyan left office, the republic appeared in desperate
need for a leader who possessed sufficient moral authority to inspire public confidence in the political system. Neither Ter Petrosyan nor his successor possessed leadership "charismata," that "transcendent call by a
divine being, believed in by both the person called and those with whom
he had to deal in exercising his calling."[31] Ter Petrosyan had emerged as a
member of the Karabagh Committee, and by the "virtue of the mission"
the legitimacy of the group's claims against the discredited Soviet regime
conferred legitimacy on his leadership as well. A charismatic leader, however, according to the sociologist Max Weber, must repeatedly prove the
fulfillment of his mission; otherwise, his "charismatic claim" is dismissed
if his mission is not realized and therefore no longer recognized by the

people.[32] A key issue concerning the newly independent state was the quality of the emerging political leadership and their parties. As evidenced time and again in the developing world, the absence of established institutions that are responsive to public demands in the process of decolonization creates a political vacuum that is often filled by authoritarian personal rulers that rely on strong, monopolistic-patrimonial institutional arrangements to safeguard their position. Once in power, the foremost priority of the top leadership is to establish the legitimacy of the regime, and only after a certain degree of stability is secured can the government devote its resources to such public goods as welfare, justice, and free and fair elections.[33] In addition to leadership, effective political parties are essential for democratization. After the fall of the Soviet one-party system in Armenia, more than seventy self-proclaimed political parties arose, most of which lacked the leadership and organizational wherewithal of actual political parties. They were, in fact, what in the West is considered "interest groups." The absence of free political space and competition in the Soviet Union had hindered the development of independent parties, and Armenians saw the collapse of the Communist Party as an opportunity for political activism. At the same time, however, they distrusted party organizations because of the close association of such concepts with the Communist Party.[34] Most emerging political parties were weak organizationally, but the few led by powerful individuals mustered sufficient support and developed personal authoritarian leadership. A central question in this process is the institutionalization of the political parties and their meaningful participation in policymaking as distinguished from the transitory political and ideological predilections of their individual leaders. Institutionalization requires that political parties transcend their individual members' proclivities and survive beyond the lifetimes of their leaders.[35] Most of the new political parties failed the test of institutionalization as they disappeared after their leaders withdrew from the political arena. The Armenian National Movement party, for example, survived as long as its leader, Ter Petrosyan, could win and maintain the presidency. Of the seventy political parties at the time of independence, only a small number have endured, including the Republican Party, the Justice Bloc (consisting of the Republic Party, the National Democratic Union, the Democratic Party, the National Democratic Party, and the People's Party), the Rule of Law Party, the Dashnaktsutiun, the National Unity Party, and the United Labor Party.

THE KOCHARYAN GOVERNMENT

Born in Stepanakert, Karabagh, Robert Kocharyan received a degree in engineering at the Erevan State Polytechnic Institute. In the 1980s he served in a number of positions in the Communist Party of Karabagh and won a seat in the first parliament of Karabagh in 1991. He became prime minister of Karabagh in 1992 and president in 1994. He won the first presidential elections in Karabagh in November 1996, and in 1997 President Ter Petrosyan appointed him as prime minister of Armenia. After Ter Petrosyan's resignation in February 1998, Kocharyan won the presidential elections held in March against former Communist chief Karen Demirchyan.

His transfer from Stepanakert to Erevan may indeed have been a rare case in the history of modern governments. Kocharyan's appointment as prime minister symbolized the significance of Karabagh to Armenian politics. As president, however, he had to address a host of policy issues, most prominently the economic situation at home (e.g., shortages in resources, unemployment, infrastructural development) and improved relations with the diasporan communities. In foreign policy, and closely related to domestic issues, his administration had to find ways to remove the blockade imposed by Turkey and Azerbaijan and to cultivate closer ties with societies that could potentially stimulate economic development and facilitate modernization. The Kocharyan government thus hoped to rely on Armenian diasporan communities with large and active organizations to lobby for economic support for the homeland, as in matters of trade and economic aid. In contrast to Ter Petrosyan, Kocharyan also promised to return the issue of international recognition of the genocide to the national agenda as a key component in the nation's foreign policy. The Ter Petrosyan government had taken steps to normalize relations with Turkey but to no avail. Upon entering office in 1998, the Kocharyan government had the unenviable task of continuing the policy, as inherited from his predecessor, of pursuing normalization with Turkey, on one hand, and recognition of the genocide, on the other hand.

The results of the parliamentary elections in May appeared to strengthen Kocharyan's hand. Defense Minister Vazgen Sargsyan and the former Communist Party boss Karen Demirchyan allied under the Union Alliance, and upon election they emerged as leaders in the National Assembly, Sargsyan securing the post of prime minister and Demirchyan, as the new Speaker of the Assembly. These parliamentary elections had enormous significance for the nation and its political institutions. The results were seen as a referendum on President Kocharyan's first year in office. Further, the elections, as promised by the Kocharyan government, in general seemed to have been free of egregious violations, in contrast to the repeated charges of electoral irregularities in previous elections. Although the electoral process was not without certain shortcomings, the elections appeared to have enhanced the credibility of the Kocharyan government, as nearly all international observers expressed satisfaction with the process.

The legitimacy of a nation's political institutions and leadership rests on the integrity of the electoral process and the ability to deliver public goods and services. Recurring failures to safeguard electoral integrity eventually undermine public confidence in, and hence the legitimacy of, the system. Diminishing legitimacy affects not only the domestic citizenry, which in the case of Armenia had ample cause for cynicism toward politics, but it also affects international confidence in the political culture and system. For better or worse, international perceptions and opinion regarding Armenia mattered because of its need for foreign trade and investments— issues closely related to its international prestige (e.g., as its membership in the Council of Europe).[36] The Armenian political system appeared to be in the process of developing some rudimentary components of procedural democracy. As Armenia's ambassador to Austria, Jivan Tabibian, has observed, "State institutions must exhibit a triple form of autonomy, that is, ultimately, non-dependence on institutions outside the country, on non-state institutions inside the country and on the idiosyncrasies of the leadership at a given moment."[37] The institutionalization of procedural democracy was a first step toward strengthening the autonomy and hence enhancing the integrity of the policymaking institutions.

By the middle of 1999, a small number of political parties had emerged with significant representation in the National Assembly. These included Unity Alliance led by Andranik Margaryan, the Party of Stability led by Hovhannes Hovhannesyan, the Communist Party led by Sergey Badalyan, the Party of Right and Unity headed by Artashes Geghamyan, Orinats Erkir led by Arthur Baghdasaryan, National Democratic Union led by Vazgen Manukyan, and the Dashnaktsutiun led by Hrand Margaryan. Parties that failed to win seats in the 1999 elections included Union of Socialist Parties, Strong Fatherland, Self-Determination Union, Armenian National Movement, Ramkavar Liberal Democrats, and Shamiram.[38] The elections of 1999 signified political leadership stability, despite initial concerns about the succession process from Ter Petrosyan to Kocharyan. The transition was the first since independence in 1991, and given Ter Petrosyan's controversial leadership and resignation, there were no guarantees for stability. The smooth succession augured well for Kocharyan, but the legitimacy of his government would depend on the political will of policymakers to manage the levers of political economy so as to deliver to the citizenry a more egalitarian distribution of resources than had been possible under the previous administration.

DEMOCRACY AND WOMEN

What mattered after the elections was the extent to which procedural democracy could facilitate the development of substantive democracy. Issues pertaining to women's rights may prove to be the litmus test for the degree of democratization Armenian social and political institutions can promote. While under the Soviet regime Armenian women, like women in other parts of the empire, had attained all economic rights associated with a modern society, their social status had not altered significantly from the views imposed by traditional, patriarchal values and customs. The ideal Armenian woman was traditionally expected to be "chaste, restrained and passive," to "care for her household" and to obey "her husband and elders without protest."[39] The constitution adopted after independence guarantees gender equality, but in practice the government thus far has failed to promote and protect women's rights. Since independence, many of the accomplishments secured under Soviet rule for Armenian women in social, economic, and political areas have been reversed with the recrudescence of patriarchal, androcentric values and attitudes toward women.[40] The International Women's Rights Action Watch commented in a report that the post-Soviet Armenian government had "done nothing to overcome the stereotypical understanding of women's role and place in society. In fact, government officials continue to refer to the 'natural' roles of women."[41] Whereas in 1990 women held 30 percent of the seats in the Armenian parliament, by 1999 that figure had dropped to 3 percent.[42] Women have found it increasingly difficult to enter politics, and those who have attempted have often found it difficult to escape the public perception that they merely represent their husbands.[43]

Domestic violence has proven particularly difficult to address. In a society dominated by notions of family honor and social shame, domestic violence, though reportedly prevalent in Armenia, has received little attention from government agencies. According to criminologist Sergey V. Arakelyan, more than 30 percent of all murders between 1988 and 1998 occurred within the family; 81 percent of domestic murders were committed by men; in 35 percent of all cases, the victims were wives or girlfriends.[44] The Minnesota Advocates for Human Rights reported in December 2000:

> Domestic violence is widespread in Armenia. In interviews conducted by Minnesota Advocates, government officials and members of the legal system initially denied the existence of the problem . . . .
> Government officials at all levels either minimize the problem or consider it a matter of private concern outside the purview of the legal system. Police reportedly discourage women from making complaints against abusive husbands, and abusers are rarely removed from their homes or jailed. The overwhelming response of the legal system to domestic violence is to urge women to reconcile with their abusers.[45]

On a positive note, in recent years, a handful of nongovernmental organizations, such as the Women's Rights Center in Erevan, have made efforts to improve conditions for women.[46]

THE NATIONAL ECONOMY

Armenia's domestic and international political and geopolitical environ-
ments pose serious obstacles toward the fulfillment of human rights and
similar objectives. After a decade of independence, the expected advantages of market economy and political liberalization and democracy had
not fully developed, although perhaps it would be too harsh to judge so
negatively a society that for long suffered the burdens and scars of the
Stalinist legacy. The Kocharyan government failed to eradicate the twin
problems of unemployment and corruption. Even as the political system
began to gain some public confidence, the national economy remained
mired in corruption at all levels of government and institutions. As one
observer has noted, "Corruption, irresponsibility and incompetence
quickly became widespread, visible and corrosive. Politics came to be seen
as a circle of self-serving intrigue rather than as a responsible attempt to
solve the country's problems."[47] The "shadow economy" is believed to
account for 40 percent of the nation's GDP. A considerable number of people are "employed" in jobs that are no longer in operation, while others
are classified under "administrative leave." The minor improvements in
economic development have not been sufficient to increase employees'
income levels. According to official data, incomes for civil servants
increased from $22 in the middle of 1990s to more than $140 per month in
2004 when the government raised salaries so as to counter bureaucratic
bribery. Employment, however, has not guaranteed mobility above the
poverty line.[48] Immediately after the parliamentary elections of 1999,
Prime Minster Vazgen Sargsyan stated in the National Assembly that the
primary task of his government would be "to overcome the economic and
social crises in the country" and "to fight against corruption at all levels of
civil service."[49] In fact, Transparency International ranked Armenia (along
with Bolivia) as eightieth on its Corruption Perceptions Index in 1999 and
eighty-eighth out of 158 countries in 2005. On a scale of 10 (least corrupt)
to 1 (most corrupt), Armenia scored 2.5 and 2.9 for the same years, joining
the ranks of such countries as Ecuador, Russia, Albania, Georgia, and
Kazakhstan.[50] The Groupe d'états contre la corruption of the European
Council reported in early 2006 that corruption permeated nearly all
spheres of Armenia's political economy but especially "the judiciary, the
police, the customs service, the tax inspectorate, education, healthcare,
licensing and privatizations."[51]

Unemployment also has remained a vexing problem. Although official
data place the unemployment rate below 8 percent of the total labor force
of 1.2 million, a more accurate figure perhaps would be about 25 percent.
In recent years an estimated 21 percent of the employed remained "very
poor," and more than 40 percent of the population remained below the

poverty line. The Armenian middle class (as understood in the West) con-
stitutes no more than 25 percent of the population. The highest 10 percent
of the population accounts for more than 41 percent of all household
incomes, while the share of the lowest 10 percent is 1.6 percent.[52]

It was not until 2000 when signs of economic improvement began to
appear, and the World Bank reported with some optimism that its poverty
reduction program would reduce the poverty levels to below 20 percent by
2015.[53] Per capita GDP (PPP) increased from $2,220 in 1999 to $4,190 in 2004.
It is common in the diasporan communities in the United States to compare
Armenia with advanced economies such as Switzerland. Yet the chasm
between the levels of economic development in Armenia and the West is so
wide as to render any such claims irrelevant. In 2004, per capita GDP (PPP)
was about $40,000 in the United States and $33,000 in Switzerland.[54]

In the meantime, in hopes of attracting capital, the government instituted laws greatly favoring foreign investments. The economic growth
was concentrated mainly in Erevan and its vicinity, which registered "50
percent of [the nation's] industrial production, 80 percent of registered
trade turnover, and 76.3 percent of services." Other parts of the country,
however, remained "in much the same miserable condition as a decade
earlier."[55] Significantly, not only was the economic growth limited to
Erevan; it also did not translate into effective social programs. Health services remained deplorable nationwide because of insufficient funding and
lack of supplies and specialists. The number of visits to medical clinics
during the first decade since independence dropped by about 60 percent
per citizen and the occupation rate of hospital beds, by 50 percent.
Education and training institutions have not fared better. Government
allocation to education has dropped considerably since the end of the
Soviet Union. Between 1989 and 1993 the resources allocated to education
fell from 8 percent of the republic's GDP to 4.9 percent; by the middle of
the decade, that figure declined to 1.9 percent. About 55 percent of schools
required structural repairs, and nearly 38 percent of vocational schools
remained vacant, as they lacked the basic infrastructure (heating, sewage,
water supplies). The Education Act of 1999 sought to rectify a number of
deficiencies in the post-Soviet educational system, with special focus on
establishing uniform standards for accreditation of institutions of higher
education, examinations, and student certification. It remains to be seen
whether such reforms can in the long-run address the problem of inequal-
ity in access to good-quality education, as the poor, especially in the rural
areas, find such institutions inaccessible. Government expenditure on
defense decreased as well, from 3.7 of GDP in 1999 to 2.7 percent in
2002 and stabilized at that level thereafter, although the shrinking share
of military expenditures has not contributed to improving the social welfare programs.[56]

No other area demanded greater attention than the region struck by the earthquake in 1988. The Kocharyan government, like its predecessor, has been unable to cope effectively with the social and economic crisis in the earthquake zone although construction of new housing beginning in 2000 gave some hope. In 1999, a decade after the earthquake, unemployment in the town of Spitak, the quake's epicenter, with a population of about 21,000, stood at 40 percent, and about 14,500 of the displaced residents continued to live in temporary housing.[57] As late as 2000, 14 percent of the population in the area was extremely poor, lacking even the minimal necessities for subsistence, with an estimated 20 to 30 percent of women (particularly in the twenty- to thirty-age group) affected by poverty and responsible for feeding their families in the absence of their husbands.[58] As one observer has noted, "An entire generation of children has grown up knowing nothing but the painful legacy of the earthquake."[59] Spitak remained a "disaster zone" for more than a decade.

Prior to the earthquake, the population in Gumri was about 211,000; by 2002 that figure had dropped to 150,000 as a result of death and migration. Gumri, twenty-five miles west of Spitak, was an industrial city during the Soviet period. Its glass and textile factories, which employed about 35,000 people, were destroyed in the quake, and by 2002 unemployment in the city stood at 45 percent. External financial assistance supplemented insufficient government allocations to reconstruct the city and its schools and medical centers.[60] Government assistance for the medical care of handicaps totaled about 22,400 drams ($40) per month, but the medical staff as at the Kuperstock Rehabilitation Center of Gumri, for example, worked for months without pay. The economic conditions left the region's inhabitants helpless and with little confidence in the government. In Gumri, when asked by a reporter her place of residence, a woman replied hopelessly, "at the devil's bosom."[61]

Rather than receive services from the formal institutions of government, an informal web of family and social ties have emerged as the more reliable institutions for support.[62] While ordinarily reliance on such relations would not represent a problem, the fact that a considerable proportion of society is unemployed and poor renders the available pool of support from family and social networks nugatory. Unemployment and poverty have led to economic hardship especially for women, whose highly precarious financial standing in the traditional patriarchal society render them vulnerable to the trappings of the informal market. International trafficking of Armenian women represents one such problem. According to the Armenian-European Center for Economic Policy and Legal Consultations, an estimated 61 percent of Armenian women trafficked were exported to Turkey, nearly 30 percent to the United States, and the rest to Eastern Europe (e.g., Bulgaria and Poland) and the Middle East (e.g., Dubai). Most of these women were from the cities of Erevan

(33 percent) and Gumri (30 percent). A large percentage decided to remain in their new host countries to work in various jobs, including prostitution.[63]

The economic difficulties have led to a large proportion of the Armenian population, perhaps as many as 1 million, to emigrate, leading to the crucial problem of brain drain. In the first half of 1990s, approximately 700,000 citizens emigrated from Armenia, about 240,000 people leaving the country in 1993 alone; by 2002 the total figure since independence had increased to 800,000. Nearly 75 percent of them emigrated to Russia and the former Soviet republics, and others to the West, especially to France and the United States. The mass exodus included the professional classes (doctors, scientists, etc.) who sought greater access to employment opportunities abroad, leaving the country with a shortage of those with the skills necessary to reinvigorate the economy.[64]

The government's failure to alleviate the economic hardships for a vast majority of the public may have been the root cause of the assassinations on October 27, 1999, when a group of five gunmen rushed into the parliament and murdered eight members. One of the gunmen, Nairi Hunanyan, reportedly shouted "Enough of drinking our blood."[65] Among those killed were Prime Minister Vazgen Sargsyan and Speaker Karen Demirchyan. Immediately after the assassinations, the military appeared prepared to seize power, as the defense ministry issued a declaration ordering the resignations of National Security Minister Serge Sargsyan, Interior Minister Suren Abramyan, and the prosecutor general. The defense ministry stated on television that "in such circumstances the national army cannot stand idly by."[66] The enormity of such a declaration for the fragile republic cannot be overemphasized. It was not clear whether the military would in fact intervene to "restore order," but Kocharyan was able to prevent such an act and to avoid a constitutional crisis. The five assassins apparently were not affiliated with any specific domestic political faction or a foreign organization, although future investigations may yield evidence to the contrary.

The assassinations had serious ramifications for the republic. The parliamentary elections earlier in the year appeared to have established a sense of political normalcy after years of political instability, particularly in the aftermath of the presidential elections in 1996. The crisis in October 1999 exposed the precarious nature of that normalcy in Armenian politics. The assassinations further weakened the economy as they heightened the saliency of the risks facing foreign investors. Moreover, the assassinations occurred at a time when the United States had become directly engaged in the negotiations over the Karabagh conflict. U.S. Deputy Secretary of State Strobe Talbott had met with Foreign Minister Vardan Oskanian and Prime Minister Vazgen Sargsyan earlier in the day on October 27. Talbott's visit gave rise to expectations that the United States could facilitate a peaceful resolution of the conflict. Sargsyan had been a staunch advocate for the continuation of close ties with Russia, and Moscow may have construed his negotiations with the United States as undermining Russian interests in the region. Speculation ran high that the five gunmen acted to forestall further negotiations, but no evidence has been brought forth to support such claims.[67] The Kocharyan government survived the crisis.

Kocharyan won his reelection bid in March 2003. Of the total 1,548,570 votes cast, 1,044,424 voted for Kocharyan, and 504,146 for Stepan Demirchyan. In the parliamentary elections, the Republican Party of Armenia, with 23.66 percent of the total votes, secured the majority (twenty-three) of seats. Significantly, the Dashnaktsutiun, which had been banned by President Ter Petrosyan in 1994, won 11.5 percent of the votes and 11 seats in the National Assembly. Ter Petrosyan's own party, the Armenian National Movement, won less than 1 (0.65) percent of the votes and gained no seats in the parliament. The Communist Party, which had dominated the republic for seven decades, also failed to win seats, as did a number of other parties, such as the Liberal Union, the Union of Industrials and Women, and the Ramkavar Azatakan Party.[68] As during the Ter Petrosyan government, economic issues determined the election outcome. Having secured his reelection, Kocharyan felt confident to address the foreign policy problems that seemed intractable under his predecessor.

KOCHARYAN'S FOREIGN POLICY

Geography, as always in international politics, is one of the primary factors influencing foreign policy. By the closing days of the millennium, the three republics in the Caucasus had become part of expanding networks of relations with their neighbors and the major powers. Geopolitical and economic considerations compelled Armenia to maintain its relations with Russia as a member of the Commonwealth of Independent States. Georgia, on the other hand, sought to distance itself from Moscow, demanded the removal of the Russian military bases from its territory, and moved closer to Turkey and the United States. Azerbaijan utilized the lure of oil as an incentive to attract the support of western corporations.

In April 1999 Armenia participated in the North Atlantic Treaty Organization (NATO) summit in Washington, DC. Although not a member, Armenia participated through NATO's Partnership for Peace program. Its participation underscored the necessity of balancing Armenia's foreign policy between the East (in this case Russia and Iran) and the West (the United States and Europe). The timing of the summit created the

particularly awkward position for Kocharyan and Oskanian of maintaining close security ties with Russia, which for its part opposed the NATO
bombing campaign in Serbia, while cultivating closer ties with NATO. At
home, the Communist Party, headed by Sergey Badalyan, led the opposition against Kocharyan's participation, claiming that Armenia's involvement in NATO could potentially undermine the republic's relations with
Russia with dire consequences for national security.[69]

In late November 1999 Kocharyan attended the Organization for
Security and Cooperation in Europe (OSCE) summit in Istanbul. The principal agenda items included the adoption of the new Charter for European
Security and the revised Treaty on Conventional Forces of Europe. There,
Kocharyan held conferences with a number of his counterparts, including
presidents Suleyman Demirel of Turkey, Jacques Chirac of France, and Bill
Clinton of the United States. The declaration issued by the summit covered a vast array of international topics, including approval of efforts by
the presidents of Armenia and Azerbaijan to resolve the Karabagh conflict
through the Minsk Group. Significantly, the declaration made no mention
of Karabagh as an independent, sovereign entity. The Istanbul summit
promised no more than support for the continuation of Armenia-
Azerbaijan negotiations but without accepting Karabagh as a legitimate
partner, a position not different from that pursued by the OSCE since the
early phases of the negotiations in 1992. In addition, several bilateral and
multilateral agreements were signed, including a Georgian-Russian
agreement to withdraw or to reduce Russian military presence in Georgia
and an agreement providing for the transit of Azerbaijani oil from Baku to
the Mediterranean port of Jeyhan in Turkey.[70] Unlike the negative assessments of the Lisbon summit of December 1996, initial public reaction to
the Istanbul summit in matters pertaining to Armenia and Karabagh was
more favorable. This was perhaps partly due to Kocharyan's statements
claiming to have achieved more positive results than his predecessor, but
the Istanbul summit failed to resolve the precarious status of Karabagh.

Among the western powers, the United States has played a significant
role in shaping the agenda for the resolution of the conflicts in the
Caucasus because of the region's oil resources and proximity to the
Middle East. The United States considered the Caspian region strategically significant because of oil interests and, after the terrorist attacks in
New York on September 11, 2001, also for its war on terrorism. The
European Union (EU) viewed the Caucasus as potentially a viable economic zone where it could expand its influence, as the three republics
sought membership in the Union or, short of that, close association with it.
Azerbaijan launched a major lobbying campaign in the United States
beginning in 1994 to secure billions of dollars' worth of investments in its
oil fields, a lucrative prospect that Azerbaijani president Heydar Aliyev

hoped to utilize in order to win U.S. support in negotiations regarding the status of Karabagh. Azerbaijan and the United States signed a security agreement in 1996, establishing a bilateral working group on mutual security concerns, and Baku expressed its determination to withdraw from the CIS security system. Azerbaijan had signed the CIS Collective Security Treaty in 1993 but refused to renew its membership and officially withdrew in 1999.[71] Similarly, having gained the confidence of Germany, Turkey, the EU, and the United States, Georgia announced its intention to leave the CIS. In November 2004, Defense Minister Giorgi Baramidze publicly expressed his preference for closer relations with NATO, and in February 2006 his government formally withdrew from the CIS Security Council. This was followed, in May, by President Mikheil Saakashvili's indication that his government would reassess its membership in the CIS. The United States increased its military presence in Georgia beginning in 2002, when the Pentagon stationed nearly 1,000 military "advisers" there to counter Iran's potentially destabilizing influence in the region.[72] Complicating matters was the security, ideological, and economic alignment between Israel and Turkey since their bilateral agreement of 1996, as the former sought allies against radical Islam. Closer ties between the two nations led Israel to lend strong support to Azerbaijan both in issues pertaining to the resolution of the status of Karabagh and in the wider international community. As of this writing in early 2007, Armenia finds itself nearly isolated in the region, with close ties only with Russia and Iran, although membership in numerous key international organizations, including the United Nations, the International Monetary Fund, the World Bank, the World Health Organization, the Council of Europe, and the World Trade Organization, may cushion the fluctuations in fortune.

THE KOCHARYAN GOVERNMENT AND DIASPORAN RELATIONS

The economic and political difficulties in Armenia continued to press the policymakers in Erevan to pay close attention to their relations with the diasporan communities. Upon entering office, Kocharyan had sought to undo the damage caused by his predecessor, and unlike Ter Petrosyan's more ad hoc style, Kocharyan adopted a more systematic approach to create a structured formulation for that relationship. In December 1998, he called for the first Armenia-diaspora conference, which met in Erevan on September 22–23, 1999, with the participation of about 800 people from the diaspora. Although it did not produce any breakthroughs in policy, the conference nevertheless set a precedent in homeland-diaspora relations and provided a forum to integrate the diasporan voices into the public debate on various issues on the national agenda. Diasporan communities clearly welcomed the initiative, and the conference perhaps would have even helped to enhance Kocharyan's international prestige. The assassinations in the parliament in October, however, eclipsed his initial efforts. Further, the new president reinstituted the legitimacy of the Dashnaktsutiun. That the second Armenia-diaspora conference was held on May 27–28, 2002, the anniversary of the first republic's independence day, carried symbolic significance in reconfirming Kocharyan's willingness to cooperate with the Dashnaktsutiun, although at the same time the latter's opposition to the Turkish-Armenian Reconciliation Commission, as discussed below, remained a serious problem. By September 2006, when the third conference met, relations between the republic and the diaspora seemed to have recovered.

Beginning in the late 1990s, homeland-diaspora relations witnessed fundamental changes. For earlier generations in the diaspora, the "homeland" referred to the lost territories in historic or Ottoman Armenia, their families' place of origin. The new generation of diasporan Armenians had little or no familiarity with the land of their forebears and saw the post-Soviet republic as the Armenian homeland. Independence from Soviet rule stimulated wide interest in travel to the republic, but with mixed results. On the positive side, the diaspora developed closer ties with Armenia and viewed the republic as the epicenter of collective national identity and aspirations; individual Armenians gained greater familiarity with the country, its problems, and its interests, a process that also demythologized the idealized Armenia that they had imagined for decades. Some Armenians even immigrated to the republic, purchased or rented houses, and established businesses. On the negative side, the economic hardship and corruption they witnessed created a certain measure of cynicism toward the country. Some Armenians who had celebrated from afar the republic's independence in 1991 grew disillusioned after they visited the country. Would diasporan Armenians hang on to the imagined republic and abandon the real, or embrace the real republic and abandon the imagined? Despite the difficulties, some organizations, such as the Land and Culture Organization, encouraged the diasporan youth to become involved in the construction of the homeland. Diasporan remittances represented a significant aspect of relations with the republic. For example, the annual telethons held by the Hayastan All-Armenia Fund (Hayastan Hamahaykakan Himnadram) between 1991 and 2006 reportedly contributed more than $160 million in various forms of assistance to Armenia and Karabagh.[73] Financial support totaling about $25 million enabled Karabagh to construct the north-south road linking Lachin and Stepanakert. These and similar diasporan contributions to the republic and Karabagh were clearly major successes in diaspora-homeland cooperation.

The Armenia-diaspora conferences also resolved to support efforts toward securing international recognition of the genocide, but such declarations were meant for diasporan consumption rather than guiding policy. The Kocharyan government appeared to follow a two-pronged approach to this issue. Its public announcements at times supported and at times refuted the claim that Erevan would insist on Turkish recognition as a precondition for normalization of relations. The Kocharyan government, however, could not control lobbying efforts and political campaigns in diasporan communities. Lobbying host governments for the recognition of the genocide had gained backing from all Armenian communities during the Cold War, when Moscow determined Armenia's foreign policy and shielded the republic from the pressures of international political economy and geopolitical competitions. In the 1990s, however, Armenia, now a sovereign state, had to assume direct responsibility for its own domestic and foreign policies. The continued practice of lobbying in diasporan communities for genocide recognition placed enormous pressure on the government in Erevan, and the Kocharyan government appeared to adopt a balanced approach to domestic economic priorities and demands to place the recognition of the genocide on the nation's foreign policy agenda.

Armenians generally believed that successes in securing recognition by host governments and international bodies would pressure Turkey into recognizing the genocide and accepting responsibility. Foreign governments adopted such resolutions for their own domestic political gains and, in the case of Europe, raised the issue within the context of debates regarding Turkey's admission to the European Union. European countries that adopted some form of resolution recognizing the genocide include Belgium, France, Germany, the Netherlands, Sweden, Switzerland. In September 2005, the European Parliament, echoing similar declarations adopted in 2002, 2000, 1998, and 1987, approved a resolution calling on the Turkish government to recognize the genocide "as a prerequisite for accession to the European Union." It further urged Ankara to work toward establishing diplomatic relations with and to terminate the economic blockade on Armenia.[74] Ostensibly a moral stance insisting on accountability for the crime of genocide, such resolutions manifest European reluctance and even opposition to the admission of Turkey (which is seen as a Muslim country) into the European Union.[75] Nevertheless, most Armenians would have been satisfied if the 2005 resolution served as a basis for Armenian-Turkish reconciliation.

The Kocharyan government attempted to normalize relations with Turkey through the Turkish-Armenian Reconciliation Commission (TARC), established in 2001 as a track-two, unofficial diplomacy under the auspices of the U.S. Department of State. The TARC process lacked the degree of transparency and representation necessary to serve as a legitimate mechanism for mediation. The Dashnaktsutiun, for example, which was excluded from the process, most vehemently opposed it. This is not to say that TARC did not produce positive results. It commissioned an independent study by the International Center for Transitional Justice (ICTJ) to determine whether the UN Genocide Convention could in fact be retroactively applicable to the Armenian case. The ICTJ correctly concluded that "the Events, viewed collectively, can thus be said to include all of the elements of the crime of genocide as defined in the Convention," but it also added that the Convention does not permit retroactive compensation for damages.[76] By early 2002, the TARC experiment appeared to have failed as an approach to Armenian-Turkish reconciliation, although one could argue that it was successful at least in setting the process in motion. Given Armenia's need for wider economic relations in the region and Turkey's need for economic development and for improved image in Europe, policymakers in both countries will be reluctant to shelve TARC permanently. It will most likely reappear in a different form, with the necessary adjustments effectuated according to assessments of the first experiment.

After seven decades of Soviet rule, Armenia regained its independence. Armenians worldwide celebrated the rebirth of the small bit of land that they inherited from the generation of genocide survivors and survivors of catastrophes at the hands of Turkish and Russian rulers. Having gained independence, however, internal difficulties, exacerbated first by efforts to recover from the earthquake in December 1988 and the war in Karabagh, rendered the task of building a modern state extremely difficult. It remains to be seen whether changes in government will lead to improvements and whether the political leadership and political culture will bring about fundamental improvements in the standard of living and democratization. Closer diaspora-homeland relations since 1991 have indicated that Armenian culture (e.g., language, religion) remains an essential part of the nation's struggle for national survival, and the republic, despite its shortcomings, is likely to reconnect diasporan Armenians with their cultural roots and homeland. As the Karabagh war has demonstrated, Armenia in the twenty-first century, as in the bygone years of monarchs and nakharars centuries earlier, remains caught between powerful neighbors and distant empires, and their geopolitical competitions directly shape the nation's domestic politics and foreign policy.

This page intentionally left blank

Notes

1   DYNASTIES AND THE GEOPOLITICS OF EMPIRE: THE ERVANDUNI AND THE ARTASHESIAN DYNASTIES

1. L.W. King and R.C. Thompson, *The Sculptures and Inscription of Darius the Great on the Rock of Behistûn in Persia* (London: Harrison and Sons, 1907), p. xxxviii; P.M. Sykes, *A History of Persia* (London: Macmillan, 1915), pp. 169–73.
2. King and Thompson, *Sculptures*, pp. 27–28, 31–32.
3. Igor M. Diakonoff, *Pre-History of the Armenian People*, trans. Lori Jennings (Delmar, NY: Caravan Books, 1984), pp. 6–7, 19–21, 58–67; the quote appears on page 65.
4. S.T. Eremyan, "Hayasa-Azzii teghvoroshume, etnikakan kazme ev lezun" [The Location of Hayasa-Azzi, Its Ethnic Composition and Language], in *Hay zhoghovrdi patmutyun* [History of the Armenian People], ed. Ts.P. Aghayan et al. (Erevan: Armenian Academy of Sciences, 1971), vol. 1, p. 191.
5. Boris B. Piotrovski, *Urartu: The Kingdom of Van*, trans. and ed. Peter S. Gelling (London: Evelyn Adams and Mackay, 1967); N.V. Arutyunyan, *Biainili (Urartu)* (Erevan: Armenian Academy of Sciences, 1970).
6. Adam T. Smith and Karen S. Rubinson, eds., *Archaeology in the Borderlands: Investigations in Caucasia and Beyond* (Los Angeles: University of California Press, 2003), esp. chapter by Ruben S. Badalyan, Adam T. Smith, and Pavel S. Avetisyan, "The Emergence of Sociopolitical Complexity in Southern Caucasia"; S.T. Eremyan, "Hay zhoghovrdi kazmavorman avarte ev Haykakan arajin petakan kazmavorumnere" [The Completion of the Formation of the Armenian People and the Formations of the First Armenian State], in Aghayan, *Hay zhoghovrdi patmutyun*, vol. 1, p. 440.
7. Robert H. Hewsen, "The Geography of Armenia," in *The Armenian People from Ancient to Modern Times*, vol. 1: *The Dynastic Periods*, ed. Richard G. Hovannisian (New York: St. Martin's Press, 1997), pp. 1–17.
8. Hakob A. Manandyan, *The Trade and Cities of Armenia in Relation to the Ancient World*, 2nd rev. ed., trans. Nina G. Garsoian (Lisbon: Calouste Gulbenkian Foundation, 1965).
9. Artak E. Movsisyan, *Vani tagavorutyan (Biaynili, Urartu, Ararat) mehenagrutyune* (Erevan: Armenian Academy of Sciences, 1998); N.V. Harutyunyan, "Urartun arajavor Asiayi hzoraguyn petutyun" [Urartu as the Strongest Government in Asia], in Aghayan, *Hay zhoghovrdi patmutyun*, vol. 1, pp. 300–1.

10. Boris B. Piotrovski, *The Ancient Civilization of Urartu*, trans. James Hogarth (London: Cresset Press, 1969).

11. J.P. Mallory, *In Search of the Indo-Europeans* (London: Thames and Hudson, 1989).

12. Boris B. Piotrovski, "Arvest, kron, gir, grakanutyun" [Profession, Religion, Letters, Literature], in Aghayan, *Hay zhoghovrdi patmutyun*, vol. 1, pp. 407–13, 415–19.

13. Harutyunyan, "Urartun arajavor Asiayi," p. 304.

14. N.V. Harutyunyan, "Urartui sotsial-tntesakan karge, petakan karutsvatske ev kaghaknere: Sotsial-tntesakan karge" [The Social-Economic Order in Urartu, the State Structure and the Cities: The Social-Economic Order], in Aghayan, *Hay zhoghovrdi patmutyun*, vol. 1, pp. 338–39.

15. Ibid., pp. 340–42.

16. N.V. Harutyunyan, "Urartui sotsial-tntesakan karge, petakan karutsvatske ev kaghaknere: petakan karutsvatske" [The Social-Economic Order in Urartu, the State Structure and the Cities: The State Structure], in Aghayan, *Hay zhoghovrdi patmutyun*, vol. 1, pp. 344–46.

17. N.V. Harutyunyan, "Urartun m.t.a. viii dari verjin ev vii darum" [Urartu in the Late Eighth Century and in the Seventh Century B.C.], in Aghayan, *Hay zhoghovrdi patmutyun*, vol. 1, pp. 332–37.

18. Robert Collins, *The Medes and Persians, Conquerors and Diplomats* (London: Cassell, 1974); Nina Garsoian, "The Emergence of Armenia," in Hovannisian, *Armenian People*, vol. 1, p. 38.

19. Eremyan, "Hay zhoghovrdi kazmavorman avarte," p. 443.

20. Ibid., pp. 423–24, 439; Diakonoff, *Pre-History*, passim.

21. David M. Lang, "Iran, Armenia and Georgia," in *The Cambridge History of Iran*, vol. 3, pt. 1, *The Seleucid, Parthian and Sasanian Periods*, ed. Ehsan Yarshater (Cambridge: Cambridge University Press, 1983), pp. 506–7; Cyril Toumanoff, *Studies in Christian Caucasian History* (Washington, DC: Georgetown University Press, 1963), pp. 277–354.

22. Xenophon, *Anabasis*, with Eng. trans. Carleton L. Brownson (Cambridge, MA: Loeb Classical Library, Harvard University Press, 1992; first published 1922), II.iv.8; III.iv.13.

23. Lang, "Iran," pp. 506–7.

24. G.A. Tiratsyan, "Haykakan mshakuyte vi-iv darerum" [The Armenian Culture in the Sixth-Fourth Centuries (B.C.)], and "Hayastane vagh hellenizmi zhamanakashrjanum" [Armenia during the Early Period of Hellenism], in Aghayan, *Hay zhoghovrdi patmutyun*, vol. 1, pp. 464–78, 504, 529.

25. Eremyan, "Hay zhoghovrdi kazmavorman avarte," pp. 437–38.

26. Andrew Robert Burn, *Persia and the Greeks: The Defence of the West, c. 546–478 B.C.* (London: E. Arnold, 1962, repr. 1970).

27. Sykes, *History*, pp. 171–72.

28. G.A. Tiratsyan, "Hayastane Akemenyan Parskastani tirapetutyan nerko" [Armenia under Achaemenian Persian Rule], in Aghayan, *Hay zhoghovrdi patmutyun*, vol. 1, pp. 448–50, 454; Tiratsyan, "Haykakan mshakuyte vi-iv darerum," p. 471.

29. Tiratsyan, "Hayastane Akemenyan," pp. 452, 455; Garsoian, "Emergence of Armenia," pp. 40, 41; Sykes, *History*, pp. 173–74.

30. Garsoian, "Emergence of Armenia," p. 41; Lang, "Iran," pp. 508–9; Sykes, *History*, pp. 173–74.

31. Manandyan, *Trade*, p. 21; Garsoian, "Emergence of Armenia," p. 41.

32. Tiratsyan, "Hayastane Akemenyan," pp. 446–50.

33. Richard N. Frye, "Continuing Iranian Influences on Armenian," in *Yād-Nāme-ye Irānī-ye Minorsky*, ed. Mujtabá Mīnovī and Īraj Afshār (Tehran: Tehran University, 1969), pp. 80–89; A. Meillet, "De l'influence parthe sur le langue arménienne," *Revue des études arméniennes* 1 (Paris, 1920): 9; Robert Bedrosian, *Armenia in Ancient and Medieval Times* (New York: Armenian National Education Committee, 1985), p. 23; Garsoian, "Emergence of Armenia," p. 42.

34. James Russell, "The Formation of the Armenian Nation," in Hovannisian, *Armenian People*, vol. 1, p. 24.

35. Manandyan, *Trade*, p. 44; Hakob Manandyan, *Knnakan tesutyun Hay zhoghovrdi patmutyan* [Critical Review of the History of the Armenian People] (Erevan: Haibedhrad, 1944), vol. 1, pp. 92–93; S.M. Krkyasharyan, "Ervanduni arkaya-tohme Hayastanum" [The Ervanduni Dynasty in Armenia], *Patma-banasirakan handes* 4:1 (1973): 179–85.

36. Edouard Will, *Histoire politique du monde hellénistique*, 2 vols. (Nancy: University of Nancy, 1966–67); Tiratsyan, "Hayastane vagh hellenizmi zhamanakashrjanum," p. 502; Manandyan, *Trade*, pp. 34, 40, 53; Manandyan, *Knnakan tesutyun*, p. 97.

37. See Russell, "Formation," p. 36; Toumanoff, *Studies*, pp. 293–94. See also Zh.G. Elchibekyan, "Ervandunineri tsagman hartsi shurj" [On the Question Concerning the Origins of the Ervandunis], *Patma-banasirakan handes* 53:2 (1971): 107–13.

38. G.A. Tiratsyan, "Ervandyan Hayastani taratske (m.t.a. vi dar)" [The Expanse of the Ervanduni Armenia (Sixth Century B.C.)], *Patma-banasirakan handes* 91:4 (1980): 92; Tiratsyan, "Ervandyan Hayastani taratske (m.t.a. vi d. verj-m.t.a. iii d. verj)" [The Expanse of the Ervanduni Armenia (Late Sixth Century B.C.-Late Third Century B.C.)], *Patma-banasirakan handes* 93:2 (1981): 68–84.

39. Tiratsyan, "Hayastane vagh hellenizmi zhamanakashrjanum," p. 519; S.M. Krkyasharyan, "Petakan aparati kazmavorume ev nra hetaga zargats-man pule hin Hayastanum" [The Formation of State Apparatus and Its Future Development Phase in Ancient Armenia], *Patma-banasirakan handes* 1–2 (1994): 225–37; Rafael Matevosyan, *Bagratuniner: Patma-tohmabanakan hanragitaran* [Bagratunis: Historic-Genealogical Encyclopedia] (Erevan: Anahit, 1997), p. 98.

40. Manandyan, *Trade*, p. 37; E. Bickerman, "The Seleucid Period," in *Cambridge History of Iran*, vol. 3, pt. 1, pp. 3–20.

41. Tiratsyan, "Hayastane vagh hellenizmi zhamanakashrjanum," pp. 514–15.

42. S.T. Eremyan, "Haykakan arajin petakan kazmavorume" [The Formation of the First Armenian State], *Patma-banasirakan handes* 3 (1968): 91–119.

43. Tiratsyan, "Hayastane vagh hellenizmi zhamanakashrjanum," p. 517; B.N. Arakelyan, "Vortegh en gtnvel Ervandashat ev Ervandakert kaghaknere?" [Where were the Cities of Ervandashat and Ervandakert Located?], *Patma-banasirakan handes* 30 (1965): 83–93.

44. Manandyan, *Trade*, pp. 36–38; Tiratsyan, "Hayastane vagh hellenizmi zhamanakashrjanum," pp. 514, 519; Arakelyan, "Vortegh en gtnvel?" p. 84.

45. Manandyan, *Trade*, pp. 42–43.

46. Tiratsyan, "Hayastane vagh hellenizmi zhamanakashrjanum," pp. 515, 520; Matevosyan, *Bagratuniner*, pp. 11–12.

47. Tiratsyan, "Hayastane vagh hellenizmi zhamanakashrjanum," p. 516; G.Kh. Sargsyan, "Hayastani miyavorume ev hzoratsume Artashes A[rajin]i orov" [The Unification and Strengthening of Armenia during the Reign of Artashes I], in Aghayan, *Hay zhoghovrdi patmutyun,* vol. 1, p. 522; Lang, "Iran," pp. 510, 512.

48. Sargsyan, "Hayastani miyavorume," pp. 524–25; Sykes, *History,* pp. 345–46; Lang, "Iran," pp. 512–13; A.D.H. Bivar, "The Political History of Iran under the Arsacids," in *Cambridge History of Iran,* vol. 3, pt. 1, pp. 28–29.

49. G.Kh. Sargsyan, "Hayastani petakan karge hellenistakan darashrjanum: Kedronakan ishkhanutyune" [The State Order of Armenia during the Period of Hellenism: The Central Government], in Aghayan, *Hay zhoghovrdi patmutyun,* vol. 1, pp. 669–70, 672.

50. Sargsyan, "Hayastani miyavorume," pp. 537–38; Sargsyan, "Kedronakan ishkhanutyune," pp. 671, 673.

51. Sargsyan, "Kedronakan ishkhanutyune," pp. 673, 674; Sargsyan, "Petakan karutsvatski tarrer" [Elements of State Structure], in Aghayan, *Hay zhoghovrdi patmutyun,* vol. 1, p. 679.

52. G.Kh. Sargsyan, "Hayastani sotsial-tntesakan karge hellenistakan darashrjanum" [The Social-Economic Order during the Period of Hellenism], in Aghayan, *Hay zhoghovrdi patmutyun,* vol. 1, pp. 656–57.

53. Ibid., p. 660; Lang, "Iran," p. 509.

54. Manandyan, *Trade,* pp. 46–49; Sargsyan, "Hayastani miyavorume," pp. 526–38, 539.

55. Sargsyan, "Hayastani sotsial-tntesakan karge," p. 641.

56. A.G. Adoyan, "Haykakan amusna-entanekan haraberutyunnere mijnadaryan orenknerum" [Armenian Marriage-Family Relations in the Laws of the Middle Ages], *Patma-banasirakan handes* 3 (1965): 49.

57. Sargsyan, "Hayastani miyavorume," p. 539; Sargsyan, "Hayastani sotsial-tntesakan karge hellenistakan darashrjanum," p. 663; Sargsyan, "Kedronakan ishkhanutyune," pp. 675, 677.

58. Sargsyan, "Kedronakan ishkhanutyune," p. 637.

59. Sargsyan, "Hayastani miyavorume," pp. 531, 534, 536–37.

60. Ibid., pp. 534–36.

61. Manandyan, *Trade,* p. 53.

62. Sargsyan, "Hayastani miyavorume," p. 543.

63. Hakob A. Manandyan, *Tigran Erkrorde ev Hrome* [Tigran II and Rome] (Erevan: Erevan State University, 1972), p. 50.

64. Sargsyan, "Hayastani miyavorume," pp. 544–47. See also Bivar, "Political History," pp. 28–29.

65. Garsoian, "Emergence of Armenia," p. 49.

66. Neilson C. Debevoise, *A Political History of Parthia* (Chicago: University of Chicago Press, 1938), pp. 249–54; Richard N. Frye, "The Political History of Iran under the Sasanians," in *Cambridge History of Iran,* vol. 3, pt. 1, p. 120.

67. Sargsyan, "Hayastani miyavorume," pp. 552–53.

68. According to Lang, Artashes I was succeeded by Tigran I (159–123 B.C.), followed by Artavazd I (123–95). Lang, "Iran," p. 513.

69. Sargsyan, "Hayastani miyavorume," p. 551; Sargsyan, "Hayastane Artavazd B-i ev nra hajordneri zhamankashrjanum" [Armenia during the Period of Artavazd II and His Successors], in Aghayan, *Hay zhoghovrdi patmutyun,* vol. 1, p. 607.

70. G.Kh. Sargsyan, "Haykakan ashkharhakal terutyune: Tigran B" [The Armenian Imperialist Government: Tigran II], in Aghayan, *Hay zhoghovrdi patmutyun*, vol. 1, pp. 556–58.

71. Manandyan and Garsoian note that until recently, historians' perceptions of the policies of the Tigran the Great were shaped largely by Roman accounts which presented his expansionism as a serious threat to Rome's interests and were therefore "hostile" in their interpretation of events in Armenia. Manandyan, *Tigran Erkrorde*, pp. 27–31; Garsoian, "Emergence of Armenia," pp. 52–59.

72. G. Khalatiantz, *Outline History of Armenia* (Moscow, 1910), p. 161, as discussed by Manandyan, *Trade*, p. 53.

73. G.Kh. Sargsyan, "Hay-Hromiakan paterazme" [The Armenian-Roman War], in Aghayan, *Hay zhoghovrdi patmutyun*, vol. 1, pp. 580–81; Manandyan, *Tigran Erkrorde*, pp. 52–55.

74. Garsoian, "Emergence of Armenia," p. 54; Sargsyan, "Haykakan ashkharhakal terutyune," p. 558.

75. Sargsyan, "Haykakan ashkharhakal terutyune," p. 560; Manandyan, *Tigran Erkrorde*, p. 50; Jörg Wagner, "Provincia Osrhoanae," in *Armies and Frontiers in Roman and Byzantine Anatolia*, ed. Stephen Mitchell (Oxford: B.A.R., 1983), pp. 103–23; Judah B. Segal, *Edessa 'The Blessed City'* (Oxford: Clarendon Press, 1970), pp. 9–15; A.H.M. Jones, *The Cities of the Eastern Roman Provinces* (Oxford: Clarendon Press, 1971), pp. 215–26.

76. Garsoian, "Emergence of Armenia," p. 54.

77. The precise location of Tigranakert has been a source of much controversy. See T. Rice Holmes, "Tigranocerta," *Journal of Roman Studies* 7 (1917): 120–38; Manandyan, *Trade*, p. 61; Manandyan, *Tigran Erkrorde*, pp. 83–84; Thomas Sinclair, "The Site of Tigranocerta. I," *Revue des études arméniennes*, n.s., 25 (1994–95): 183–254; Ronald Syme, "Tigranocerta: A Problem Misconceived," in Mitchell, *Armies and Frontiers*, pp. 61–70; Levon Avdoyan, "Tigranocerta: The City 'Built by Tigranes'," in *Armenian Tigranakert/Diarbekir and Edessa/Urfa*, ed. Richard G. Hovannisian (Costa Mesa, CA: Mazda, 2006), pp. 81–95.

78. Manandyan, *Trade*, p. 62.

79. Nikoghayos Adonts, *Hayastane Hustinianosi darashrjanum* [Armenia during the Period of Justinian] (Erevan: Hayastan, 1987); *Armenia in the Period of Justinian*, trans. Nina G. Garsoian (Lisbon: Calouste Gulbenkian Foundation, 1970), p. 165. It was in the Arshakuni period, however, that the nakharar system attained its final developed or mature form. According to Krkyasharyan, the system emerged no earlier than the Arshakuni era. See Krkyasharyan, "Petakan aparati kazmavorume," pp. 225–37.

80. Sargsyan, "Haykakan ashkharhakal terutyune," p. 570; Manandyan, *Trade*, pp. 64–65; Manandyan, *Tigran Erkrorde*, pp. 67–72.

81. This system differed from the more centralized political and administrative system developed under Artashes I. Sargsyan, "Hayastani miyavorume," p. 537.

82. Manandyan, *Tigran Erkrorde*, pp. 110–11; Garsoian, "Emergence of Armenia," pp. 58–59; Sargsyan, "Hay-Hromiakan paterazme," p. 583; Syme, "Tigranocerta," p. 61; Sykes, *History*, p. 368.

83. Niccolò Machiavelli, *The Art of War*, rev. ed. Ellis Farneworth, translation, with an introduction by Neal Wood (Cambridge, MA: Perseus Books, Da Capo Press, 2001; first published 1521), pp. 52–53.

84. Garsoian, "Emergence of Armenia," p. 59.
85. Lang, "Iran," p. 516; Manandyan, *Tigran Erkrorde*, pp. 148–50, 171–73; Sargsyan, "Hay-Hromiakan paterazme," pp. 585, 589–90; Sykes, *History*, p. 368.
86. Bivar, "Political History," pp. 46–47.
87. Manandyan, *Tigran Erkrorde*, pp. 186, 203–09; Sargsyan, "Hay-Hromiakan paterazme," p. 602; Garsoian, "Emergence of Armenia," p. 59; Sykes, *History*, p. 370.
88. Sykes, *History*, p. 371.
89. Ibid., p. 374.
90. Bivar, "Political History," p. 53; Sargsyan, "Hayastane Artavazd B-i," pp. 606–7; Sykes, *History*, p. 374.
91. Bivar, "Political History," p. 49.
92. Sargsyan, "Hayastane Artavazd B-i," p. 608; Sykes, *History*, p. 379.
93. Plutarch, *Lives*, "Crassus," trans. Bernadotte Perrin (Cambridge, MA: Loeb Classical Library, Harvard University Press, 1996; first published 1916), III.xxxiii, pp. 420/421.
94. Sykes, *History*, p. 382.
95. Ibid., p. 387; Bivar, "Political History," pp. 58–59.
96. Vladimir Minorsky, "Roman and Byzantine Campaigns in Atropatene," *Bulletin of the School of Oriental and African Studies* 11:2 (1944): 243–65; Sykes, *History*, pp. 388–89; Bivar, "Political History," pp. 64–65.
97. Sargsyan, "Hayastane Artavazd B-i," p. 622.
98. Ibid., p. 627; Manandyan, *Knnakan tesutyun*, p. 293;
99. Manandyan, *Tigran Erkrorde*, pp. 39–44.
100. Brian Campbell, "War and Diplomacy: Rome and Parthia, 31 BC-AD 235," in *War and Society in the Roman World*, ed. John Rich (London: Routledge, 1993), pp. 214–16, 220–25, 228–32.
101. Sargsyan, "Hayastane Artavazd B-i," p. 629.
102. Ibid., pp. 631, 633; Debevoise, *Political History*, pp. 143, 147.

2   CULTURE, LANGUAGE, AND WARS OF RELIGION: KINGS, MARZPANS, OSTIKANS

1. Nina Garsoian, "The Aršakuni Dynasty (A.D. 12-[180?]-428)," in *The Armenian People from Ancient to Modern Times*, vol. 1: *The Dynastic Periods*, ed. Richard G. Hovannisian (New York: St. Martin's Press, 1997), p. 64; P.M. Sykes, *A History of Persia* (London: Macmillan, 1915), p. 403; A.D.H. Bivar, "The Political History of Iran under the Arsacids," in *The Cambridge History of Iran*, vol. 3, pt. 1, *The Seleucid, Parthian and Sasanian Periods*, ed. Ehsan Yarshater (Cambridge: Cambridge University Press, 1983), pp. 67–69.
2. S.T. Eremyan, "Mets Hayki paykare ankakhutyan hamar Artashesyan dinasti-ayi ankumits heto" [The Struggle for the Independence of Greater Armenia after the Collapse of the Artashesian Dynasty], in *Hay zhoghovrdi patmutyun* [History of the Armenian People], ed. Ts.P. Aghayan et al. (Erevan: Armenian Academy of Sciences, 1971), vol. 1, pp. 730–31; Bivar, "Political History," p. 79.
3. Sykes, *History*, p. 407; Miriam T. Griffin, *Nero* (New Haven, CT: Yale University Press, 1984), pp. 61, 62, 226–27.
4. Bivar, "Political History," pp. 82–85; S.T. Eremyan, "Tasnamya paterazme Hromyatsineri ev Hay-Partevakan zorkeri mijev" [The Decade-Long War

between the Roman and Armeno-Parthian Forces], in Aghayan, *Hay zhoghovrdi patmutyun*, vol. 1, pp. 735, 739, 752; Garsoian, "Aršakuni Dynasty," pp. 66–67.

5. Eremyan, "Tasnamya paterazme," pp. 757, 759; Garsoian, "Aršakuni Dynasty," p. 67; Sykes, *History*, p. 408.

6. Garsoian, "Aršakuni Dynasty," p. 67; Griffin, *Nero*, p. 122.

7. Dio, LXII, viii, pp. 142/43, 146/47, in Garsoian, "Aršakuni Dynasty," pp. 67–68.

8. Eremyan, "Tasnamya paterazme," pp. 760, 761–62; Garsoian, "Aršakuni Dynasty," p. 68.

9. S.T. Eremyan, "Hayastani kaghakakan vichake m.t. ii darum" [The Political Situation in Armenia in the Second Century], in Aghayan, *Hay zhoghovrdi patmutyun*, vol. 1, pp. 779–80; Garsoian, "Aršakuni Dynasty," p. 68.

10. Bivar, "Political History," pp. 90–91; F.A. Lepper, *Trajan's Parthian War* (Oxford: Oxford University Press, 1948); Garsoian, "Aršakuni Dynasty," p. 69; Eremyan, "Hayastani kaghakakan vichake m.t. ii darum," pp. 768–74; Sykes, *History*, pp. 410–12.

11. Edward N. Luttwak, *Grand Strategy of the Roman Empire* (Baltimore: Johns Hopkins University Press, 1976); on Armenia as a buffer state, see pp. 104–5; on Parthia, pp. 108, 110, 113, 145; Garsoian, "Aršakuni Dynasty," p. 70.

12. Garsoian, "Aršakuni Dynasty," p. 76.

13. On Oriental despotism, see Karl A. Wittfogel, *Oriental Despotism: A Comparative Study of Total Power* (New Haven, CT: Yale University Press, 1957).

14. See S.T. Eremyan, "Mets Hayki tagavorutyan petakan karutsvatske m.t. i-ii darerum" [The State Structure of Greater Armenia in I-II Centuries], in Aghayan, *Hay zhoghovrdi patmutyun*, vol. 1, p. 827.

15. S.Kh. Sargsyan, "Hayastani petakan karge hellenistakan darashrjanum: Kedronakan ishkhanutyune" [The State Order of Armenia during the Period of Hellenism: The Central Government], in Aghayan, *Hay zhoghovrdi patmutyun*, vol. 1, pp. 668, 671; Eremyan, "Mets Hayki tagavorutyan," pp. 823, 825–26; Garsoian, "Aršakuni Dynasty," p. 76.

16. Sargsyan, "Hayastani petakan," pp. 672–73; S.T. Eremyan, "Agrarayin haraberutyunnere hin Hayastanum" [The Agricultural Relations in Ancient Armenia], in Aghayan, *Hay zhoghovrdi patmutyun*, vol. 1, pp. 797–99; Eremyan, "Mets Hayki tagavorutyan," pp. 829–35.

17. Garsoian, "Aršakuni Dynasty," p. 76.

18. Eremyan, "Mets Hayki tagavorutyan," pp. 842–43.

19. Hakob A. Manandyan, *The Trade and Cities of Armenia in Relation to the Ancient World*, 2d rev. ed., trans. Nina G. Garsoian (Lisbon: Calouste Gulbenkian Foundation, 1965), p. 70.

20. Garsoian, "Aršakuni Dynasty," pp. 77–78.

21. Ibid.; Eremyan, "Mets Hayki tagavorutyan," p. 831; Nikoghayos Adonts, *Hayastane Hustinianosi darashrjanum* [Armenia during the Period of Justinian] (Erevan: Hayastan, 1987); trans. with annotations, Nina G. Garsoian *Armenia in the Period of Justinian* (Lisbon: Calouste Gulbenkian Foundation, 1970).

22. Garsoian, "Aršakuni Dynasty," p. 78; Hakob A. Manandyan, *Knnakan tesutyun Hay zhoghovrdi patmutyan* [A Critical Review of the History of the Armenian People], vol. 2, pt. 1 (Erevan: Haypethrat, 1957), pp. 327–29.

23. Garsoian, "Aršakuni Dynasty," pp. 78–79.

24. Eremyan, "Mets Hayki tagavorutyan," pp. 840–42.

25. Ibid., pp. 824–25.

26. Garsoian, "Aršakuni Dynasty," pp. 70–71.

27. Eremyan, "Hayastani kaghakakan vichake m.t. ii darum," p. 793.

28. Richard N. Frye, "The Political History of Iran under the Sasanians," in *Cambridge History of Iran*, vol. 3, pt. 1, pp. 116–19; Sykes, *History*, p. 425.

29. Garsoian, "Aršakuni Dynasty," p. 75.

30. Eremyan, "Hayastani kaghakakan vichake m.t. ii darum," p. 794; Frye, "Political History," p. 125; Sykes, *History*, pp. 432–33.

31. Cyrill Toumanoff, *Studies in Christian Caucasian History* (Washington, DC: Georgetown University, 1963); S.T. Eremyan, "Hayastani kaghakakan vichake iii dari verjin karordum" [The Political Situation in Armenia in the Last Quarter of the Third Century], in Ts.P. Aghayan et al., eds., *Hay zhoghovrdi patmutyun* (Erevan: Armenian Academy of Sciences, 1984), vol. 2, p. 64.

32. J.D. Howard-Johnston, "Byzantine Anzitene," in *Armies and Frontiers in Roman and Byzantine Anatolia*, ed. Stephen Mitchell (Oxford: B.A.R., 1983), p. 239; Frye, "Political History," pp. 124–25, 130; Garsoian, "Aršakuni Dynasty," pp. 74–75; R.C. Blockley, *East Roman Foreign Policy* (Leeds: Francis Cairns, 1992), pp. 5–7; Eremyan, "Hayastani kaghakakan vichake iii dari verjin karordum," pp. 66, 70.

33. Historians disagree on the reigns of Trdat III and Trdat IV. While traditionally it was believed that the Armenian conversion to Christianity occurred during the reign of Trdat III as Trdat the Great, Manandyan, Toumanoff, and Garsoian maintain that it was Trdat IV who led the conversion.

34. Eremyan, "Hayastani kaghakakan vichake iii dari verjin karordum," pp. 65, 67, 70.

35. Leo (Arakel Babakhanian), *Erkeri zhoghovatsu* [Collected Works], vol. 1 (Erevan: Hayastan, 1966), pp. 414–15.

36. Ibid., pp. 416–18.

37. Ibid., pp. 418–19; Blockley, *East Roman*, pp. 10–11.

38. Blockley, *East Roman*, pp. 10–11; Eremyan, "Hayastani kaghakakan vichake iii dari verjin karordum," p. 71; Garsoian, "Aršakuni Dynasty," pp. 81, 82.

39. Eremyan, "Hayastani kaghakakan vichake iii dari verjin karordum," pp. 71–72.

40. Leo, *Erkeri zhoghovatsu*, pp. 423–24; Eremyan, "Tasnamya paterazme," p. 761; George Bournoutian, *A History of the Armenian People* (Costa Meza, CA: Mazda Publishers, 1993), vol. 1, p. 63.

41. Leo, *Erkeri zhoghovatsu*, pp. 420–23; Eremyan, "Hayastani kaghakakan vichake iii dari verjin karordum," pp. 77–79; A.G. Adoyan, "Haykakan amusnaentanekan haraberutyunnere mijnadaryan orenknerum" [Armenian Matrimonial-Familial Relations According to the Laws of the Middle Ages], *Patma-banasirakan handes* 3 (1965): 50, 51.

42. Adoyan, "Haykakan," pp. 51–52.

43. Leo, *Erkeri zhoghovatsu*, pp. 424–28.

44. Ibid., pp. 430–31, 434; S.T. Eremyan, "Paykar Mets Hayki tagavorutyan ankakhutyan hamar" [The Struggle for the Independence of the Greater Armenian Kingdom], in Aghayan, *Hay zhoghovrdi patmutyun*, vol. 2, pp. 82, 106–9; Iskanyan, *Hay-Buzandakan haraberutyunnere*, pp. 44–47; K.G. Ghafadaryan, "Dvin kaghaki himnadrman zhamanaki ev Mijnaberdi hetanosakan mehyani masin" [Concerning the Period of the Founding of Dvin City and the Pagan Temple of Mijnaberd], *Patma-banasirakan handes* 2 (1966): 44–45.

45. Leo, *Erkeri zhoghovatsu*, pp. 429, 432–33; Mark Whittow, *The Making of Byzantium, 600–1025* (Berkeley: University of California Press, 1996), p. 97;

Eremyan, "Paykar Mets Hayki," p. 106; Blockley, *East Roman*, pp. 11–12; Frye, "Political History," p. 137.

46. Blockley, *East Roman*, pp. 28–29.

47. Adontz, *Armenia*, p. 34; Rafael Matevosyan, *Bagratuniner: Patma-tohmabanakan hanragitaran* [Bagratunis: Historic-Genealogical Encyclopedia] (Erevan: Anahit, 1997), p. 84.

48. Frye, "Political History," p. 138.

49. Adontz, *Armenia*, p. 93; Garsoian, "Aršakuni Dynasty," p. 92; Nina G. Garsoian, "The Problem of Armenian Integration into the Byzantine Empire," in *Studies on the Internal Diaspora of the Byzantine Empire*, ed. Hélène Ahrweiler and Angeliki E. Laiou (Washington, DC: Dumbarton Oaks, 1998), p. 54; S.T. Eremyan, "Mets Hayki tagavorutyan trohumn u ankume" [The Division and Fall of the Greater Armenian Kingdom], in Aghayan, *Hay zhoghovrdi patmutyun*, vol. 2, p. 120; Iskanyan, *Hay-Buzandakan haraberutyunnere*, pp. 55–57.

50. Manandyan, *Knnakan tesutyun*, p. 246; Eremyan, "Mets Hayki tagavorutyan trohumn," pp. 121–22.

51. Michel Foucault, *Le souci de soi* (Paris: Gallimard, 1984), as discussed by Averil Cameron, *Christianity and the Rhetoric of Empire* (Berkeley: University of California Press, 1991), pp. 2–3.

52. Frye, "Political History," pp. 144–45; Garsoian, "Aršakuni Dynasty," p. 93.

53. Nina Garsoian, "The *Marzpanate*," in Hovannisian, *Armenian People*, vol. 1, p. 96.

54. For an interesting debate on the causes of the conflict and the role of the Armenian leadership, see Hrant K. Armen, *Marzpane ev sparapete* [The Governor and the Commander] (Los Angeles: Horizon, 1952); James Mantalian, *Vardanants paterazme* [The War of Vardanants] (Boston: Hayrenik, 1954).

55. Frye, "Political History," pp. 146–47; Armen, *Marzpane*, pp. 205–7; Garsoian, "*Marzpanate*," p. 98; Iskanyan, *Hay-Buzandakan haraberutyunnere*, pp. 68–69.

56. Garsoian, "*Marzpanate*," p. 99; Iskanyan, *Hay-Buzandakan haraberutyunnere*, pp. 71–76; Armen, *Marzpane*, pp. 208–12, 232; Mantalian, *Vardanants*, pp. 221–29, 230–31.

57. Frye, "Political History," pp. 146–47; Armen, *Marzpane*, pp. 219–21; Mantalian, *Vardanants*, p. 232.

58. Iskanyan, *Hay-Buzandakan haraberutyunnere*, pp. 83–85; Armen, *Marzpane*, pp. 223–26; Mantalian, *Vardanants*, pp. 56–69.

59. Armen, *Marzpane*, pp. 227–32.

60. Ibid., p. 232.

61. Ibid., pp. 233–35.

62. Eghishe, *Vasn Vardanay ev Hayots paterazmin* [About Vardan and the Armenian War], ed. E. Ter-Minasyan (Erevan: Armenian Academy of Sciences, 1957), facs. reprod., *The History of Vardan and the Armenian War*, intro. Robert W. Thomson (Delmar, NY: Caravan Books, 1993), p. 100; Garsoian, "*Marzpanate*," p. 100; Armen, *Marzpane*, pp. 237–39, 242–45.

63. Ehsan Yarshater, "Iranian National History," in *Cambridge History of Iran*, vol. 3, pt. 1, p. 477; Frye, "Political History," p. 147.

64. Matevosyan, *Bagratuniner*, pp. 13, 84; Iskanyan, *Hay-Buzandakan haraberutyunnere*, pp. 94–95, 99, 124–25; Garsoian, "*Marzpanate*," pp. 100–2; Frye, "Political History," p. 149.

65. Garsoian, "*Marzpanate*," p. 102.

66. Adoyan, "Haykakan," p. 53; Iskanyan, *Hay-Buzandakan haraberutyunnere*, pp. 147–48; H.M. Bartikyan, "Hustinianos A[rajin]i varchakaghakakan u

razmakan mijotsarumnere Buzantakan Hayastanum ev Hayeri entvzumnere kaysrutyan dem" [The Political-Administrative and Military Approaches of Justinian I in Byzantine Armenia and the Armenian Opposition against the Empire], in Aghayan, *Hay zhoghovrdi patmutyun*, vol. 2, p. 232; George Ostrogorsky, *History of the Byzantine State*, rev. ed., trans. Joan Hussey (New Brunswick, NJ: Rutgers University Press, 1969), p. 71; Frye, "Political History," pp. 153–59.

67. Iskanyan, *Hay-Buzandakan haraberutyunnere*, p. 170; Garsoian, "*Marzpanate*," pp. 103–04; Adonts, *Armenia*, pp. 76, 80, 94.

68. Adonts, *Armenia*, pp. 103–11, 133–36, 151–52; Garsoian, "*Marzpanate*," p. 104.

69. Bartikyan, "Hustinianos," pp. 246–47.

70. Adonts, *Armenia*, p. 153.

71. Garsoian, "Problem of Armenian Integration," p. 68.

72. Ostrogorsky, *Byzantine State*, p. 79; Bartikyan, "Hustinianos," p. 242; Garsoian, "*Marzpanate*," pp. 108–9; Frye, "Political History," pp. 159, 163–65; Ostrogorsky, *Byzantine State*, p. 80; V.K. Iskanyan, "Marzpanakan Hayastane vi darum" [Marzpanate Armenia in the Sixth Century], in Aghayan, *Hay zhoghovrdi patmutyun*, vol. 2, pp. 263–66; Iskanyan, *Hay-Buzantakan haraberutyunnere*, pp. 370–94.

73. A.N. Ter-Ghevondyan, "Hayastani kaghakakan inknuruynutyune vii dari 30–90-akan tt." [The Distinct Characteristics of Armenian Politics during the 30s-90s of the Seventh Century], in Aghayan, *Hay zhoghovrdi patmutyun*, vol. 2, p. 306.

74. Nina Garsoian, "The Arab Invasions and the Rise of the Bagratuni (640–884)," in Hovannisian, *Armenian People*, vol. 1, p. 121. Ter-Ghevondyan, "Hayastani kaghakakan inknuruynutyune," pp. 311–12.

75. Garsoian, "Arab Invasions," pp. 120–22; A.N. Ter-Ghevondyan, *Arabakan amirayutyunnere Bagratuniats Hayastanum* [The Arab Emirates in Bagratuni Armenia] (Erevan: Armenian Academy of Sciences, 1965), pp. 42–43.

76. A.N. Ter-Ghevondyan, "Hay zhoghovrdi paykare khalifayutyun ltsi dem" [The Struggle of the Armenian People against the Yoke of the Caliphate], in Aghayan, *Hay zhoghovrdi patmutyun*, vol. 2, pp. 325–26; Ter-Ghevondyan, *Arabakan amirayutyunnere*, p. 43.

77. Ter-Ghevondyan, "Hay zhoghovrdi paykare," p. 329; Matevosyan, *Bagratuniner*, p. 17.

78. Nina G. Garsoian, *The Paulician Heresy* (The Hague: Mouton, 1967); Seta B. Dadoyan, *The Fatimid Armenians: Cultural and Political Interaction in the Near East* (Leiden: Brill, 1997); S.T. Melik-Pakhshian, *Pavlikyan sharzhume hayastanum* [The Paulician Movement in Armenia] (Erevan: Erevan State University, 1953); Leo, *Erkeri zhoghovatsu*, p. 418; H.M. Bartikyan, "Pavlikyan sharzhume Hayastanum vii-ix darerum" [The Paulician Movement in Armenia from the Seventh to Ninth Centuries], in Aghayan, *Hay zhoghovrdi patmutyun*, vol. 2, pp. 389–403.

79. Ter-Ghevondyan, "Hay zhoghovrdi paykare," pp. 335–36, 340–41; Garsoian, "Arab Invasions," p. 129; Nikoghayos Adonts, "Bagratuniats parke" [The Bagratuni Dynasty], in *Patmakan usumnasirutyunner* [Historical Studies] (Paris: A. Ghukasian, 1948), p. 51.

80. B.N. Arakelyan, "Haykakan petakanutyan verakangnume," in Aghayan, *Hay zhoghovrdi patmutyun*, vol. 3, p. 14; Ter-Ghevondyan, *Arabakan amirayutyunnere*, pp. 44–45.

81. Howard-Johnston, "Byzantine Anzitene," pp. 258–61; Garsoian, "Arab Invasions," p. 133.

82. Matevosyan, *Bagratuniner*, p. 19.

83. Arakelyan, "Haykakan petakanutyan verakangnume," pp. 14–15.
84. Minorsky, *Studies*, p. 118; Matevosyan, *Bagratuniner*, pp. 20–21.
85. Ostrogorsky, *Byzantine State*, p. 237.

3 THE BAGRATUNI KINGDOM AND DISINTEGRATION

1. A. Ter-Ghevondyan, *Arabakan amirayutyunnere Bagratuniats Hayastanum* [The Arab Emirates in Bagratuni Armenia] (Erevan: Armenian Academy of Sciences, 1965), p. 101; Yovhannēs Drasxanakertcʻi (Hovhannes Draskhanakerttsi), *History of Armenia*, trans. and comm. Krikor H. Maksoudian (Atlanta: Scholars Press, 1987), p. 128.
2. George Ostrogorsky, *History of the Byzantine State*, rev. ed., trans. Joan Hussey (New Brunswick, NJ: Rutgers University Press, 1969), p. 237.
3. For example, he minted no coins of his own. Nina Garsoian, "The Independent Kingdoms of Medieval Armenia," in *The Armenian People from Ancient to Modern Times*, vol. 1: *The Dynastic Periods*, ed. Richard G. Hovannisian (New York: St. Martin's Press, 1997), p. 148.
4. Babgen N. Arakelyan, "Haykakan petakanutyan verakangnume" [The Revival of the Armenian Government], in *Hay zhoghovrdi patmutyun* [History of the Armenian People], ed. Ts.P. Aghayan et al. (Erevan: Armenian Academy of Sciences, 1976), vol. 3, pp. 19, 23; Rafael Matevosyan, *Bagratuniner: Patmatohmabanakan hanragitaran* [Bagratunis: Historic-Genealogical Encyclopedia] (Erevan: Anahit, 1997), p. 22.
5. Garsoian, "Independent," p. 150.
6. Rafael Matevosyan, *Bagratunyats Hayastani petakan karutsvatskn u varchakan karge* [The State Structure and Administrative Organization of Bagratuni Armenia] (Erevan: Armenian Academy of Sciences, 1990), pp. 158–59.
7. Hakob A. Manandyan, *The Trade and Cities of Armenia in Relation to the Ancient World*, 2nd rev. ed., trans. Nina G. Garsoian (Lisbon: Calouste Gulbenkian Foundation, 1965), p. 137; Garsoian, "Independent," p. 144.
8. Matevosyan, *Bagratunyats Hayastani*, pp. 97, 220.
9. Babgen N. Arakelyan, "Erkri miavorman dzgtume ev paykar otar nerkhuzhman dem" [The Aspiration toward the Unity of the Land and Struggle against Foreign Invasion], in Aghayan, *Hay zhoghovrdi patmutyun*, vol. 3, pp. 26–28; Charles Burney and David Marshall Lang, *The Peoples of the Hills: Ancient Ararat and Caucasus* (London: Weidenfeld and Nicolson, 1971; repr. London: Phoenix Press, 2001), p. 209; Matevosyan, *Bagratuniner*, p. 21; Garsoian, "Independent Kingdoms," pp. 150–52.
10. Ter-Ghevondyan, *Arabakan*, p. 112; Arakelyan, "Erkri," p. 29.
11. Manandyan, *Trade*, pp. 139–40.
12. Arakelyan, "Erkri," pp. 30–31; Garsoian, "Independent," p. 154.
13. Arakelyan, "Erkri," p. 31.
14. Ibid., pp. 31–32.
15. Ibid., pp. 32–34.
16. Ibid., pp. 34–37; Ter-Ghevondyan, *Arabakan*, pp. 123–24.
17. Matevosyan, *Bagratunyats Hayastani*, p. 116.
18. Garsoian, "Independent," pp. 156–58; Arakelyan, "Erkri," pp. 38–39.
19. Arakelyan, "Erkri," p. 39.
20. Ibid., pp. 40–41.

21. Drasxanakertc'i, *History of Armenia*, p. 185.

22. Ter-Ghevondyan, *Arabakan*, p. 132; George A. Bournoutian, *A History of the Armenian People*, vol. 1: *Pre-History to 1500 A.D.* (Costa Mesa, CA: Mazda, 1993), p. 109.

23. Garsoian, "Independent," p. 159; Bournoutian, *History*, p. 110.

24. Garsoian, "Independent," p. 160; Matevosyan, *Bagratunyats Hayastani*, p. 116; Arakelyan, "Erkri," pp. 37–38, 43; A.N. Ter-Ghevondyan, "Arabakan amirayutyunnere Hayastanum" [The Arab Emirates in Armenia], in Aghayan, *Hay zhoghovrdi patmutyun*, vol. 3, p. 62.

25. Garsoian, "Independent," p. 176.

26. Kh.A. Torosyan, "Datavarutyune mijnadaryan Hayastanum" [The Court System in Armenia during the Middle Ages], *Patma-banasirakan handes* 3 (1966): 39–52; A.G. Adoyan, "Haykakan amusna-entanekan haraberutyunnere mijnadaryan orenknerum" [Armenian Matrimonial-Familial Relations According to the Laws of the Middle Ages], *Patma-banasirakan handes* 3 (1965): 63.

27. Torosyan, "Datavarutyune," pp. 39–41, 44–45, 49–51.

28. Ibid., p. 47; Adoyan, "Haykakan," pp. 56–58; S.G. Barkhudaryan, "Hay knoj iravakan vichake mijin darerum" [The Legal Situation of Armenian Women during the Middle Ages], *Patma-banasirakan handes* 2 (1966): 34–35.

29. V.M. Harutyunyan, "Mijnadaryan Hayastani kaghakashinakan kulturan" [The Culture of City Construction in Armenia in the Middle Ages], *Patma-bansirakan handes* 2 (1963): 85–99; Babken Arakelyan, *Hayastani kaghaknere xi-xiii darerum* [The Cities of Armenia during the Eleventh-Thirteenth Centuries] (Erevan: Armenian Academy of Sciences, 1956).

30. Manandyan, *Trade*, pp. 148–49; Harutyunyan, "Mijnadaryan," p. 86.

31. Babgen N. Arakelyan, "Hayastani mijnadaryan kaghakneri bnakchutyan sotsialakan kazme" [The Social Composition of Urban Population in Armenia during the Middle Ages], *Patma-banasirakan handes* 2 (1958): 43.

32. Ibid., pp. 37–65.

33. Ashot Hovhannisyan, "Ardyok mijnadaryan Hayastanum teghi unetsel e kapitali nakhaskzbnakan kutakum" [Did Preliminary Accumulation of Capital Appear in Armenia during the Middle Ages?], *Patma-banasirakan handes* 1 (1959): 202–23; V.K. Chaloyan, "Norits kapitali nakhaskzbnakan kutakman ev harakits hartseri masin" [Once More Regarding Accumulation of Capital and Related Issues], *Patma-banasirakan handes* 3 (1960): 152–71.

34. Arakelyan, "Hayastani mijnadaryan kaghakneri," pp. 37–65; Babgen N. Arakelyan, "Aprankayin artadrutyan ev arhestagortsutyan tekhnikayi zargatsume Hayastanum ix-xiii darerum" [The Development of Production of Goods and Industrial Technology in Armenia during the Ninth-Thirteenth Centuries], *Patma-banasirakan handes* 2–3 (1959): 97–107; Hovhannisyan, "Mijnadaryan Hayastanum," pp. 202–23; Chaloyan, "Norits," pp. 152–71.

35. Manandyan, *Trade*, pp. 150–53; Garsoian, "Independent," pp. 181, 183, 184; Hovhannisyan, "Mijnadaryan Hayastanum," p. 219.

36. Garsoian, "Independent," p. 182.

37. Nina G. Garsoian, *The Paulician Heresy* (The Hague: Mouton, 1967); Garsoian, "Independent," pp. 173–74; S.T. Melik-Pakhshyan, *Pavlikyan sharzhume Hayastanum* [The Paulician Movement in Armenia] (Erevan: Erevan State University, 1953); Vrej Nersessian, *The Tondrakian Movement* (Allison Park, PA: Pickwick Publications, 1988); Ter-Ghevondyan, *Arabakan*, pp. 234–38.

38. Ter-Ghevondyan, *Arabakan*, pp. 137, 147; Garsoian, "Independent," p. 161; Arakelyan, "Erkri," pp. 44–45.

39. Babgen N. Arakelyan, "Bagratunyats tagavorutyan bargavachume" [The Prosperity of the Bagratuni Kingdom], in Aghayan, *Hay zhoghovrdi patmutyun*, vol. 3, pp. 48–49; S.T. Eremyan, "Karse ix-xi darerum" [Kars in the Ninth-Eleventh Centuries], in Aghayan, *Hay zhoghovrdi patmutyun*, vol. 3, p. 94; Garsoian, "Independent," p. 163.

40. Matevosyan, *Bagratuniner*, p. 43; Ter-Ghevondyan, *Arabakan*, pp. 168–71.

41. Matevosyan, *Bagratuniner*, pp. 90–91; T.M. Sahakyan, "Syunyats tagavorutyan himnume ev nra kaghakakan dere xi darum" [The Establishment of the Kingdom of Siunik and Its Political Role in the Eleventh Century], *Patma-banasirakan handes* 3 (1966): 221–28; R.I. Matevosyan, *Tashir-Dzoraget* (Erevan: Armenian Academy of Sciences, 1982); Vrezh M. Vardanyan, *Vaspurakani Artsrunyats tagavorutyune, 908–1021 tt.* [The Artsruni Kingdom of Vaspurakan, 908–1021] (Erevan: Erevan State University, 1969).

42. Nina G. Garsoian, "The Problem of Armenian Integration into the Byzantine Empire," in *Studies on the Internal Diaspora of the Byzantine Empire*, ed. Hélène Ahrweiler and Angeliki E. Laiou (Washington, DC: Dumbarton Oaks, 1998), p. 99.

43. Torosyan, "Datavarutyune," pp. 39–52.

44. Matevosyan, *Bagratuniner*, pp. 91–92; Sahakyan, "Syunyats," p. 222.

45. T.Kh. Hakobyan, *Patmakan Hayastani kaghaknere* [The Cities of Historic Armenia] (Erevan: Hayastan, 1987), p. 39.

46. Matevosyan, *Bagratuniner*, pp. 100–1; Matevosyan, *Bagratunyats Hayastani*, pp. 208–9.

47. Matteos Urhayetsi, *Zhamanakagrutyun* [Chronicle], ed. and trans. Ara Dostourian, *Armenia and the Crusades: The Chronicle of Matthew of Edessa* (Lanham, MD: University Press of America, 1993), pp. 20–21.

48. Matevosyan, *Bagratuniner*, p. 101; Arakelyan, "Bagratunyats tagavorutyan bargavachume," pp. 52–53.

49. Arakelyan, "Bagratunyats tagavorutyan bargavachume," pp. 54–55; Bournoutian, *History*, p. 114.

50. Matevosyan, *Bagratuniner*, p. 86.

51. Garsoian, "Independent," p. 167; Matevosyan, *Bagratuniner*, pp. 32–33.

52. Leo (Arakel Babakhanian), *Ani* (Erevan: Haypethrat, 1946), pp. 232–34; Arakelyan, "Bagratunyats tagavorutyan bargavachume," pp. 52–56.

53. See Sargis V. Bornazyan, *Hayastane ev Selchuknere, xi-xii tt.* [Armenia and the Seljuks, Eleventh-Twelfth Centuries] (Erevan: Armenian Academy of Sciences, 1980).

54. J.D. Howard-Johnston, "Byzantine Anzitene," in *Armies and Frontiers in Roman and Byzantine Anatolia*, ed. Stephen Mitchell (Oxford: B.A.R., 1983), p. 249; Warren Treadgold, *A History of the Byzantine State and Society* (Stanford, CA: Stanford University Press, 1997), pp. 512–14; Babgen N. Arakelyan, "Bagratunyats tagavorutyune x dari verjin ev xi dari skzbnerin" [The Bagratuni Kingdom during the Late 10th Century and Early 11th Century], in Aghayan, *Hay zhoghovrdi patmutyun*, vol. 3, p. 129.

55. Garsoian, "Independent," pp. 168–69.

56. Arakelyan, "Bagratunyats tagavorutyune x dari verjin," pp. 135–37; Garsoian, "Independent," p. 169; Mesrop Chanashian, *Davit Kurapaghat* (Venice: Mekhiterist Press, 1972), pp. 53–57.

57. Matevosyan, *Bagratuniner*, p. 35; Matevosyan, *Bagratuniats Hayastani*, pp. 221–22; Sahakyan, "Syunyats," p. 224.

58. Garsoian, "Independent," p. 170; Nina Garsoian, "Byzantine Annexation of the Armenian Kingdoms in the Eleventh Century," in Hovannisian, *Armenian People*, vol. 1, pp. 188–90.
59. Matevosyan, *Bagratuniner*, pp. 37–38, 41–42.
60. Aristakes Lastiverttsi, *Patmutyun* [History], ed. Karen N. Yuzbashyan (Erevan: Armenian Academy of Sciences, 1963), English trans. Robert Bedrosian (New York: n.p., 1985), p. 16; Matevosyan, *Bagratuniner*, pp. 41–42.
61. H.M. Bartikyan, "Bagratunyats tagavorutyan chknazhame" [The Crisis of the Bagratuni Kingdom], in Aghayan, *Hay zhoghovrdi patmutyun*, vol. 3, pp. 145–46; Matevosyan, *Bagratuniner*, pp. 41–42.
62. Matevosyan, *Bagratuniner*, p. 38; Bartikyan, "Bagratunyats tagavorutyan chknazhame," pp. 144–45.
63. Sahakyan, "Syunyats," p. 225.
64. Quoted in Garsoian, "Problem of Armenian Integration," p. 117.
65. H.M. Bartikyan, "Bagratunyats tagavorutyan ankume" [The Fall of the Bagratuni Kingdom], in Aghayan, *Hay zhoghovrdi patmutyun*, vol. 3, p. 151; Matevosyan, *Bagratuniner*, p. 106; Garsoian, "Problem of Armenian Integration," pp. 58–59, 71; Garsoian, "Byzantine Annexation," p. 192.
66. Vladimir Minorsky, *Studies in Caucasian History* (London: Taylor's Foreign Press, 1953), pp. 79–80; Garsoian, "Byzantine Annexation," p. 192; Garsoian, "Problem of Armenian Integration," pp. 58–59, 71, 79; Bartikyan, "Bagratunyats tagavorutyan ankume," p. 151; Matevosyan, *Bagratuniner*, pp. 39, 106.
67. Matevosyan, *Bagratuniner*, pp. 40–41.
68. V.M. Vardanyan, "Byuzandakan kaysrutyan arajkhaghatsume ev Vaspurakani tagavorutyan veratsume" [The Advance of the Byzantine Empire and the Removal of the Vaspurakan Kingdom], in Aghayan, *Hay zhoghovrdi patmutyun*, vol. 3, pp. 141–43; Garsoian, "Byzantine Annexation," p. 190; Robert H. Hewsen, "Van in This World; Paradise in the Next": The Historical Geography of Van/Vaspurakan," in *Armenian Van/Vaspurakan*, ed. Richard G. Hovannisian (Costa Mesa, CA: Mazda, 2000), pp. 28–29.
69. Lastiverttsi, *Patmutyun*, p. 19; V.K. Iskanyan, "Artsrunyats artagaghti masin" [Regarding the Emigration of the Artsrunis], *Patma-banasirakan handes* 3 (1965): 67–72, 82. On the Paulician community in the region, see Seda B. Dadoyan, *The Fatimid Armenians* (Leiden: Brill, 1997), pp. 49–53; Hrach Bartikyan, "Vaspurakantsiner Buzandakan kaysrutyan tsarayutyan mej xi-xii darerum" [Vaspurakanians in the Service of the Byzantine Empire in the Eleventh-Twelfth Centuries], *Patma-banasirkan handes* 3 (2000): 134–35.
70. Lastiverttsi, *Patmutyun*, pp. 91–92; Garsoian, "Byzantine Annexation," p. 192; Matevosyan, *Bagratunyats Hayastani*, p. 203; Matevosyan, *Bagratuniner*, p. 44.
71. Matevosyan, *Bagratuniner*, p. 46; Sahakyan, "Syunyats," p. 225.
72. Matevosyan, *Bagratuniner*, p. 46.
73. Ibid., p. 47.
74. Lastiverttsi, *Patmutyun*, pp. 76–77.

4   THE CILICIAN KINGDOM, THE CRUSADES, AND THE INVASIONS FROM THE EAST

1. M.K. Zulalyan, "Haykakan ishkhanutyan himnume Kilikiayum" [The Establishment of the Armenian Principality in Cilicia], in *Hay zhoghovrdi*

patmutyun [History of the Armenian People], ed. Ts.P. Aghayan et al. (Erevan: Armenian Academy of Sciences, 1976), vol. 3, p. 673; A.H.M. Jones, *The Cities of the Eastern Roman Provinces* (Oxford: Clarendon Press, 1937; repr. Sandpiper Books, 1998), pp. 192–97, 210–12.

2. Keith Hopwood, "Policing the Hinterland: Rough Cilicia and Isauria," in *Armies and Frontiers in Roman and Byzantine Anatolia*, ed. Stephen Mitchell (Oxford: B.A.R., 1983), pp. 173–87.

3. Sirarpie Der Nersessian, "The Kingdom of Cilician Armenia," in *A History of the Crusades*, vol. 2: *The Later Crusades, 1189–1311*, ed. Kenneth M. Setton (Philadelphia: University of Pennsylvania Press, 1962), pp. 630–31.

4. Zulalyan, "Haykakan," p. 674.

5. T.S.R. Boase, ed., *The Cilician Kingdom of Armenia* (Edinburgh: Scottish Academic Press, 1978), p. 2.

6. Angus Donal Stewart, *The Armenian Kingdom and the Mamluks: War and Diplomacy during the Reigns of Het'um II (1289–1307)* (Leiden: Brill, 2001), pp. 7–18.

7. Der Nersessian, "Kingdom," p. 631.

8. Zulalyan, "Haykakan," p. 675; A.K. Sukiasyan, *Kilikiayi Haykakan petutyan ev iravunki patmutyun (xi-xiv darer)* [History of the Cilician Armenian Government and Jurisprudence (XI-XIV Centuries)] (Erevan: Erevan State University, 1978), pp. 22–23; A.S. Tritton, *The Caliphs and Their Non-Muslim Subjects* (London: Frank Cass, 1970), pp. 153–54; Boase, *Cilician*, p. 4; Seta B. Dadoyan, *The Fatimid Armenians: Cultural and Political Interaction in the Near East* (Leiden: Brill, 1997).

9. Zulalyan, "Haykakan," p. 675; Stewart, *Armenian*, p. 33.

10. Ira M. Lapidus, *A History of Islamic Societies* (Cambridge: Cambridge University Press, 1988), p. 345; Hugh Kennedy, *The Prophet and the Age of the Caliphates: The Islamic Near East from the Sixth to the Eleventh Century* (London: Longman, 1986), pp. 309–18.

11. Lapidus, *History*, pp. 132–36, 349; Kennedy, *Prophet*, p. 184.

12. Mark Whittow, *The Making of Byzantium, 600–1025* (Berkeley: University of California Press, 1996), p. 327; Kennedy, *Prophet*, pp. 282–84; Stephen W. Reinert, "The Muslim Presence in Constantinople, 9th-15th Centuries: Some Preliminary Observations," in *Studies on the Internal Diaspora of the Byzantine Empire*, ed. Hélène Ahrweiler and Angeliki E. Laiou (Washington, DC: Dumbarton Oaks, 1998), pp. 136–39.

13. Dadoyan, *Fatimid*, Chs. 2–3, passim; see also Nina G. Garsoian, *The Paulician Heresy* (The Hague: Mouton, 1967); Vrej Nersessian, *The Tondrakian Movement* (Allison Park, PA: Pickwick, 1987).

14. Dadoyan, *Fatimid*, pp. 106–16.

15. Dadoyan, *Fatimid*, Chs. 4–6, pp. 81–168 passim.

16. Zulalyan, "Haykakan," p. 677.

17. See Desmond Seward, *The Monks of War: The Military Religious Orders*, rev. ed. (London: Penguin Books, 1995).

18. S.V. Bornazyan, "Khachakir ordenneri ev Kilikyan Hayastani kaghakakan u tntesakan arnchutyunneri patmutyunits" [From the History of the Political and Economic Relations between the Crusader Orders and Cilician Armenia], *Patma-banasirakan handes* 22:3 (1963): 176–84; René Grousset, *Histoire des croisades et du royaume franc de Jérusalem*, 3 vols. (Paris: Plon, 1934–36); Aziz S. Atiya, "The Crusades: Old Ideas and New Conceptions," *Journal of World History* 2:2 (1954): 471–72. For a contemporary observer's criticism of the role of the Crusaders in Cilicia, see Matthew of Edessa, *The Chronicle of Matthew of*

Edessa, trans. Ara E. Dostourian, *Armenia and the Crusades* (Lanham, MD: University Press of America, 1993).

19. Zulalyan, "Haykakan," pp. 677–79; Der Nersessian, "Kingdom," pp. 635, 650.
20. See Claude Cahen, *La Syrie du Nord à l'époque des croisades* (Paris: Paul Geuthner, 1940); Zulalyan, "Haykakan," pp. 680–81.
21. Zulalyan, "Haykakan," p. 680; Claude Mutafian, "L'enjeu cilicien et les prétentions normandes," in *Autour de la première croisade*, ed. Michel Balard (Paris: Publications de la Sorbonne, 1996).
22. Der Nersessian, "Kingdom," pp. 637–38; Stewart gives 1145 as the date for Toros's escape. Stewart, *Armenian*, p. 34.
23. Zulalyan, "Haykakan," p. 680; Ani Atamian Bournoutian, "Cilician Armenia," in *The Armenian People from Ancient to Modern Times*, vol. 1: *The Dynastic Periods: From Antiquity to the Fourteenth Century*, ed. Richard G. Hovannisian (New York: St. Martin's Press, 1997), p. 279; Der Nersessian, "Kingdom," p. 640; Harutiun Ter Ghazarian, *Haykakan Kilikia* [Armenian Cilicia] (Antelias: Catholicosate of Cilicia, 1966), p. 41; Stewart, *Armenian*, p. 34.
24. P.M. Holt, *The Age of the Crusades: The Near East from the Eleventh Century to 1517* (London: Longman, 1986), pp. 38–52; V.A. Ter-Ghevondyan, "Kilikyan Hayastann u Syrian xii dari 40–70-akan tvakannerin" [Cilician Armenia and Syria during the 40s-70s of the Twelfth Century], *Patma-banasirakan handes* 2 (1986): 123.
25. Azat Bozoyan, *Buzandiayi arevelyan kaghakakanutyune ev Kilikyan Hayastane* [The Eastern Policy of Byzantium and Cilician Armenia] (Erevan: Armenian Academy of Sciences, 1988).
26. A.A. Bozoyan, "Kilikiayi Buzandakan karavarichnere ev Rubenian ishkhanu-tiune xii dari 40–70-akan tvakannerin" [The Byzantine Governors of Cilicia and the Rubenian Principality during the 40s-70s of the Twelfth Century], *Patma-banasirakan handes* 3 (1984): 85; Der Nersessian, "Kingdom," p. 639.
27. Ter-Ghevondyan, "Kilikyan," p. 124; Zulalyan, "Haykakan," pp. 682–83; Der Nersessian, "Kingdom," p. 640.
28. Robert Browning, *The Byzantine Empire*, rev. ed. (Washington, DC: Catholic University of America Press, 1992), pp. 184–86; 223–54; Steven Runciman, *History of the Crusades* (Cambridge: Cambridge University Press, 1951), vol. 3, pp. 121–23; George Ostrogorsky, *History of the Byzantine State*, trans. Joan Hussey (New Brunswick, NJ: Rutgers University Press, 1969), pp. 416–17; Bozoyan, "Kilikiayi," pp. 74–86; Zulalyan, "Haykakan," p. 680.
29. Bozoyan, "Kilikiayi," p. 84; Ter-Ghevondyan, "Kilikyan," pp. 125–27; Der Nersessian, "Kingdom," p. 643; Stewart, *Armenian*, p. 25; Zulalyan, "Haykakan," pp. 684–85.
30. Runciman, *History*, vol. 2, pp. 445–64, vol. 3, p. 107; Stewart, *Armenian*, pp. 40–41.
31. M.K. Zulalyan, "Kilikiayi Haykakan tagavorutyan arajatsume ev nra pokhharaberutyunnere harevan erkrneri het" [The Emergence of the Armenian Kingdom of Cilicia and Its Relations with Southern Neighbors], in Aghayan, *Hay zhoghovrdi patmutyun*, vol. 3, p. 689; Runciman, *History*, vol. 3, p. 77.
32. Stewart, *Armenian*, p. 34. Sources give different dates for the coronation, ranging from 1196 to 1199. For example, according to Der Nersessian, the corona-tion took place in 1198, but Zulalyan mentions 1199. See Der Nersessian, "Kingdom," p. 648; Zulalyan, "Haykakan," pp. 684–85.
33. Dickran Kouymjian, "Armenia from the Fall of the Cilician Kingdom (1375) to the Forced Emigration under Shah Abbas (1604)," in *The Armenian People from*

Ancient to Modern Times, vol. 2: *Foreign Dominion to Statehood: The Fifteenth Century to the Twentieth Century*, ed. Richard G. Hovannisian (New York: St. Martin's Press, 1997), p. 2.

34. S.V. Bornazyan, "Arevture" [The Trade], in Aghayan, *Hay zhoghovrdi patmutyun*, vol. 3, pp. 729–32; Stewart, *Armenian*, p. 34.

35. Der Nersessian, "Kingdom," p. 651.

36. S.V. Bornazyan, "Kaghaknere ev kaghakayin kyanki zargatsume" [The Cities and the Development of Urban Life], in Aghayan, *Hay zhoghovrdi patmutyun*, vol. 3, pp. 724–25; Stewart, *Armenian*, p. 30.

37. S.V. Bornazyan, "Kilikiayi Haykakan petutyan sotsialakan karutsvatske ev hoghatirutyan dzevere" [The Social Structure of the Armenian Government of Cilicia and the Methods of Landownership], in Aghayan, *Hay zhoghovrdi patmutyun*, vol. 3, pp. 715–16.

38. S.V. Bornazyan, "Kilikiayi petakan karge" [The Organization of the Government of Cilicia], in Aghayan, *Hay zhoghovrdi patmutyun*, vol. 3, pp. 742–45.

39. Ibid., pp. 745–46; Sukiasyan, *Kilikiayi*, pp. 106–13.

40. On different views concerning the foreign influences on the Cilician legal system, see A. Galstyan, review of Rüdt-Collenberg's work, *Patma-banasirakan handes* 3 (1964): 167–70; W.H. Rüdt-Collenberg, *The Rupenides, Hethumides and Lusignans: The Structure of the Armeno-Cilician Dynasties* (Lisbon: Calouste Gulbenkian Foundation Armenian Library; Paris: Librairie C. Klincksieck, 1963). See also Der Nersessian, "Kingdom," p. 651; Robert W. Edwards, *The Fortifications of Armenian Cilicia* (Washington, DC: Dumbarton Oaks, 1987), pp. 47–48 and n37.

41. Sukiasyan, *Kilikiayi*, pp. 181, 203, 206–10. See, for example, on Mekhitar Gosh, Kh.A. Torosyan, "Datavarutyune mijnataryan Hayastanum" [The Court System in Armenia during the Middle Ages], *Patma-banasirakan handes* 3 (1966): 39–52.

42. Bornazyan, "Petakan karge," p. 748.

43. Ibid., pp. 748–49; Sukiasyan, *Kilikiayi*, pp. 178, 269–372.

44. Sukiasyan, *Kilikiayi*, pp. 176–77; Bornazyan, "Petakan karge," p. 748.

45. See Azat A. Bozoyan, "Armenian Political Revival in Cilicia," in *Armenian Cilicia*, ed. Richard G. Hovannisian and Simon Payaslian (Costa Mesa, CA: Mazda, forthcoming), Ch. 3.

46. Ibid.; Robert H. Hewsen, "Armenia Maritima: The Historical Geography of Cilicia," in Hovannisian and Payaslian, *Armenian Cilicia*, Ch. 2.

47. Bernard Coulie, "Manuscripts and Libraries: Scriptorial Activity in Cilicia," in Hovannisian and Payaslian, *Armenian Cilicia*, Ch. 10; see also Bozoyan, "Armenian Political Revival in Cilicia"; Hewsen, "Armenia Maritima."

48. Rüdt-Collenberg, *Rupenides*; Galstyan, review of Rüdt-Collenberg's book, pp. 167–70. See also Bournoutian, "Cilician," pp. 281–82. For example, on Baghras, see A.W. Lawrence, "The Castle of Baghras," in Boase, *Cilician*, pp. 34–83. See also C.E. Bosworth, "Christian and Jewish Religious Dignitaries in Mamluk Egypt and Syria," *International Journal of Middle East Studies* 3:1 (Jan. 1972): 59–74, and 3:2 (April 1972): 199–216.

49. Bournoutian, "Cilician," p. 282; Der Nersessian, "Kingdom," p. 650; Edwards, *Fortifications*, pp. 31–32; J.S.C. Riley-Smith, "The Templars and the Teutonic Knights in Cilician Armenia," in Boase, *Cilician*, pp. 92–117.

50. Sukiasyan, *Kilikiayi*, pp. 30–31.

51. Bournoutian, "Cilician," p. 282.

52. Ibid., p. 285.

53. Zulalyan, "Kilikiayi Haykakan tagavorutyan arajatsume," pp. 692–93.

54. Bournoutian, "Cilician," p. 285; Der Nersessian, "Kingdom," p. 652; Stewart, *Armenian*, p. 34.

55. David Morgan, *The Mongols* (Cambridge: Basil Blackwell, 1986).

56. Der Nersessian, "Kingdom," p. 652. According to Bornazyan, the Smbat mission to Qaraqorum took place in 1246. See S.V. Bornazyan, "Kilikiayi Haykakan tagavorutyan zoreghatsume ev mijazgayin haraberutyunnere xiii darum" [The Strengthening of the Armenian Kingdom of Cilicia and Its International Relations in the Thirteenth Century], in Aghayan, *Hay zhoghovrdi patmutyun*, vol. 3, pp. 699–701.

57. Hakob Manandyan, *Erker* [Works] (Erevan: Armenian Academy of Sciences, 1977), vol. 3, pp. 131–55, passim.

58. H.A. Stepanyan, "Vrats-Haykakan entvzumnere Tatar-Mongolakan brnadirutyan dem 1247–1249 tt" [Georgian-Armenian Rebellions against Tatar-Mongolian Repression, 1247–1249], *Patma-banasirakan handes* 1 (1986): 97–105; Stewart, *Armenian*, p. 44.

59. Bornazyan, "Zoreghatsume," p. 703; Bournoutian, "Cilician," p. 286; Der Nersessian, "Kingdom," p. 653.

60. Bornazyan, "Zoreghatsume," pp. 703–4; Sukiasyan, *Kilikiayi*, pp. 73–75.

61. Holt, *Age of the Crusades*, pp. 87–88, 93–94.

62. M. Canard, "Le royaume d'Arménie-Cilicie et les Mamelouks jusqu'au traité de 1285," *Revue des études arméniennes* 4 (1967): 217–59; Bornazyan, "Zoreghatsume," pp. 702, 706–7; Stewart, *Armenian*, pp. 39, 44.

63. Sukiasyan, *Kilikiayi*, pp. 76–77, 109.

64. Ibid., p. 77; Bornazyan, "Zoreghatsume," p. 701. The size of the Armenian military was about 60,000 but was greater in times of war. Bornazyan, "Petakan karge," p. 753.

65. Stewart, *Armenian*, p. 45; Lapidus, *History*, p. 278.

66. Morgan, *Mongols*, p. 156; Sukiasyan, *Kilikiayi*, p. 77; Stewart, *Armenian*, pp. 39, 46–47.

67. Bornazyan, "Zoreghatsume," pp. 712–13; Stewart, *Armenian*, pp. 48–49; Bournoutian, "Cilician," pp. 286–87; Der Nersessian, "Kingdom," pp. 653–54.

68. Sukiasyan, *Kilikiayi*, p. 214; S.V. Bornazyan, "Kilikiayi Haykakan tagavorutyan nerkin ev mijazgayin drutyune xiii dari verjerin ev xiv dari skzbin" [The Internal and International Situation of the Armenian Kingdom of Cilicia in the Late Thirteenth Century and the Early Fourteenth Century], in Aghayan, *Hay zhoghovrdi patmutyun*, vol. 3, pp. 755–56; Stewart, *Armenian*, pp. 50–51.

69. Bornazyan, "Nerkin," pp. 758–59; Sukiasyan, *Kilikiayi*, p. 214; Stewart, *Armenian*, pp. 53–55.

70. P.M. Holt, "The Treaties of the Early Mamluk Sultans with the Frankish States," *Bulletin of the School of Oriental and African Studies* 43:1 (1980): 67–76.

71. Stewart, *Armenian*, pp. 55–59; Sukiasyan, *Kilikiayi*, pp. 217–25.

72. Claude Mutafian, *Le Royaume arménien de Cilicie* (Paris: CNRS Editions, 1993).

73. Stewart, *Armenian*, pp. 60, 94–95.

74. Bornazyan, "Nerkin," p. 759; Stewart, *Armenian*, p. 60.

75. Stewart, *Armenian*, pp. 71–75, 80–81, 97. The marriage of Hetum's sister into the Lusignan house established close relations between the two families; a generation later the Lusignans inherited the Cilician throne.

76. Stewart, *Armenian*, pp. 98, 100–2; Der Nersessian, "Kingdom," p. 257; Bournoutian, "Cilician," p. 287; Bornazyan, "Nerkin," pp. 762–63.

77. Bournoutian, "Cilician," p. 287; Bornazyan, "Nerkin," p. 764; Stewart, *Armenian*, pp. 84–87, 103–4.

78. Bornazyan, "Nerkin," p. 766; Stewart, *Armenian*, pp. 136–37, 153–56, 159, 164–66; Kouymjian, "Armenia," p. 33.

79. Al-Ayni, *Iqd*, vol. 4, p. 48, quoted in Stewart, *Armenian*, p. 142. *Al-bāb al-sharqī* refers to the eastern gate of Damascus and *bāb al-jābiya*, to the western gate.

80. Lapidus, *History*, p. 279.

81. Sukiasyan, *Kilikiayi*, p. 87; Bornazyan, "Nerkin," p. 767; Stewart, *Armenian*, pp. 173–79.

82. Bornazyan, "Khachakir," p. 178; Bornazyan, "Nerkin," pp. 766–67; S.V. Bornazyan, "Kilikiayi Haykakan tagavorutyan goyamarte xiv darum ev ankume" [The Struggle of the Armenian Kingdom of Cilicia in the Fourteenth Century and Its Fall], in Aghayan, *Hay zhoghovrdi patmutyun*, vol. 3, pp. 768–70.

83. Beatrice Forbes Manz, *The Rise and Rule of Tamerlane* (Cambridge: Cambridge University Press, 1989; Canto ed., 1999), p. 73; Warren Treadgold, *A History of the Byzantine State and Society* (Stanford, CA: Stanford University Press, 1997), p. 782; Lapidus, *History*, p. 306. See also Charles J. Halperin, *Russia and the Golden Horde* (Bloomington: Indiana University Press, 1985).

84. See Avedis K. Sanjian, *The Armenian Communities in Syria under Ottoman Dominion* (Cambridge, MA: Harvard University Press, 1965).

85. Bournoutian, "Cilician," p. 288; Bornazyan, "Goyamarte," pp. 769, 770–71.

86. Lapidus, *History*, pp. 280–81; Stewart, *Armenian*, pp. 185–86; Bornazyan, "Goyamarte," p. 771.

87. Bornazyan, "Goyamarte," pp. 772–74.

88. Ibid., pp. 774–75; Bournoutian, "Cilician," p. 288.

89. Bournoutian, "Cilician," p. 288; Bornazyan, "Goyamarte," pp. 775–76.

90. Bornazyan, "Goyamarte," pp. 776–78.

91. David Ayalon, "The Plague and Its Effects upon the Mamluk Army," in *Studies on the Mamluks of Egypt (1250–1517)*, ed. David Ayalon (London: Variorum Reprints, 1977), pp. 67–73; Holt, *Age of the Crusades*, pp. 194–95.

92. Bournoutian, "Cilician," pp. 288–90; Bornazyan, "Goyamarte," pp. 775–76; Stewart, *Armenian*, pp. 185–86.

93. Bornazyan, "Goyamarte," p. 785; Bournoutian, "Cilician," p. 290; Stewart, *Armenian*, pp. 185–87.

5 ARMENIA UNDER OTTOMAN, PERSIAN, AND RUSSIAN RULE

1. Beatrice Forbes Manz, *The Rise and Rule of Tamerlane* (Cambridge: Cambridge University Press, 1989; Canto ed., 1999); Levon S. Khachikyan, "Hayastani kaghakakan vichake ev sotsial-tntesakan haraberutyunnere xiv-xv darerum" [The Political Situation in Armenia and Social-Economic Relations in the 14th–15th Centuries], in *Hay zhoghovrdi patmutyun*, ed. Ts.P. Aghayan et al. (Erevan: Armenian Academy of Sciences, 1972), vol. 4, pp. 24–27.

2. Ira Lapidus, *A History of Islamic Societies* (Cambridge: Cambridge University Press, 1988), pp. 280–81; Manz, *Tamerlane*, p. 13; Khachikyan, "Hayastani,"

p. 32; Vladimir Minorsky, "A Civil and Military Review in Fārs in 881/1476," *British School of Oriental Studies* 10:1 (1939): 141–78; repr. in Minorsky, *The Turks, Iran and the Caucasus in the Middle Ages* (London: Variorum, 1978).

3. The two dynasties of the Kara Koyunlu (Black Sheep) and the Ak Koyunlu (White Sheep) took their names from the emblems on their banners. John E. Woods, *The Aqquyunlu: Clan, Federation, Empire*, rev. ed. (Salt Lake City: University of Utah Press, 1999), pp. 48–49.

4. Dickran Kouymjian, "Armenia from the Fall of the Cilician Kingdom (1375) to the Forced Emigration under Shah Abbas (1604)," in *The Armenian People from Ancient to Modern Times*, vol. 2: *Foreign Dominion to Statehood*, ed. Richard G. Hovannisian (New York: St. Martin's Press, 1997), pp. 3–5; Khachikyan, "Hayastani," p. 35. See also H.G. Turshyan, "Shah-i-Armenner" [Shah-i Armens], *Patma-banasirakan handes* 4 (1964): 117–33.

5. Kouymjian, "Armenia," pp. 5–6, 35–39; Khachikyan, "Hayastani," pp. 38–39.

6. Kouymjian, "Armenia," p. 40.

7. P.P. Antabyan, "Dprots ev mankavarzhutyun" [School and Education], L.R Azaryan, "Kerparvest," and R.A. Ishkhanyan, "Tpagrutyun" [Printing], in Aghayan, *Hay zhoghovrdi patmutyun*, vol. 4, pp. 437–50, 577–93, 607–26. See also Dickran Kouymjian, "Dated Armenian Manuscripts as a Statistical Tool for Armenian Studies," in *Medieval Armenian Culture*, ed. Thomas Samuelian and Michael Stone (Chico, CA: Scholars Press, 1983), pp. 425–38.

8. Warren Treadgold, *A History of the Byzantine State and Society* (Stanford, CA: Stanford University Press, 1997), pp. 782, 796–97; Lapidus, *History*, pp. 306–8; Khachikyan, "Hayastani," p. 49; Steven Runciman, *The Fall of Constantinople, 1453* (Cambridge: Cambridge University Press, 1965).

9. See Avedis K. Sanjian, *The Armenian Communities in Syria under Ottoman Dominion* (Cambridge, MA: Harvard University Press, 1965); H.M. Ghazaryan, "Kostandnupolisi ev Zmurniayi gaghtochakhnere" [The Colonies in Constantinople and Smyrna], in Aghayan et al., *Hay zhoghovrdi patmutyun*, vol. 4, pp. 301–2; Kouymjian, "Armenia," pp. 10–13. See also Kevork B. Bardakjian, "The Rise of the Armenian Patriarchate of Constantinople," in *Christians and Jews in the Ottoman Empire: The Functioning of a Plural Society*, vol. 1: *The Central Lands*, ed. Benjamin Braude and Bernard Lewis (New York: Holmes and Meier Publishers, 1982), pp. 89-100.

10. Lapidus, *History*, p. 342; Bernard Lewis, *The Emergence of Modern Turkey*, 2nd ed. (London: Oxford University Press, 1968), p. 36; Andrew C. Hess, "The Evolution of the Ottoman Seaborne Empire in the Age of the Oceanic Discoveries, 1453–1525," *American Historical Review* 75 (Dec. 1970): 1870–1919; Hess, "The Ottoman Conquest of Egypt (1517) and the Beginning of the Sixteenth-Century World War," *International Journal of Middle East Studies* 4:1 (Jan. 1973): 55–76; Kouymjian, "Armenia," pp. 14–15; A.G. Hovhannisyan, "Hayastani kaghakakan vichake Sefyan Irani ev Osmanyan Turkiayi tirapetutyan tak" [The Political Situation in Armenia under the Rule of Safavid Iran and Ottoman Turkey], in Aghayan, *Hay zhoghovrdi patmutyun*, vol. 4, p. 85; Kouymjian, "Armenia," pp. 15, 17.

11. Kouymjian, "Armenia," pp. 18–21, 25; George A. Bournoutian, "Eastern Armenia from the Seventeenth Century to the Russian Annexation," in Hovannisian, *Armenian People*, vol. 2, p. 81.

12. Omer L. Barkan, "The Price Revolution of the Sixteenth Century: A Turning Point in the History of the Near East," *International Journal of Middle East Studies* 6:1 (Jan. 1975): 3–28; Halil Inalcik, *An Economic and Social History of the*

Ottoman Empire, vol. 1: *1300–1600* (Cambridge: Cambridge University Press, 1994), pp. 50–51, 95–98.

13. Inalcik, *Economic*, pp. 64–75.

14. Hovhannisyan, "Hayastani," pp. 112–14.

15. Kouymjian, "Armenia," pp. 21–23, 26, 27–28; Ronald C. Jennings, "Urban Population in Anatolia in the Sixteenth Century: A Study of Kayseri, Karaman, Amasya, Trabzon and Erzurum," *International Journal for Middle Eastern Studies* 7:1 (Jan. 1976): 21–57.

16. Kouymjian, "Armenia," pp. 22–24; Hovhannisyan, "Hayastani," pp. 124–26; A.E. Redgate, *The Armenians* (Oxford: Blackwell, 1998), p. 263.

17. George A. Bournoutian, *A History of Qarabagh* (Costa Mesa, CA: Mazda, 1994), p. 17.

18. Hovhannisyan, "Hayastani," p. 108.

19. Kouymjian, "Armenia," pp. 24–26; Nina G. Garsoian, "The Problem of Armenian Integration into the Byzantine Empire," in *Studies on the Internal Diaspora of the Byzantine Empire*, ed. Hélène Ahrweiler and Angeliki E. Laiou (Washington, DC: Dumbarton Oaks, 1998), p. 59.

20. Redgate, *Armenians*, pp. 264, 266.

21. Bournoutian, "Eastern Armenia," p. 84; Hovhannisyan, "Hayastani kaghakakan vichake," p. 133.

22. Bournoutian, "Eastern Armenia," p. 85; Kouymjian, "Armenia," p. 31.

23. Hovhannisyan, "Hayastani," pp. 124–26, 128; Bournoutian, "Eastern Armenia," pp. 86–87.

24. Bournoutian, "Eastern Armenia," p. 89; Lapidus, *History*, p. 300; V.R. Grigoryan, "Arevelyan Hayastane xviii dari 50–70-akan tvakannerin" [Eastern Armenia during the 50s-70s of the 18th Century], in Aghayan, *Hay zhoghovrdi patmutyun*, vol. 4, p. 190.

25. A.G. Hovhannisyan, "Hay azatagrakan sharzhume Iranakan tirapetutyan ev Turk zavtichneri dem xviii dari arajin kesum" [The Armenian Liberation Movement against Iranian Rule and Turkish Tyranny during the First Half of the 18th Century], in Aghayan, *Hay zhoghovrdi patmutyun*, vol. 4, p. 138.

26. Lapidus, *History*, pp. 299–30; A.G. Hovhannisyan, "Haykakan sghnakhneri paykare Iranakan tirapetutyan dem ev Gandzaki 1724 tvakani Hay-Adrbejanakan paymanagire" [The Struggle of the Armenian Regions against Iranian Rule and the 1724 Armeno-Azerbaijan Treaty of Gandzak/Ganja], in Aghayan, *Hay zhoghovrdi patmutyun*, vol. 4, p. 154.

27. Krikor Maksoudian, "Armenian Communities in Eastern Europe," in Hovannisian, *Armenian People*, vol. 2, pp. 55–59; Catherine Evtuhov et al., *A History of Russia: Peoples, Legends, Events, Forces* (Boston: Hougton Miflin, 2004), pp. 276–78.

28. Evtuhov et al., *History of Russia*, p. 306. For excellent analyses of Russian imperial expansion in the eighteenth century, see Christopher Duffy, *Russia's Military Way to the West: The Origins and Nature of Russian Military Power, 1700–1800* (London: Routledge, 1981); Aleksandr B. Kamenskii, *The Russian Empire in the Eighteenth Century*, trans. David Griffiths (Armonk, NY: M.E. Sharpe, 1997); Benedict H. Sumner, *Peter the Great and the Ottoman Empire* (Oxford: Blackwell, 1949).

29. Bournoutian, "Eastern Armenia," pp. 91–93; Grigoryan, "Arevelyan Hayastane," pp. 194–95; V.G. Grigoryan, "Hay-Rusakan haraberutyunnere xviii dari 80–90-akan tvakannerin" [Armenian-Russian Relations during the 80s-90s of the 18th Century], in Aghayan, *Hay zhoghovrdi patmutyun*, vol. 4, p. 227.

30. Grigoryan, "Hay-Rusakan haraberutyunnere," pp. 224–26; Vahé Oshagan, "Modern Armenian Literature and Intellectual History from 1700 to 1915," in Hovannisian, *Armenian People*, vol. 2, pp. 145–46.
31. Grigoryan, "Hay-Rusakan haraberutyunnere," pp. 227–41.
32. Ibid., p. 246; Z.T. Grigoryan, "Hayastani hyusis-arevelyan shrjanneri miatsume Rusastanin" [The Unification of the Northeastern Regions of Armenia with Russia], in *Hay zhoghovrdi patmutyun*, ed. Ts.P. Aghayan et al. (Erevan: Armenian Academy of Sciences, 1974), vol. 5, p. 114; Grigoryan, "Hayastani," pp. 119–26; Bournoutian, "Eastern Armenia," pp. 100–1.
33. Bournoutian, "Eastern Armenia," pp. 102–3; Grigoryan, "Hayastani," pp. 134–35.
34. Bournoutian, "Eastern Armenia," pp. 104–5; Z.T. Grigoryan, "Arevelyan Hayastani azatagrume parskakan ltsits" [The Liberation of Eastern Armenia from the Persian Yoke], in Aghayan, *Hay zhoghovrdi patmutyun*, vol. 5, pp. 144–58, 170; H.F.B. Lynch, *Armenia: Travels and Studies*, 2 vols. (Beirut: Khayats, 1965), vol. 1, pp. 232–33.
35. M.S. Anderson, *The Eastern Question, 1774–1923: A Study in International Relations* (London: Macmillan, 1966); A.J.P. Taylor, *The Struggle for Mastery in Europe, 1848–1918* (Oxford: Oxford University Press, 1954).
36. Z.T. Grigoryan, "1828–1829 tt. Rus-Turkakan paterazme ev arevmtahayutyune" [The Russo-Turkish War of 1828–1829 and the Western Armenians], in Aghayan, *Hay zhoghovrdi patmutyun*, vol. 5, pp. 189–201; Ronald Grigor Suny, "Eastern Armenians under Tsarist Rule," in Hovannisian, *Armenian People*, vol. 2, p. 112. For different figures, see Bournoutian, "Eastern Armenia," p. 105; Bournoutian, "The Ethnic Composition and the Socio-Economic Condition of Eastern Armenia in the First Half of the Nineteenth Century," in *Transcaucasia, Nationalism, and Social Change*, ed. Ronald Gregory Suny (Ann Arbor: University of Michigan Press, 1996), p. 79.
37. Suny, "Eastern Armenians," pp. 113, 115; Lynch, *Armenia*, vol. 1, pp. 233–34; V.A. Diloyan and V.H. Rshtuni, "Arevelyan Hayastane Rusastani kazmum: Tsarizmi gaghutayin kaghakakanutyune" [Eastern Armenia in the Russian System: The Colonial Policy of Tsarism], in *Hay zhoghovrdi patmutyun*, vol. 5, p. 214.
38. Diloyan and Rshtuni, "Arevelyan Hayastane," in Aghayan, *Hay zhoghovrdi patmutyun*, pp. 211, 214.
39. See Suny, "Eastern Armenians," pp. 115–17.
40. The millet system, as a structural arrangement for community representation and administration, dated back to the Sasanian empire. See R.N. Frye, "The Political History of Iran under the Sasanians," in *The Cambridge History of Iran*, vol. 3, pt. 1, *The Seleucid, Parthian and Sasanian Periods*, ed. Ehsan Yarshater (Cambridge: Cambridge University Press, 1983), p. 132.
41. Lapidus, *History*, p. 316.
42. Hagop Barsoumian, "The Eastern Question and the Tanzimat Era," in Hovannisian, *Armenian People*, vol. 2, pp. 180–82.
43. See Stephan H. Astourian, "Genocidal Process: Reflections on the Armeno-Turkish Polarization," in *The Armenian Genocide: History, Politics, Ethics*, ed. Richard G. Hovannisian (New York: St. Martin's Press, 1992), pp. 53–79.
44. See Karl A. Wittfogel, *Oriental Despotism: A Comparative Study of Total Power* (New Haven, CT: Yale University Press, 1957).
45. Maghakia Ormanian, *Azgapatum* [History of the Nation], vol. 3 (Jerusalem: St. James Press, 1927; reprinted, Antelias: Catholicosate of Cilicia, 2001), col. 4068.
46. Barsoumian, "Eastern Question," pp. 199–200; Christopher J. Walker, *Armenia: The Survival of a Nation* (New York: St. Martin's Press, 1980), pp. 94–100.

47. Kemal H. Karpat, "The Transformation of the Ottoman State, 1789–1908," *International Journal of Middle East Studies* 3:3 (July 1972): 243–81.
48. Barsoumian, "Eastern Question," pp. 199–200; Richard G. Hovannisian, "The Armenian Question in the Ottoman Empire, 1876–1914," in Hovannisian, *Armenian People*, p. 203; Walker, *Armenia*, pp. 100–2, 108–17; Louise Nalbandian, *The Armenian Revolutionary Movement* (Berkeley: University of California Press, 1963), pp. 74–78, 80–85.
49. Christopher Clay, "The Origins of Modern Banking in the Levant: The Branch Network of the Imperial Ottoman Bank, 1890–1914," *International Journal of Middle East Studies* 26 (1994): 610; Michelle Raccagni, "The French Economic Interests in the Ottoman Empire," *International Journal of Middle East Studies* 11 (1980): 348.
50. Levon A. Bayramyan, *Arevmtyan Hayastane Angliakan imperializmi plannerum* [Western Armenia in English Imperialist Plans] (Erevan: Hayastan, 1982).
51. Suny, "Eastern Armenians," p. 127; Hovannisian, "Armenian Question," pp. 207–8.
52. See excerpt in Hovannisian, "Armenian Question," pp. 208–9; Suny, "Eastern Armenians," p. 127.
53. See Richard Shannon, *The Crisis of Imperialism, 1865–1915* (London: Paladin, Granada Publishing, 1974), p. 121; Hovannisian, "Armenian Question," pp. 209–10; William L. Langer, *The Diplomacy of Imperialism, 1890–1902*, 2nd ed. (New York: Alfred A. Knopf, 1951), p. 151.
54. Hovannisian, "Armenian Question," p. 210; Akaby Nassibian, *Britain and the Armenian Question, 1915–1923* (London: Croom Helm, 1984), p. 17.
55. Bayramyan, *Arevmetyan Hayastane*, pp. 113–15; Dwight E. Lee, *Great Britain and the Cyprus Convention Policy of 1878* (Cambridge, MA: Harvard University Press, 1934); Anderson, *Eastern Question*, pp. 204–9.
56. An earlier draft of this section, titled "Sources of Armenian Nationalism in the Ottoman Empire: An Historiographical Assessment," was presented at the fourth Workshop of Armenian-Turkish Scholarship, Salzburg, Austria, April 15–17, 2005.
57. Eric J. Hobsbawm, *Nations and Nationalism since 1780: Programme, Myth, Reality*, 2nd ed. (Cambridge: Cambridge University Press, 1992), p. 102.
58. See Fatma Müge Göçek, *Rise of the Bourgeoisie, Demise of Empire: Ottoman Westernization and Social Change* (New York: Oxford University Press, 1996), pp. 134–37. On Armenian identity, see Razmik Panossian, *The Armenians: From Kings and Priests to Merchants and Commissars* (New York: Columbia University Press, 2006).
59. Ronald Gregory Suny, *Looking toward Ararat: Armenia in Modern History* (Bloomington: Indiana University Press, 1993), p. 21; James Etmekjian, *The French Influence on the Western Armenian Renaissance, 1843–1915* (New York: Twayne, 1964), p. 98.
60. Etmekjian, *French*, pp. 71–74; Minas Tololyan, *Ardi Hay grakanutiun*, vol. 1: *1850–1920*, 2nd pr. (Boston: Steven Day Press, 1977; 1st pr., Cairo: Husaber, 1955), pp. 35–44.
61. Etmekjian, *French*, pp. 71–72, 73.
62. A.S. Hambaryan, *Hay hasarakakan kaghakakan mitke arevmtahayutyan azatagrutyan ughineri masin, xix dari verj-xx dari skizb* [Armenian Popular Political Thought Regarding the Ways of Western Armenian Liberation, Late 19th–Early 20th Centuries] (Erevan: Hayastan Press, 1990). See also Andrzej Walicki, *A History of Russian Thought from the Enlightenment to Marxism*, trans.

Hilda Andrews-Rusiecka (Stanford, CA: Stanford University Press, 1979); Ewa M. Thompson, ed., *The Search for Self-Definition in Russian Literature* (Houston: Rice University Press, 1991).

63. Tololyan, *Ardi Hay grakanutiun*, p. 31.

64. For a useful survey of Armenian literature, see Agop J. Hacikyan et al., eds., *The Heritage of Armenian Literature*, vol. 3: *From the Eighteenth Century to Modern Times* (Detroit, MI: Wayne State University Press, 2005). See also Oshagan, "Modern Armenian Literature," pp. 139–174.

65. V.D. Azatyan et al., "Bnakan gitutyunner" [Natural Sciences], in *Hay zhoghovrdi patmutyun*, ed. Ts.P. Aghayan et al. (Erevan: Armenian Academy of Sciences, 1981), vol. 6, pp. 942–47.

66. Ibid., pp. 948–49, 950–51.

67. See Anaide Ter Minassian, *Nationalism and Socialism in the Armenian Revolutionary Movement, 1887–1912* (Cambridge, MA: Zoryan Institute, 1984), pp. 5–6; Nalbandian, *Armenian Revolutionary Movement*, pp. 90–178, passim; M.G. Nersissyan, *Hay zhoghovrdi azatagrakan paykare Turkakan brnapetutyan dem, 1850–1870* [The Armenian People's Struggle for Liberation against Turkish Tyrannical Rule, 1850–1870] (Erevan: Armenian Academy of Sciences, 1955).

68. Suny, *Looking*, p. 20.

69. Hovannisian, "Armenian Question," pp. 218, 222; Christopher J. Walker, "From Sassun to the Ottoman Bank: Turkish Armenians in the 1890s," *Armenian Review* 30 (March 1979): 227–64; Johannes Lepsius, *Armenia and Europe: An Indictment*, trans. and ed. J. Rendel Harris (London: Hodder and Stoughton, 1897), pp. 330–31. According to Armen Garo, the total number of Armenians massacred was about 300,000. Armen Garo, "Aprvadz orer" [Days Lived], *Hayrenik amsagir* 1:9 (July 1923): 94.

70. Lynch, *Armenia*, vol. 1, p. 459; Suny, "Eastern Armenians," pp. 128–29; Mary K. Matossian, *The Impact of Soviet Policies in Armenia* (Leiden: E.J. Brill, 1962), p. 19; Manoug Joseph Somakian, *Empires in Conflict: Armenia and the Great Powers, 1895–1920* (London: I.B. Tauris, 1995).

71. Suny, "Eastern Armenians," pp. 115–17.

72. See, for example, Armenian Revolutionary Federation, Bureau, *Hushapatum H.H. Dashnaktsutian, 1890–1950* [History of the Armenian Revolutionary Federation, 1890–1950] (Boston: Hayrenik, 1950), p. 602.

73. Ibid.; Mikayel Varandyan, *Hay Heghapokhakan Dashnaktsutyan patmutyun* [History of the Armenian Revolutionary Federation] (Paris: n.p., 1932).

74. Gerard J. Libaridian, "Revolution and Liberation in the 1892 and 1907 Programs of the Dashnaktsutiun," in Suny, *Transcaucasia*, pp. 194–97.

75. Abraham Ascher, *The Revolution of 1905: Russia in Disarray* (Stanford, CA: Stanford University Press, 1988).

76. D.A. Muradyan, *Hayastane Rusakan arajin revolutsiayi tarinerin (1905–1907)* [Armenia During the Years of the First Russian Revolution (1905–1907)] (Erevan: Armenian Academy of Sciences, 1964); Ts.B. Aghayan, *Revolutsion sharzhumnere Hayastanum, 1905–1907* [The Revolutionary Movements in Armenia, 1905–1907] (Erevan: Armenian Academy of Sciences, 1955); D.A. Muradyan, "Heghapokhakan sharzhumnere arevelyan Hayastanum, 1905–1907 tvakannerin" [The Revolutionary Movements in Eastern Armenia During the Years 1905–1907], in Aghayan, *Hay zhoghovrdi patmutyun*, vol. 6, pp. 368–71.

77. Ter Minassian, *Nationalism and Socialism*, pp. 13–14, 23–30.

78. Rosa Luxemburg, "Social Democracy and the National Struggles in Turkey," trans. Ian Birchall, *Revolutionary History* 8:3 (2003).

79. Richard G. Hovannisian, *Armenia on the Road to Independence, 1918* (Berkeley: University of California Press, 1967), pp. 18–20.

80. Suny, "Eastern Armenians," p. 135; Matossian, *Impact*, p. 19.

81. Suny, "Eastern Armenians," p. 135. Aleksandr Kerenski and Pavel Miliukov, both prominent lawyers in 1912, successfully defended some members of Dashnaktsutiun. Kerenski and Miliukov became prime minister and foreign minister, respectively, of Russia in 1917.

82. Jacob M. Landau, *Pan-Turkism: From Irredentism to Cooperation*, 2nd rev. ed. (Bloomington: Indiana University Press, 1995); Uriel Heyd, *Foundations of Turkish Nationalism: The Life and Teachings of Ziya Gökalp* (London: Luzac, 1950); Taha Parla, *The Social and Political Thought of Ziya Gökalp, 1876–1924* (Leiden: E.J. Brill, 1985).

83. A.J.P. Taylor, *The Struggle for Mastery in Europe, 1848–1918* (Oxford: Oxford University Press, 1954), p. 451.

84. Hovannisian, *Armenia on the Road to Independence*, pp. 29–30; Walker, *Armenia*, pp. 182–88.

85. Anderson, *Eastern Question*, p. 291; Taylor, *Struggle*, pp. 474, 489, 490; Lewis, *Emergence*, p. 214; M.E. Yapp, *The Making of the Modern Near East, 1792–1923* (London: Longman, 1987), p. 64.

86. Lewis, *Emergence*, p. 225; Feroz Ahmad, *The Young Turks: The Committee of Union and Progress in Turkish Politics, 1908–1914* (Oxford: Clarendon Press, 1969), pp. 116–20.

87. W.E.D. Allen and Paul Muratoff, *Caucasian Battlefields: A History of the Wars on the Turco-Caucasian Border, 1828–1921* (Cambridge: Cambridge University Press, 1953), pp. 228–29; Ulrich Trumpener, *Germany and the Ottoman Empire, 1914–1918* (Princeton, NJ: Princeton University Press, 1968), pp. 13–14; see also Vahakn N. Dadrian, *German Responsibility in the Armenian Genocide: A Review of the Historical Evidence of German Complicity* (Watertown, MA: Blue Crane Books, 1996), p. 20; Dadrian, *The History of the Armenian Genocide: Ethnic Conflict from the Balkans to Anatolia to the Caucasus* (Providence, RI: Berghahn Books, 1995), p. 204.

6 THE ARMENIAN GENOCIDE

1. Ronald Grigor Suny, "Eastern Armenians under Tsarist Rule," and Richard G. Hovannisian, "The Armenians in the Ottoman Empire, 1876–1914," in *The Armenian People from Ancient to Modern Times*, vol. 2: *Foreign Dominion to Statehood*, ed. Richard G. Hovannisian (New York: St. Martin's Press, 1997), pp. 136, 233–38.

2. See FO 43989/19208/13/44, Marling to Grey, Sept. 26, 1913, in Great Britain, *British Documents on the Origins of the War, 1898–1914*, vol. 10: *The Near and Middle East on the Eve of War*, ed. G.P. Gooch and Harold Temperely (London: H.M.S.O., 1928–1936), p. 517.

3. FO 6328/98/14/44 (No. 97), Sir L. Mallet to Sir Edward Grey, Feb. 11, 1914, ibid., p. 229.

4. *Internationalen Beziehungen*, 1st series, I, no. 210, as quoted in Roderic H. Davison, "The Armenian Crisis, 1912–1914," *American Historical Review* 53 (April 1948): 504.

5. FO 32430/19208/13/44, Marling to Grey, July 13, 1913, *British Documents*, vol. 10, p. 496.
6. Rostom to Simon Vratsian, Feb. 12, 1914, in *Rostom: Namakani* [Rostom: Collection of Letters] (Beirut: Hamazkayin, 1999), pp. 611–12.
7. Great Britain, Parliament, *The Treatment of Armenians in the Ottoman Empire, 1915–1916*. Documents Presented to Viscount Grey of Fallodon, Secretary of State for Foreign Affairs, ed. and comp. Arnold Toynbee, 3rd ed. (Beirut: G. Doniguian and Sons, 1988 [London: Sir Joseph Causton and Sons, 1916]), pp. 635–36 (hereafter *Treatment*).
8. Djemal Pasha, *Memories of a Turkish Statesman, 1913–1919* (New York: George H. Doran, 1922), p. 276.
9. Simon Vratsian, *Hayastani Hanrapetutiun* [Republic of Armenia] (Paris: A.R.F. Central Committee of America, 1928; repr., Erevan: Hayastan, 1993), pp. 5–6; W.E.D. Allen and Paul Muratoff, *Caucasian Battlefields: A History of the Wars on the Turco-Caucasian Border, 1828–1921* (Cambridge: Cambridge University Press, 1953), p. 234; Vahakn N. Dadrian, *The History of the Armenian Genocide: Ethnic Conflict from the Balkans to Anatolia to the Caucasus* (Providence, RI: Berghahn Books, 1995), pp. 220–21; Dadrian, "Genocide as a Problem of National and International Law: The World War I Armenian Case and Its Contemporary Legal Ramifications," *Yale Journal of International Law* 14:2 (Summer 1989): 265.
10. William L. Langer, *The Diplomacy of Imperialism, 1890–1902*, 2 vols. (New York: Alfred A. Knopf, 1935), vol. 1, pp. 162, 202–10.
11. Vahakn N. Dadrian, *German Responsibility in the Armenian Genocide: A Review of the Historical Evidence of German Complicity* (Watertown, MA: Blue Crane Books, 1996), p. 47.
12. Richard G. Hovannisian, "The Historical Dimensions of the Armenian Question, 1878–1923," in *The Armenian Genocide in Perspective*, ed. Richard G. Hovannisian (New Brunswick, NJ: Transaction Books, 1986), p. 28; Christopher J. Walker, *Armenia: The Survival of a Nation* (London: Croom Helm, 1980), pp. 197–98; Dadrian, *History*, pp. 236–39, 246n26. On the origins of the *Teshkilat-i Makhsusa*, see Philip H. Stoddard, "The Ottoman Government and the Arabs, 1911 to 1918: A Preliminary Study of the Teşkilât-ı Mahsusa," Ph.D. diss., Princeton University, 1963.
13. Vahan Minakhorian, *1915 tvakane* [The Year 1915] (Venice: Mekhitarist Press, 1949), pp. 66–71.
14. Dadrian, *German*, p. 47.
15. *Treatment*, Doc. 122; Grigor H. Galustian, comp. and ed., *Marash kam Germanik ev heros Zeitun* [Marash or Germanica and Heroic Zeitun], 2nd ed. (New York: Compatriotic Union of Marash, 1934; Long Island City, NY: Union of Marash Armenians, 1988), pp. 171–72; Levon Norashkharyan, *Zeytune, 1914–1921 tt.* [Zeitun, 1914–1921] (Erevan: Armenian Academy of Sciences, 1984), p. 9; Sebuh Akuni, *Milion me Hayeru jardi patmutyune* [The Story of the Massacre of a Million Armenians] (Constantinople: Hayastan, 1921), p. 298.
16. Simon Payaslian, "The Death of Armenian Karin/Erzerum," in *Armenian Karin/Erzerum*, ed. Richard G. Hovannisian (Costa Mesa, CA: Mazda, 2003), pp. 341–42; Minakhorian, *1915*, pp. 90–93; Johannes Lepsius, *Rapport secret sur les massacres d'Armenie* (Beirut: Hamazkayin, 1980; first published Paris: Payot, 1918), p. 59.

17. France, Archives du Ministère des Affaires Étrangères (A.M.A.E.), Guerre 1914–1918, *Turquie*, Dépêche no. 34, Barthe de Sandfort, Vice-Consul of France at Van, to Bompard, Ambassador of France at Constantinople, Sept. 19, 1914, in Arthur Beylerian, ed. and comp., *Les grandes puissances l'empire ottoman et les arméniens dans les archives françaises (1914–1918)* (Paris: Université de Paris I, Panthéon-Sorbonne, 1983), p. 4; Payaslian, "Death of Armenian Karin/ Erzerum," pp. 342–43.
18. Turkish Ambassador, Rustem, to Secretary of State, Sept. 10, 1914, in U.S. Department of State, *Papers Relating to the Foreign Relations of the United States, 1914* (Washington, DC: Government Printing Office, 1922), pp. 1090–91.
19. Simon Payaslian, *United States Policy toward the Armenian Question and the Armenian Genocide* (New York: Palgrave Macmillan, 2005), pp. 49–50.
20. S.L.A. Marshall, *World War I* (Boston: Houghton Mifflin, 1964; repr. Mariner Books, 2001), p. 121.
21. Simon Payaslian, "United States Policy toward the Armenian Question and the Armenian Genocide," Ph.D. diss., UCLA, 2003, p. 154.
22. Haigazn G. Ghazarian, *Tseghaspan Turke* [The Genocidal Turk] (Beirut: Hamazkayin, 1968), p. 113.
23. Ibid., p. 112; *Treatment*, p. 637; Dadrian, *History*, pp. 220–21.
24. Henry H. Riggs, *Days of Tragedy in Armenia: Personal Experiences in Harpoot, 1915–1917* (Ann Arbor, MI: Gomidas Institute, 1997), p. 38.
25. France, A.M.A.E., Guerre 1914–1918, *Opérations stratégiques*, tome 1027, folio 12, télégramme no. 1174, Paléologue, Ambassador of France at Petrograd, to Declassé, Minister of Foreign Affairs, Dec. 30, 1914, in Beylerian, *Les grandes puissances*, p. 6; Allen and Muratoff, *Caucasian Battlefields*, pp. 243–44.
26. Payaslian, "United States Policy," p. 195; Dzitogh had become a military garrison in September 1914. See Vartiter K. Hovannisian, *Dzitogh, dashti Karno* [Dzitogh of the Karin Plain] (Beirut: Hamazkayin, 1972), pp. 95–96, 196–98.
27. *Treatment*, Doc. 21; Dadrian, "Genocide as a Problem," p. 260.
28. Maria Jacobsen, *Oragrutiun 1907–1919: Kharpert* [Diary 1907–1919: Kharpert], trans. from Danish by Bishop Nerses Bakhtikian and Mihran Simonian (Antelias: Catholicosate of Antelias, 1979), pp. 63, 64, 69–70.
29. Anahide Ter Minassian, "Van 1915," in *Armenian Van/Vaspurakan*, ed. Richard G. Hovannisian (Costa Mesa, CA: Mazda, 2000), pp. 214–15.
30. *Treatment*, pp. 637–38; Allen and Muratoff, *Caucasian Battlefields*, pp. 245–47, 250–53, 261–62, 283n2, 284, 270, 271; Marshall, *World War I*, pp. 116–17; Keegan, *First World War*, p. 222; Walker, *Armenia*, p. 199.
31. Akuni, *Milion*, p. 29.
32. Zaven Der Yeghiayan, *My Patriarchal Memoirs*, translated from the Armenian by Ared Misirliyan, annotated by Vatche Ghazarian (Barrington, RI: Mayreni Publishing, 2002), p. 63.
33. Allen and Muratoff, *Caucasian Battlefields*, p. 286; Donald M. McKale, *War by Revolution: Germany and Great Britain in the Middle East in the Era of World War I* (Kent, OH: Kent State University Press, 1998), p. 86.
34. Payaslian, "United States Policy," p. 207; McKale, *War*, pp. 90, 92.
35. "Battle of the Suez Canal: A First-Hand Account of the Unsuccessful Turkish Invasion," *Times* (London), Feb. 19, 1915, reprinted in *Current History* 2 (April 1915): 85–88; Keegan, *First World War*, pp. 219–21; McKale, *War*, pp. 97–100.
36. Langer, *Diplomacy*, pp. 162, 202–10.

37. *Treatment*, p. 638.
38. Henry Morgenthau, *Ambassador Morgenthau's Story* (New York: Doubleday, 1918), pp. 20, 323.
39. Dadrian, *History*, pp. 4–5, 240; Simon Payaslian, "The Destruction of the Armenian Church during the Genocide," *Genocide Studies and Prevention* 1:2 (Fall 2006): 156.
40. Leslie A. Davis, *The Slaughterhouse Province: An American Diplomat's Report on the Armenian Genocide, 1915–1917*, ed. with introduction and notes by Susan K. Blair (New Rochelle, NY: Aristide D. Caratzas, 1989), pp. 39, 59, 71.
41. Payaslian, *United States*, pp. 58–59.
42. Bertha B. Morley, *Marsovan 1915: The Diaries of Bertha B. Morley*, ed. Hilmar Kaiser (Ann Arbor, MI: Gomidas Institute, 1999), pp. 2–3.
43. Levon Chormisian, *Hamapatker arevmtahay mek daru patmutyan* [A Panorama of One Century of Western Armenian History], 3 vols. (Beirut: Sevan, 1975), vol. 3, p. 359; *Treatment*, Docs. 29, 30, 31, 36; Lepsius, *Rapport*, pp. 227–28. See also United States, National Archives, Record Group 59 (hereafter RG 59), 867.00/760, Charles F. Brissel to Secretary of State, April 1, 1915.
44. Akuni, *Milion*, pp. 26–28; Chormisian, *Hamapatker*, pp. 343–45. See also Nuri Bey to Jemal Bey, Feb. 18, 1915, in Aram Antonian, *Mets vochire* [The Colossal Crime] (Boston: Bahak, 1921; repr. Erevan: Arevik, 1990), pp. 129–30, 133; Vahakn N. Dadrian, "The Secret Young-Turk Ittihadist Conference and the Decision for the World War I Genocide of the Armenians," *Holocaust and Genocide Studies* 7:2 (Fall 1993), reprinted with revisions in "The Armenian Genocide in Official Turkish Records," *Journal of Political and Military Sociology* 22:1 (Summer 1994): 173–201.
45. Chormisian, *Hamapatker*, pp. 343–45; Antonian, *Mets vochire*, pp. 129–33.
46. "Chronology of the War," *Current History* 2 (April 1915): 197; *Current History* 2 (May 1915): 405; *Treatment*, Docs. 21, 27, 28, 31, 36; Payaslian, *United States*, p. 61; Allen and Muratoff, *Caucasian Battlefields*, pp. 295–99.
47. Bibliothèque Nubar (Paris), Boghos Nubar, "The War and the Armenians of Cilicia," Memorandum, 918–923, Cairo, Feb. 3, 1915, in *Boghos Nubar's Papers and the Armenian Question, 1915–1918*, trans. and ed. Vatche Ghazarian (Waltham, MA: Mayrnei Publishing, 1996), pp. 3–5 (hereafter *Boshos Nubar Papers*).
48. Akuni, *Milion*, pp. 294–95; Lepsius, *Rapport*, pp. 33–34; Haykaz M. Poghosyan, *Zeytuni patmutyune, 1409–1921 tt.* [The History of Zeitun, 1409–1921] (Erevan: Hayastan, 1969), p. 387.
49. Poghosyan, *Zeytuni patmutyune*, pp. 393–95.
50. *Treatment*, Doc. 123.
51. Ibid., Doc. 119, 120, 122, 123, 124, and editor's note, "Cilicia," pp. 466–67; Bibliothèque Nubar (Paris), 1107–1110, Levon Meguerditchian to Boghos Nubar, May 28, 1915, and [no file number] Yacoub Artin Pasha to Boghos Nubar, June 27, 1915, and 1249–1252, H. Mutafoff to Boghos Nubar, July 5, 1915, *Boghos Nubar Papers*, pp. 65, 115, 134; Abraham H. Hartunian, *Neither to Laugh Nor to Weep: A Memoir of the Armenian Genocide* (Boston: Beacon Press, 1968), pp. 54–56; Lepsius, *Rapport*, pp. 27–31, 33; 225–26; Norashkharyan, *Zeytune*, pp. 33, 44–45, 56; Poghosyan, *Zeytuni patmutyune*, pp. 388–90, 395–99; Galustian, *Marash*, pp. 176–77; Chormisian, *Hamapatker*, pp. 440–41, 477.
52. RG 59, 867.4016/373, Jackson to Secretary of State, March 4, 1918; Lepsius, *Rapport*, pp. 28–29, 38–39, 194; *Treatment*, Docs. 29–31, 36, 137; Khoren K. Davidson, *Odyssey of an Armenian of Zeitoun* (New York: Vantage Press, 1985),

p. 65; Zakaria Pztikian, comp., *Kilikian kskidzner: Vaveragrer Kilikio katoghikosakan divanen, 1903–1915* [Cilician Pains: Documents from the Archives of the Cilician Catholicosate] (Beirut: Hrazdan, 1927), p. 136; Buzand Eghiayan, *Zhamanakakits patmutiun Katoghikosutian Hayots Kilikio, 1914–1972* [Contemporary History of the Catholicosate of Cilician Armenians, 1914–1972] (Antelias: Catholicosate of Cilicia, 1975), pp. 43–44.

53. RG 59, 867.4016/59, Morgenthau to Secretary of State, April 30, 1915; RG 59, 867.4016/60, Bryan to Bakhméteff, May 3, 1915; Akuni, *Milion*, pp. 303–5; France, A.M.A.E., Guerre 1914–1918, *Turquie*, Kévork V, Catholicos de tous les Arméniens, à Sa Majesté Victor-Emmanuel, Roi d'Italie, April 22, 1915, in Beylerian, *Les grandes puissances*, p. 14; Catholicos Kevork V to Boghos Nubar, April 22, 1915, in *Boghos Nubar Papers*, p. 17.

54. For the minutes of the meeting, see Der Yeghiayan, *Memoirs*, pp. 62–63.

55. *Treatment*, Docs. 64, 94; Lepsius, *Rapport*, pp. 44–45; Nazaret Piranian, *Kharberdi egherne* [The Genocide in Kharpert] (Boston: Baykar, 1937), p. 99; Asatur H. Makarian, "Ampop hamaynapatker" [Concise Overview], in *Hushamatian Mets Egherni, 1915–1965* [Memorial Volume of the Colossal Crime, 1915–1965], comp. and ed. Gersam Aharonian (Beirut: Atlas, 1965), p. 309.

56. Walker, *Armenia*, pp. 209–10; Grigoris Palakian, *Hay Goghgotan* [The Armenian Calvary] (Erevan: Hayastan, 1991), pp. 46–109 passim; Lepsius, *Rapport*, pp. 48, 228–29, 231, 233–34.

57. RG 59, 867.4016/59, Morgenthau to Secretary of State, April 30, 1915.

58. Morgenthau, *Story*, pp. 184–85, 194, 197–99, 202–04; Marshall, *World War I*, pp. 149–53; Niall Ferguson, *The Pity of War* (London: Penguin Press, 1998; New York: Basic Books, 1999), pp. 290–91; Jean Giraudoux, "The Dardanelles," *North American Review* 206 (Aug. 1917): 285–91; Brigadier General Cecil Faber Aspinall-Oglander, comp., *Military Operations, Gallipoli* (London: W. Heinemann, 1929–1932); Alan Moorehead, *Gallipoli* (London: H. Hamilton, 1956); *Current History* 2 (May 1915): 400.

59. James L. Stokesbury, *A Short History of World War I* (New York: William Morrow, 1981), pp. 115–20; "Battle of the Dardanelles," *Current History* 2 (May 1915): 219–22; Marshall, *World War I*, p. 154.

60. Morgenthau, *Story*, p. 274.

61. Lewis Einstein, *A Diplomat Looks Back* (New Haven, CT: Yale University Press, 1968), pp. 118, 133. For a similar argument, see Joseph L. Grabill, *Protestant Diplomacy and the Near East: Missionary Influence on American Policy, 1810–1927* (Minneapolis: University of Minnesota Press, 1971), p. 63.

62. For general history of the genocide, see Richard G. Hovannisian, *The Armenian Genocide: History, Politics, Ethics* (New York: St. Martin's Press, 1992); Hovannisian, *Armenian Genocide in Perspective*; Dadrian, *History*; Taner Akçam, *A Shameful Act: The Armenian Genocide and the Question of Turkish Responsibility* (New York: Metropolitan Books, 2006).

63. Chormisian, *Hamapatker*, pp. 439–40.

64. Allen and Muratoff, *Caucasian Battlefields*, p. 299.

65. Lepsius, *Rapport*, pp. 130–32; Anahide Ter Minassian, "Van 1915," in *Armenian Van/Vaspurakan*, ed. Richard G. Hovannisian (Costa Mesa, CA: Mazda, 2000), p. 239.

66. Lepsius, *Rapport*, pp. 130–32; Ter Minassian, "Van 1915," pp. 239, 242; Allen and Muratoff, *Caucasian Battlefields*, pp. 300–1.

67. "The Petrograd Plan," [Handed to Boghos Nubar by Dr. Zavriev], 1065–1068, [May 1915], in *Boghos Nubar Papers*, pp. 19–20. See also Jon Kirakosyan, comp., *Hayastane mijazgayin ev Sovetakan artakin kaghakanutyan pastatghterum,*

1828–1923 [Armenia in the Documents of International and Soviet Foreign Policy, 1828–1923] (Erevan: Hayastan, 1972), pp. 371–74.

68. "The Petrograd Plan," pp. 19–20.

69. RG 59, 867.4016/97, Hollis to Secretary of State, July 6, 1915; *Treatment*, Docs. 120, 123–25, 128–30, 133, 138; Lepsius, *Rapport*, pp. 34–35, 45; Chormisian, *Hamapatker*, p. 479; Makarian, "Ampop hamaynapatker," p. 309.

70. *Treatment*, Docs. 6, 15, 19, 21–23, 27–31, 36, 53, 60, 120, 123, 124, 128, 137–39; Henry Barby, *Au pays de l'épouvante: L'Arménie martyre* (Beirut: Hamazkayin, 1972; first published 1917), p. 74; Hovannisian, *Dzitogh*, p. 96.

71. A.M.A.E., Guerre 1914–1918, *Turquie*, "Communication de l'Ambassade de Russie au Département," May 11, 1915, "Communication de l'Ambassade de Grande-Bretagne au Département," May 19, 1915, "Communication de l'Ambassade de Grande-Bretagne au Département," May 21, 1915, "Note du Département à l'Agence Havas," May 24, 1915, and M. William Sharp, Ambassadeur des États-Unis à Paris, à M. Declassé, Ministre des Affaires étrangères, May 28, 1915, in Beylerian, *Les grandes puissances*, pp. 23, 25–26, 27–28, 29, 31; RG 59, 867.4016/67, Sharp to Secretary of State, May 28, 1915; RG 59, 867.4016/67, Secretary of State Bryan to American Embassy, Constantinople, May 29, 1915.

72. Hikmet Yusuf Bayur, *Türk İnkılâbı Tarihi*, vol. 3: *1914–1918 Genel Savaşı*, pt. 3, *1915–1917 Vuruşmaları ve Bunların Siyasal Tepkileri* [History of the Turkish Revolution, vol. 3: The 1914–1918 World War, the Battles of 1915–1917 and Their Political Effects] (Ankara: Türk Tarih Kurumu, 1957), pp. 37–38, cited in Richard G. Hovannisian, *Armenia on the Road to Independence, 1918* (Berkeley: University of California Press, 1967), p. 50.

73. Henry H. Riggs, *Days of Tragedy in Armenia: Personal Experiences in Harpoot, 1915–1917* (Ann Arbor: Gomidas Institute, 1997), p. 92.

74. Bibliothèque Nubar (Paris), 1090–1091, Boghos Nubar to Lieutenant-Colonel G.M. Gregory, May 25, 1915, *Boghos Nubar Papers*, p. 54.

75. Ibid., 1107–1110, Levon Meguerditchian to Boghos Nubar, May 28, 1915, *Boghos Nubar Papers*, p. 65.

76. Ibid., 1534–1537, Boghos Nubar to Bishop Ghevont Tourian, Aug. 10, 1915, *Boghos Nubar Papers*, pp. 255–56; Der Yeghiayan, *Memoirs*, p. 89; Lepsius, *Rapport*, pp. 237–38; Barby, *Pays*, p. 57.

77. Ghazar Chareg, *Karinapatum: Hushamatian Bardzr Hayki* [Karin: Memorial Volume of upper Armenia] (Beirut: Karin Compatriotic Union of the United States and Lebanon, 1957), pp. 469–70; Lepsius, *Rapport*, p. 69.

78. Ibid., pp. 466–67; *Treatment*, Doc. 56; Ghazarian, *Tseghaspan*, p. 114.

79. Payaslian, "Death of Armenian Karin/Erzerum," pp. 352–53.

80. Davis, *Slaughterhouse Province*, p. 7.

81. RG 59, 867.4016/85/105/114, Heizer to Morgenthau, June 28, 1915, Morgenthau to Secretary of State, July 26, 1915, Heizer to Secretary of State, July 12, 1915, encl. Heizer to Morgenthau, June 28, 1915; Ghazarian, *Tseghaspan*, pp. 74–77; M. Gushakchian, "Trapizoni ev Samsoni teghahanu-tiunn u jardere" [The Deportation and Massacres of Trebizond and Samson], in Aharonian, *Hushamatian*, p. 468.

82. RG 59, 876.4016/122, Morgenthau to Secretary of State, Aug. 10, 1915, encl., Doc. 3, report by Dashnaktsutiun Committee, Balkan Section.

83. RG 59, 867.4016/288, Hoffman Philip to Secretary of State, June 12, 1916, encl., report by Dr. C.E. Clark, May 31, 1916.

84. Barby, *Pays*, p. 116.

85. *Treatment*, Doc. 86, 87, and p. 647; Lepsius, *Rapport*, p. 62.
86. RG 59, 867.4016/288, Hoffman Philip to Secretary of State, June 12, 1916, encl., report by Dr. C.E. Clark, May 31, 1916; Hayk Naggashian, "Sebastahayutian brnagaghtn u jarde" [The Forced Deportation and Massacre of the Armenians of Sebastia], in Aharonian, *Hushamatian*, pp. 368–69.
87. RG 59, 867.4016/106, Morgenthau to Secretary of State, July 26, 1915, encl., report on "Conditions in Marsovan"; Ghazarian, *Tseghaspan*, pp. 93–94; Chormisian, *Hamapatker*, p. 452.
88. Simon Payaslian, "The Armenian Resistance at Shabin-Karahisar, 1915," in *Armenian Sebastia/Sivas and Lesser Armenia*, ed. Richard G. Hovannisian (Costa Mesa, CA: Mazda, 2004), pp. 403–26.
89. RG 59, 867.4016/225/241/373, Jackson to Secretary of State, Oct. 16, 1915, encl., "Armenian Exodus from Harpoot"; Morgenthau to Secretary of State, Nov. 17, 1915, encl., "Miss Alma Johanson's Report"; Jackson to Secretary of State, report, "Armenian Atrocities," March 4, 1918; *Treatment*, Docs. 23, 66; Akuni, *Milion*, pp. 153–55. Tacy W. Atkinson, "Statement of Dr. Tacy W. Atkinson," Ruth A. Parmelee, "A Visit to the Exile Camp in Mezereh," and "Statement by Isabelle Harley," in *"Turkish Atrocities": Statements of American Missionaries on the Destruction of Christian Communities in Ottoman Turkey, 1915–1917*, comp. James L. Barton (Ann Arbor, MI: Gomidas Institute, 1998), pp. 41, 59, 65; Tacy Atkinson, *"The German, the Turk and the Devil Made a Triple Alliance": Harpoot Diaries, 1908–1917* (Princeton, NJ: Gomidas Institute, 2000), pp. 40–41.
90. Atkinson, *Harpoot*, p. 39.
91. Ghazarian, *Tseghaspan*, pp. 149–52; Krieger, *Yosghati hayaspanutyan vaveragrakan patmutyune* [The Documentary History of the Armenocide in Yozgat] (New York: Vosketar, 1980), pp. 142–43; Clara Childs Richmond, "The Turkish Atrocities," in Barton, *"Turkish Atrocities,"* p. 123; *Treatment*, Docs. 93–98; Vardan, *Zhamanakagrutiun*, p. 49.
92. Der Yeghiayan, *Memoirs*, p. 82.
93. Akuni, *Milion*, pp. 193–94; Chormisian, *Hamapatker*, pp. 480–81.
94. Akuni, *Milion*, p. 228.
95. *Treatment*, Docs. 105, 106, 107, 109, 110, 113, 143.
96. *Horizon* (Armenian daily), Tiflis, Aug. 21, 1915, as reported by Barby, *Au pays de l'épouvante*, pp. 189–90. Barby puts the number of refugees in Echmiadzin at 45,000 (p. 188). *Treatment*, Docs. 46, 48, 49, 50.
97. Morgenthau, *Story*, p. 314; Walker, *Armenia*, p. 226.
98. *Treatment*, Docs. 9, 139.
99. RG 59, 867.4016/148, Morgenthau to Secretary of State, Aug. 30, 1915, encl., Jackson to Morgenthau, Aug. 19, 1915; RG 59, 867.4016/219, Morgenthau to Secretary of State, Nov. 1, 1915, encl., Jackson to Morgenthau, Sept. 29, 1915. See also *Treatment*, Docs. 134, 136, 139, 143; Der Yeghiayan, *Memoirs*, p. 96; Akuni, *Milion*, pp. 126–35.
100. Adamantios Polyzoides, "The Passing of Turkey," *Current History* 15 (Oct. 1921): 33; Dadrian, "Genocide as a Problem," pp. 221–334.

7 THE REPUBLIC OF ARMENIA: THE FIRST REPUBLIC

1. Hayastani Hanrapetutyun, Arvesti, Grakanutyan ev Mamuli Pastatghteri Petakan Kentronakan Arkhiv [Republic of Armenia, State Central Archives of Art, Literature, and Media], *Vaveragrer Hay ekeghetsu patmutyan*, Girk G: *Artak*

Episkopos Smbatyants: Hogevor, grakan, patma-banakan gortsuneutyune ev gndaka-harutyune, 1876–1937 tt.) [Documents of the History of the Armenian Church, Book 3: Bishop Artak Smbatyants: His Spiritual, Literary, Historical-Philological Works and Execution (1867–1937)], comp. Sandro Behbudyan (Erevan: Anahit, 1999), Doc. 67, pp. 126–30.

2. Simon Vratsian, *Hayastani Hanrapetutiun* [The Republic of Armenia], 2nd pr. (Beirut: Mshak, 1958), p. 17; Simon Vratsian, *Kianki ughinerov: Depker, demker, aprumner* [Along Life's Ways: Episodes, Figures, Experiences] (Beirut: Mshak, 1963), vol. 3, p. 150.

3. Richard G. Hovannisian, *Armenia on the Road to Independence, 1918* (Berkeley: University of California Press, 1967), pp. 70–71.

4. *Vaveragrer*, Girk G, Doc. 81, pp. 143–44.

5. Hovannisian, *Armenia on the Road to Independence*, pp. 71–72; Richard G. Hovannisian, "Armenia and the Caucasus in the Genesis of the Soviet-Turkish Entente," *International Journal of Middle East Studies* 4:2 (April 1973): 129–47.

6. James Bunyan and H.H. Fisher, *The Bolshevik Revolution, 1917–1918: Documents and Materials* (Stanford, CA: Stanford University Press, 1934), pp. 282–83; Merle Fainsod, *How Russia Is Ruled* (Cambridge, MA: Harvard University Press, 1953), pp. 80–83. See also Alfred D. Low, *Lenin on the Question of Nationality* (New York: Bookman, 1958); Bertram D. Wolfe, *Three Who Made a Revolution*, rev. ed. (New York: Dell, 1964).

7. Hovannisian, *Armenia on the Road to Independence*, pp. 96, 111–13; A.N. Mnatsakanyan, *V.I. Lenine ev Hay zhoghovrdi azatagrakan paykare* [V.I. Lenin and the Armenian People's Struggle for Freedom] (Erevan: Armenian Academy of Sciences, 1962), p. 272; Stepan Shahumyan, *Erker* [Works] (Erevan: Armenian Academy of Sciences, 1958), vol. 3, pp. 37–39. On Shahumyan, see Lendrush A. Khurshudyan, *Stepan Shahumyan: Petakan ev partiakan gortsuneu-tyune, 1917–1918 tvakannerin* [Stepan Shahumyan: Governmental and Party Activity during the Years 1917–1918] (Erevan: Armenian Academy of Sciences, Institute of History, 1959).

8. Mary K. Matossian, *The Impact of Soviet Policies in Armenia* (Leiden: E.J. Brill, 1962), p. 25; Vratsian, *Hayastani Hanrapetutiun*, pp. 53–54.

9. Hovannisian, *Armenia on the Road to Independence*, pp. 109–10.

10. Ibid., p. 114.

11. W.E.D. Allen and Paul Muratoff, *Caucasian Battlefields: A History of the Wars on the Turco-Caucasian Border, 1828–1921* (Cambridge: Cambridge University Press, 1953), pp. 458–62; Antoine Poidebard, "Rôle militaire des Arméniens sur le front du Caucase après la défection de l'armée russe (décembre 1917-novembre 1919)," *Revue des études arméniennes* 1 (1920): 141–42.

12. See Hovannisian, *Armenia on the Road to Independence*, p. 104.

13. Allen and Muratoff, *Caucasian Battlefields*, pp. 463–64; Vratsian, *Hayastani Hanrapetutiun*, pp. 86–87.

14. Vahan Minakhorian, "Karsi ankume" [The Fall of Kars], *Hayrenik amsagir* 13 (Aug. 1935): 84; Hovannisian, *Armenia on the Road to Independence*, pp. 162–66; Vratsian, *Hayastani Hanrapetutiun*, pp. 104, 108–10, 112–13; Aleksandr Khatisian, *Hayastani Hanrapetutian tsagumn u zargatsume* [The Creation and Development of the Republic of Armenia], 2nd pr. (Beirut: Hamazkayin, 1968), pp. 42–44.

15. Khatisian, *Hayastani Hanrapetutian*, pp. 63–65; Richard Pipes, *The Formation of the Soviet Union* (Cambridge, MA: Harvard University Press, 1997 [1954]), pp. 193–95; Vahan Minakhorian, "Batumi khorhrdazhoghove" [The Batum

Conference], *Hayrenik amsagir* 12 (March 1936): 94; Vratsian, *Hayastani Hanrapetutiun*, pp. 113–15; Firuz Kazemzadeh, *The Struggle for Transcaucasia, 1917–1921* (New York: Philosophical Library, 1951), p. 147.

16. Vratsian, *Hayastani Hanrapetutiun*, pp. 152–53; Hovannisian, *Armenia on the Road to Independence*, pp. 189–91.

17. See Aleksandr Khatisian, "Kaghakapeti me hishataknere" [The Memories of a Mayor], *Hayrenik amsagir*, part I, 9 (May 1932): 86–93.

18. Pipes, *Formation*, p. 208.

19. Jacques Kayaloff, *The Battle of Sardarabad* (The Hague: Mouton, 1973); Vratsian, *Hayastani Hanrapetutiun*, pp. 116, 143.

20. See excerpt in Hovannisian, *Armenia on the Road to Independence*, pp. 196–97.

21. Ibid., p. 201; Vratsian, *Hayastani Hanrapetutiun*, p. 154.

22. Vratsian, *Hayastani Hanrapetutiun*, p. 181.

23. Richard G. Hovannisian, *The Republic of Armenia*, vol. 1: *The First Years, 1918–1919* (Berkeley: University of California Press, 1971), pp. 42–43, 45–46; Vratsian, *Hayastani Hanrapetutiun*, pp. 183–87.

24. Harry R. Rudin, *Armistice, 1918* (New Haven, CT: Yale University Press, 1944), pp. 410–11; H.W.V. Temperely, *A History of the Peace Conference of Paris* (London: H. Frowde, and Hodder & Stoughton, 1920), vol. 1, pp. 495–97.

25. Hovannisian, *Republic*, vol. 1, pp. 55–56, 60–62.

26. See Edouard Brémond, *La Cilicie en 1919–1920* (Paris: Imprimerie nationale, 1921); Dikran Boyajian (Tigran Poyajian), *Haykakan legione* [The Armenian Legion] (Watertown, MA: Baykar, 1965).

27. Hovannisian, *Republic*, vol. 1, pp. 257–60. See also E.J. Dillon, *The Inside Story of the Peace Conference* (New York: Harper, 1920).

28. Hovannisian, *Republic of Armenia*, vol. 2: *From Versailles to London, 1919–1920* (Berkeley: University of California Press, 1982), pp. 22, 26, 27, 35–37.

29. Simon Payaslian, *United States Policy toward the Armenian Question and the Armenian Genocide* (New York: Palgrave Macmillan, 2005); Laurence Evans, *United States Policy and the Partition of Turkey, 1914–1924* (Baltimore: Johns Hopkins Press, 1965); Richard H. Ullman, *Anglo-Soviet Relations, 1917–1921*, vol. 2: *Britain and the Russian Civil War, November 1918-February 1920* (Princeton, NJ: Princeton University Press, 1968), pp. 65–80.

30. Hovannisian, *Republic*, vol. 1, pp. 109–14, 121; Vratsian, *Hayastani Hanrapetutiun*, pp. 214–21.

31. Vratsian, *Hayastani Hanrapetutiun*, pp. 211–13; Arno J. Mayer, *Politics and Diplomacy of Peacemaking: Containment and Counterrevolution at Versailles, 1918–1919* (New York: Alfred A. Knopf, 1967), pp. 373–409, 853–56; Pierre Renaudel, *L'internationale à Berne: Faits et documents* (Paris: B. Grasset, 1919), pp. 87–91.

32. See E. Ishkhanian, "Depkere Gharabaghum: Chshtumner ev ditoghutiunner" [The Events in Karabagh: Corrections and Observations], *Hayrenik amsagir* 11 (Sept. 1933): 85–91.

33. A. Babalian, *Ejer Hayastani ankakhutyan patmutyunits* [Pages from the History of Armenian Independence] (Cairo: Husaber, 1959), pp. 30–33; Vratsian, *Hayastani Hanrapetutiun*, pp. 296–99; Hovannisian, *Republic*, vol. 1, pp. 90, 175–76.

34. Arsen Mikayelian, "Gharabaghi verjin depkere" [The Recent Events in Karabagh], *Hayrenik amsagir* 1 (May 1923): 162–63; Khatisian, *Hayastani Hanrapetutian*, pp. 152–54; Sarur, "Gharabaghi ktsume Adrbejani" [The Annexation of Karabagh to Azerbaijan], *Hayrenik amsagir* 7 (June 1929): 133–36; Vratsian, *Hayastani Hanrapetutiun*, pp. 285, 312–13.

35. Grigor Agababian, "The Economic Situation of the Armenian Republic," *Armenian Review* 16 (April 1920): 308–15.

36. Vratsian, *Hayastani Hanrapetutiun*, pp. 174–75, 226–27; Khatisian, *Hayastani Hanrapetutian*, pp. 113–14; Ruben Ter Minasian, *Hay heghapokhakani me hishataknere* [The Memories of an Armenian Revolutionary] (Los Angeles: Horizon, 1952), vol. 3, pp. 228–32, 271–76, 329–39; Hovannisian, *Republic*, vol. 1, pp. 152–53.

37. George Stewart, *The White Armies of Russia: A Chronicle of Counter-Revolution and Allied Intervention* (New York: Macmillan, 1933), pp. 155–163; Ullman, *Anglo-Soviet Relations*, vol. 2, pp. 62–70, 212–30; Mayer, *Politics and Diplomacy*, pp. 308–15; Kazemzadeh, *Struggle*, pp. 181–82, 234–38.

38. Zarevand, *Krnank hashtvil Turkin het?* [Can We Reconcile with the Turk?] (n.p., 1926).

39. Lord Kinross, *Ataturk: The Rebirth of a Nation* (London: Weidenfeld and Nicolson, 1964), pp. 202–19; Uluğ İğdemir, *Sivas kongresi tutanakları* [Minutes of the Sivas Congress] (Ankara: Türk Tarih Kurumu Basımevi, 1969); Hovannisian, *Republic*, vol. 1, pp. 434–36.

40. Khatisian, *Hayastani Hanrapetutian*, pp. 129–31; Hovannisian, *Republic*, vol. 1, pp. 460–61; Vratsian, *Hayastani Hanrapetutiun*, pp. 237–38, 254–65.

41. Hovannisian, *Republic*, vol. 1, pp. 464–66, vol. 2, p. 17; Vratsian, *Hayastani Hanrapetutiun*, pp. 239–40, 278–80.

42. Ter Minasian, *Hay heghapokhakani*, vol. 7, pp. 225–36, 271–339, 340–43; Hovannisian, *Republic*, vol. 2, pp. 280–83.

43. Hovannisian, *Republic*, vol. 2, pp. 286–89, 291, 292.

44. Ibid., pp. 294–95.

45. Ibid., pp. 295–97, 301; *Vaveragrer*, Girk G, Doc. 104, pp. 173–74.

46. Payaslian, *United States*, Chs. 10–11, pp. 142–78.

47. President Wilson appointed Henry Churchill King, president of Oberlin College, and Charles R. Crane, an industrialist and a close friend, to head the commission. The King-Crane Commission visited Jaffa, Jerusalem, Beirut, Aleppo, Adana, and Constantinople. Harry N. Howard, *The King-Crane Commission: An American Inquiry in the Middle East* (Beirut: Khayat, 1963), p. 32; Hovannisian, *Republic*, vol. 2, p. 323. James B. Gidney, *A Mandate for Armenia* (Kent: Kent State University Press, 1967), pp. 143–51; On the expectations of the Wilson administration regarding the U.S. role in international relations after the war, see Payaslian, *United States*, Chs. 9–12; William C. Redfield, "America's International Trade as Affected by the European War," *Annals of the American Academy of Political and Social Science* 60 (July 1915): 14–15.

48. H. Khachaturian, "Amerikian zinvorakan arakelutiune depi Hayastan" [The American Military Mission to Armenia], *Hayrenik amsagir*, parts I-II, 19 (Nov.–Dec. 1940): 119–30, 64–80; Payaslian, *United States*, pp. 157–60; 166–67.

49. On Wilson, see Lloyd E. Ambrosius, *Wilsonian Statecraft* (Wilmington, DE: Scholarly Resource Books, 1991); Thomas J. Knock, *To End All Wars* (Princeton, NJ: Princeton University Press, 1992); Arno J. Mayer, *Political Origins of the New Diplomacy, 1917–1918* (New Haven, CT: Yale University Press, 1959). Armenian political organizations in the United States are discussed in Manuk G. Chizmechian, *Patmutiun Amerikahay kaghakakan kusaktsutiants, 1890–1925* [History of American Armenian Political Parties, 1890–1925] (Fresno, CA: Nor Or, 1930).

50. Payaslian, *United States*, pp. 161–70; Hovannisian, *Republic*, vol. 2, pp. 401–2, 431–33.

51. Ruben G. Sahakyan, *Turk-Fransiakan haraberutyunnere ev Kilikian 1919–1921 tt.* [Turkish-French Relations and Cilicia, 1919–1921] (Erevan: Armenian Academy of Sciences, 1970); Paul du Véou, *La passion de la Cilicie, 1919–1922*, rev. ed. (Paris: Librarie Orientaliste, 1954); Robert Farrer Zeidner, "The Tricolor Over the Taurus: The French in Cilicia and Vicinity, 1918–1922," Ph.D. diss., University of Utah, 1991; Edouard Brémond, "The Brémond Mission, Cilicia in 1919–1920," *Armenian Review*, part I, 29 (Winter 1976–1977): 339–72; Brémond, "The Brémond Mission, Cilicia in 1919–1920," *Armenian Review*, part II, 30 (Spring 1977): 34–72; Kinross, *Ataturk*, pp. 202–4.

52. On British policy toward Armenian issues within the context of regional geopolitical considerations, see, for example, Briton Cooper Busch, *Mudros to Lausanne: Britain's Frontier in West Asia, 1918–1923* (Albany, NY: State University of New York Press, 1976); Busch, *Britain, India, and the Arabs, 1914–1921* (Berkeley: University of California Press, 1971). For a historical perspective, see Levon A. Bayramyan, *Arevmetyan Hayastane Angliakan imperializmi plannerum* [Western Armenia in British Imperialist Plans] (Erevan: Hayastan, 1982); and Ram Lakhan Shukla, *Britain, India and the Turkish Empire 1853–1882* (New Delhi: People's Publishing House, 1973).

53. Payaslian, *United States*, pp. 170–71; Hovannisian, *Republic*, vol. 2, pp. 501, 512, 518–19.

54. On the London Conference in general, see Paul C. Helmreich, *From Paris to Sèvres: The Partition of the Ottoman Empire at the Peace Conference of 1919–1920* (Columbus: Ohio State University Press, 1974). On matters pertaining to Armenia, see Avetis Aharonian, *Sardarapatits minchev Sevr ev Lozan* [From Sardarapat to Sèvres and Lausanne] (Boston: Hayrenik, 1943); Richard G. Hovannisian, *The Republic of Armenia*, vol. 3: *From London to Sèvres, February–August 1920* (Berkeley: University of California Press, 1996), pp. 21–27.

55. Hovannisian, *Republic*, vol. 3, pp. 51–66.

56. Payaslian, *United States*, pp. 175–76.

57. Hovannisian, *Republic*, vol. 3, pp. 90–93, 106.

58. Simon Vratsian, "How Armenia Was Sovietized," *Armenian Review* 1:2 (1948): 81; Matossian, *Impact*, p. 27; Hovannisian, *Republic*, vol. 3, p. 210.

59. See Khikar H. Barseghyan, *Hayastani komunistakan partiayi kazmavorume* [The Formation of the Communist Party of Armenia] (Erevan: Hayastan, 1965); Gevorg B. Gharibjanyan, *Hayastani komunistakan kazmakerputyunnere Sovetakan ishkhanutyan haghtanaki mghvats paykarum* [The Communist Organizations in Armenia during the Struggle for the Victory of the Soviet Government] (Erevan: Hayastan, 1955).

60. Karo Sasuni, *Mayisian khrovutiunnere ev Tatarakan apstamb shrjannere* [The May Disturbances and the Rebellious Tatar Districts] (Beirut: Sevan, 1968); Hovhannes S. Karapetyan, *Mayisyan apstambutyune Hayastanum, 1920* [The May Rebellion in Armenia, 1920] (Erevan: Armenian Academy of Sciences, 1961); A.H. Melkonyan, *Mayisyan apstambutyan patmutyan hartsi shurj* [Regarding the Issue of the History of the May Rebellion] (Erevan: Armenian Academy of Sciences, 1965).

61. Grigor A. Hovhannisyan, *Sovetakan ishkhanutyan hastatume Lernayin Gharabaghum* [The Establishment of Soviet Government in Mountainous Karabagh] (Erevan: Erevan State University, 1971), pp. 140–42.

62. Hovannisian, *Republic*, vol. 3, pp. 222–24, 235–47.

63. Ibid., pp. 279, 284–85.

64. Ibid., pp. 290–324 passim.

65. Payaslian, *United States*, pp. 179–80.

66. Richard G. Hovannisian, *The Republic of Armenia*, vol. 4: *Between Crescent and Sickle: Partition and Sovietization* (Berkeley: University of California Press, 1996), p. 33.

67. Ibid., pp. 40–44 n105; Payaslian, *United States*, pp. 180–82.

68. *Vaveragrer*, Girk G, Doc. 108, pp. 177–78; Hovannisian, *Republic*, vol. 4, pp. 188–96, 267–69. See also Edik A. Zohrapyan, *1920 t. Turk-Haykakan paterazme ev terutyunnere* [The Turkish-Armenian War of 1920 and the Powers] (Erevan: Oskan Erevantsi, 1997); Zohrapyan, *Sovetakan Rusastane ev Hay-Turkakan haraberutyunnere, 1920–1922 tt.* [Soviet Russia and Armenian-Turkish Relations, 1920–1922] (Erevan: Erevan State University, 1979); Saribek Karapetyan, *1920 tvakani Hay-Turkakan paterazme ev Sovetakan Rusastane* [The Armenian-Turkish War of 1920 and Soviet Russia] (Erevan: Hayastan, 1965).

69. Artashes Badalian, "Karsi ankume" [The Fall of Kars], *Hayrenik amsagir* 1 (Oct. 1923): 52–68; Dikran Baghdasarian (Tigran Paghtasarian), "Hayastani Hanrapetutian verjaluysin" [At the Twilight of the Republic of Armenia], in *Ejer mer azatagrakan patmutenen* [Pages from Our National Liberation Movement] (Paris: Union of Armenian Volunteers and Soldiers, 1937), pp. 193–280.

70. Vratsian, *Hayastani Hanrapetutiun*, pp. 428–31; Karo Sasuni, *Hay-Trkakan paterazme 1920-in* [The Armenian-Turkish War in 1920] (Beirut: Hamazkayin, 1969), pp. 100–17; Hovannisian, *Republic*, vol. 4, pp. 249–58, 270–71, 291.

71. *Vaveragrer*, Girk G, Doc. 112, pp. 180–81.

72. Khatisian, *Hayastani Hanrapetutian*, pp. 252–57, 260–69; Vratsian, *Hayastani Hanrapetutiun*, pp. 510–20.

73. See the text in Hovannisian, *Republic*, vol. 4, p. 364.

74. Ibid., pp. 368, 370–71.

75. H.M. Elchipekyan, "Sovetakan ishkhanutyan hastatume Hayastanum" [The Establishment of the Soviet Government in Armenia], in *Hay zhoghovrdi patmutyun*, ed. Ts.P. Aghayan et al. (Erevan: Armenian Academy of Sciences, 1967), vol. 7, pp. 116–21.

76. Hovannisian, *Republic*, vol. 4, pp. 369, 379, 385–87; Matossian, *Impact*, p. 28.

77. Ronald Grigor Suny, "Soviet Armenia," in *The Armenian People from Ancient to Modern Times*, vol. 2: *Foreign Dominion to Statehood: The Fifteenth Century to the Twentieth Century*, ed. Richard G. Hovannisian (New York: St. Martin's Press, 1997), pp. 348–50; H. Marmandian, "The Exile of the Armenian Army Officers," *Armenian Review* 11 (Spring 1958): 102–15. In early 1922 famine and death continued unabated; about 200,000 people were reported starving, and in some regions, such as Dilijan, nearly 100 died each day. Matossian, *Impact*, p. 53.

78. Karo Sasuni, *Petrvarian apstambutiune, 1921* [The February Rebellion, 1921] (Beirut: Hamazkayin, 1970); Ervand Hayrapetian, "The February 18, 1921 Armenian Revolt," *Armenian Review*, part II, 10 (Summer 1957): 101–20; parts IV-VI, 11 (Spring-Autumn 1958): 143–52, 153–60, 151–56; Matossian, *Impact*, pp. 29–30.

79. Bakhshi Ishkhanian, *Erku amis bolshevikyan bantum* [Two Months in Bolshevik Prison] (Cairo: Husaber, 1924).

80. Suny, "Soviet Armenia," p. 351.

81. Hovannisian, *Republic*, vol. 4, pp. 405–6; Matossian, *Impact*, p. 30.

8 THE LENINIST-STALINIST LEGACY: SEVENTY YEARS OF SOVIET RULE

1. Ronald Grigor Suny, "Soviet Armenia," in Richard G. Hovannisian, ed., *The Armenian People from Ancient to Modern Times*, vol. 2: *Foreign Dominion to Statehood* (New York: St. Martin's Press, 1997), pp. 348, 353; Mary K. Matossian, *The Impact of Soviet Policies in Armenia* (Leiden: E.J. Brill, 1962), Ch. 2, passim.
2. Matossian, *Impact*, p. 53; Suny, "Soviet Armenia," pp. 351–52.
3. Matossian, *Impact*, p. 55.
4. Adam B. Ulam, *Stalin: The Man and His Era* (New York: Viking Press, 1973), pp. 204–5; on Ordjonikidze as "satrap of the Caucasus," see 214, 220–21; Bertram D. Wolfe, *Three Who Made a Revolution*, rev. ed. (New York: Dell, 1964), p. 436; Richard Pipes, *The Formation of the Soviet Union* (Cambridge, MA: Harvard University Press, 1997 [1954]), pp. 221–25.
5. Matossian, *Impact*, pp. 37–39. Suny, "Soviet Armenia," p. 353.
6. Richard G. Hovannisian, *The Republic of Armenia*, vol. 4: *Between Crescent and Sickle: Partition and Sovietization* (Berkeley: University of California Press, 1996), p. 391.
7. Matossian, *Impact*, pp. 39–40.
8. Ibid., pp. 37–42, 78–95; Suny, "Soviet Armenia," pp. 351, 355.
9. Hayastani Hanrapetutyun, Arvesti, Grakanutyan ev Mamuli Pastatghteri Petakan Kentronakan Arkhiv [Republic of Armenia, State Central Archives of Art, Literature, and Media], *Vaveragrer Hay ekeghetsu patmutyan*, Girk G: *Artak Episkopos Smbatyants: Hogevor, grakan, patma-banakan gortsuneutyune ev gndakaharutyune (1876–1937 tt.)* [Documents of the History of the Armenian Church, Book 3: Bishop Artak Smbatyants: His Spiritual, Literary, Historical-Philological Works and Execution (1867–1937)], comp. Sandro Behbudyan (Erevan: Anahit, 1999), Docs. 123, 124, pp. 195–96, 197–98.
10. Matossian, *Impact*, pp. 55–57, 58.
11. Ibid., p. 57; Astghik Mirzakhanyan, "Economic and Social Development," in *The Armenians: Past and Present in the Making of National Identity*, ed. Edmund Herzig and Marina Kurkchiyan (London: Routledge, 2005), p. 197.
12. Suny, "Soviet Armenia," p. 353; Levon Chorbajian, Patrick Donabedian, and Claude Mutafian, *The Caucasian Knot: The History and Geopolitics of Nagorno-Karabagh* (London: Zed Books, 1994), p. 136.
13. Chorbajian, *Caucasian Knot*, p. 136.
14. Ibid., p. 138.
15. Suny, "Soviet Armenia," pp. 356–57.
16. Suny, "Soviet Armenia," pp. 358–59.
17. Mirzakhanyan, "Economic," p. 198; Suny, "Soviet Armenia," p. 359.
18. Mirzakhanyan, "Economic," p. 198.
19. Suny, "Soviet Armenia," p. 362.
20. Ibid., p. 364; Matossian, *Impact*, p. 173.
21. Suny, "Soviet Armenia," pp. 364–65.
22. *Vaveragrer*, Girk G, Docs. 127, 141, pp. 201–7, 235–39.
23. Ibid., Docs. 135, 136, pp. 217–18, 218–20.
24. S. Surgunyan, "Lrtesutyan orje" [The Den of Espionage], *Proletar* (Tiflis), June 11, 1938, p. 2, in *Vaveragrer Hay ekeghetsu patmutyan (1938–1955)*, Girk Z: *Gevorg Z*

Chorekchyan, Katoghikos Amenayn Hayots [Documents of the History of the Armenian Church (1938–1955), Book 6: Gevorg VI Chorekchyan, Catholicos of All Armenians], ed. and comp. Santro Behbudyan (Erevan: Oskan Erevantsi, 1999), Doc. 4, pp. 13–16.

25. Matossian, *Impact*, p. 149.
26. Ibid., pp. 149–50, 161; Vahe Sarafian, "The Soviet and the Armenian Church," *Armenian Review* 8:2 (1955): 97.
27. *Vaveragrer*, Girk G., Docs. 120, 121, 123, 125, 378, pp. 191–94, 195–96, 199–200, 436–37, 614.
28. Ibid., pp. 617–30.
29. Ibid., pp. 631–32.
30. Suny, "Soviet Armenia," pp. 365–67.
31. Matossian, *Impact*, pp. 194–95.
32. Suny, "Soviet Armenia," p. 368.
33. Chorbajian, *Caucasian Knot*, p. 145.
34. Matossian, *Impact*, p. 166.
35. Suny, "Soviet Armenia," p. 367.
36. Mirzakhanyan, "Economic," p. 198.
37. Suny, "Soviet Armenia," p. 371.
38. Hedrick Smith, *The New Russians* (New York: Random House, 1990), pp. 8–9, 14–15.
39. Richard F. Staar, *Communist Regimes in Eastern Europe*, 4th ed. (Stanford, CA: Hoover Institution Press, 1982), p. 137; Michael G. Roskin, *The Rebirth of East Europe*, 2nd ed. (Englewood Cliffs, NJ: Prentice-Hall, 1994), p. 101.
40. Buzant Eghiayan, *Zhamanakakits patmutiun Katoghikosutian Hayots Kilikio, 1914–1972* [Contemporary History of the Armenian Catholicosate of Cilicia, 1914–1972] (Antelias: Catholicosate of Cilicia, 1975), pp. 663–83; R. Hrair Dekmejian, "The Armenian Diaspora," in *The Armenian People from Ancient to Modern Times*, vol. 2: *Foreign Dominion to Statehood*, ed. Richard G. Hovannisian (New York: St. Martin's Press, 1997), p. 418; Matossian, *Impact*, p. 208. See also "The Catholicosate of Cilicia, Her Place and Status in the Armenian Church: Text of an Official Statement of the Catholicosate of Cilicia, Antelias, Lebanon," *Armenian Review* 15:1 (Spring 1962): 11–26.
41. Suny, "Soviet Armenia," pp. 372–73.
42. Ibid., p. 373.
43. Supreme Soviet of Armenia, *Haykakan SSR hingerord gumarman geraguyn Soveti nistere* [The Fifth Conference of the Supreme Soviet of the Armenian S[oviet] S[ocialist] R[epublic], 3rd sess., March 24–25, 1960 (Erevan: Presidium, Supreme Soviet of Armenia, 1960), pp. 6–7.
44. Ibid., pp. 10–32.
45. Ibid., pp. 157–98.
46. Ronald Gregory Suny, "On the Road to Independence: Cultural Cohesion and Ethnic Revival in a Multinational Society," in *Transcaucasia, Nationalism, and Social Change: Essays in the History of Armenia, Azerbaijan, and Georgia*, ed. Ronald Gregory Suny (Ann Arbor: University of Michigan Press, 1996), p. 392.
47. Suny, "Soviet Armenia," pp. 376–77.
48. Chorbajian, *Caucasian Knot*, pp. 145–46.
49. Staar, *Communist Regimes*, pp. 71–72; Roskin, *East Europe*, pp. 118–20.
50. Suny, "On the Road to Independence," p. 379.
51. Chorbajian, *Caucasian Knot*, pp. 146–47.
52. Suny, "Soviet Armenia," p. 377; *Soviet News*, Feb. 13, 1977, p. 44; *New York Times*, Feb. 3, 1980, p. 29.

53. Mirzakhanyan, "Economic," p. 198.
54. Marina Kurkchiyan, "Society in Transition," in Herzig and Kurkchiyan, *Armenians*, pp. 216–17.
55. Simon Payaslian, "Hovannes Shiraz, Paruyr Sevak, and the Memory of the Armenian Genocide," *Journal of the Society for Armenian Studies* (forthcoming).
56. Kurkchiyan, "Society," pp. 216–17.
57. Matossian, *Impact*, pp. 63–64.
58. Quoted in Mark R. Beissinger, *Nationalist Mobilization and the Collapse of the Soviet State* (Cambridge: Cambridge University Press, 2002), p. 57.
59. Mikhail Gorbachev, *Memoirs*, trans. Georges Peronasky and Tatjana Varsavsky (New York: Doubleday, 1996), p. 168.
60. Smith, *New Russians*, pp. 14–15.
61. Simon Payaslian, "From Perestroika to Uncertainty: Will Gorbachev's Experiment Survive Forces Pounding at Kremlin Gates?" *Armenian International Magazine* (July 1990): 42–44 (hereafter *AIM*).
62. Smith, *New Russians*, pp. 326–27.
63. Hakob Asatrian, "The Other Jolt," *AIM* (Dec. 1993): 30–31.
64. See, for example, Marshall I. Goldman, *U.S.S.R. in Crisis: The Failure of an Economic System* (New York: W.W. Norton, 1983); Zbigniew Brzezinski, *The Grand Failure* (New York: Collier Books, 1990).
65. Quoted in Beissinger, *Nationalist Mobilization*, p. 58.
66. Ibid., pp. 58–59.
67. Ibid., pp. 58, 60–61. Italics in the original.
68. Payaslian, "From Perestroika," pp. 42–44.
69. Barbara A. Anderson and Brian D. Silver, "Population Redistribution and the Ethnic Balance in Transcaucasia," in Suny, *Transcaucasia*, p. 503.
70. Chorbajian, *Caucasian Knot*, p. 156.
71. Ibid., p. 149; Suny, "Soviet Armenia," p. 379; Lalig Papazian, "A People's Will: Armenian Irredentism over Nagorno-Karabagh," in Levon Chorbajian, ed., *The Making of Nagorno-Karabagh: From Secession to Republic* (New York: Palgrave Macmillan, 2001), pp. 68–69; Joseph R. Masih and Robert O. Krikorian, *Armenia at the Crossroads* (Amsterdam: Harwood Academic Publishers, 1999), pp. 4–7.
72. Beissinger, *Nationalist Mobilization*, p. 186.
73. Samvel Shahmuratian, comp. and ed. *The Sumgait Tragedy: Pogroms against Armenians in Soviet Azerbaijan*, trans. Steven Jones (New Rochelle, NY: Aristide D. Caratzas; Cambridge, MA: Zoryan Institute, 1990).
74. Smith, *New Russians*, p. 337.
75. Shahmuratian, *Sumgait*, pp. 38, 56, 179–80, 224, 261.
76. Beissinger, *Nationalist Mobilization*, pp. 66–69.
77. Quoted in Brzezinski, *Grand Failure*, p. 90.
78. Gerard J. Libaridian, *Modern Armenia: People, Nation, State* (New Brunswick, NJ: Transaction Publishers, 2004), p. 206.
79. Beissinger, *Nationalist Mobilization*, p. 187.
80. Ibid., pp. 187–88, 390–91.
81. Marina Kurkchiyan, "The Karabagh Conflict: From Soviet Past to post-Soviet Uncertainty," in Herzig and Kurkchiyan, *Armenians*, p. 154.
82. Razmik Panossian, "The Diaspora and the Karabagh Movement: Oppositional Politics between the Armenian Revolutionary Federation and the Armenian National Movement," in Chorbajian, *Making of Nagorno-Karabagh*, p. 159.
83. See the text in Gerard J. Libaridian, ed., *Armenia at the Crossroads* (Watertown, MA: Blue Crane, 1991), Appendix A/1, pp. 127–29.

84. Panossian, "Diaspora and the Karabagh Movement," p. 161.
85. Michael P. Croissant, *Armenian-Azerbaijan Conflict: Causes and Implications* (Westport, CT: Praeger, 1998), p. 33.
86. Chorbajian, *Caucasian Knot*, p. 155.
87. Beissinger, *Nationalist Mobilization*, p. 188.
88. Croissant, *Armenian-Azerbaijan Conflict*, p. 35; Thomas de Waal, *Black Garden: Armenia and Azerbaijan through Peace and War* (New York: New York University Press, 2003), pp. 108–9.
89. Kurkchiyan, "Karabagh," p. 155; Suny, "Soviet Armenia," pp. 381–82; Chorbajian, *Caucasian Knot*, pp. 155–56; Beissinger, *Nationalist Mobilization*, pp. 189–90.
90. Dekmejian, "The Armenian Diaspora," pp. 413–35; Robin Cohen, *Global Diasporas* (Seattle: University of Washington Press, 1997), Figure 2.1, p. 48.
91. Asatrian, "The Other Jolt," 30–31.
92. Suren Deherian, "Unlucky Anniversary: Gumri Marks 13 Years as a Disaster Zone," *AIM* (Jan.–Feb. 2002): 45.
93. For a brief background, see Betsy Gidwitz, "Labor Unrest in the Soviet Union," *Problems of Communism* (Nov.–Dec. 1982): 33–34; see also Stephen Crowley, *Hot Coal, Cold Steel: Russian and Ukrainian Workers from the End of the Soviet Union to the Post-Communist Transformations* (Ann Arbor, MI: University of Michigan Press, 1997), pp. 25–45; Peter Rutland, "Labor Unrest and Movements in 1989 and 1990," *Soviet Economy* 6:3 (1990): 354.
94. Payaslian, "From Perestroika," pp. 42–44.
95. Ibid.
96. Ibid.
97. Beissinger, *Nationalist Mobilization*, p. 392.
98. Payaslian, "From Perestroika," pp. 42–44; Anatol Lieven, *The Baltic Revolution: Estonia, Latvia, Lithuania and the Path to Independence* (New Haven, CT: Yale University Press, 1993); Rein Taagepera, *Estonia: Return to Independence* (Boulder, CO: Westview Press, 1993); Rasma Karklins, *Ethnopolitics and Transition to Democracy: The Collapse of the USSR and Latvia* (Washington, DC: Woodrow Wilson Center Press, 1994).
99. See Vera Tolz, *The USSR in 1990: A Record of Events* (Boulder, CO: Westview Press, 1992), pp. 807–8.
100. Beissinger, *Nationalist Mobilization*, p. 405.
101. Masih and Krikorian, *Armenia*, pp. 11–12; Libaridian, *Modern Armenia*, pp. 207–8.
102. Beissinger, *Nationalist Mobilization*, p. 404.
103. Helsinki Watch, *Bloodshed in the Caucasus*, p. 8.
104. Payaslian, "From Perestroika," pp. 42–44.
105. Libaridian, *Modern Armenia*, p. 208. Suny, "Soviet Armenia," pp. 383, 385–86.
106. *Rossiiskaia gazeta*, Dec. 12, 1991, p. 1, cited in Beissinger, *Nationalist Mobilization*, p. 386.

9 INDEPENDENCE AND DEMOCRACY: THE SECOND REPUBLIC

1. Robert Mirak, "The Armenians in America," in *The Armenian People from Ancient to Modern Times*, vol. 2: *Foreign Dominion to Statehood*, ed. Richard G. Hovannisian (New York: St. Martin's Press, 1997), p. 403; Gerard J. Libaridian,

The Challenge of Statehood: Armenian Political Thinking since Independence (Watertown, MA: Blue Crane, 1999), p. ix.

2. *Armenian International Magazine* (Jan. 1996): 14 (hereafter *AIM*); Tony Halpin, "Up the Down Escalator," *AIM* (Oct. 1992): 14–15, 20; Astghik Mirzakhanyan, "Economic and Social Development," in *The Armenians: Past and Present in the Making of National Identity*, ed. Edmund Herzig and Marina Kurkchiyan (London: Routledge, 2005), pp. 201–3, 207.

3. *AIM* (Jan. 1996): 14; Mirzakhanyan, "Economic," pp. 201–3; Halpin, "Up the Down Escalator," p. 20; Nancy L. Najarian, "A Fair Shake," interview with Pavel Khaltakchian, *AIM* (Oct. 1992): 20–21.

4. Hakob Asatrian, "The Other Jolt," *AIM* (Dec. 1993): 30–31.

5. Ken Curtin, "Vanishing Points," *AIM* (Oct. 1993): 22.

6. Mirzakhanyan, "Economic," p. 208.

7. *AIM* (Dec. 1993): 20–21.

8. Interview by Salpi Haroutinian Ghazarian, *AIM* (Mar. 1994): 32–35.

9. *AIM* (Nov.–Dec. 1996): 17; Republic of Armenia, National Statistical Services, Economic and Financial Data, *Statistical Yearbook 2001* (Erevan: National Statistical Services, 2001); Mirzakhanyan, "Economic," p. 204.

10. Rachel Denber and Robert Goldman, *Bloodshed in the Caucasus* (New York: Helsinki Watch, 1992), p. 12; Halpin, "Up the Down Escalator," p. 19.

11. See, for example, Stockholm International Peace Research Institute, Military Expenditure Database, 1988–2006, SIPRI online, at sipri.org.

12. United Nations, Security Council, S/RES/822, 3205th meeting, Apr. 30, 1993; S/RES/853, 3259th meeting, July 29, 1993; S/RES/874, 3292nd meeting, Oct. 14, 1993; S/RES/884, 3313th meeting, Nov. 12, 1993.

13. Marina Kurkchiyan, "The Karabagh Conflict: From Soviet Past to post-Soviet Uncertainty," in Herzig and Kurkchiyan, *Armenians*, p. 158.

14. The Conference on Security and Co-operation in Europe (CSCE) was renamed as the Organization for Security and Co-operation in Europe (OSCE) in December 1994. The Minsk Group is comprised of nine countries in addition to Armenia and Azerbaijan.

15. Kurkchiyan, "Karabagh," pp. 158–59.

16. Graine Zeitlian, "The Shifting Ensemble," *AIM* (Mar. 1994): 28–29.

17. *OMRI Daily Digest*, no. 55, Mar. 18, 1996; *AIM* (Mar. 1996): 14–15.

18. For the politics of MGM's refusal to produce the film, see Vahram Leon Shemmassian, "The Armenian Villagers of Musa Dagh: A Historical-Ethnographic Study, 1840–1915," Ph.D. diss., University of California, Los Angeles, 1996, pp. 249–61.

19. Graham E. Fuller, "Turkey's New Eastern Orientation," in *Turkey's New Geopolitics: From the Balkans to Western China*, ed. Graham E. Fuller and Ian O. Lesser (Boulder, CO: Westview Press, 1993), pp. 76–80; Libaridian, *Challenge*, pp. 81–84, 87–90.

20. The BSEC founding members are Albania, Armenia, Azerbaijan, Bulgaria, Georgia, Greece, Moldova, Romania, Russia, Turkey, and Ukraine.

21. Simon Payaslian, "Ozal's Last Stand," *AIM* (April/May 1993); *Azg* (Sept. 14, 1993).

22. Fuller, "Turkey's New Eastern Orientation," p. 78.

23. Kurkchiyan, "Karabagh," p. 159.

24. International Monetary Fund, *Direction of Trade Statistics Yearbook* (Washington, DC: International Monetary Fund, 1997).

25. See *Noyan Tapan*, 1994–96, various issues. See also Jalil Rawshandil and Rafik Qulipur, *Siasat va Hokumat dar Armenistan* [Politics and Government in Armenia] (Tehran: Muassasah-i Chap va Intisharat-i Vizarat-i Umur-i Khariji, 1373 [1994/5]).

26. Quoted in Salpi Haroutinian Ghazarian, "He Came, He Saw, He Conquered," *AIM* (Feb. 1996): 23.

27. *AIM* (Apr. 1999): 45.

28. David D. Laitin and Ronald Grigor Suny, "Armenia and Azerbaijan: Thinking a Way Out of Karabakh," *Middle East Policy* 7:1 (Oct. 1999): 165–66; Ronald Grigor Suny, "The Fall of a President," *AIM* (Feb. 1998): 13–14.

29. Tony Halpin, "The End of an Era," *AIM* (Feb. 1998): 15–18.

30. Razmik Panossian, "Homeland-Diaspora Relations and Identity Differences," in Herzig and Kurkchiyan, *Armenians*, p. 238; Gerard Libaridian, interview, *AIM* (Apr. 1999): 46; Halpin, "End of an Era."

31. Carl J. Friedrich, "Political Leadership and the Problem of Charismatic Power," *Journal of Politics* 23 (1961): 14.

32. Max Weber, "The Sociology of Charismatic Leadership," in *From Max Weber: Essays in Sociology*, trans. and ed. H.H. Gerth and C. Wright Mills (New York: Oxford University Press, 1946), pp. 246–47; Max Weber, *On Charisma and Institution Building* (Chicago: University of Chicago Press, 1968).

33. Samuel P. Huntington, *Political Order in Changing Societies* (New Haven, CT: Yale University Press, 1968); R.H. Jackson and C.E. Rosberg, "Personal Rule: Theory and Practice in Africa," *Comparative Politics* 16:4 (July 1984): 421–42; Taketsugu Tsurutani, *The Politics of National Development* (New York: Abeland-Schuman, 1973).

34. Gerard Libaridian, interview, *AIM* (Apr. 1999): 46.

35. Huntington, *Political Order*, p. 410.

36. A.H. Alexandrian, "Armenia's New Parliament," *AIM* (June 1999): 24–25.

37. Jivan Tabibian, "Building Institutions," *AIM* (June 1999): 29.

38. Alexandrian, "Armenia's New Parliament," pp. 24–25.

39. Mary K. Matossian, *The Impact of Soviet Policies in Armenia* (Leiden: E.J. Brill, 1962), pp. 3, 11; Nora Dudwick, "Out of the Kitchen into the Crossfire: Women in Independent Armenia," in *Post-Soviet Women: From the Baltic to Central Asia*, ed. Mary Buckley (Cambridge: Cambridge University Press, 1997), pp. 235–48; Larissa Lissyutkina, "Soviet Women at the Crossroads of Perestroika," in *Gender Politics and Post-Communism*, ed. Nanette Funk and Magda Mueller (New York: Routledge, 1993), pp. 274–86.

40. Valentine Moghadam, "Gender Dynamics of Economics and Political Change: Efficiency, Equality, and Women," in *Democratic Reform and the Position of Women in Transitional Economies*, ed. Valentine M. Moghadam (Oxford: Clarendon Press, 1993).

41. International Women's Rights Action Watch (IWRAW), *Country Report: Armenia*, submitted to the Committee on the Elimination of Discrimination Against Women (CEDAW), (Minneapolis, MN: International Women's Rights Action Watch, 1997), p. 3.

42. Republic of Armenia, Ministry of Statistics, *Women and Men in Armenia* (Erevan: Ministry of Statistics, 1999), pp. 48–49.

43. Dudwick, "Out of the Kitchen," p. 245.

44. Sergey Vaganovich Arakelyan, "Ubistva v sfere semeino-bitovikh otnoshenii i ikh preduprezhdeniye" [Murder in the Sphere of Domestic Relations and Its Prevention], Ph.D. diss. (Erevan: Erevan State University, 1999), sections 1.1., 1.2,

as cited in Minnesota Advocates for Human Rights, *Domestic Violence in Armenia* (Minneapolis, MN: Minnesota Advocates for Human Rights, Dec. 2000), at www.mnadvocates.org.

45. Minnesota Advocates for Human Rights, *Domestic Violence in Armenia*, p. 3.
46. Laurence Ritter, "Under Pressure," *AIM* (Mar. 2002): 29–35.
47. Marina Kurkchiyan, "Society in Transition," in Herzig and Kurkchiyan, *Armenians*, p. 227.
48. Republic of Armenia, National Statistical Services, Economic and Financial Data, *Statistical Yearbook 2005* (Erevan: National Statistical Services, 2006); Freedom House, *Nations in Transition 2005* (New York: Freedom House, 2006); Mirzakhanyan, "Economic," pp. 204–5, 208–9; Kurkchiyan, "Society in Transition," p. 211.
49. *AIM* (July 1999): 24.
50. Transparency International, *Corruption Perceptions Index (CPI)* (Berlin: Transparency International, 1999, 2005); www.transparency.org.
51. Council of Europe, Groupe d'etats contre la corruption (GRECO), *Evaluation Report on Armenia*, 27th Plenary Meeting, Strasbourg, Mar. 6–10, 2006.
52. Central Intelligence Agency, *The World Factbook* (2007), www.cia.gov/library/publications.
53. Mirzakhanyan, "Economic," p. 210.
54. World Bank, *World Development Indicators* (Washington, DC: World Bank, 2007); United Nations, Human Development Program, *Human Development Report, 2006* (New York: United Nations, 2007).
55. Mirzakhanyan, "Economic," pp. 204–5.
56. Ibid., p. 208; Kurkchiyan, "Society in Transition," pp. 217–19, 220–21; SIPRI, Military Expenditures Database, 1988–2006.
57. Matthew Karanian, "Epicenter Spitak," *AIM* (Jan. 1999): 22.
58. Mirzakhanyan, "Economic," p. 209.
59. *AIM* (Jan.–Feb. 2002): 12.
60. Suren Deherian, "Unlucky Anniversary: Gumri Marks 13 Years as a Disaster Zone," *AIM* (Jan.–Feb. 2002): 43–47.
61. Marianna Grigorian, "Homes Too Long: 13 Years of Temporary Living," and Nara Markossian, "A Stressful Inheritance," *AIM* (Jan.–Feb. 2002): 48, 51.
62. Kurkchiyan, "Society in Transition," p. 211.
63. "Armenia Supplying Prostitutes to International Markets," Arminfo, Dec. 1, 2004. Hedq (online).
64. *AIM* (Feb. 1996): 14. See also *Noyan Tapan*, Feb. 18, 2000, where it is estimated that about 600,000 people emigrated from Armenia during the decade. ANN/Groong (online).
65. Quoted in Tony Halpin, "What Now?" *AIM* (Nov. 1999): 26–31.
66. Ibid.
67. Ibid.
68. Republic of Armenia, Central Electoral Commission, Parliamentary Elections, May 25, June 14, 15, 29, July 30, 2003, and Presidential Elections, Feb. 19, Mar. 5, 2003 (www.elections.am).
69. *AIM* (May 1999): 24–26; Badalyan died of a heart attack in November 1999 during his visit in Moscow. *AIM* (Dec. 1999): 19.
70. Hratch Tchilingirian, "The Istanbul Summit," *AIM* (Dec. 1999): 24–25.
71. Tony Halpin, "Geography of Friendship," *AIM* (Mar. 1999): 40–41.
72. Hooman Peimani, "Iran Fights to Loosen America's Noose," *Asia Times*, May 1, 2003, online, www.atimes.com/atimes/Middle_East.

73. Hayastan All-Armenian Fund, www.himnadram.org, accessed Oct. 22, 2006.
74. See, for example, Armenian National Institute, www.armenian-genocide.org.
75. Tony Halpin, "History's Reckoning," *AIM* (Apr. 2002): 28.
76. David L. Phillips, *Unsilencing the Past: Track Two Diplomacy and Turkish-Armenian Reconciliation* (New York: Berghahn Books, 2005); Simon Payaslian, "Anatomy of Post-Genocide Reconciliation," in *The Armenian Genocide: Cultural and Ethical Legacies*, ed. Richard G. Hovannisian (New Brunswick, NJ: Transaction, forthcoming).

Selected Bibliography

BOOKS

Adonts, Nicholas. *Armenia in the Period of Justinian: The Political Conditions Based on the Nakharar System*, trans. Nina Garsoian. Lisbon: Calouste Gulbenkian Foundation, 1970.

Adonts, Nikoghayos. *Patmakan usumnasirutyunner* [Historical Studies]. Paris: Ghukasian, 1948.

Aghayan, Ts.P. et al., eds. *Hay zhoghovrdi patmutyun* [History of the Armenian People]. 8 vols. Erevan: Armenian Academy of Sciences, 1967–84.

Aharonian, Avetis. *Sardarapatits minchev Sevr ev Lozan* [From Sardarabad to Sèvres and Lausanne]. Boston: Hayrenik, 1943.

Aharonian, Gersam, ed. and comp. *Hushamatian Mets Egherni, 1915–1965* [Memorial Volume of the Colossal Crime, 1915–1965]. Beirut: Atlas, 1965.

Ahmad, Feroz. *The Young Turks: The Committee of Union and Progress in Turkish Politics, 1908–1914*. Oxford: Clarendon Press, 1969.

Ahrweiler, Hélène, and Angeliki E. Laiou, ed. *Studies on the Internal Diaspora of the Byzantine Empire*. Washington, DC: Dumbarton Oaks, 1998.

Akçam, Taner. *A Shameful Act: The Armenian Genocide and the Question of Turkish Responsibility*. New York: Metropolitan Books, 2006.

Akuni, Sebuh. *Milion me Hayeru jardi patmutiune* [The Story of the Massacre of a Million Armenians]. Constantinople: Hayastan, 1921.

Allen, W.E.D., and Paul Muratoff. *Caucasian Battlefields: A History of the Wars on the Turco-Caucasian Border, 1828–1921*. Cambridge: Cambridge University Press, 1953.

Ambrosius, Lloyd E. *Wilsonian Statecraft: Theory and Practice of Liberal Internationalism during World War I*. Wilmington, DE: Scholarly Resource Books, 1991.

Anderson, M.S. *The Eastern Question, 1774–1923: A Study in International Relations*. London: Macmillan, 1966.

Antonian, Aram. *Mets vochire* [The Colossal Crime]. Boston: Bahak, 1921; repr. Erevan: Arevik, 1990.

Arakelyan, Babken. *Hayastani kaghaknere xi-xiii darerum* [The Cities of Armenia during the Eleventh-Thirteenth Centuries]. Erevan: Armenian Academy of Sciences, 1956.

Armen, Hrant K. *Marzpane ev sparapete* [The Governor and the Commander]. Los Angeles: Horizon, 1952.

Artsruni, Tovma. *Patmutiun tann Artsruniats,* ed. Kerobe Patkanian. St. Petersburg, 1887; repr. Delmar, NY: Caravan Books, 1991. Trans. Robert W. Thomson. *The History of the House of Artsrunik.* Detroit: Wayne State University Press, 1985.

Arutyunyan, N.V. *Biainili (Urartu).* Erevan: Armenian Academy of Sciences, 1970.

Ascher, Abraham. *The Revolution of 1905: Russia in Disarray.* Stanford: Stanford University Press, 1988.

Ayalon, David, ed. *Studies on the Mamluks of Egypt (1250–1517).* London: Variorum Reprints, 1977.

Babalyan, A. *Ejer Hayastani ankakhutyan patmutyunits* [Pages from the History of Armenian Independence]. Cairo: Husaber, 1959.

Balard, Michel, ed. *Autour de la première croisade.* Paris: Publications de la Sorbonne, 1996.

Barby, Henry. *Au pays de l'épouvante: L'Arménie martyre.* Beirut: Hamazkayin, 1973; first published 1917.

Barseghyan, Khikar H. *Hayastani komunistakan partiayi kazmavorume* [The Formation of the Communist Party of Armenia]. Erevan: Hayastan, 1965.

Bayramyan, Levon A. *Arevmtyan Hayastane angliakan imperializmi blannerum* [Western Armenia in English Imperialist Plans]. Erevan: Hayastan, 1982.

Bedrosian, Robert. *Armenia in Ancient and Medieval Times.* New York: Armenian National Education Committee, 1985.

Behbudyan, Sandro, comp. *Vaveragrer Hay ekeghetsu patmutyan,* Girk G: *Artak Episkopos Smbatyants: Hogevor, grakan, patma-banakan gortsuneutyune ev gndakaharutyune, 1876–1937 tt.)* [Documents of the History of the Armenian Church, Book 3: Bishop Artak Smbatyants: His Spiritual, Literary, Historical-Philological Works and Execution (1867–1937)]. Erevan: Anahit, 1999.

Behbudyan, Sandro, ed. and comp. *Vaveragrer Hay ekeghetsu patmutyan (1938–1955),* Girk Z: *Gevorg VI Chorekchyan, Katoghigos Amenayn Hayots* [Documents of the History of the Armenian Church (1938–1955), Book 6: Gevorg VI Chorekchyan, Catholicos of All Armenians]. Erevan: Oskan Erevantsi, 1999.

Beissinger, Mark R. *Nationalist Mobilization and the Collapse of the Soviet State.* Cambridge: Cambridge University Press, 2002.

Beylerian, Arthur, ed. and comp. *Les grandes puissances l'empire ottoman et les arméniens dans les archives françaises (1914–1918).* Paris: Université de Paris I, Panthéon-Sorbonne, 1983.

Blockley, R.C. *East Roman Foreign Policy.* Leeds: Francis Cairns, 1992.

Boase, T.S.R., ed. *The Cilician Kingdom of Armenia.* Edinburgh: Scottish Academic Press, 1978.

Bornazyan, Sargis V. *Hayastane ev selchuknere, xi-xii tt.* [Armenia and the Seljuks, 11th-12th Centuries]. Erevan: Armenian Academy of Sciences, 1980.

Bournoutian, George A. *A History of Qarabagh.* Costa Mesa, CA: Mazda, 1994.

Boyajian, Dikran (Tigran Poyajian). *Haykakan legione* [The Armenian Legion]. Watertown, MA: Baikar, 1965.

Bozoyan, Azat. *Byuzandiayi arevelyan kaghakakanutyune ev Kilikian Hayastane* [The Eastern Policy of Byzantium and Cilician Armenia]. Erevan: Armenian Academy of Sciences, 1988.

Brémond, Edouard. *La Cilicie en 1919–1920*. Paris: Imprimerie nationale, 1921.

Browning, Robert. *The Byzantine Empire*. Rev. ed. Washington, DC: Catholic University of America Press, 1992.

Brzezinski, Zbigniew. *The Grand Failure*. New York: Collier Books, 1990.

Buckley, Mary, ed. *Post-Soviet Women: From the Baltic to Central Asia*. Cambridge: Cambridge University Press, 1997.

Bunyan, James, and H.H. Fisher. *The Bolshevik Revolution, 1917–1918: Documents and Materials*. Stanford, CA: Stanford University Press, 1934.

Burn, Andrew Robert. *Persia and the Greeks: The Defense of the West, c. 546–478 B.C.* London: E. Arnold, 1962, repr. 1970.

Burney, Charles, and David Marshall Lang. *The Peoples of the Hills: Ancient Ararat and Caucasus*. London: Weidenfeld and Nicolson, 1971; repr. London: Phoenix Press, 2001.

Busch, Briton Cooper. *Britain, India, and the Arabs, 1914–1921*. Berkeley: University of California Press, 1971.

Busch, Briton Cooper. *Mudros to Lausanne: Britain's Frontier in West Asia, 1918–1923*. Albany: State University of New York Press, 1976.

Buzandatsi, Pavstos. *Patmutiun Hayots*. Trans. Nina G. Garsoian. *The Epic Histories (Buzanadaran Patmutiunk)*. Cambridge, MA: Harvard University Press, 1989.

Cahen, Claude. *La Syrie du Nord à l'époque des Croisades*. Paris: Paul Geuthner, 1940.

Cameron, Averil. *Christianity and the Rhetoric of Empire*. Berkeley: University of California Press, 1991.

Chareg, Ghazar. *Karinapatum: Hushamatian Bartsr Hayki* [Karin: Memorial Volume of Bardzr Hayk]. Beirut: Karin Compatriotic Union of the United States and Lebanon, 1957.

Chorbajian, Levon, ed. *The Making of Nagorno-Karabagh: From Secession to Republic*. New York: Palgrave Macmillan, 2001.

Chorbajian, Levon, Patrick Donabedian, and Claude Mutafian. *The Caucasian Knot: The History and Geopolitics of Nagorno-Karabagh*. London: Zed Books, 1994.

Chormisian, Levon. *Hamapatker arevmtahay mek daru patmutian* [A Panorama of One Century of Western Armenian History], vol. 3. Beirut: Sevan, 1975.

Collins, Robert. *The Medes and Persians, Conquerors and Diplomats*. London: Cassell, 1974.

Council of Europe. Groupe d'etats contre la corruption (GRECO). *Evaluation Report on Armenia*. 27th Plenary Meeting. Strasbourg, March 6–10, 2006.

Croissant, Michael P. *Armenian-Azerbaijan Conflict: Causes and Implications*. Westport, CT: Praeger, 1998.

Crowley, Stephen. *Hot Coal, Cold Steel: Russian and Ukrainian Workers from the End of the Soviet Union to the Post-Communist Transformations*. Ann Arbor: University of Michigan Press, 1997.

Dadoyan, Seta B. *The Fatimid Armenians: Cultural and Political Interaction in the Near East*. Leiden: Brill, 1997.

Dadrian, Vahakn N. *The History of the Armenian Genocide: Ethnic Conflict from the Balkans to Anatolia to the Caucasus*. Providence, RI: Berghahn Books, 1995.

Dadrian, Vahakn N. *German Responsibility in the Armenian Genocide: A Review of the Historical Evidence of German Complicity*. Watertown, MA: Blue Crane Books, 1996.

Debevoise, Neilson C. *A Political History of Parthia*. Chicago: University of Chicago Press, 1938.

Der Yeghiayan, Zaven. *My Patriarchal Memoirs.* Trans. from the Armenian by Ared Misirliyan, annotated by Vatche Ghazarian. Barrington, RI: Mayreni Publishing, 2002.

Diakonoff, Igor M. *Pre-History of the Armenian People.* Trans. Lori Jennings. Delmar, NY: Caravan Books, 1984.

Dillon, E.J. *The Inside Story of the Peace Conference.* New York: Harper, 1920.

Dio, Cassius. *Dio's Roman History.* Ed. and trans. Earnest Cary. 9 vols. Cambridge, MA: Harvard University Press, Loeb Classical Library, 1970–87.

Djemal Pasha. *Memories of a Turkish Statesman, 1913–1919.* New York: George H. Doran, 1922.

Drasxanakertci, Yovhannēs (Hovhannes Draskhanakerttsi). *History of Armenia.* Trans. and comm. Krikor H. Maksoudian. Atlanta, GA: Scholars Press, 1987.

Edwards, Robert W. *The Fortifications of Armenian Cilicia.* Washington, DC: Dumbarton Oaks, 1987.

Eghiayan, Buzand. *Zhamanakakits patmutiun katoghikosutian Hayots Kilikio, 1914–1972* [Contemporary History of the Catholicosate of Cilician Armenians, 1914–1972]. Antelias: Catholicosate of Cilicia, 1975.

Einstein, Lewis. *A Diplomat Looks Back.* New Haven: Yale University Press, 1968.

Etmekjian, James. *The French Influence on the Western Armenian Renaissance, 1843–1915.* New York: Twayne, 1964.

Evans, Laurence. *United States Policy and the Partition of Turkey, 1914–1924.* Baltimore: Johns Hopkins Press, 1965.

Fainsod, Merle. *How Russia Is Ruled.* Cambridge, MA: Harvard University Press, 1953.

Ferguson, Niall. *The Pity of War.* New York: Basic Books, 1999.

Freedom House. *Nations in Transition 2005.* New York: Freedom House, 2006.

Funk, Nanette, and Magda Mueller. *Gender Politics and Post-Communism.* New York: Routledge, 1993.

Galustian, Grigor H., comp. and ed. *Marash kam Germanik ev heros Zeitun* [Marash or Germanica and Heroic Zeitun]. 2nd ed. New York: Compatriotic Union of Marash, 1934; Long Island City, NY: Union of Marash Armenians, 1988.

Garsoian, Nina G. *The Paulician Heresy.* The Hague: Mouton, 1967.

Gharibchanyan, Gevorg B. *Hayastani kominastakan kazmakerputyunnere Sovetakan ishkhanutyan haghtanaki mghvats paykarum* [The Communist Organizations in Armenia during the Struggle for the Victory of Soviet Government]. Erevan: Hayastan, 1955.

Ghazarian, Haigazn G. *Tseghaspan Turke* [The Genocidal Turk]. Beirut: Hamazkayin, 1968.

Gidney, James B. *A Mandate for Armenia.* Kent, OH: Kent State University Press, 1967.

Göçek, Fatma Müge. *Rise of the Bourgeoisie, Demise of Empire: Ottoman Westernization and Social Change.* New York: Oxford University Press, 1996.

Goldman, Marshall I. *U.S.S.R. in Crisis: The Failure of an Economic System.* New York: W.W. Norton, 1983.

Gorbachev, Mikhail. *Memoirs.* Trans. Georges Peronasky and Tatjana Varsavsky. New York: Doubleday, 1996.

Grabill, Joseph L. *Protestant Diplomacy and the Near East: Missionary Influence on American Policy, 1810–1927.* Minneapolis: University of Minnesota Press, 1971.

Great Britain. *British Documents on the Origins of the War, 1898–1914,* vol. 10: *The Near and Middle East on the Eve of War.* G.P. Gooch and Harold Temperely, eds. London: H.M.S.O., 1928–1936.

Great Britain. Parliament. *The Treatment of Armenians in the Ottoman Empire, 1915–1916.* Documents Presented to Viscount Grey of Fallodon, Secretary of State for Foreign Affairs. Arnold Toynbee, ed. and comp. 3rd ed. Beirut: G. Doniguian and Sons, 1988 [London: Sir Joseph Causton and Sons, 1916].

Griffin, Miriam T. *Nero: The End of a Dynasty.* New Haven: Yale University Press, 1984.

Grousset, René. *Histoire des croisades et du royaume franc de Jérusalem.* 3 vols. Paris: Plon, 1934–36.

Hakobyan, T.Kh. *Patmakan Hayastani kaghaknere* [The Cities of Historic Armenia]. Erevan: Hayastan, 1987.

Halperin, Charles J. *Russia and the Golden Horde: The Mongol Impact on Medieval Russian History.* Bloomington: Indiana University Press, 1985.

Hambaryan, A.S. *Hay hasarakakan kaghakakan mitke arevmtahayutyan azatagrutyan ughineri masin, xix dari verj-xx dari skizb* [Armenian Popular Political Thought Regarding Western Armenian Liberation, Late 19th-Early 20th Centuries]. Erevan: Hayastan, 1990.

Helmreich, Paul C. *From Paris to Sèvres: The Partition of the Ottoman Empire at the Peace Conference of 1919–1920.* Columbus: Ohio State University Press, 1974.

Helsinki Watch. *Bloodshed in the Caucasus: Escalation of the Armed Conflict in Nagorno-Karabagh.* Helsinki Watch, 1992.

Herzig, Edmund, and Marina Kurkchiyan, ed. *The Armenians: Past and Present in the Making of National Identity.* London: Routledge, 2005.

Heyd, Uriel. *Foundations of Turkish Nationalism: The Life and Teachings of Ziya Gökalp.* London: Luzac, 1950.

Holt, P.M. *The Age of the Crusades: The Near East from the Eleventh Century to 1517.* London: Longman, 1986.

Holt, P.M. *Early Mamluk Diplomacy (1260–1290): Treaties of Baybars and Qalāwūn with Christian Rulers.* Leiden: E.J. Brill, 1995.

Hovannisian, Richard G. *Armenia on the Road to Independence, 1918.* Berkeley: University of California Press, 1967.

Hovannisian, Richard G. *The Republic of Armenia.* 4 vols. Berkeley: University of California Press, 1971–96.

Hovannisian, Richard G., ed. *The Armenian Genocide in Perspective.* New Brunswick, NJ: Transaction Books, 1986.

Hovannisian, Richard G., ed. *The Armenian Genocide: History, Politics, Ethics.* New York: St. Martin's Press, 1992.

Hovannisian, Richard G., ed. *The Armenian People from Ancient to Modern Times.* 2 vols. New York: St. Martin's Press, 1997.

Hovannisian, Richard G., ed. *Armenian Van/Vaspurakan.* Costa Mesa, CA: Mazda, 2000.

Hovannisian, Richard G., ed. *Armenian Karin/Erzerum.* Costa Mesa, CA: Mazda, 2003.

Hovannisian, Richard G., ed. *Armenian Sebastia/Sivas and Lesser Armenia.* Costa Mesa, CA: Mazda, 2004.

Hovannisian, Richard G., ed. *Armenian Tigranakert/Diarbekir and Edessa/Urfa.* Costa Mesa, CA: Mazda, 2006.

Hovannisian, Richard G., and Simon Payaslian, eds. *Armenian Cilicia.* Costa Mesa, CA: Mazda [forthcoming].

Hovhannisyan, Grigor A. *Sovetakan ishkhanutyan hastatume Lernayin Gharabaghum* [The Establishment of Soviet Government in Mountainous Karabagh]. Erevan: Erevan State University, 1971.

Howard, Harry N. *The King-Crane Commission: An American Inquiry in the Middle East.* Beirut: Khayat, 1963.

Huntington, Samuel P. *Political Order in Changing Societies.* New Haven: Yale University Press, 1968.

İğdemir, Uluğ. *Sivas Kongresi tutanakları* [Minutes of the Sivas Congress]. Ankara: Türk Tarih Kurumu Bas1mevi, 1969.

Inalcik, Halil. *An Economic and Social History of the Ottoman Empire*, vol. 1: *1300–1600.* Cambridge: Cambridge University Press, 1994.

Ishkhanian, Bakhshi. *Erku amis bolshevikian bantum* [Two Months in Bolshevik Prison]. Cairo: Husaber, 1924.

Iskanyan, V.K. *Hay-Buzantakan haraberutyunnere iv-vii dd.* [Armenian-Byzantine Relations during the Fourth-Seventh Centuries]. Erevan: Gitelik, 1991.

Jones, A.H.M. *The Cities of the Eastern Roman Provinces.* Oxford: Clarendon Press, 1937; repr. Sandpiper Books, 1998.

Karapetyan, Hovhannes S. *Mayisyan apstambutyune Hayastanum, 1920* [The May Rebellion in Armenia, 1920]. Erevan: Armenian Academy of Sciences, 1961.

Karapetyan, Saribek. *1920 tvakani Hay-Turkakan paterazme ev Sovetakan Rusastane* [The Armenian-Turkish War of 1920 and Soviet Russia]. Erevan: Hayastan, 1965.

Karklins, Rasma. *Ethnopolitics and Transition to Democracy: The Collapse of the USSR and Latvia.* Washington, DC: Woodrow Wilson Center, 1994.

Kazemzadeh, Firuz. *The Struggle for Transcaucasia, 1917–1921.* New York: Philosophical Library, 1951.

Keegan, John. *The First World War.* New York: Vintage Books, 1998.

Kennedy, Hugh. *The Prophet and the Age of the Caliphates: The Islamic Near East from the Sixth to the Eleventh Century.* London: Longman, 1986.

Khatisian, Aleksandr. *Hayastani Hanrapetutian tsagumn u zargatsume* [The Creation and Development of the Republic of Armenia]. Beirut: Hamazkayin, 1968.

Khurshudyan, Lendrush A. *Stepan Shahumyan: Petakan ev partiakan gortsuneutyune, 1917–1918 tvakannerin* [Stepan Shahumyan: Governmental and Party Activity during the Years 1917–1918]. Erevan: Armenian Academy of Sciences, Institute of History, 1959.

King, L.W., and R.C. Thompson. *The Sculptures and Inscription of Darius the Great on the Rock of Behistûn in Persia.* London: Harrison and Sons, 1907.

Kinross, Lord. *Ataturk: The Rebirth of a Nation.* London: Weidenfeld and Nicolson, 1964.

Kirakosyan, Jon, comp. *Hayastane mijazgayin ev Sovetakan artakin kaghakanutyan pastatghterum, 1828–1923* [Armenia in the Documents of

International and Soviet Foreign Policy, 1828–1923]. Erevan: Hayastan, 1972.

Krikorian, Mesrob K. *Armenians in the Service of the Ottoman Empire, 1860–1908.* London: Routledge, 1977.

Landau, Jacob M. *Pan-Turkism: From Irredentism to Cooperation.* 2nd rev. ed. Bloomington: Indiana University Press, 1995.

Langer, William L. *The Diplomacy of Imperialism, 1890–1902.* 2 vols. New York: Alfred A. Knopf, 1935.

Lapidus, Ira M. *A History of Islamic Societies.* Cambridge: Cambridge University Press, 1988.

Lastiverttsi, Aristakes. *Patmutyun* [History]. Ed. Karen N. Yuzbashyan. Erevan: Armenian Academy of Sciences, 1963. English trans. Robert Bedrosian. New York: n.p., 1985.

Laurent, Joseph. *L'Arménie entre Byzance et l'Islam depuis la conquete arabe jusqu'en 836.* Paris: Fontemoing, 1919.

Lee, Dwight E. *Great Britain and the Cyprus Convention Policy of 1878.* Cambridge, MA: Harvard University Press, 1934.

Leo (Arakel Babakhanian). *Ani.* Erevan: Haypethrat, 1946.

Leo (Arakel Babakhanian). *Erkeri zhoghovatsu* [Collection of Works]. 10 vols. Erevan: Hayastan, 1966.

Lepper, F.A. *Trajan's Parthian War.* London: Oxford University Press, 1948.

Lepsius, Johannes. *Armenia and Europe: An Indictment.* Trans. and ed. J. Rendel Harris. London: Hodder and Stoughton, 1897.

Lepsius, Johannes. *Rapport secret sur les massacres d'Armenie.* Beirut: Hamazkayin, 1980; first published Paris: Payot, 1918.

Lewis, Bernard. *The Emergence of Modern Turkey.* 2nd ed. London: Oxford University Press, 1968.

Libaridian, Gerard J. *Modern Armenia: People, Nation, State.* New Brunswick, NJ: Transaction Publishers, 2004.

Low, Alfred D. *Lenin on the Question of Nationality.* New York: Bookman, 1958.

Luttwak, Edward N. *Grand Strategy of the Roman Empire.* Baltimore: Johns Hopkins University Press, 1976.

Lynch, H.F.B. *Armenia: Travels and Studies.* 2 vols. Beirut: Khayats, 1965.

Machiavelli, Niccolò. *The Art of War.* Rev. ed. and trans. Ellis Farneworth. Cambridge, MA: Perseus Books, 2001; first published, 1521.

Mallory, J.P. *In Search of the Indo-Europeans.* London: Thames and Hudson, 1989.

Manandyan, Hakob A. *Knnakan tesutyun Hay zhoghovrdi patmutyan* [Critical Review of the History of the Armenian People]. 3 vols. Erevan: Haypethrat, 1944–60.

Manandyan, Hakob A. *The Trade and Cities of Armenia in Relation to the Ancient World.* 2nd rev. ed.. Trans. Nina G. Garsoian. Lisbon: Calouste Gulbenkian Foundation, 1965.

Manandyan, Hakob A. *Tigran Erkrorte ev Hrome* [Tigran II and Rome]. Erevan: Erevan State University, 1972 [1940].

Manandyan, Hakob A. *Erker* [Works]. 6 vols. Erevan: Armenian Academy of Sciences, 1977–78.

Mantalian, James. *Vardanants paterazme* [The War of Vardanants]. Boston: Hayrenik, 1954.

Manz, Beatrice Forbes. *The Rise and Rule of Tamerlane.* Cambridge: Cambridge University Press, 1989; Canto ed., 1999.

Marshall, S.L.A. *World War I*. Boston: Houghton Mifflin, 1964; repr. Mariner Books, 2001.

Masih, Joseph R., and Robert O. Krikorian. *Armenia at the Crossroads*. Amsterdam: Harwood Academic Publishers, 1999.

Matevosyan, Rafael I. *Bagratuniats Hayastani petakan karutsvatskn u varchakan karge*. Erevan: Armenian Academy of Sciences, 1990.

Matevosyan, Rafael I. *Bagratuniner: Patma-tohmabanakan hanragitaran* [Bagratunis: Historic-Genealogical Encyclopedia]. Erevan: Anahit, 1997.

Matossian, Mary K. *The Impact of Soviet Policies in Armenia*. Leiden: E.J. Brill, 1962.

Matthew of Edessa. *Zhamanakagrutyun/Matteos Urhayetsi* [Chronicle/ Matthew of Edessa]. Ed. and trans., Ara E. Dostourian. *Armenia and the Crusades*. Lanham, MD: University Press of America, 1993.

Mayer, Arno J. *Politics and Diplomacy of Peacemaking: Containment and Counterrevolution at Versailles, 1918–1919*. New York: Alfred A. Knopf, 1967.

McKale, Donald M. *War by Revolution: Germany and Great Britain in the Middle East in the Era of World War I*. Kent, OH: Kent State University Press, 1998.

Melik-Pakhshyan, S.T. *Pavlikian sharzhume Hayastanum* [The Paulician Movement in Armenia]. Erevan: Erevan State University, 1953.

Melkonyan, A.H. *Mayisyan apstambutyan patmutian hartsi shurje* [Regarding the Issue of the History of the May Rebellion]. Erevan: Armenian Academy of Sciences, 1965.

Minakhorian, Vahan. *1915 tvakane* [The Year 1915]. Venice: Mekhitarist Press, 1949.

Minorsky, Vladimir. *Studies in Caucasian History*. London: Taylor's Foreign Press, 1953.

Minorsky, Vladimir. *The Turks, Iran and the Caucasus in the Middle Ages*. London: Variorum, 1978.

Minuvi, Mujtaba, and Iraj Afshar, ed. *Yād-Nāme-ye Irānī-ye Minorsky*. Tehran: Tehran University, 1969.

Mitchell, Stephen, ed. *Armies and Frontiers in Roman and Byzantine Anatolia*. Oxford: B.A.R., 1983.

Mnatsakanyan, A.N. *V.I. Lenine ev Hay zhoghovrdi azatagrakan paykare* [V.I. Lenin and the Armenian People's Struggle for Freedom]. Erevan: Armenian Academy of Sciences, 1962.

Moghadam, Valentine M., ed. *Democratic Reform and the Position of Women in Transitional Economies*. Oxford: Clarendon Press, 1993.

Moorehead, Alan. *Gallipoli*. London: H. Hamilton, 1956.

Morgan, David. *The Mongols*. Cambridge: Basil Blackwell, 1986.

Morgenthau, Henry. *Ambassador Morgenthau's Story*. New York: Doubleday, 1918.

Mutafian, Claude. *Le Royaume arménien de Cilicie*. Paris: CNRS Editions, 1993.

Nalbandian, Louise. *The Armenian Revolutionary Movement*. Berkeley: University of California Press, 1963.

Nassibian, Akaby. *Britain and the Armenian Question, 1915–1923*. London: Croom Helm, 1984.

Nersessian, Vrej. *The Tondrakian Movement*. Allison Park, PA: Pickwick, 1987.

Nersissyan, M.G. *Hay zhoghvrdi azatagrakan paykare Turkakan brnapetutyan dem, 1850–1870* [The Armenian People's Struggle for Liberation against Turkish Tyrannical Rule, 1850–1870]. Erevan: Armenian Academy of Sciences, 1955.

Nicol, Donald M. *The End of the Byzantine Empire*. London: Edward Arnold Publishers, 1985.

Norashkharyan, Levon. *Zeytune, 1914–1921 tt.* [Zeitun, 1914–1921]. Erevan: Armenian Academy of Sciences, 1984.

Nubar, Boghos. *Boghos Nubar's Papers and the Armenian Question, 1915–1918*. Trans. and ed. Vatche Ghazarian. Waltham, MA: Mayrnei Publishing, 1996.

Ormanian, Maghakia. *Azgapatum* [History of the Nation]. 3 vols. Jerusalem: St. James Press, 1927; reprinted, Antelias: Catholicosate of Cilicia, 2001.

Ostrogorsky, George. *History of the Byzantine State*. Trans. Joan Hussey. New Brunswick, NJ: Rutgers University Press, 1969.

Palakian, Grigoris. *Hay Goghgotan* [The Armenian Calvary]. Erevan: Hayastan, 1991.

Panossian, Razmik. *The Armenians: From Kings and Priests to Merchants and Commissars*. New York: Columbia University Press, 2006.

Parla, Taha. *The Social and Political Thought of Ziya Gökalp, 1876–1924*. Leiden: E.J. Brill, 1985.

Payaslian, Simon. *United States Policy toward the Armenian Question and the Armenian Genocide*. New York: Palgrave Macmillan, 2005.

Phillips, David L. *Unsilencing the Past: Track Two Diplomacy and Turkish-Armenian Reconciliation*. New York: Berghahn Books, 2005.

Piotrovski, Boris B. *Urartu: The Kingdom of Van*. Trans. from the Russian and ed. Peter S. Gelling. London: Evelyn Adams and Mackay, 1967.

Piotrovski, Boris B. *The Ancient Civilization of Urartu*. Trans. from the Russian James Hogarth. London: Cresset Press, 1969.

Pipes, Richard. *The Formation of the Soviet Union*. Cambridge, MA: Harvard University Press, 1997 [1954].

Poghosyan, Haikaz M. *Zeytuni Patmutyune, 1409–1921 tt.* [The History of Zeitun, 1409–1921]. Erevan: Hayastan, 1969.

Pztikian, Zakaria, comp. *Kilikian Kskidzner: Vaveragrer Kilikio katoghikosakan divanen* [Cilician Pains: Documents from the Archives of the Cilician Catholicosate]. Beirut: Hrazdan, 1927.

Redgate, A.E. *The Armenians*. Oxford: Blackwell, 1998.

Renaudel, Pierre. *L'internationale à Berne: Faits et documents*. Paris: B. Grasset, 1919.

Republic of Armenia. Ministry of Statistics. State Register and Analysis. *Women and Men in Armenia*. Erevan: Ministry of Statistics, 1999.

Republic of Armenia. National Statistical Services. Economic and Financial Data. *Statistical Yearbook 2001, 2005*. Erevan: National Statistical Services, 2001, 2005.

Rich, John, ed. *War and Society in the Roman World*. New York: Routledge, 1993.

Riggs, Henry H. *Days of Tragedy in Armenia: Personal Experiences in Harpoot, 1915–1917*. Ann Arbor, MI: Gomidas Institute, 1997.

Roskin, Michael G. *The Rebirth of East Europe*. 2nd ed. Englewood Cliffs, NJ: Prentice-Hall, 1994.

Rostom. *Rostom: Namakani* [Rostom: Collection of Letters]. Beirut: Hamazkayin, 1999.

Rudin, Harry R. *Armistice, 1918*. New Haven, CT: Yale University Press, 1944.

Rüdt-Collenberg, W.H. *The Rupenides, Hethumides and Lusignans: The Structure of the Armeno-Cilician Dynasties*. Lisbon: Calouste Gulbenkian Foundation Armenian Library, 1963.

Runciman, Steven. *History of the Crusades*, 3 vols. Cambridge: Cambridge University Press, 1951.

Runciman, Steven. *The Fall of Constantinople, 1453*. Cambridge: Cambridge University Press, 1965.

Sahakyan, Ruben G. *Turk-Fransiakan haraberutyunnere ev Kilikian 1919–1921 tt.* [Turkish-French Relations and Cilicia, 1919–1921]. Erevan: Armenian Academy of Sciences, 1970.

Samuelian, Thomas and Michael Stone, eds. *Medieval Armenian Culture*. Chico, CA: Scholars Press, 1983.

Sanjian, Avedis K., *The Armenian Communities in Syria under Ottoman Dominion*. Cambridge, MA: Harvard University Press, 1965.

Sasuni, Karo. *Mayisian khrovutiunnere ev Tatarakan apstamb shrjannere* [The May Disturbances and the Rebellious Tatar Districts]. Beirut: Sevan, 1968.

Sasuni, Karo. *Hay-Trkakan paterazme 1920-in* [The Armenian-Turkish War in 1920]. Beirut: Hamazkayin, 1969.

Sasuni, Karo. *Petrvarian apstambutiune, 1921* [The February Rebellion, 1921]. Beirut: Hamazkayin, 1970.

Setton, Kenneth M., ed. *A History of the Crusades*. vol. 2: *The Later Crusades, 1189–1311*. Philadelphia: University of Pennsylvania, 1962.

Seward, Desmond. *The Monks of War: The Military Religious Orders*. Rev. ed. London: Penguin Books, 1995.

Shannon, Richard. *The Crisis of Imperialism, 1865–1915*. London: Paladin, Granada Publishing, 1974.

Shukla, Ram Lakhan. *Britain, India and the Turkish Empire 1853–1882*. New Delhi: People's Publishing House, 1973.

Smith, Adam T., and Karen S. Rubinson, eds. *Archaeology in the Borderlands: Investigations in Caucasia and Beyond*. Los Angeles: University of California Press, 2003.

Smith, Hedrick. *The New Russians*. New York: Random House, 1990.

Somakian, Manoug Joseph. *Empires in Conflict: Armenia and the Great Powers, 1895–1920*. London: I.B. Tauris, 1995.

Staar, Richard F. *Communist Regimes in Eastern Europe*. 4th ed. Stanford, CA: Hoover Institution Press, 1982.

Stewart, Angus Donald. *The Armenian Kingdom and the Mamluks: War and Diplomacy during the Reigns of Het'um II (1289–1307)*. Leiden: Brill, 2001.

Stewart, George. *The White Armies of Russia: A Chronicle of Counter-Revolution and Allied Intervention*. New York: Macmillan, 1933.

Stoddard, Philip H. *The Ottoman Government and the Arabs, 1911 to 1918: A Preliminary Study of the Teşkilât-ı Mahsusa*. Ph.D. diss. Princeton University, 1963.

Sukiasyan, A.K. *Kilikiayi Haykakan petutyan ev iravunki patmutyun (xi-xiv Darer)* [History of the Cilician Armenian Government and Jurisprudence (xi-xiv Centuries)]. Erevan: Erevan State University, 1978.

Suny, Ronald Gregory. *Looking toward Ararat: Armenia in Modern History*. Bloomington: Indiana University Press, 1993.

Suny, Ronald Gregory, ed. *Transcaucasia, Nationalism, and Social Change: Essays in the History of Armenia, Azerbaijan, and Georgia*. Rev. Ed. Ann Arbor: University of Michigan Press, 1996.

Supreme Soviet of Armenia. *Haykakan SSR hingerord gumarman geraguyn soveti nistere* [The Fifth Conference of the Supreme Soviet of the Armenian S[oviet] S[ocialist] R[epublic]. 3rd Sess. March 24–25, 1960. Erevan: Presidium, Supreme Soviet of Armenia, 1960.

Sykes, P.M. *A History of Persia*. London: Macmillan, 1915.

Taagepera, Rein. *Estonia: Return to Independence*. Boulder, CO: Westview Press, 1993.

Taylor, A.J.P. *The Struggle for Mastery in Europe, 1848–1918*. Oxford: Oxford University Press, 1954.

Temperely, H.W.V. *A History of the Peace Conference of Paris*. London: H. Frowde and Hodder & Stoughton, 1920.

Ter Ghazarian, Harutiun. *Haykakan Kilikia* [Armenian Cilicia]. Antelias: Catholicosate of Cilicia, 1966.

Ter-Ghevondyan, Aram N. *Arabakan amirayutyunnere Bagratuniats hayastanum* [The Arab Emirates in Bagratuni Armenia]. Erevan: Armenian Academy of Sciences, 1965.

Ter-Ghevondyan, V.A. *Kilikian Hayastane ev mertsavor arevelki arabakan erkirnere 1145–1226 Tvakannerin* [Cilician Armenia and the Near Eastern Arab Countries in the Years 1145–1226]. Erevan: Kidutiun, 1994.

Ter Minassian, Anaide. *Nationalism and Socialism in the Armenian Revolutionary Movement, 1887–1912*. Cambridge, MA: Zoryan Institute, 1984.

Ter Minasian, Ruben. *Hay heghapokhakani me hishataknere* [The Memories of an Armenian Revolutionary]. Los Angeles: Horizon, 1952.

Tololyan, Minas. *Ardi Hay grakanutiun* [Modern Armenian Literature], vol. 1: *1850–1920*. 2nd pr. Boston: Steven Day Press, 1977.

Tolz, Vera. *The USSR in 1990: A Record of Events*. Boulder, CO: Westview Press, 1992.

Toumanoff, Cyril. *Studies in Christian Caucasian History*. Washington, DC: Georgetown University Press, 1963.

Treadgold, Warren. *A History of the Byzantine State and Society*. Stanford, CA: Stanford University Press, 1997.

Tritton, A.S. *The Caliphs and Their Non-Muslim Subjects*. London: Frank Cass, 1970.

Trumpener, Ulrich. *Germany and the Ottoman Empire, 1914–1918*. Princeton, NJ: Princeton University Press, 1968.

Tsurutani, Taketsugu. *The Politics of National Development*. New York: Abeland-Schuman, 1973.

Ullman, Richard H. *Anglo-Soviet Relations, 1917–1921*, vol. 2: *Britain and the Russian Civil War, November 1918-February 1920*. Princeton, NJ: Princeton University Press, 1968.

U.S. Department of State. *Papers Relating to the Foreign Relations of the United States, 1914*. Washington, DC: Government Printing Office, 1922.

Vardanyan, V.M. *Vaspurakani Artsruniats tagavorutyune, 908–1021 tt.* [The Artsruni Kingdom of Vaspurakan, 908–1021]. Erevan: Erevan State University Press, 1969.

Vratsian, Simon. *Hayastani Hanrapetutiun* [Republic of Armenia]. Paris: A.R.F. Central Committee of America, 1928; repr., Erevan: Hayastan, 1993.

Walicki, Andrzej. *A History of Russian Thought from the Enlightenment to Marxism.* Trans. Hilda Andrews-Rusiecka. Stanford, CA: Stanford University Press, 1979.

Walker, Christopher J. *Armenia: The Survival of a Nation.* London: Croom Helm, 1980.

Weber, Max. *From Max Weber: Essays in Sociology.* Trans. and ed. H.H. Gerth and C. Wright Mills. New York: Oxford University Press, 1946.

Will, Edouard. *Histoire politique du monde hellénistique.* 2 vols. Nancy: University of Nancy, 1966–67.

Wittfogel, Karl A. *Oriental Despotism: A Comparative Study of Total Power.* New Haven, CT: Yale University Press, 1957.

Whittow, Mark. *The Making of Byzantium, 600–1025.* Berkeley: University of California Press, 1996.

Wolfe, Bertram D. *Three Who Made a Revolution,* rev. ed. New York: Dell Publishing, 1964.

Woods, John E. *The Aqquyunlu: Clan, Federation, Empire.* Rev. and exp. ed. Salt Lake City: University of Utah Press, 1999.

Yapp, M.E. *The Making of the Modern Near East, 1792–1923.* London: Longman, 1987.

Yarshater, Ehsan, ed. *The Cambridge History of Iran,* vol. 3, pt. 1, *The Seleucid, Parthian and Sasanian Periods.* Cambridge: Cambridge University Press, 1983.

Zohrapyan, Edik A. *Sovetakan Rusastane ev Hay-Turkakan haraberutyunnere, 1920–1922 tt.* [Soviet Russia and Armenian-Turkish Relations, 1920–1922]. Erevan: Erevan State University, 1979.

Zohrapyan, Edik A. *1920 t. Turk-Haykakan paterazme ev terutyunnere* [The Turkish-Armenian War of 1920 and the Powers]. Erevan: Oskan Erevantsi, 1997.

Xenophon. *Anabasis.* Trans. Carleton L. Brownson. Loeb Classical Library, 1947.

ARTICLES

Adoyan, A.G. "Haykakan amusna-entanekan haraberutyunnere mijnadaryan orenknerum" [Armenian Marriage-Family Relations in the Laws of the Middle Ages]. *Patma-banasirakan handes* 3 (1965): 49–66.

Arakelyan, B.N. "Hayastani mijnadaryan kaghakneri bnakchutyan sotsialakan kazme" [The Social Structure of Urban Population in Armenia during the Middle Ages]. *Patma-banasirakan handes* 2 (1958): 37–65.

Arakelyan, B.N. "Aprankayin artadrutyan ev arhestagortsutyan tekhnikayi zargatsume hayastanum ix-xiii darerum" [The Development of Production of Goods and Industrial Technology in Armenia during the Ninth-Thirteenth Centuries]. *Patma-banasirakan handes* 2–3 (1959): 97–107.

Arakelyan, B.N. "Vortegh en gtnvel Ervandashat ev Ervandakert kaghaknere?" [Where were the Cities of Ervandashat and Ervandagert Located?]. *Patma-banasirakan handes* 30 (1965): 83–93.

Atiya, Aziz S. "The Crusades: Old Ideas and New Conceptions." *Journal of World History* 2:2 (1954): 469–75.

Barkan, Omer L. "The Price Revolution of the Sixteenth Century: A Turning Point in the History of the Near East." *International Journal of Middle East Studies* 6:1 (Jan. 1975): 3–28.

Barkhudaryan, S.G. "Hay knoj iravakan vichake mijin darerum" [The Legal Situation of Armenian Women during the Middle Ages]. *Patma-banasirakan handes* 2 (1966): 25–40.

Bartikyan, Hrach. "Vaspurakantsiner Buzandakan kaysrutyan tsarayutyan mej xi-xii darerum" [Vaspurakanians in the Service of the Byzantine Empire in the eleventh-twelfth Centuries]. *Patma-banasirakan handes* 3 (2000): 131–51.

Bornazyan, S.V. "Khachakir ordenneri ev Kilikian Hayastani kaghakakan u tntesakan arnchutyunneri patmutyunits" [From the History of the Political and Economic Relations between the Crusader Orders and Cilician Armenia]. *Patma-banasirakan handes* 3 (1963): 176–84.

Bosworth, C.E. "Christian and Jewish Religious Dignitaries in Mamluk Egypt and Syria," *International Journal of Middle East Studies.* Part I, 3:1 (Jan. 1972): 59–74; Part II, 3:2 (April 1972): 199–216.

Bozoyan, Azat A. "Kilikiayi Buzandakan karavarichnere ev Rubenyan ishkhanutyune xii dari 40–70-akan tvakannerin" [The Byzantine Governors of Cilicia and the Rubenian Principality during the 40s-70s of the XII Century]. *Patma-banasirakan handes* 3 (1984): 74–86.

Brémond, Edouard. "The Bremond Mission, Cilicia in 1919–1920." *Armenian Review.* Part I, 29 (Winter 1976–1977): 339–72; Part II, 30 (Spring 1977): 34–72.

Canard, M. "Le royaume d'Arménie-Cilicie et les Mamelouks jusqu'au traité de 1285." *Revue des études arméniennes* 4 (1967): 217–59.

Chaloyan, V.K. "Norits kapitali nakhaskzbnakan kutakman ev harakits hart-seri masin" [Once More Regarding Accumulation of Capital and Related Issues]. *Patma-banasirakan handes* 3 (1960): 152–71.

Clay, Christopher. "The Origins of Modern Banking in the Levant: The Branch Network of the Imperial Ottoman Bank, 1890–1914." *International Journal of Middle East Studies* 26:4 (Nov. 1994): 589–614.

Cornell, Svante E. "Undeclared War: The Nagorno-Karabakh Conflict Reconsidered." *Journal of Asian and Middle Eastern Studies* 20:4 (Summer 1997): 1–23.

Dadrian, Vahakn N. "Genocide as a Problem of National and International Law: The World War I Armenian Case and Its Contemporary Legal Ramifications." *Yale Journal of International Law* 14:2 (Summer 1989): 221–334.

Davison, Roderic H. "The Armenian Crisis, 1912–1914." *American Historical Review* 53 (April 1948): 481–505.

Dédéyan, Gérard. "L'immigration arménienne en Capadoce au XIe siècle." *Byzantion* 45 (1975): 41–117.

Deherian, Suren. "Unlucky Anniversary: Gumri Marks 13 Years as a Disaster Zone." *Armenian International Magazine* [hereafter *AIM*] (Jan.–Feb. 2002): 43–47.

Elchibekian, Zh.G. "Ervandunineri tsagman hartsi shurj" [On the Question Concerning the Origins of the Ervandunis]. *Patma-banasirakan handes* 2 (1971): 107–15.

Eremyan, S.T. "Haykakan arajin petakan kazmavorumnere" [The Structures of the First Armenian State]. *Patma-banasirakan handes* 3 (1968): 91–119.

Friedrich, Carl J. "Political Leadership and the Problem of Charismatic Power." *Journal of Politics* 23:1 (Feb. 1961): 3–24.

Ghafadaryan, K.G. "Dvin kaghaki himnadrman zhamanaki ev Mijnaberdi hetanosakan mehyanimasin" [Concerning the Period of the Founding of Dvin City and the Pagan Temple of Mijnaberd]. *Patma-banasirakan handes* 2 (1966): 41–58.

Giraudoux, Jean. "The Dardanelles." *North American Review* 206 (Aug. 1917): 285–91.

Halpin, Tony. "What Now?" *AIM* (Nov. 1999): 26–31.

Halpin, Tony. "Up the Down Escalator." *AIM* (Oct. 1992): 14–15.

Harutyunyan, V.M. "Mijnadaryan Hayastani kaghakashinakan kulturan" [The Culture of City Construction in Armenia in the Middle Ages]. *Patma-bansirakan handes* 2 (1963): 85–99.

Hayrapetian, Ervand. "The February 18, 1921 Armenian Revolt." *Armenian Review*. Parts I-III, 10 (Summer-Winter 1957): 101–20, 146–57, 147–58; Parts IV-VI, 11 (Spring-Autumn 1958): 143–52, 153–60, 151–56.

Hess, Andrew C. "The Evolution of the Ottoman Seaborne Empire in the Age of the Oceanic Discoveries, 1453–1525." *American Historical Review* 75:7 (Dec. 1970): 1892–1919.

Hess, Andrew C. "The Ottoman Conquest of Egypt (1517) and the Beginning of the Sixteenth-Century World War." *International Journal of Middle East Studies* 4:1 (Jan. 1973): 55–76.

Holmes, T. Rice. "Tigranocerta." *Journal of Roman Studies* 7 (1917):120–38.

Holt, P.M. "The Treaties of the Early Mamluk Sultans with the Frankish States." *Bulletin of the School of Oriental and African Studies* 43:1 (1980): 67–76.

Hovannisian, Richard G. "Armenia and the Caucasus in the Genesis of the Soviet-Turkish Entente." *International Journal of Middle East Studies* 4:2 (April 1973): 129–47.

Hovhannisyan, Ashot. "Ardyok mijnadaryan Hayastanum teghi unetsel e kapitali nakhaskzbnakan kutakum" [Was There Accumulation of Capital in Armenia during the Middle Ages?]. *Patma-banasirakan handes* 1 (1959): 202–23.

Ishkhanian, E. "Depkere Gharabaghum: Chshtumner ev ditoghutiunner." *Hayrenik amsagir.* Parts I-II, 11 (Sept.–Oct. 1933): 85–93, 111–27.

Iskanyan, V.K. "Artsrunyats artagaghti masin." *Patma-banasirakan handes* 3 (1965): 67–82.

Jennings, Ronald C. "Urban Population in Anatolia in the Sixteenth Century: A Study of Kayseri, Karaman, Amasya, Trabzon and Erzurum." *International Journal for Middle Eastern Studies* 7:1 (Jan. 1976): 21–57.

Karo, Armen. "Aprvadz orer" [Days Lived]. *Hayrenik amsagir* 1:9 (July 1923): 93–96.

Karpat, Kemal H. "The Transformation of the Ottoman State, 1789–1908." *International Journal of Middle East Studies* 3:3 (July 1972): 243–81.

Khatisian, Aleksandr. "Kaghakaptei me hishataknere." *Hayrenik amsagir.* Parts I-VI, 10 (May 1932-Oct. 1932): 86–93, 124–34, 91–103, 97–106, 111–25, 155–62; Parts VII-XI, 11 (Nov. 1932-March 1933): 133–41, 127–41, 129–33, 122–25, 143–47.

Krkyasharyan, S.M. "Bteshkhutyunneri arajatsume hayastanum." *Patma-banasirakan handes* 4 (1966): 257–62.

Krkyasharyan, S.M. "Ervanduni arkayatohme Hayastanum" [The Ervanduni Dynasty in Armenia]. *Patma-banasirakan handes* 4:1 (1973): 179–85.

Krkyasharyan, S.M. "Petakan aparati kazmavorume ev nra hetaga zargatsman pule hin Hayastanum" [The Formation of State Apparatus and Its Future Development Phase in Ancient Armenia]. *Patma-banasirakan handes* 1–2 (1994): 225–37.

Laitin, David D. and Ronald Grigor Suny. "Armenia and Azerbaijan: Thinking a Way Out of Karabakh." *Middle East Policy* 7:1 (Oct. 1999): 145–76.

Mardin, Şerif. "The Influence of the French Revolution on the Ottoman Empire." *International Social Science Journal* 119 (Feb. 1989): 17–30.

Marmandian, H. "The Exile of the Armenian Army Officers." *Armenian Review* 11 (Spring 1958): 102–15.

Meillet, A. "De l'influence parthe sur le langue arménienne." *Revue des études arméniennes* 1 (1920): 9–14.

Minakhorian, Vahan. "Batumi khorhrdazhoghove" [The Batum Conference]. *Hayrenik amsagir.* Part I-II, 14 (Mar.–Apr. 1936): 91–99, 123–31.

Minakhorian, Vahan. "Karsi ankume" [The Fall of Kars]. *Hayrenik amsagir.* Parts I-III, 13 (Aug.–Oct. 1935): 79–87, 83–96, 79–92; Parts VI-V, 14 (Dec.–Jan. 1936): 133–39, 145–52.

Minorsky, Vladimir. "Roman and Byzantine Campaigns in Atropatene." *Bulletin of the School of Oriental and African Studies* 11:2 (1944): 243–65.

Payaslian, Simon. "From Perestroika to Uncertainty: Will Gorbachev's Experiment Survive Forces Pounding at Kremlin Gates?" *AIM* (July 1990): 42–44.

Payaslian, Simon. "The Destruction of the Armenian Church during the Genocide." *Genocide Studies and Prevention* 1:2 (Fall 2006): 149–71.

Poidebard, Antoine. "Rôle militaire des Arméniens sur le front du Caucase, après la défection de l'armée russe (décembre 1917-novembre 1918)." *Revue des études arméniennes* 1 (1920): 141–42.

Raccagni, Michelle. "The French Economic Interests in the Ottoman Empire." *International Journal of Middle East Studies* 11:3 (1980): 339–76.

Redfield, William C. "America's International Trade as Affected by the European War." *Annals of the American Academy of Political and Social Science* 60 (July 1915): 7–15.

Ritter, Laurence. "Under Pressure." *AIM* (March 2002): 29–35.

Rutland, Peter. "Labor Unrest and Movements in 1989 and 1990." *Soviet Economy* 6:4 (1990): 345–84.

Sahakyan, T.M. "Syunyats tagavorutyan himnume ev nra kaghakakan dere xi darum" [The Establishment of the Kingdom of Siunik and Its Political Role in the Eleventh Century]. *Patma-banasirakan handes* 3 (1966): 221–28.

Sarafian, Vahe. "The Soviet and the Armenian Church." *Armenian Review* 8:2 (Summer 1955): 83–107.

Sarur. "Gharabaghi ktsume Adrbejani" [The Annexation of Karabagh to Azerbaijan]. *Hayrenik amsagir* 7 (June 1929): 128–46.

Sinclair, Thomas. "The Site of Tigranocerta. I." *Revue des études arméniennes,* n.s. 25 (1994–95): 183–253.

Stepanyan, H.A. "Vratz-Haykakan entvzumnere Tatar-Mongolakan brnatirutyan dem 1247–1249 tt" [Georgian-Armenian Rebellions against Tatar-Mongolian Repression, 1247–1249], *Patma-banasirakan handes* 1 (1986): 97–105.

Ter-Ghevondyan, V.A. "Kilikian Hayastann u Syrian xii dari 40–70-akan tvakannerin" [Cilician Armenia and Syria during the 40s–70s of the XII Century]. *Patma-banasirakan handes* 2 (1986): 122–29.

Tiratsyan, G.A. "Ervandyan Hayastani taratske (m.t.a. vi dar)" [The Expanse of the Ervanduni Armenia (Sixth Century B.C.)]. *Patma-banasirakan handes* 4 (1980): 84–95.

Tiratsyan, G.A. "Ervandyan Hayastani taratske (m.t.a. vi d. verj-m.t.a. iii d. verj)" [The Expanse of the Ervanduni Armenia (Late Sixth Century B.C.-Late Third Century B.C.)]. *Patma-banasirakan handes* 2 (1981): 68–84.

Torosyan, Kh.A. "Datavarutyune mijnataryan hayastanum" [The Court System in Armenia during the Middle Ages]. *Patma-banasirakan handes* 3 (1966): 39–52.

Turshyan, H.G. "Shah-i-Armenner" [Shah-i Armens]. *Patma-banasirakan handes* 4 (1964): 117–33.

Vratsian, Simon. "How Armenia Was Sovietized." *Armenian Review.* Parts I-IV, 1:1–4 (Winter-Autumn 1948): 74–84, 79–91, 59–75, 87–103; Part V, 2:1 (Spring 1949): 118–27.

Walker, Christopher J. "From Sassun to the Ottoman Bank: Turkish Armenians in the 1890s." *Armenian Review* 30 (March 1979): 227–64.

Yuzbashyan, Karen N. "L'administration byzantine en arménie aux Xᵉ–XIᵉ siècles." *Revue des études arméniennes* 10 (1973–74): 139–83.

Zeitlian, Garine. "The Shifting Ensemble." *AIM* (Mar. 1994): 28–29.

INTERNET LINKS

armenianhouse.org
armenica.org (historical maps)
armstat.am
aua.am/extens/N_maps/ (in Armenian and English)
cilicia.com
digilib.am (in Armenian)
eurasianet.org
groong.usc.edu/news/
worldstatesmen.org

Index

27252493R00171

Printed in Great Britain
by Amazon